HOW EVERYTHING WORKS

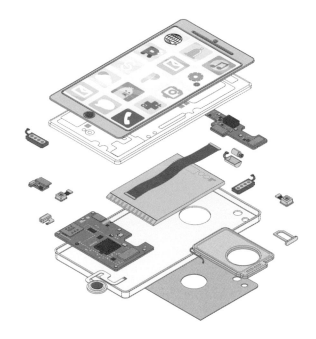

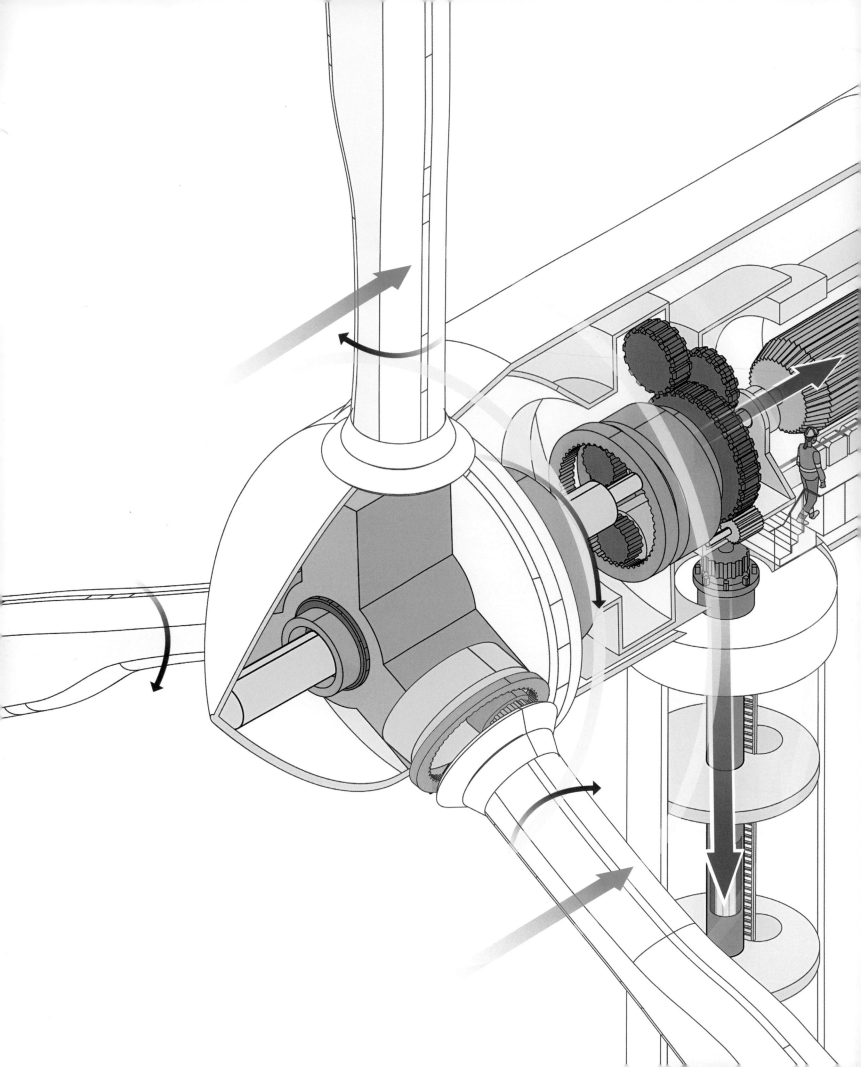

HOW EVERYTHING WORKS

DK LONDON

Senior Editors Peter Frances, Rob Houston
Senior Art Editor Ina Stradins
Project Art Editors Francis Wong, Steve Woosnam-Savage
Editors Helen Fewster, Sarah MacLeod, Annie Moss,
Gill Pitts, Hannah Westlake
Art Editors Karen Constanti, Alison Gardner,
Mik Gates, Simon Murrell
Design Assistant Clarisse Hassan
Managing Editor Angeles Gavira Guerrero
Managing Art Editor Michael Duffy
Illustrators Peter Bull, Ed Byrne, Dan Crisp,
Mark Franklin, Phil Gamble, Julian@KJA-artists,
Max@KJA-artists, Simon Tegg
DK Media Archive Romaine Werblow
Picture Researcher Laura Barwick
Production Editor Jacqueline Street-Elkayam
Production Controller Laura Andrews
Jacket Designer Akiko Kato
Jacket Design Development Manager Sophia MTT
Associate Publishing Director Liz Wheeler
Art Director Karen Self
Publishing Director Jonathan Metcalf
Design Director Phil Ormerod

DK DELHI

Senior Art Editor Vaibhav Rastogi
Project Art Editor Rupanki Arora Kaushik
Art Editors Nobina Chakravorty, Sonakshi Singh
Illustrator Priyal Motel
DTP Designers Jaypal Chauhan, Bimlesh Tiwary
Senior Picture Researcher Surya Sankash Sarangi
Senior Jackets Coordinator Priyanka Sharma-Saddi
Jackets DTP Designer Rakesh Kumar

CONTRIBUTORS

Jack Challoner, Clive Gifford
Wendy Horobin, Tom Jackson

CONSULTANTS

Roger Bridgman, Hilary Lamb,
Professor Mark Viney
Dr Rebecca Williams

First published in Great Britain in 2022 by
Dorling Kindersley Limited
DK, One Embassy Gardens, 8 Viaduct Gardens,
London SW11 7BW

The authorised representative in the EEA is
Dorling Kindersley Verlag GmbH. Arnulfstr. 124,
80636 Munich, Germany

A CIP catalogue record for this book
is available from the British Library.
ISBN: 978-0-2415-0923-4

Printed and bound in the United Arab Emirates

For the curious
www.dk.com

This book was made with Forest
Stewardship Council ™ certified paper
– one small step in DK's commitment
to a sustainable future. For more
information go to www.dk.com/
our-green-pledge

Contents

City and Industry (continued)

Living World

If you carefully explore the detailed illustrations in this book, you might find something fun, or not going to plan.

Our Planet

Space

Beneath your skin, activities are going on that deliver oxygen and food to every microscopic cell in your body. There, the cell's molecular machinery, such as DNA and proteins, carries out the processes your body needs to run, sing, and operate domestic appliances.

You

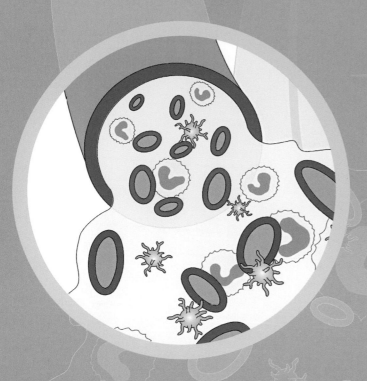

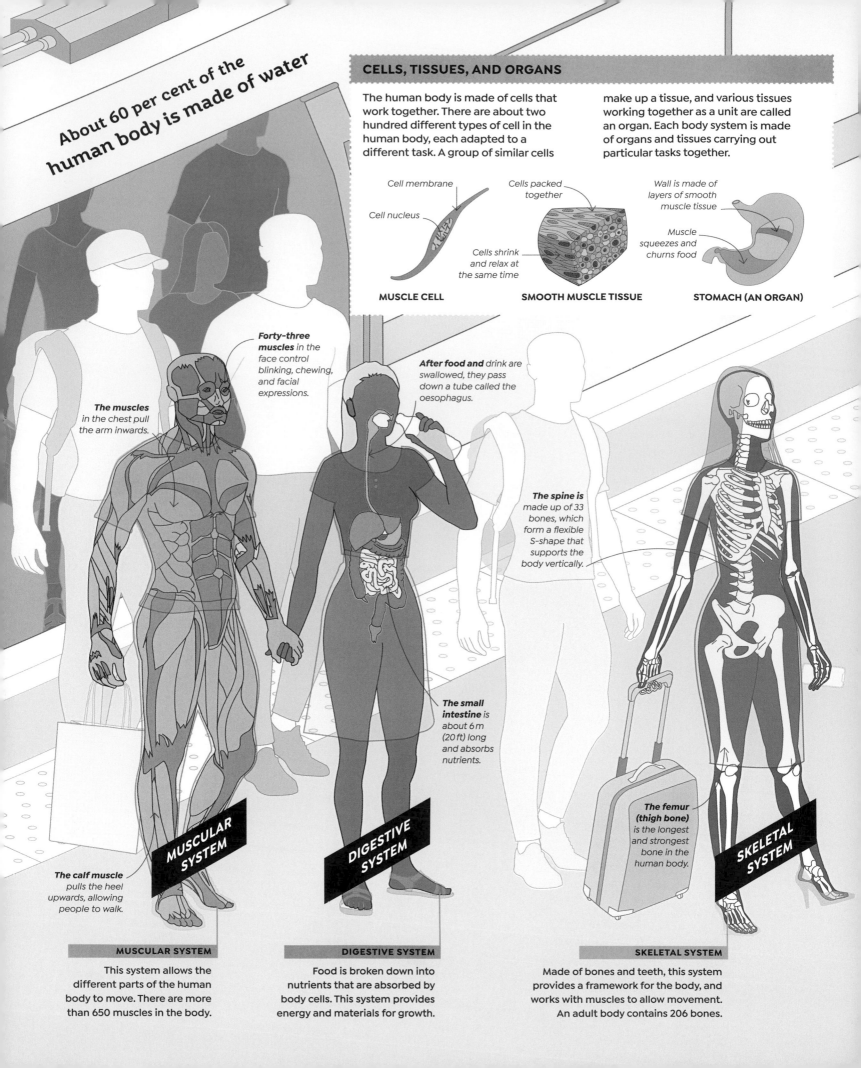

About 60 per cent of the human body is made of water

CELLS, TISSUES, AND ORGANS

The human body is made of cells that work together. There are about two hundred different types of cell in the human body, each adapted to a different task. A group of similar cells make up a tissue, and various tissues working together as a unit are called an organ. Each body system is made of organs and tissues carrying out particular tasks together.

Cell membrane

Cell nucleus

Cells shrink and relax at the same time

MUSCLE CELL

Cells packed together

SMOOTH MUSCLE TISSUE

Wall is made of layers of smooth muscle tissue

Muscle squeezes and churns food

STOMACH (AN ORGAN)

Forty-three muscles in the face control blinking, chewing, and facial expressions.

The muscles in the chest pull the arm inwards.

After food and drink are swallowed, they pass down a tube called the oesophagus.

The spine is made up of 33 bones, which form a flexible S-shape that supports the body vertically.

The small intestine is about 6 m (20 ft) long and absorbs nutrients.

The femur (thigh bone) is the longest and strongest bone in the human body.

The calf muscle pulls the heel upwards, allowing people to walk.

MUSCULAR SYSTEM

DIGESTIVE SYSTEM

SKELETAL SYSTEM

MUSCULAR SYSTEM

This system allows the different parts of the human body to move. There are more than 650 muscles in the body.

DIGESTIVE SYSTEM

Food is broken down into nutrients that are absorbed by body cells. This system provides energy and materials for growth.

SKELETAL SYSTEM

Made of bones and teeth, this system provides a framework for the body, and works with muscles to allow movement. An adult body contains 206 bones.

Body basics

The human body is made up of several systems working together. Each system has a job to do. For example, the respiratory system takes in oxygen from the air and passes it onto the body's blood vessels. Each system is made of tissues and organs that help it do its job.

GROWTH AND DEVELOPMENT

Humans start off as a single cell in the womb. By the time they are born, this has grown to around 26 billion cells. An adult has around 37 trillion cells in their body.

REPRODUCTIVE SYSTEM

This system produces new humans. Both a male and female reproductive system are needed to make a baby.

INTEGUMENTARY SYSTEM

Made up of skin, hair, and nails, this system protects the body from the outside world.

The spinal cord connects the brain to the rest of the nervous system.

A large muscle called the diaphragm helps air to enter the lungs.

Blood vessels carry oxygen, sugar, nutrients, and waste products around the body.

The sciatic nerve is the longest, running from the spine to the sole of the foot.

REPRODUCTIVE SYSTEM

INTEGUMENTARY SYSTEM

NERVOUS SYSTEM

RESPIRATORY SYSTEM

CIRCULATORY SYSTEM

CIRCULATORY SYSTEM

This is made up of the heart and blood vessels. The heart pumps blood around the body to all organs and tissues.

RESPIRATORY SYSTEM

This system draws oxygen into your lungs, where it is absorbed into the bloodstream. It releases carbon dioxide as a waste product.

NERVOUS SYSTEM

The nervous system senses the world and controls the body. The brain receives messages from sensory nerves and sends control signals to muscles.

YOU

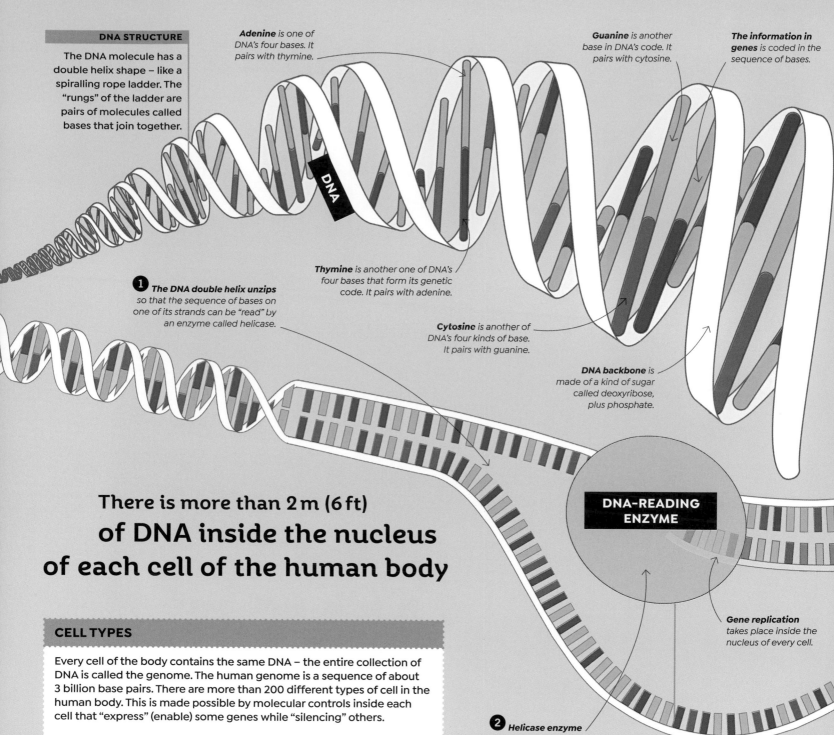

DNA STRUCTURE

The DNA molecule has a double helix shape – like a spiralling rope ladder. The "rungs" of the ladder are pairs of molecules called bases that join together.

Adenine is one of DNA's four bases. It pairs with thymine.

Guanine is another base in DNA's code. It pairs with cytosine.

The information in genes is coded in the sequence of bases.

DNA

Thymine is another one of DNA's four bases that form its genetic code. It pairs with adenine.

Cytosine is another of DNA's four kinds of base. It pairs with guanine.

DNA backbone is made of a kind of sugar called deoxyribose, plus phosphate.

❶ *The DNA double helix unzips* so that the sequence of bases on one of its strands can be "read" by an enzyme called helicase.

There is more than 2 m (6 ft) of DNA inside the nucleus of each cell of the human body

DNA-READING ENZYME

Gene replication takes place inside the nucleus of every cell.

CELL TYPES

Every cell of the body contains the same DNA – the entire collection of DNA is called the genome. The human genome is a sequence of about 3 billion base pairs. There are more than 200 different types of cell in the human body. This is made possible by molecular controls inside each cell that "express" (enable) some genes while "silencing" others.

❷ *Helicase enzyme* reads the genetic code and creates a copy in RNA – a molecule closely related to DNA.

A gene (therefore the length of DNA that must be unzipped) is a sequence of hundreds, thousands, or millions of DNA bases.

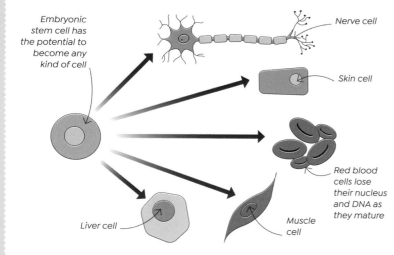

Embryonic stem cell has the potential to become any kind of cell

Nerve cell

Skin cell

Red blood cells lose their nucleus and DNA as they mature

Liver cell

Muscle cell

MAKING A COPY OF A GENE

The first step in making a protein is copying the gene from DNA, inside the cell nucleus. The copy is a single-stranded molecule called RNA (ribonucleic acid). To do this, the DNA double helix is first "unzipped".

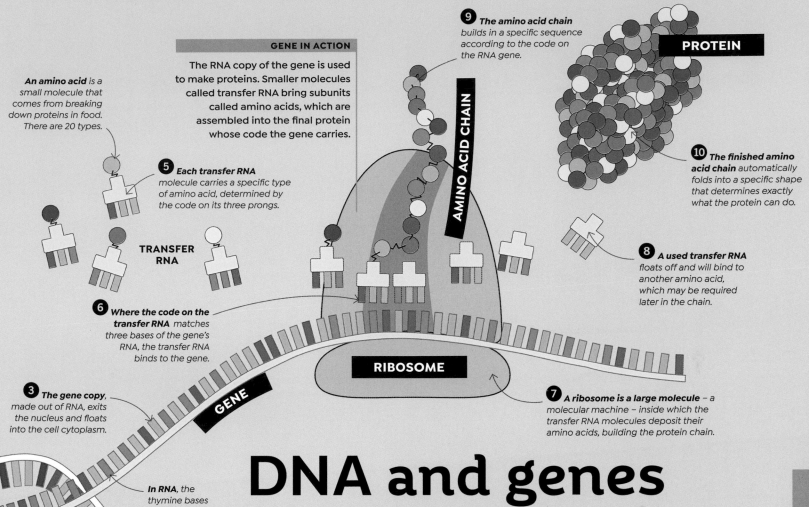

An amino acid is a small molecule that comes from breaking down proteins in food. There are 20 types.

GENE IN ACTION

The RNA copy of the gene is used to make proteins. Smaller molecules called transfer RNA bring subunits called amino acids, which are assembled into the final protein whose code the gene carries.

9 *The amino acid chain* builds in a specific sequence according to the code on the RNA gene.

PROTEIN

AMINO ACID CHAIN

5 *Each transfer RNA* molecule carries a specific type of amino acid, determined by the code on its three prongs.

TRANSFER RNA

10 *The finished amino acid chain* automatically folds into a specific shape that determines exactly what the protein can do.

8 *A used transfer RNA* floats off and will bind to another amino acid, which may be required later in the chain.

6 *Where the code on the transfer RNA* matches three bases of the gene's RNA, the transfer RNA binds to the gene.

GENE

RIBOSOME

7 *A ribosome is a large molecule* – a molecular machine – inside which the transfer RNA molecules deposit their amino acids, building the protein chain.

3 *The gene copy,* made out of RNA, exits the nucleus and floats into the cell cytoplasm.

In RNA, the thymine bases are replaced by a base called uracil.

DNA and genes

DNA (deoxyribonucleic acid) is a chemical found in the nucleus of every cell. It is a long, thin molecule that carries information along its length. Genes are particular sections of DNA – human cells carry about 20,000 genes. In many cases, the information carried by genes is used to make proteins – each with a different job in the body. DNA is the reason why certain characteristics are passed down through generations: a baby gets half of its DNA from each of its parents.

4 *Once the DNA is copied,* another enzyme, called ligase, zips it together again.

The proteins made by genes (see left) help to determine simple characteristics such as eye colour, but also complicated ones such as susceptibility to diseases, athletic ability, and even, to some extent, whether you can roll your tongue. Many of these characteristics are also affected by how much we learn and practise.

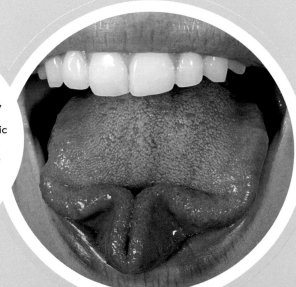

GENETIC ABILITIES

Skeleton

Made up of about 270 bones when you're a baby and 206 bones in adulthood, your skeleton is the light and strong framework that supports and protects your body, gives it shape, and allows it to move. Bones are held together at joints by tough connective fibres, stringy ligaments, or cartilage.

Fibrous joints *use strong fibres, made mostly of a substance called collagen, to join bones, including the 22 bones that make up the skull, or cranium.*

PROTECTION

Some bones offer protection – the skull protects the brain and the ribs protect internal organs.

CRANIUM

PROSTHETIC LIMBS

When someone loses a body part, they may receive an artificial version, called a prosthetic. A prosthetic limb can provide some of the support, flexibility, and motion that bones give in a natural limb.

More than half the bones in the human body are in the hands and feet

Clavicle *is the formal name for the collarbone.*

CLAVICLE

Spongy bone *is porous (full of holes) and contains blood vessels. It is usually found at the ends of long bones, like the humerus.*

Compact bone *is the hard outer shell on most of the body's bones.*

Blood vessels *in spongy bone supply oxygen and nutrients.*

Scapula *is the formal name for the shoulder blade.*

SCAPULA

Yellow bone marrow, *found at the centre of some adult bones, stores fats but can change to red marrow when needed.*

Hinge joints *open and close like a hinge and are found in the fingers, toes, and elbows.*

VERTEBRAE

The spine *(backbone, or vertebral column) is made up of 33 bones called vertebrae.*

RADIUS

ULNA

Cartilaginous joints *join bones that need to move a little. They are connected with cartilage – a strong but flexible connective tissue.*

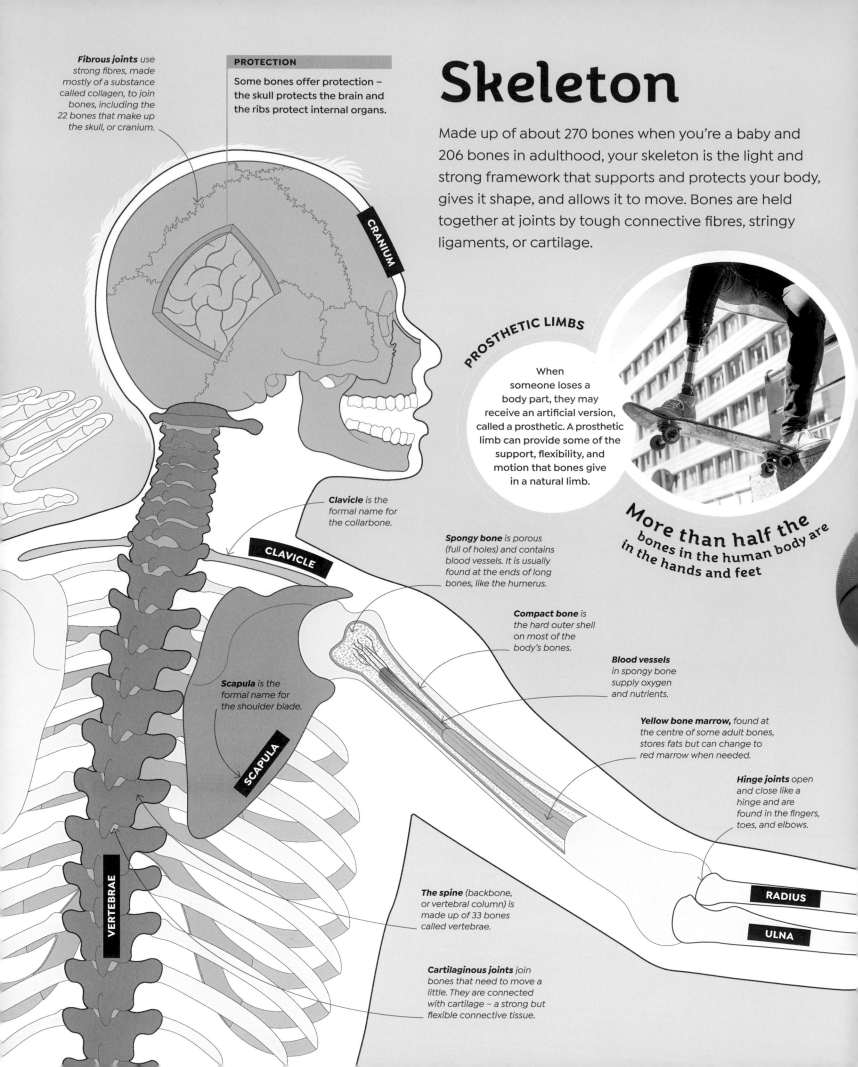

TYPES OF FRACTURES

Bones are strong, but with enough force, they can be broken in several different ways, from cracklike greenstick fractures partway into a bone, to open fractures that tear through the skin. Luckily, old bone cells are always being replenished by new ones, so bones don't stay broken forever – but they may need the support of a splint or cast while they heal.

  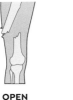 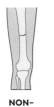

CLOSED   **OPEN**   **NON-DISPLACED**   **DISPLACED**

  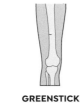 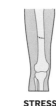

COMMINUTED   **IMPACTED**   **GREENSTICK**   **STRESS**

Ligament

Cartilage

Synovial membrane

Synovial fluid

Muscle

At many of the skeleton's joints, the ends of the bones are coated in tough cartilage and separated by a pocket of fluid. This slippery fluid holds the bones apart and makes movement more smooth.

SYNOVIAL JOINT

Irregular bones have an unusual shape, and include the bones of the face and of the spinal column (vertebrae).

BLOOD CELL PRODUCTION

Blood cells are produced in red bone marrow, which is found inside most bones. Marrow produces billions of blood cells every day.

Flat bones such as the sternum (chest bone) and skull bones are flattened into plates.

Long bones, such as the humerus (upper arm), are strong and wider at the ends than the middle.

Cartilage is a tough, flexible tissue found in your joints, nose, ears, windpipe, and ribs. In childhood, a lot of your skeleton is made of cartilage that gradually turns to bone as you age.

HUMERUS

RIBS

Sesamoid bones found in the wrist, ankle, and knee are small bones that are embedded within tendons.

SHAPE AND SUPPORT

Together, bones give shape and support to the body, keeping it upright and providing the foundation for muscles and other tissues.

The heart and lungs are well protected by the strong ribcage.

A joint is a point where two or more bones meet. There are three types of joint: synovial, fibrous, and cartilaginous.

Short bones are found in the wrist and ankle. They are rounded and made mostly of spongy bone.

PELVIS

Synovial joints are found between bones that need to move freely, like those in the arm and leg. The bones in these joints are cushioned by a capsule filled with synovial fluid.

FEMUR

Ball and socket joints at the hip and shoulder allow a long bone to rotate its rounded end inside a cup-shaped dent in another bone.

SUPPLE SPINE

The spine is an incredible piece of structural engineering. This slender column supports the head, protects the spinal cord, and acts as a framework for the limbs and ribs. It is made up of 33 bones held in place by ligaments. Between the bones are spongy discs that act as shock absorbers and allow the spinal bones to move in various directions without rubbing. The discs contain a jelly-like substance encased in a stretchy fibrous sheath that can flex and compress. Exercise keeps the spine flexible by strengthening the muscles that support it to protect against pain and injury.

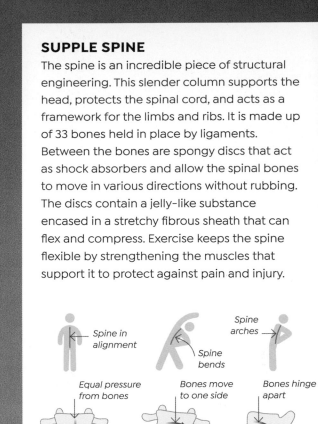

← Spine in alignment

Spine arches →

Spine bends

Equal pressure from bones

Bones move to one side

Bones hinge apart

Disc in resting state

Disc bulges in opposite direction

Disc bulges forward

STANDING UPRIGHT

BENDING SIDEWAYS

BENDING BACKWARD

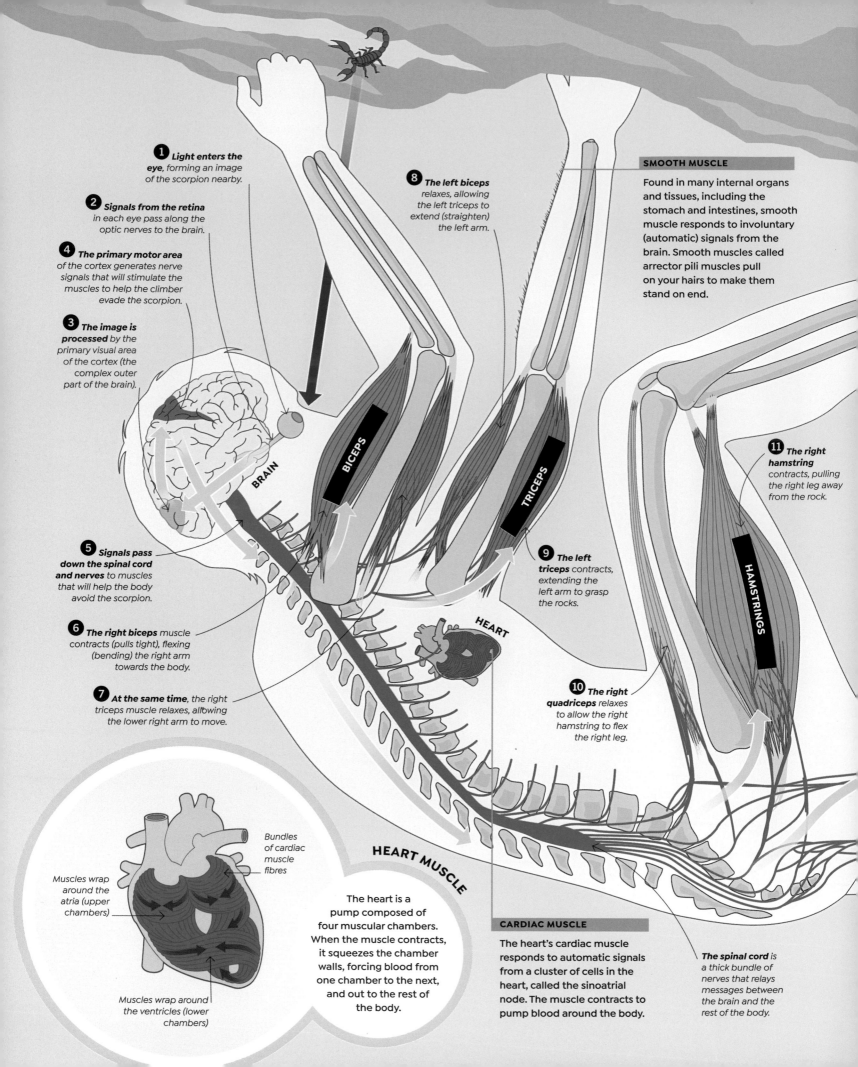

1 *Light enters the eye*, forming an image of the scorpion nearby.

2 *Signals from the retina* in each eye pass along the optic nerves to the brain.

4 *The primary motor area* of the cortex generates nerve signals that will stimulate the muscles to help the climber evade the scorpion.

3 *The image is processed* by the primary visual area of the cortex (the complex outer part of the brain).

5 *Signals pass down the spinal cord and nerves* to muscles that will help the body avoid the scorpion.

6 *The right biceps* muscle contracts (pulls tight), flexing (bending) the right arm towards the body.

7 *At the same time*, the right triceps muscle relaxes, allowing the lower right arm to move.

8 *The left biceps* relaxes, allowing the left triceps to extend (straighten) the left arm.

9 *The left triceps* contracts, extending the left arm to grasp the rocks.

10 *The right quadriceps* relaxes to allow the right hamstring to flex the right leg.

11 *The right hamstring* contracts, pulling the right leg away from the rock.

BRAIN

BICEPS

TRICEPS

HAMSTRINGS

HEART

SMOOTH MUSCLE

Found in many internal organs and tissues, including the stomach and intestines, smooth muscle responds to involuntary (automatic) signals from the brain. Smooth muscles called arrector pili muscles pull on your hairs to make them stand on end.

HEART MUSCLE

Bundles of cardiac muscle fibres

Muscles wrap around the atria (upper chambers)

Muscles wrap around the ventricles (lower chambers)

The heart is a pump composed of four muscular chambers. When the muscle contracts, it squeezes the chamber walls, forcing blood from one chamber to the next, and out to the rest of the body.

CARDIAC MUSCLE

The heart's cardiac muscle responds to automatic signals from a cluster of cells in the heart, called the sinoatrial node. The muscle contracts to pump blood around the body.

The spinal cord is a thick bundle of nerves that relays messages between the brain and the rest of the body.

When muscles are worked hard, they become damaged. As the body repairs this damage, the muscle fibres fuse together, increasing the size of the muscle. Bodybuilders rely on this process during regular training to build their muscle mass to astounding degrees.

BODY BUILDING

Skeletal muscle is surrounded by a protective layer of connective tissue called the epimysium.

A fascicle is a bundle of muscle fibres, surrounded by a tough membrane called the perimysium.

A muscle fibre is a long, single muscle cell.

A myofibril is a structure within a muscle fibre that contracts when the muscle is activated.

MUSCLE FIBRES

Skeletal muscle consists of bundles of hundreds or thousands of cylindrical muscle fibres that are just 0.02–0.08 mm wide.

The human body has nearly 700 skeletal muscles

Pairs of opposing muscles are known as antagonistic pairs, as each one relaxes when the other contracts.

12 *The left quadriceps* contracts, extending the left leg in readiness for the next manoeuvre.

13 *The left hamstring* relaxes, to allow the left leg to extend

QUADRICEPS

SKELETAL MUSCLE

Skeletal muscle is made of long fibres, which attach to bones via tendons. These fibres respond to voluntary (intentional) signals from the brain. The main role of skeletal muscle is to move the skeleton.

Tendons are pieces of connective tissue that attach skeletal muscles firmly to bones.

MUSCULAR SYSTEM

Skeletal muscle, smooth muscle, and cardiac muscle together make up the muscular system. They require a lot of energy and produce heat as a result, keeping the body warm. Muscles near the surface of the body are called superficial muscles, and those closer to the bones and internal organs are called deep muscles.

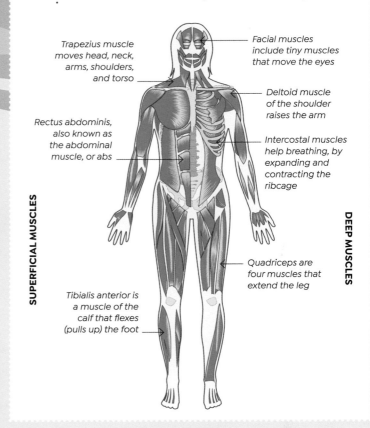

Trapezius muscle moves head, neck, arms, shoulders, and torso

Facial muscles include tiny muscles that move the eyes

Deltoid muscle of the shoulder raises the arm

Rectus abdominis, also known as the abdominal muscle, or abs

Intercostal muscles help breathing, by expanding and contracting the ribcage

SUPERFICIAL MUSCLES

DEEP MUSCLES

Quadriceps are four muscles that extend the leg

Tibialis anterior is a muscle of the calf that flexes (pulls up) the foot

YOU

Muscles

From the thick muscular walls that squeeze the chambers of your heart, to the tiny arrector pili muscles beneath your skin that make your arm hairs stand on end, muscles are the tissues that allow parts of your body to move. All muscles except those in the heart are activated by signals originating in the brain, sent along nerves. These signals stimulate your muscles to contract (pull tight), creating movement.

Nerves and brain

A column of nerves called the spinal cord passes through the hollow bones of the spine, sending electrical signals between the brain and the rest of the body. Each nerve is a bundle of neurons (nerve cells). Signals arrive at the brain from the senses. Outgoing signals move body parts and are voluntary (intentional) or involuntary (unintentional - for example, to control breathing).

Brain and spinal cord make up the central nervous system

Pairs of nerves spread out from the brain and spinal cord

Nerves in the body make up the peripheral nervous system

Sensory and motor nerves are highly branched

Each neuron in the brain can communicate with up to 10,000 others

Dendrites link with axons of other neurons

Axon is a long nerve fibre that carries electrical signals

Nucleus

Cell body of neuron

Each neuron has a cell body with a nucleus, branching threads called dendrites that bring signals to the cell body, and a tail called an axon that carries signals away.

NEURON

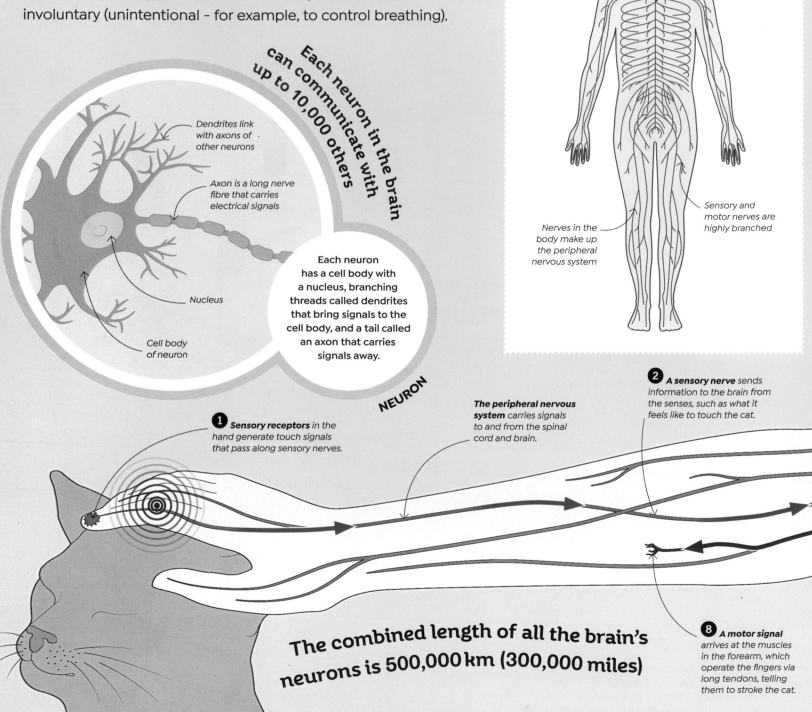

1 *Sensory receptors* in the hand generate touch signals that pass along sensory nerves.

The peripheral nervous system carries signals to and from the spinal cord and brain.

2 *A sensory nerve* sends information to the brain from the senses, such as what it feels like to touch the cat.

8 *A motor signal* arrives at the muscles in the forearm, which operate the fingers via long tendons, telling them to stroke the cat.

The combined length of all the brain's neurons is 500,000 km (300,000 miles)

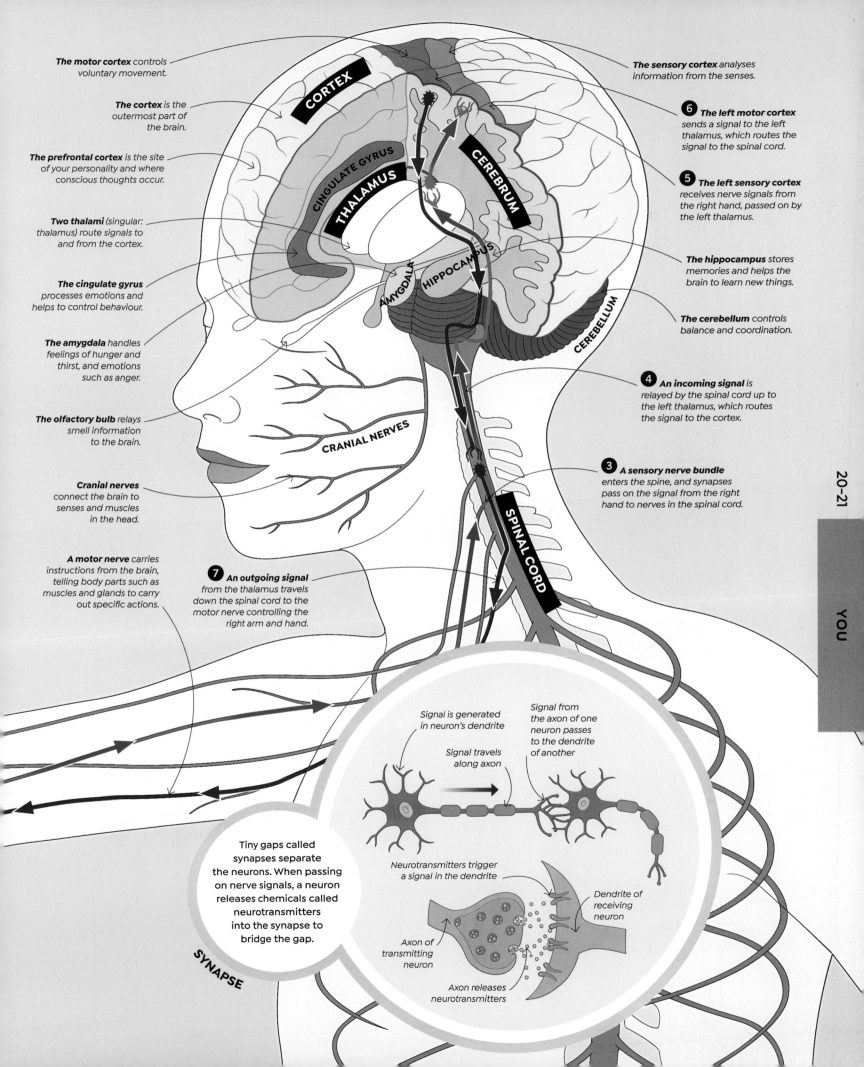

The motor cortex controls voluntary movement.

The cortex is the outermost part of the brain.

The prefrontal cortex is the site of your personality and where conscious thoughts occur.

Two thalami (singular: thalamus) route signals to and from the cortex.

The cingulate gyrus processes emotions and helps to control behaviour.

The amygdala handles feelings of hunger and thirst, and emotions such as anger.

The olfactory bulb relays smell information to the brain.

Cranial nerves connect the brain to senses and muscles in the head.

A motor nerve carries instructions from the brain, telling body parts such as muscles and glands to carry out specific actions.

CORTEX

CINGULATE GYRUS

THALAMUS

CEREBRUM

AMYGDALA

HIPPOCAMPUS

CEREBELLUM

CRANIAL NERVES

SPINAL CORD

The sensory cortex analyses information from the senses.

6 **The left motor cortex** sends a signal to the left thalamus, which routes the signal to the spinal cord.

5 **The left sensory cortex** receives nerve signals from the right hand, passed on by the left thalamus.

The hippocampus stores memories and helps the brain to learn new things.

The cerebellum controls balance and coordination.

4 **An incoming signal** is relayed by the spinal cord up to the left thalamus, which routes the signal to the cortex.

3 **A sensory nerve bundle** enters the spine, and synapses pass on the signal from the right hand to nerves in the spinal cord.

7 **An outgoing signal** from the thalamus travels down the spinal cord to the motor nerve controlling the right arm and hand.

Tiny gaps called synapses separate the neurons. When passing on nerve signals, a neuron releases chemicals called neurotransmitters into the synapse to bridge the gap.

Signal is generated in neuron's dendrite

Signal from the axon of one neuron passes to the dendrite of another

Signal travels along axon

Neurotransmitters trigger a signal in the dendrite

Dendrite of receiving neuron

Axon of transmitting neuron

Axon releases neurotransmitters

SYNAPSE

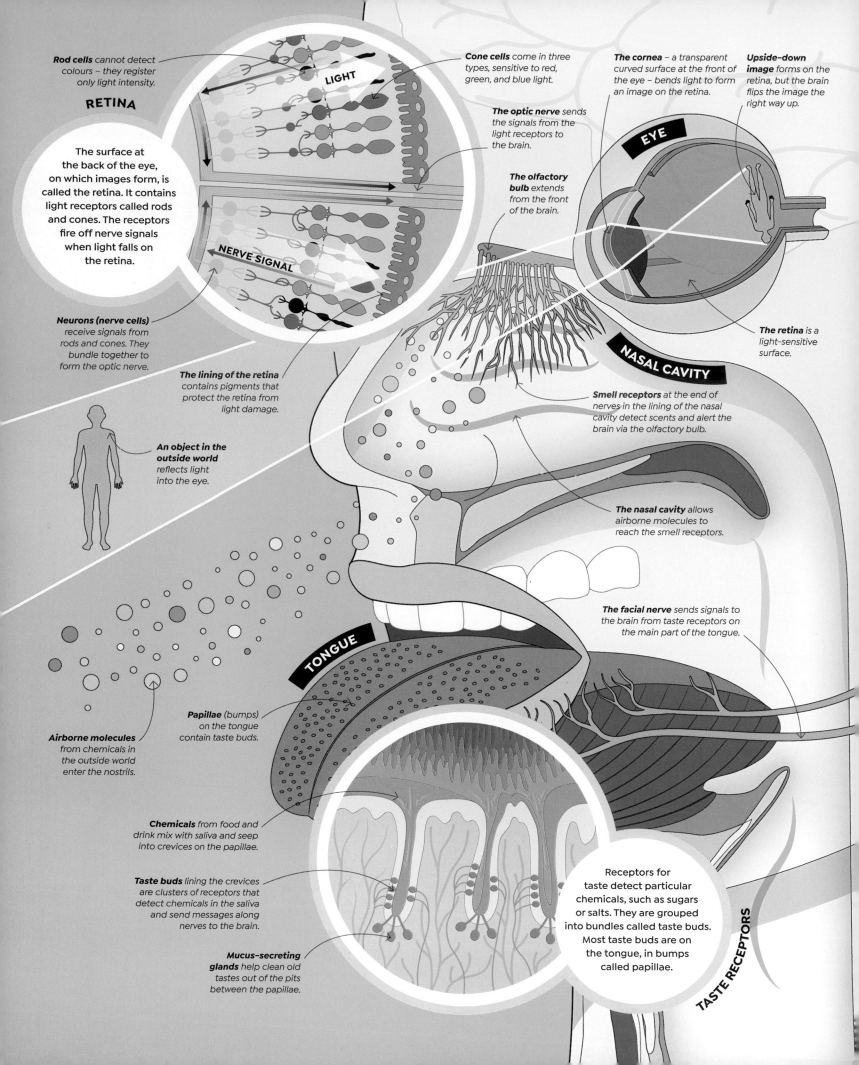

Rod cells cannot detect colours – they register only light intensity.

RETINA

The surface at the back of the eye, on which images form, is called the retina. It contains light receptors called rods and cones. The receptors fire off nerve signals when light falls on the retina.

Neurons (nerve cells) receive signals from rods and cones. They bundle together to form the optic nerve.

The lining of the retina contains pigments that protect the retina from light damage.

An object in the outside world reflects light into the eye.

Airborne molecules from chemicals in the outside world enter the nostrils.

LIGHT

NERVE SIGNAL

Cone cells come in three types, sensitive to red, green, and blue light.

The optic nerve sends the signals from the light receptors to the brain.

The olfactory bulb extends from the front of the brain.

The cornea – a transparent curved surface at the front of the eye – bends light to form an image on the retina.

Upside-down image forms on the retina, but the brain flips the image the right way up.

EYE

NASAL CAVITY

The retina is a light-sensitive surface.

Smell receptors at the end of nerves in the lining of the nasal cavity detect scents and alert the brain via the olfactory bulb.

The nasal cavity allows airborne molecules to reach the smell receptors.

The facial nerve sends signals to the brain from taste receptors on the main part of the tongue.

TONGUE

Papillae (bumps) on the tongue contain taste buds.

Chemicals from food and drink mix with saliva and seep into crevices on the papillae.

Taste buds lining the crevices are clusters of receptors that detect chemicals in the saliva and send messages along nerves to the brain.

Mucus-secreting glands help clean old tastes out of the pits between the papillae.

Receptors for taste detect particular chemicals, such as sugars or salts. They are grouped into bundles called taste buds. Most taste buds are on the tongue, in bumps called papillae.

TASTE RECEPTORS

The inner ear processes sound information, but it also contains miniature organs that detect turning movement, gravity, and acceleration.

1 **The auricle** – the outer ear flap – helps to capture sounds and tell you where they are coming from.

The vestibule contains sensors for gravity and acceleration.

Semicircular canals contain turning movement sensors.

AURICLE

INNER EAR

FACIAL NERVE

GLOSSOPHARYNGEAL NERVE

2 **Sounds vibrate the eardrum**, a thin sheet of tissue at the end of the ear canal.

4 **The cochlea** is a coiled, fluid-filled tube. Waves of vibration travel through the cochlea and shake receptor cells, causing them to send signals to the brain.

3 **Three small bones**, called ossicles, pass vibrations from the eardrum to the cochlea.

The glossopharyngeal nerve carries signals from taste receptors at the back of the tongue.

A child has about 10,000 taste buds, an old person may have fewer than 5,000

Our sense of balance relies partly on information from the eyes and from receptors in the skin and joints. But the inner ear's fluid-filled vestibule and semicircular canals also play a key role. Tiny hairs on receptors inside these structures feed information to the brain about the position and movement of the head – both vital to help us stay upright.

BALANCE

Senses

Our senses – including sight, hearing, taste, smell, and touch – supply our brain with information about our surroundings. Each sense has structures called receptors, which lie at the end of nerves. When triggered by a stimulus, such as light, heat, sound, or chemicals, the receptors fire off electrical nerve signals to the brain. The brain uses the information it gets from the senses to produce our awareness of the world, called perception.

The retina has about 95 million light-sensitive **receptor cells**

MAKING SENSE OF IT ALL

Signals created by receptors travel along nerves into the brain. There, they meet at structures known as thalami (see p.21) – there is one thalamus for each side of the body. The thalami relay the signals from the senses to the appropriate areas of the brain's outermost layer, called the cortex. The cortex processes these sensory signals, allowing us to perceive the world around us.

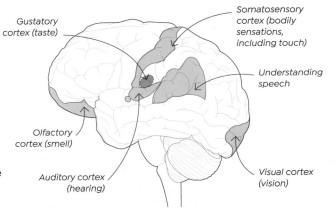

Gustatory cortex (taste)

Somatosensory cortex (bodily sensations, including touch)

Understanding speech

Olfactory cortex (smell)

Auditory cortex (hearing)

Visual cortex (vision)

SIXTH SENSE

Proprioception, sometimes called the sixth sense, is the body's inbuilt way of knowing where it is and how it is moving in space. Sensors in the muscles, skin, and joints join forces with the eyes and balance organs in the ears to send messages to the brain. The brain then sends messages to tell the body to change position or stop moving.

Inner ear sends information about rotation, acceleration, and gravity

Eyes provide information on position

Nerve signals from limbs travel up spine to brain

Sensors in joints tell brain that arms are extended

Input from pressure and tension sensors in legs and feet

UNCONSCIOUS AWARENESS

The body is constantly adjusting its position to maintain balance. Most of the time we are completely unaware of it happening.

Heart and lungs

Since before birth, every person's heart has been beating more than 60 times each minute to keep them alive. This vital organ is a muscular pump, consisting of four chambers. With every beat, it pushes blood around the body through a closed network of blood vessels. The blood delivers oxygen, absorbed from the air in the lungs, to the body's cells, and removes the waste product carbon dioxide, which is then exhaled from the lungs.

BLOOD CIRCULATION

Capillaries are tiny blood vessels that form an extensive network throughout every part of the body. Oxygen passes from the blood inside, through their thin walls, into the cells of nearby tissues, and the carbon dioxide that cells produce as a waste product passes from cells into the blood. Blood also carries nutrients absorbed from digested food.

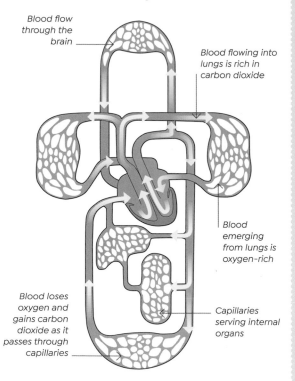

Blood flow through the brain

Blood flowing into lungs is rich in carbon dioxide

Blood emerging from lungs is oxygen-rich

Blood loses oxygen and gains carbon dioxide as it passes through capillaries

Capillaries serving internal organs

The heart beats more than 36 million times every year

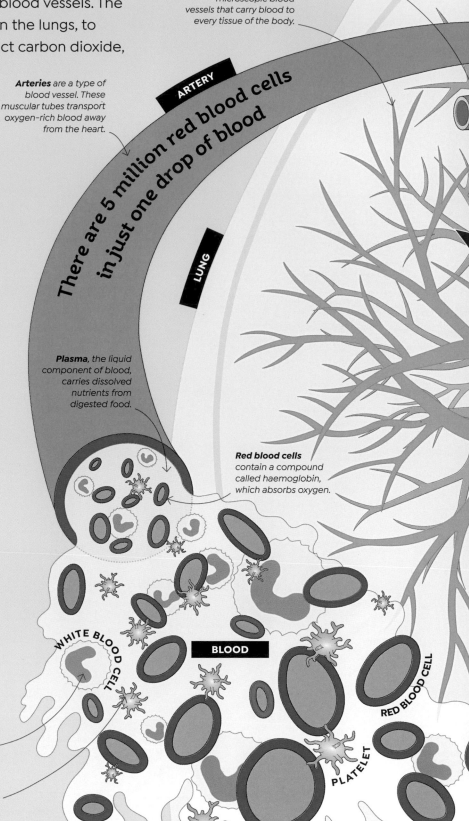

Lungs take in oxygen-rich air from outside the body with each inhale, and expel carbon-dioxide-rich air with each exhale.

Veins are blood vessels that carry blood towards the heart.

Capillaries are microscopic blood vessels that carry blood to every tissue of the body.

Arteries are a type of blood vessel. These muscular tubes transport oxygen-rich blood away from the heart.

ARTERY

There are 5 million red blood cells in just one drop of blood

LUNG

Plasma, the liquid component of blood, carries dissolved nutrients from digested food.

Red blood cells contain a compound called haemoglobin, which absorbs oxygen.

BLOOD

WHITE BLOOD CELL

RED BLOOD CELL

PLATELET

White blood cells are an essential part of the immune system, which fights disease.

Platelets help to make the blood thick when it needs to clot at the site of an injury.

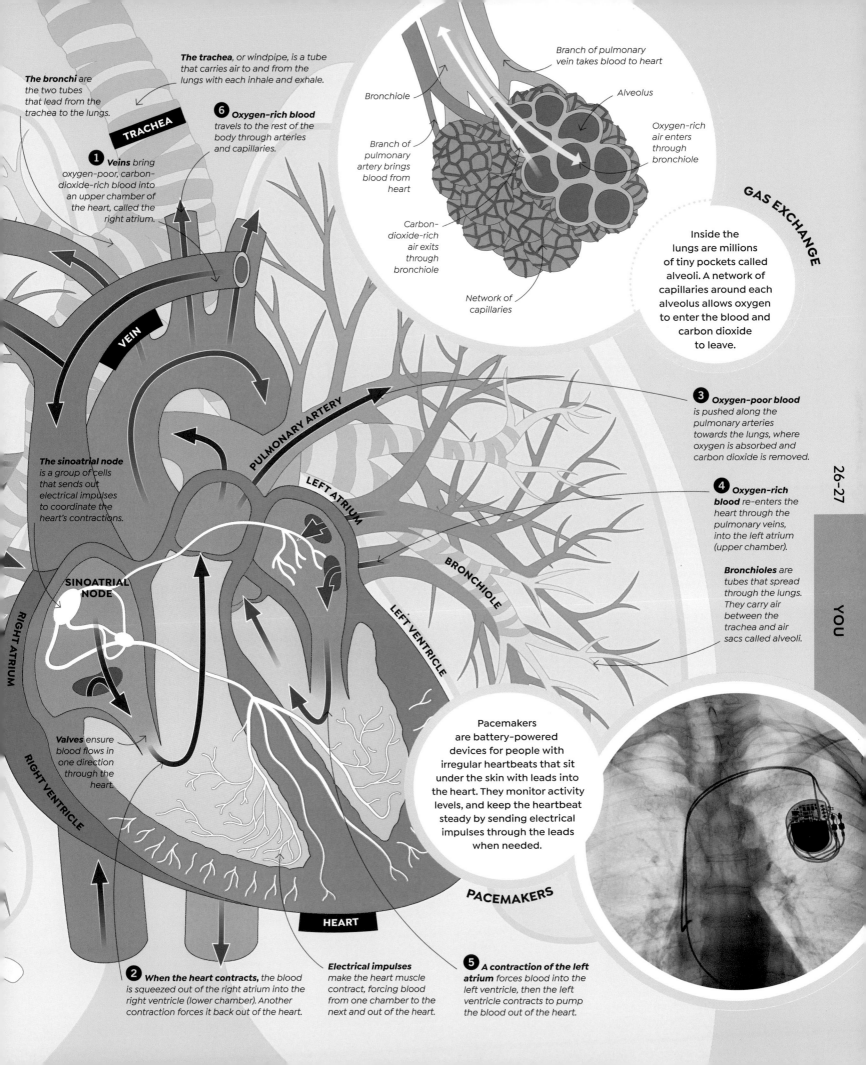

The bronchi are the two tubes that lead from the trachea to the lungs.

The trachea, or windpipe, is a tube that carries air to and from the lungs with each inhale and exhale.

6 **Oxygen-rich blood** travels to the rest of the body through arteries and capillaries.

1 **Veins** bring oxygen-poor, carbon-dioxide-rich blood into an upper chamber of the heart, called the right atrium.

TRACHEA

VEIN

Branch of pulmonary vein takes blood to heart

Bronchiole

Branch of pulmonary artery brings blood from heart

Alveolus

Oxygen-rich air enters through bronchiole

Carbon-dioxide-rich air exits through bronchiole

Network of capillaries

GAS EXCHANGE

Inside the lungs are millions of tiny pockets called alveoli. A network of capillaries around each alveolus allows oxygen to enter the blood and carbon dioxide to leave.

PULMONARY ARTERY

3 **Oxygen-poor blood** is pushed along the pulmonary arteries towards the lungs, where oxygen is absorbed and carbon dioxide is removed.

LEFT ATRIUM

4 **Oxygen-rich blood** re-enters the heart through the pulmonary veins, into the left atrium (upper chamber).

BRONCHIOLE

Bronchioles are tubes that spread through the lungs. They carry air between the trachea and air sacs called alveoli.

The sinoatrial node is a group of cells that sends out electrical impulses to coordinate the heart's contractions.

LEFT VENTRICLE

SINOATRIAL NODE

RIGHT ATRIUM

Valves ensure blood flows in one direction through the heart.

RIGHT VENTRICLE

Pacemakers are battery-powered devices for people with irregular heartbeats that sit under the skin with leads into the heart. They monitor activity levels, and keep the heartbeat steady by sending electrical impulses through the leads when needed.

PACEMAKERS

HEART

2 **When the heart contracts,** the blood is squeezed out of the right atrium into the right ventricle (lower chamber). Another contraction forces it back out of the heart.

Electrical impulses make the heart muscle contract, forcing blood from one chamber to the next and out of the heart.

5 **A contraction of the left atrium** forces blood into the left ventricle, then the left ventricle contracts to pump the blood out of the heart.

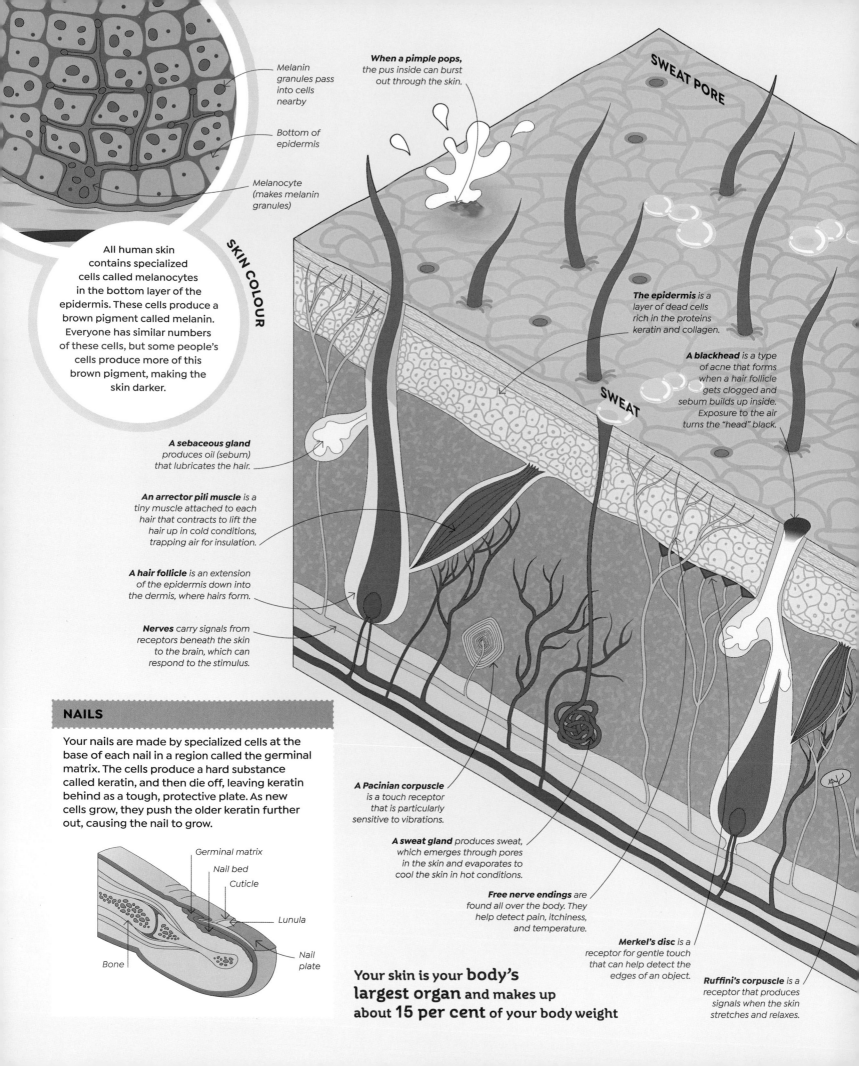

Melanin granules pass into cells nearby

Bottom of epidermis

Melanocyte (makes melanin granules)

When a pimple pops, the pus inside can burst out through the skin.

SWEAT PORE

SKIN COLOUR

All human skin contains specialized cells called melanocytes in the bottom layer of the epidermis. These cells produce a brown pigment called melanin. Everyone has similar numbers of these cells, but some people's cells produce more of this brown pigment, making the skin darker.

The epidermis is a layer of dead cells rich in the proteins keratin and collagen.

A blackhead is a type of acne that forms when a hair follicle gets clogged and sebum builds up inside. Exposure to the air turns the "head" black.

SWEAT

A sebaceous gland produces oil (sebum) that lubricates the hair.

An arrector pili muscle is a tiny muscle attached to each hair that contracts to lift the hair up in cold conditions, trapping air for insulation.

A hair follicle is an extension of the epidermis down into the dermis, where hairs form.

Nerves carry signals from receptors beneath the skin to the brain, which can respond to the stimulus.

NAILS

Your nails are made by specialized cells at the base of each nail in a region called the germinal matrix. The cells produce a hard substance called keratin, and then die off, leaving keratin behind as a tough, protective plate. As new cells grow, they push the older keratin further out, causing the nail to grow.

Germinal matrix

Nail bed

Cuticle

Lunula

Nail plate

Bone

A Pacinian corpuscle is a touch receptor that is particularly sensitive to vibrations.

A sweat gland produces sweat, which emerges through pores in the skin and evaporates to cool the skin in hot conditions.

Free nerve endings are found all over the body. They help detect pain, itchiness, and temperature.

Merkel's disc is a receptor for gentle touch that can help detect the edges of an object.

Your skin is your **body's largest organ** and makes up about **15 per cent** of your body weight

Ruffini's corpuscle is a receptor that produces signals when the skin stretches and relaxes.

Skin, hair, and nails

Known as the integumentary system, your skin, hair, and nails form a barrier to the outside world. Skin protects your body against heat, light, and injury, and detects pressure and temperature change. It also works together with your hair to keep you at the right temperature, trapping air to insulate your skin when it is cold, and sweating to cool you when you are hot.

The hair shaft extends from the follicle, above the epidermis.

❶ *An injury to the skin* allows bacteria to enter your body, which could cause a dangerous infection, so your immune system (see pp.38–39) leaps into action to eradicate the threat.

HAIR

CUT IN THE SKIN

A whitehead is a type of acne that forms when a hair follicle gets blocked. Sebum, skin cells, and bacteria build up, forming pus and causing a swollen white "head".

EPIDERMIS

DERMIS

HYPODERMIS

❷ *Nearby cells recognize* the invaders as non-human, and release chemicals, called cytokines, which spread out to nearby tissues.

❸ *Cytokines cause nearby blood vessels to expand* (causing redness and swelling) and attract white blood cells, including neutrophils and macrophages, which attack the bacteria.

❹ *The macrophages and neutrophils* engulf and destroy the bacteria, slowing or stopping the infection.

Meissner's corpuscle is a nerve ending that detects very gentle pressure.

An arteriole is a small blood vessel that brings oxygen and nutrients to the skin.

The skin is composed of three layers: the epidermis, dermis, and hypodermis.

A venule is a small blood vessel that takes away carbon dioxide and other waste products.

This image shows the tails of eyelash mites poking out of their host's hair follicles. These tiny arachnids live harmlessly within your eyelash follicles, where they feed on your dead skin cells.

EYELASH MITES

YOU

HAIR GROWTH

Hairs are "shafts" made mostly of keratin that grow from structures found in the dermis called follicles. They develop in three phases. Anagen, the most active phase, lasts for several years for hairs on your scalp.

Base of follicle produces hair shaft

ANAGEN
Cells at root divide rapidly, pushing out old hair.

Hair can no longer grow

CATAGEN
Hair shaft breaks away from base of follicle.

New hair will replace lost hair

TELOGEN
Resting phase, in which hair is ready to be pushed out.

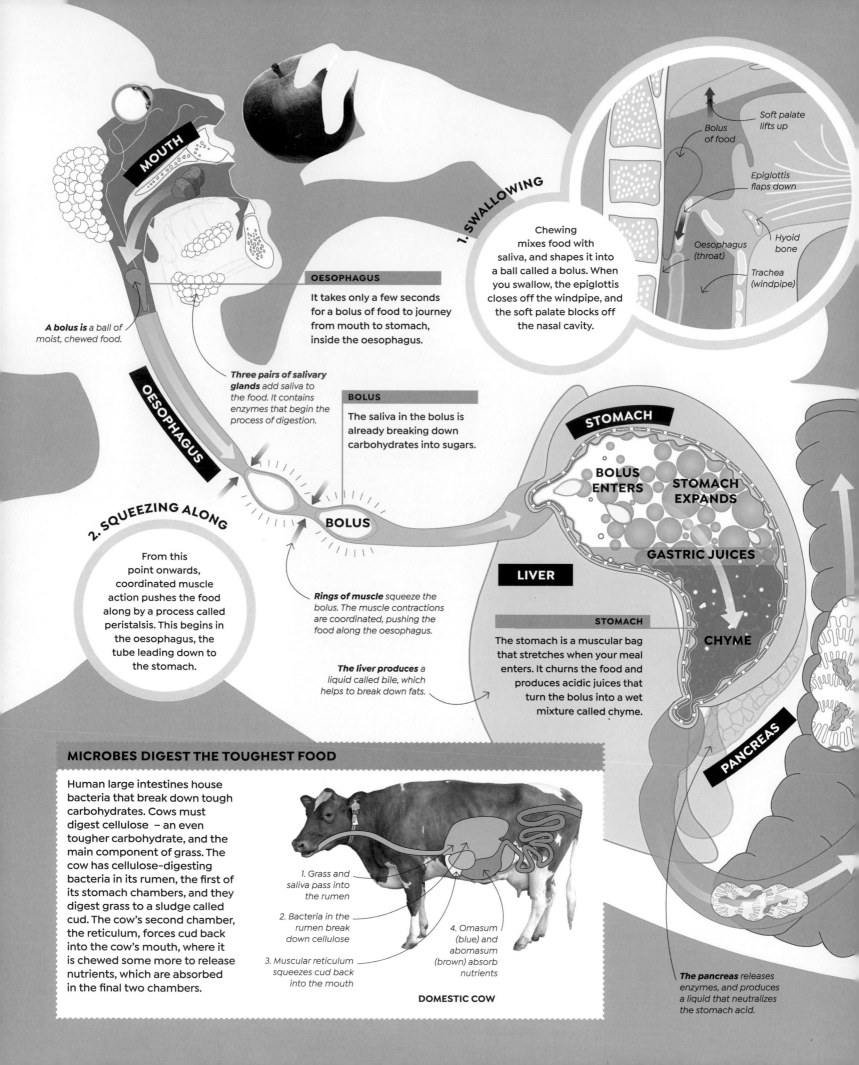

MOUTH

OESOPHAGUS

A bolus is a ball of moist, chewed food.

OESOPHAGUS

It takes only a few seconds for a bolus of food to journey from mouth to stomach, inside the oesophagus.

Three pairs of salivary glands add saliva to the food. It contains enzymes that begin the process of digestion.

BOLUS

The saliva in the bolus is already breaking down carbohydrates into sugars.

1. SWALLOWING

Chewing mixes food with saliva, and shapes it into a ball called a bolus. When you swallow, the epiglottis closes off the windpipe, and the soft palate blocks off the nasal cavity.

Bolus of food

Soft palate lifts up

Epiglottis flaps down

Oesophagus (throat)

Hyoid bone

Trachea (windpipe)

2. SQUEEZING ALONG

From this point onwards, coordinated muscle action pushes the food along by a process called peristalsis. This begins in the oesophagus, the tube leading down to the stomach.

BOLUS

Rings of muscle squeeze the bolus. The muscle contractions are coordinated, pushing the food along the oesophagus.

The liver produces a liquid called bile, which helps to break down fats.

STOMACH

BOLUS ENTERS

STOMACH EXPANDS

GASTRIC JUICES

LIVER

STOMACH

The stomach is a muscular bag that stretches when your meal enters. It churns the food and produces acidic juices that turn the bolus into a wet mixture called chyme.

CHYME

PANCREAS

The pancreas releases enzymes, and produces a liquid that neutralizes the stomach acid.

MICROBES DIGEST THE TOUGHEST FOOD

Human large intestines house bacteria that break down tough carbohydrates. Cows must digest cellulose – an even tougher carbohydrate, and the main component of grass. The cow has cellulose-digesting bacteria in its rumen, the first of its stomach chambers, and they digest grass to a sludge called cud. The cow's second chamber, the reticulum, forces cud back into the cow's mouth, where it is chewed some more to release nutrients, which are absorbed in the final two chambers.

1. Grass and saliva pass into the rumen

2. Bacteria in the rumen break down cellulose

3. Muscular reticulum squeezes cud back into the mouth

4. Omasum (blue) and abomasum (brown) absorb nutrients

DOMESTIC COW

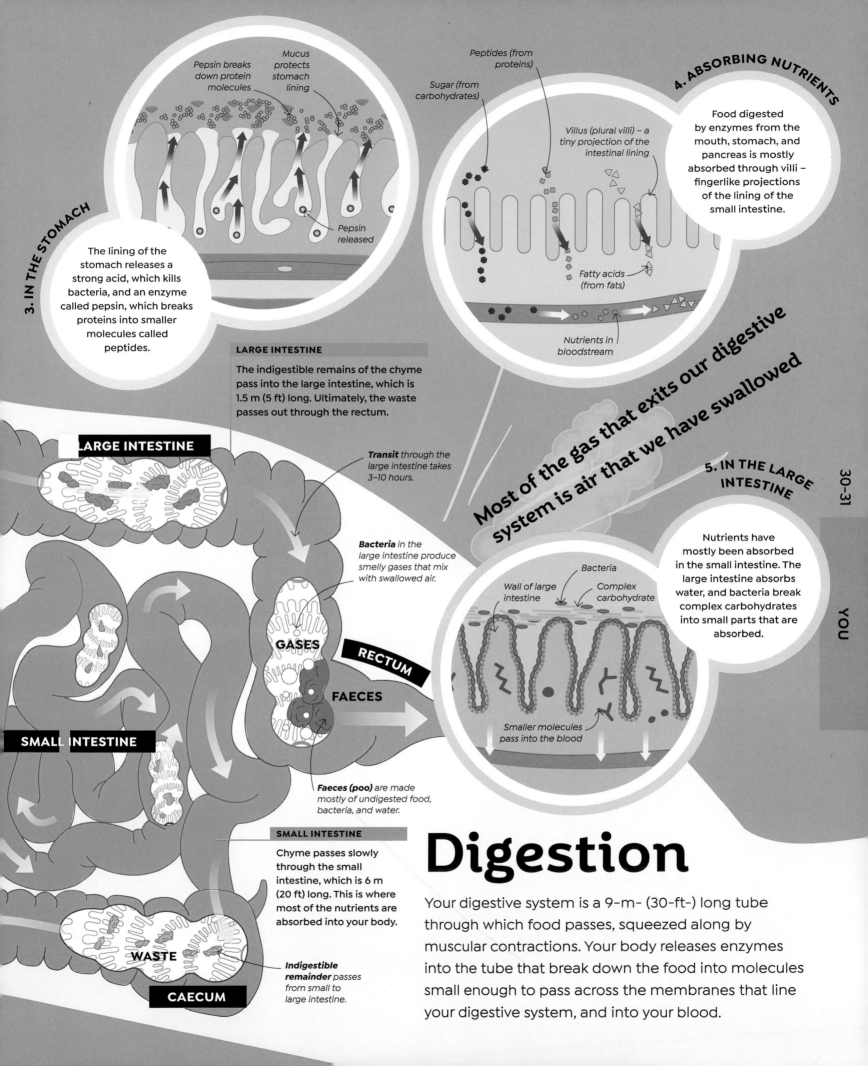

3. IN THE STOMACH

Pepsin breaks down protein molecules

Mucus protects stomach lining

Pepsin released

The lining of the stomach releases a strong acid, which kills bacteria, and an enzyme called pepsin, which breaks proteins into smaller molecules called peptides.

4. ABSORBING NUTRIENTS

Peptides (from proteins)

Sugar (from carbohydrates)

Villus (plural villi) – a tiny projection of the intestinal lining

Food digested by enzymes from the mouth, stomach, and pancreas is mostly absorbed through villi – fingerlike projections of the lining of the small intestine.

Fatty acids (from fats)

Nutrients in bloodstream

LARGE INTESTINE

The indigestible remains of the chyme pass into the large intestine, which is 1.5 m (5 ft) long. Ultimately, the waste passes out through the rectum.

Transit through the large intestine takes 3–10 hours.

Bacteria in the large intestine produce smelly gases that mix with swallowed air.

Most of the gas that exits our digestive system is air that we have swallowed

5. IN THE LARGE INTESTINE

Nutrients have mostly been absorbed in the small intestine. The large intestine absorbs water, and bacteria break complex carbohydrates into small parts that are absorbed.

Bacteria

Wall of large intestine

Complex carbohydrate

Smaller molecules pass into the blood

LARGE INTESTINE

GASES

RECTUM

FAECES

SMALL INTESTINE

Faeces (poo) are made mostly of undigested food, bacteria, and water.

SMALL INTESTINE

Chyme passes slowly through the small intestine, which is 6 m (20 ft) long. This is where most of the nutrients are absorbed into your body.

Indigestible remainder passes from small to large intestine.

WASTE

CAECUM

Digestion

Your digestive system is a 9-m- (30-ft-) long tube through which food passes, squeezed along by muscular contractions. Your body releases enzymes into the tube that break down the food into molecules small enough to pass across the membranes that line your digestive system, and into your blood.

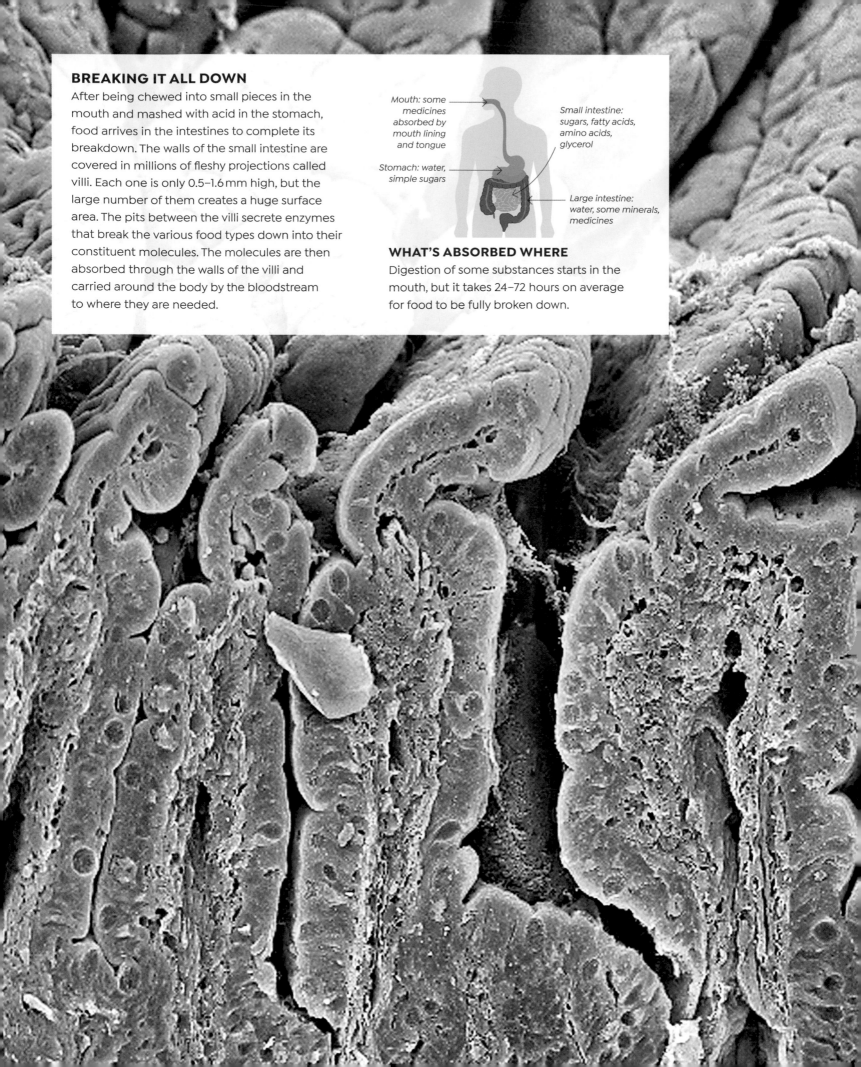

BREAKING IT ALL DOWN

After being chewed into small pieces in the mouth and mashed with acid in the stomach, food arrives in the intestines to complete its breakdown. The walls of the small intestine are covered in millions of fleshy projections called villi. Each one is only 0.5–1.6 mm high, but the large number of them creates a huge surface area. The pits between the villi secrete enzymes that break the various food types down into their constituent molecules. The molecules are then absorbed through the walls of the villi and carried around the body by the bloodstream to where they are needed.

Mouth: some medicines absorbed by mouth lining and tongue

Stomach: water, simple sugars

Small intestine: sugars, fatty acids, amino acids, glycerol

Large intestine: water, some minerals, medicines

WHAT'S ABSORBED WHERE

Digestion of some substances starts in the mouth, but it takes 24–72 hours on average for food to be fully broken down.

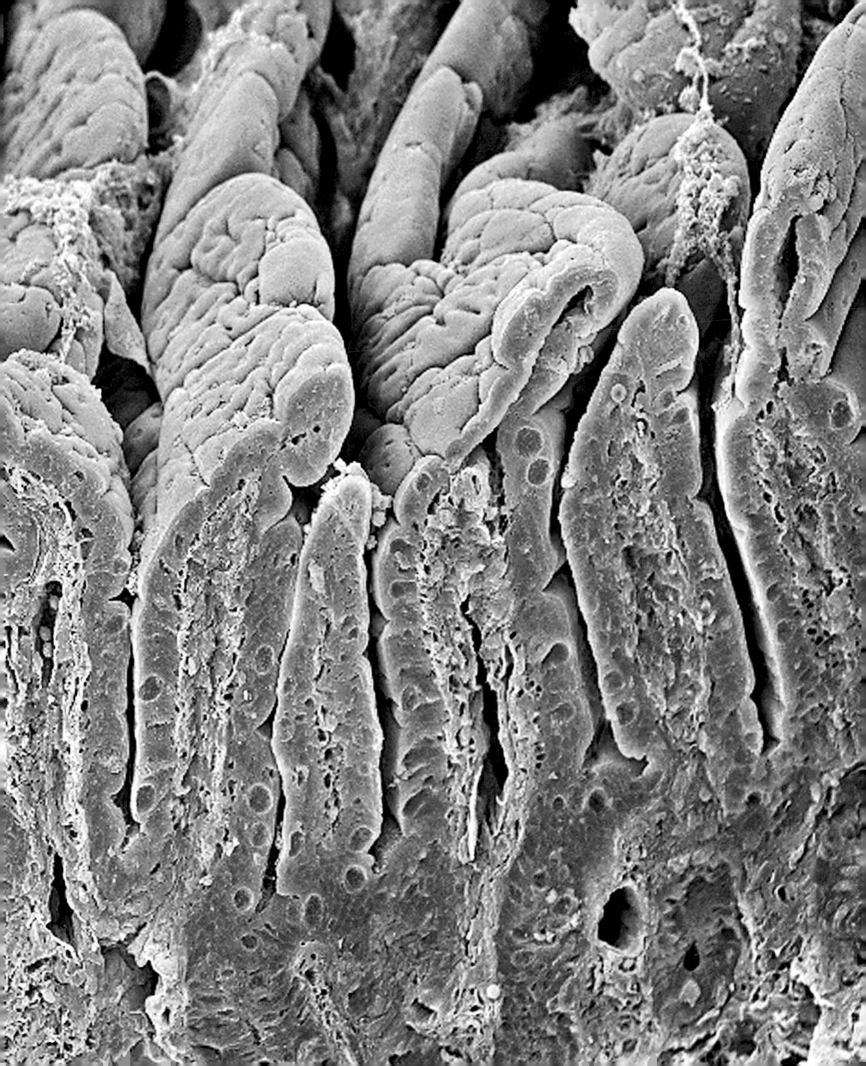

FATS

Fats are needed in every cell of the body to build cell membranes, and help your body absorb nutrients. Unsaturated fats, found in foods like vegetable oils, nuts, and fish, lower your risk of disease.

Dairy products include milk, butter, and cheese. They are sources of proteins and fat.

Vegetables are vital to a healthy diet, because they are rich in fibre, vitamins, and minerals. These nutrients help prevent diseases such as heart disease and some types of cancer.

Sugar provides rapid energy that is hard for your body to regulate unless you are exercising hard. This is why it can lead to weight gain and diabetes.

Caffeine, found in coffee and tea, does not have any nutritional value.

FATS

VEGETABLES

Dairy alternatives, such as soy milk, often have calcium added to them by their manufacturers to make sure people who don't consume dairy products get the nutrients they need.

Fruits are rich in water, vitamins, minerals, and fibre, which help with digestion and disease prevention.

Fish is an excellent source of protein and unsaturated fats, which have many health benefits.

WATER

From helping your body to digest food, to keeping it at the right temperature, water is an essential part of many of your body's processes.

Meat has been hunted by humans for food for 2 million years. It is rich in protein and B vitamins.

A healthy diet is achieved by eating a variety of foods, ensuring you consume all the food types, and avoiding too much sugar.

MEAT

How do you fancy a grasshopper burger topped with juicy mealworms? About two billion people around the world regularly eat insects. That number is set to grow due to climate change, since producing insect-based food uses much less energy, water, and land than producing other high-protein foods like beef.

Fermented food such as kimchee, sauerkraut, and yoghurt, help balance the good bacteria that live in your gut.

EATING INSECTS

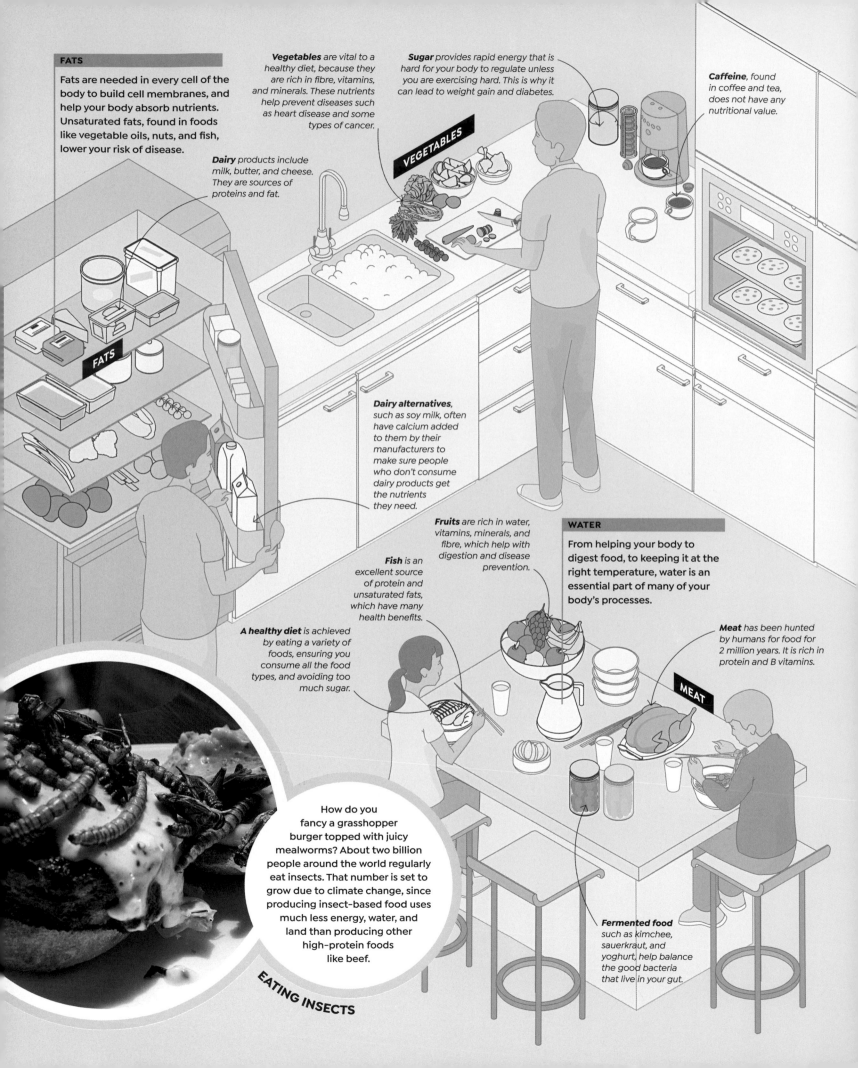

The energy available in food is measured in units called kilocalories (kcal). A large egg provides 80 kcal

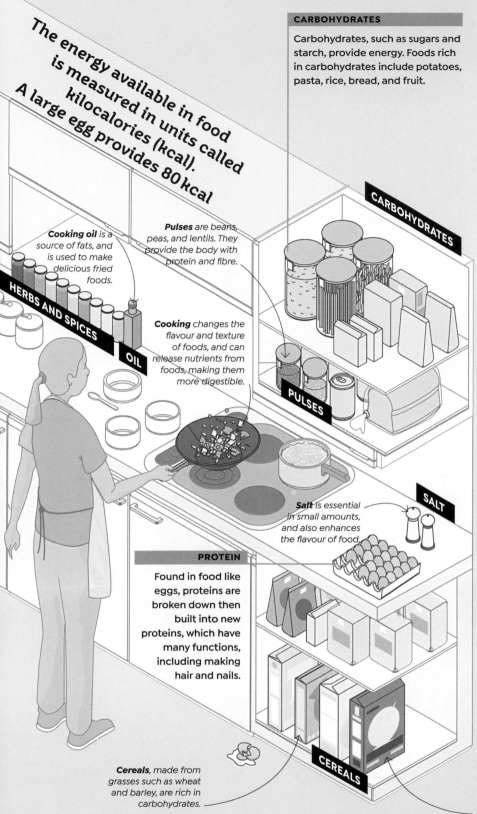

Cooking oil is a source of fats, and is used to make delicious fried foods.

Pulses are beans, peas, and lentils. They provide the body with protein and fibre.

Cooking changes the flavour and texture of foods, and can release nutrients from foods, making them more digestible.

HERBS AND SPICES

OIL

CARBOHYDRATES

Carbohydrates, such as sugars and starch, provide energy. Foods rich in carbohydrates include potatoes, pasta, rice, bread, and fruit.

CARBOHYDRATES

PULSES

SALT

Salt is essential in small amounts, and also enhances the flavour of food.

PROTEIN

Found in food like eggs, proteins are broken down then built into new proteins, which have many functions, including making hair and nails.

Cereals, made from grasses such as wheat and barley, are rich in carbohydrates.

CEREALS

Fibre is a type of carbohydrate the body cannot digest, but it keeps the digestive system healthy.

VITAMINS AND MINERALS

Vitamins and minerals are nutrients that are needed in small amounts, but are essential to keep the body healthy. Deficiencies in these micronutrients can lead to fatigue and diseases such as scurvy and rickets.

VITAMIN A
Important for a healthy immune system.

VITAMIN B
A group of eight vitamins, with a variety of roles.

VITAMIN C
Helps in many processes, such as wound healing.

VITAMIN D
Vitamin that keeps bones and muscles healthy.

VITAMIN E
Helps keep skin and eyes healthy, and fights disease.

CALCIUM
Mineral that keeps bones healthy and muscles working.

IODINE.
Mineral involved in the production of some hormones.

IRON
Mineral needed for the production of red blood cells.

ZINC
Mineral needed for making new cells and wound healing.

FAT CELLS

When you consume excess carbohydrates, your body converts them into fat. Along with other excess fats from foods, this fat is stored in fat cells, found under the skin and around the liver. It acts as a vital energy reserve for when food is scarce or your activity has increased, and helps keep the body warm.

Fat cells are called adipocytes

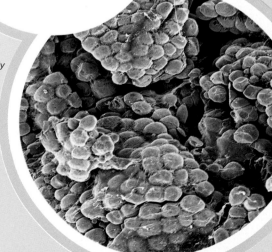

Food and nutrition

The food and drinks you consume should supply everything you need to keep your body working, heal injuries, and fight off disease. Food provides your body with two types of nutrients: macronutrients (such as carbohydrates, proteins, and fats) and micronutrients (such as vitamins and minerals).

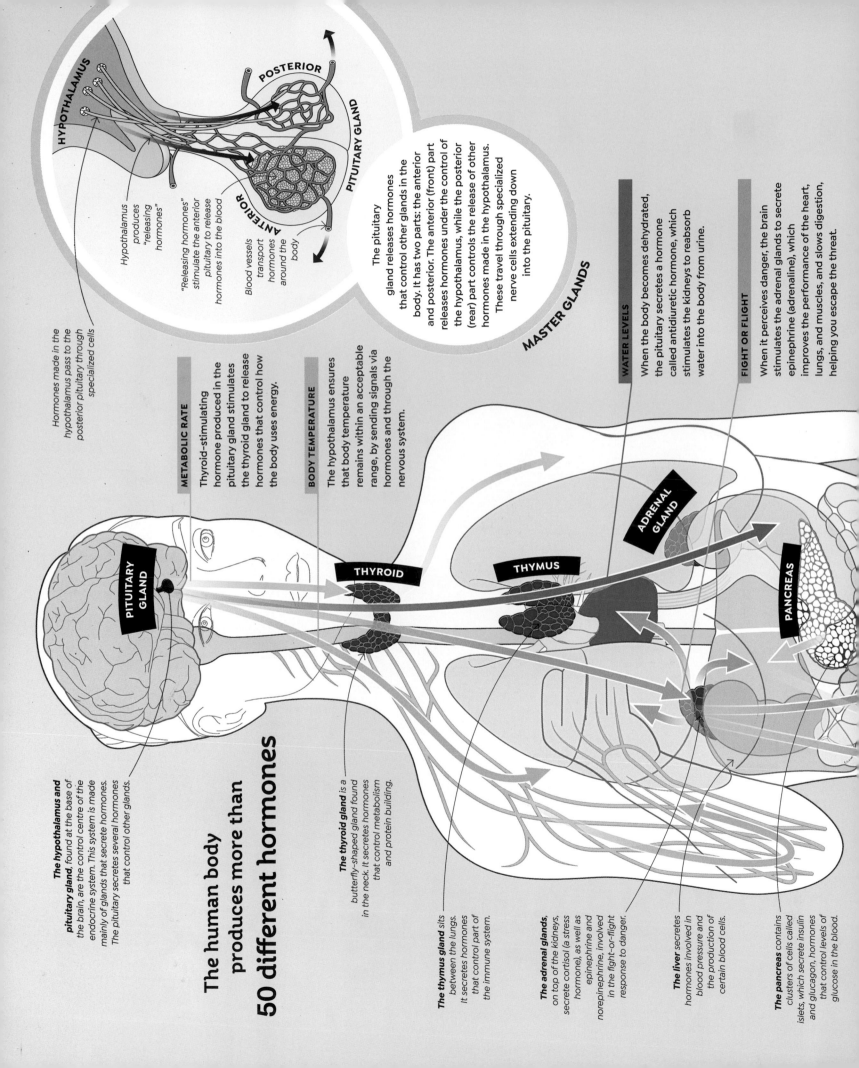

The human body produces more than 50 different hormones

The hypothalamus and pituitary gland, found at the base of the brain, are the control centre of the endocrine system. This system is made mainly of glands that secrete hormones. The pituitary secretes several hormones that control other glands.

HYPOTHALAMUS

POSTERIOR

ANTERIOR

PITUITARY GLAND

Hypothalamus produces "releasing hormones"

"Releasing hormones" stimulate the anterior pituitary to release hormones into the blood

Blood vessels transport hormones around the body

Hormones made in the hypothalamus pass to the posterior pituitary through specialized cells

MASTER GLANDS

The pituitary gland releases hormones that control other glands in the body. It has two parts: the anterior and posterior. The anterior (front) part releases hormones under the control of the hypothalamus, while the posterior (rear) part controls the release of other hormones made in the hypothalamus. These travel through specialized nerve cells extending down into the pituitary.

METABOLIC RATE
Thyroid-stimulating hormone produced in the pituitary gland stimulates the thyroid gland to release hormones that control how the body uses energy.

BODY TEMPERATURE
The hypothalamus ensures that body temperature remains within an acceptable range, by sending signals via hormones and through the nervous system.

WATER LEVELS
When the body becomes dehydrated, the pituitary secretes a hormone called antidiuretic hormone, which stimulates the kidneys to reabsorb water into the body from urine.

FIGHT OR FLIGHT
When it perceives danger, the brain stimulates the adrenal glands to secrete epinephrine (adrenaline), which improves the performance of the heart, lungs, and muscles, and slows digestion, helping you escape the threat.

PITUITARY GLAND

THYROID

THYMUS

ADRENAL GLAND

PANCREAS

The thyroid gland is a butterfly-shaped gland found in the neck. It secretes hormones that control metabolism and protein building.

The thymus gland sits between the lungs. It secretes hormones that control part of the immune system.

The adrenal glands, on top of the kidneys, secrete cortisol (a stress hormone), as well as epinephrine and norepinephrine, involved in the fight-or-flight response to danger.

The liver secretes hormones involved in blood pressure and the production of certain blood cells.

The pancreas contains clusters of cells called islets, which secrete insulin and glucagon, hormones that control levels of glucose in the blood.

Hormones

Hormones are the body's chemical messengers. They control how the body uses energy, as well as how it grows and develops. A hormone is secreted (released) into the blood by groups of cells called glands. When the hormone reaches its target cells and tissues, it causes them to work in a new or special way.

BLOOD GLUCOSE

Insulin and glucagon, secreted by the pancreas, regulate levels of the sugar glucose in the blood. They stimulate the liver to release glucose when needed, or absorb it for storage when there is an excess.

NEGATIVE FEEDBACK

Hormones help ensure the body's systems remain in balance. Some do this by negative feedback: when something goes out of balance, hormones are released to correct the change. A good example is blood glucose, which is controlled by a negative feedback loop involving insulin and glucagon.

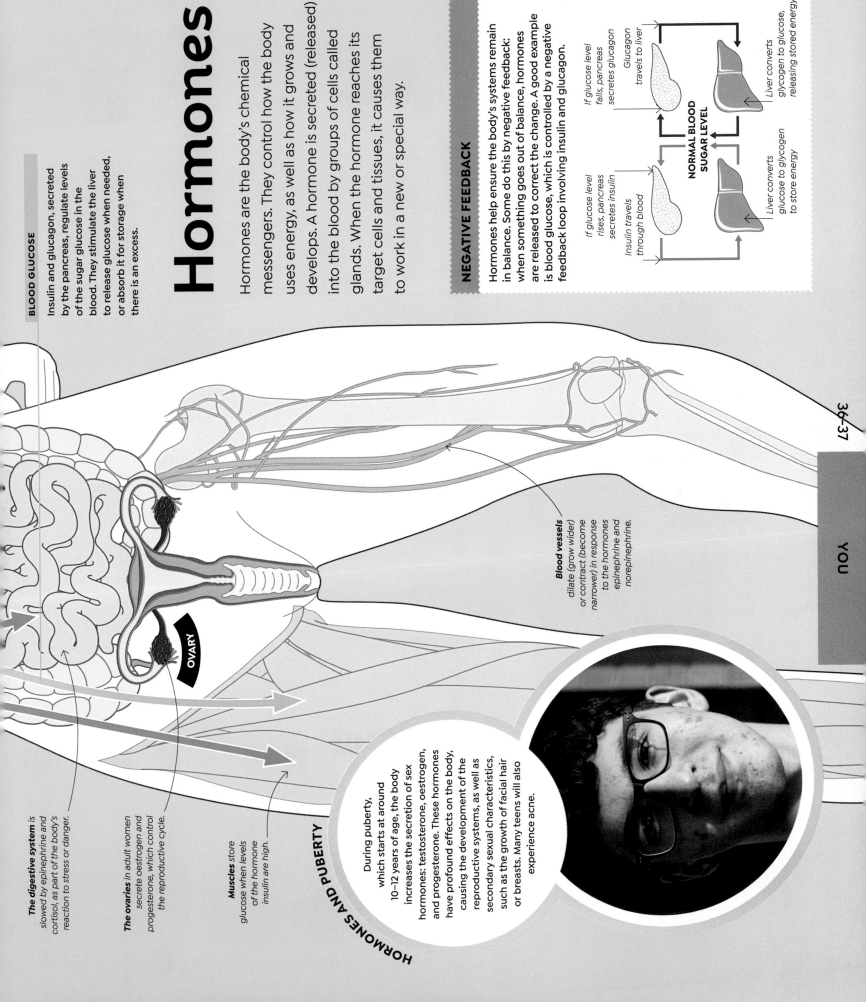

NORMAL BLOOD SUGAR LEVEL

If glucose level rises, pancreas secretes insulin

Insulin travels through blood

Liver converts glucose to glycogen to store energy

If glucose level falls, pancreas secretes glucagon

Glucagon travels to liver

Liver converts glycogen to glucose, releasing stored energy

The digestive system *is slowed by epinephrine and cortisol, as part of the body's reaction to stress or danger.*

The ovaries *in adult women secrete oestrogen and progesterone, which control the reproductive cycle.*

OVARY

Muscles *store glucose when levels of the hormone insulin are high.*

Blood vessels *dilate (grow wider) or contract (become narrower) in response to the hormones epinephrine and norepinephrine.*

HORMONES AND PUBERTY

During puberty, which starts at around 10–12 years of age, the body increases the secretion of sex hormones: testosterone, oestrogen, and progesterone. These hormones have profound effects on the body, causing the development of the reproductive systems, as well as secondary sexual characteristics, such as the growth of facial hair or breasts. Many teens will also experience acne.

HOW VIRUSES WORK

A virus is a germ that is even smaller than a bacterium. It is not alive, but it does contain DNA or closely related RNA – chemicals that carry genes with instructions on how to replicate itself (make new copies of itself). Viruses hijack the replication process used by the body's own cells (which takes place inside the nucleus of the body cell) to make copies of themselves. The copies leave the host body cell and can go on to infect and replicate within many more.

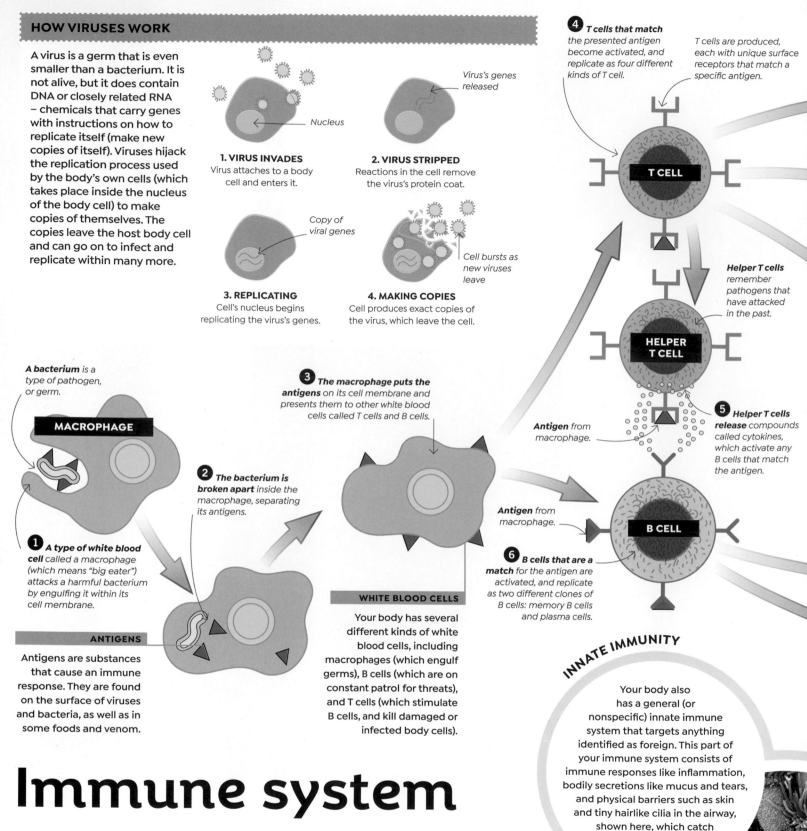

Nucleus

1. VIRUS INVADES
Virus attaches to a body cell and enters it.

Virus's genes released

2. VIRUS STRIPPED
Reactions in the cell remove the virus's protein coat.

Copy of viral genes

3. REPLICATING
Cell's nucleus begins replicating the virus's genes.

Cell bursts as new viruses leave

4. MAKING COPIES
Cell produces exact copies of the virus, which leave the cell.

4 *T cells that match* the presented antigen become activated, and replicate as four different kinds of T cell.

T cells are produced, each with unique surface receptors that match a specific antigen.

T CELL

Helper T cells remember pathogens that have attacked in the past.

HELPER T CELL

Antigen from macrophage.

5 *Helper T cells release* compounds called cytokines, which activate any B cells that match the antigen.

B CELL

Antigen from macrophage.

6 *B cells that are a match* for the antigen are activated, and replicate as two different clones of B cells: memory B cells and plasma cells.

A bacterium is a type of pathogen, or germ.

MACROPHAGE

1 *A type of white blood cell* called a macrophage (which means "big eater") attacks a harmful bacterium by engulfing it within its cell membrane.

2 *The bacterium is broken apart* inside the macrophage, separating its antigens.

3 *The macrophage puts the antigens* on its cell membrane and presents them to other white blood cells called T cells and B cells.

ANTIGENS

Antigens are substances that cause an immune response. They are found on the surface of viruses and bacteria, as well as in some foods and venom.

WHITE BLOOD CELLS

Your body has several different kinds of white blood cells, including macrophages (which engulf germs), B cells (which are on constant patrol for threats), and T cells (which stimulate B cells, and kill damaged or infected body cells).

INNATE IMMUNITY

Your body also has a general (or nonspecific) innate immune system that targets anything identified as foreign. This part of your immune system consists of immune responses like inflammation, bodily secretions like mucus and tears, and physical barriers such as skin and tiny hairlike cilia in the airway, shown here, which catch breathed-in pathogens.

Immune system

When pathogens (germs) such as bacteria and viruses infect your body, your immune system leaps into action to defend against the invaders. The immune system is composed of a huge team of specialized cells that work together to neutralize threats. At the heart of this system are white blood cells and molecules called antibodies that are tailor-made to fight a specific pathogen.

KILLER T CELLS

KILLER T CELL

Killer T cells, or cytotoxic T cells, destroy the body's own damaged or infected cells.

REGULATOR T CELL

Regulator T cells calm down the immune system when an infection has died down.

MEMORY T CELL

Memory T cells that match the antigen live for many years, allowing a faster response if the same pathogen tries to attack again in future.

A killer T cell recognizes and attaches to an antigen on infected body cells, then releases compounds that open up pores (small holes) in the cell, causing it to die.

Every day, your body makes 100 billion white blood cells

Killer T cell recognizes antigen and releases compounds

Cell spills its contents and dies

Pores (small holes) open in membrane

Body's own cell is infected, and contains antigens

PATHOGENS

A pathogen, or germ, is anything that causes an infection. Pathogens cause a wide range of infectious diseases, including the common cold. They replicate (reproduce) inside your body, and can then infect other people, when you sneeze near them, for example.

BACTERIA
These pathogens can cause pneumonia, cholera, and tetanus.

VIRUSES
Viruses cause colds, flu, COVID-19, and chickenpox.

PROTISTS
These single-celled organisms can cause malaria.

FUNGI
Fungal infections like athlete's foot are caused by fungi.

Memory B cells replicated from matching B cells will live in the body for many years, ready to respond if reinfection occurs.

Millions of different B cells are produced, so there is a matching one for every different antigen.

MEMORY B CELL

8 *Some antibodies attach to bacteria* (or other pathogens), causing the bacteria to clump together and become inactive.

9 *Attached antibodies* also prevent pathogens from binding to the body's cells, where they could invade and multiply.

7 *The plasma B cells release* large numbers of antibodies.

ANTIBODY

PLASMA CELL

Plasma cells are B cells that produce antibodies specific to a particular pathogen.

An antibody is a substance that attacks a pathogen and marks it for destruction by white blood cells. Antibodies live in the blood for many years after infection.

BACTERIA

BODY CELLS

10 *Antibodies coating* bacteria, or other pathogens, attract macrophages, and mark the pathogen for elimination.

NEUTRALIZING PATHOGENS

When antibodies attach to a pathogen, they may "neutralize" it – prevent it from causing an infection. A neutralized virus, for example, cannot attach to the body's cells.

13 *The macrophage releases* the destroyed bacterium, which is now unable to replicate and infect the body's cells.

11 *A macrophage engulfs* the bacterium in a process called phagocytosis, which means "cell eating".

12 *The macrophage surrounds* the bacterium and encloses it in a space called a vacuole, where it is digested (broken down).

VACCINATION DELIVERY

Most vaccines are delivered by a hypodermic syringe pushed into muscles or the fatty tissue under your skin. But some are sprayed up a nostril or simply swallowed.

1 *A vaccine is injected* under your skin, typically through a hypodermic syringe.

TYPES OF VACCINE

There are several different kinds of vaccine, including the three shown below. In each case, they teach your immune system to recognize a particular pathogen, or germ.

Weakened pathogen vaccines contain an entire pathogen, or germ, weakened so that it will not cause disease.

Empty "shell" vaccines use disabled pathogens. They present the pathogen's antigens to the body.

Antigens are a substance found on the surface of pathogens.

ANTIGENS

Subunit vaccines contain just the antigens. The antigens create an immune reaction in your body without the pathogen being present.

VACCINES

DISEASE TRANSMISSION

Some microscopic pathogens travel from victim to victim through other living organisms, called vectors, such as mosquitoes and ticks (shown here).

Vaccines prevent more than 2.5 million deaths each year

2 *A type of white blood cell* called a B cell binds to the antigens in the vaccine. This activates the B cell and stimulates it to replicate as plasma cells and memory cells.

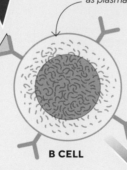

B CELL

3 *The plasma B cells* are "fooled" into releasing large amounts of antibodies into the body to attack the false threat.

PLASMA B CELLS

Antibodies attack pathogens and mark them for destruction by white blood cells. They can live in your body for many years after infection.

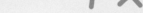

ANTIBODIES

VACCINE DEVELOPMENT

New vaccines go through rigorous safety testing. They are tested on animals before being given to a small number of humans, and undergo trials on different groups before they are rolled out to the wider population.

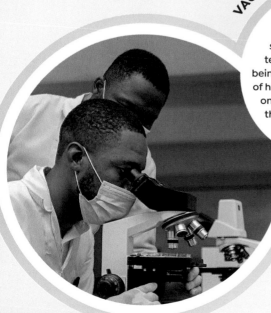

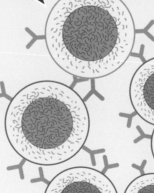

4 *Memory B cells* that match the antigen of the pathogen injected in the vaccine remain in your body for many years.

LONG-TERM IMMUNITY

Memory B cells live for many years, ready to clone if the same threat returns. If the pathogen used in the vaccine tries to infect your body in the future, the B cells will copy themselves once again to take down the invader.

MEMORY B CELLS

Vaccination

Infectious diseases are caused by pathogens (germs). Your immune system (see pp.38–39) is equipped to rapidly produce molecules called antibodies to fight any infection. Some of your immune cells remain alive in your body for years, providing future immunity against the disease. Vaccines stimulate your body to produce this immune reaction without you having to suffer the disease, giving you immunity.

HERD IMMUNITY

Vaccination saves millions every year from deadly infectious diseases such as smallpox, tetanus, flu, measles, and COVID-19. Vaccinating the large majority of people gives the population "herd immunity" – it prevents pathogens spreading to the people who cannot be vaccinated. Without new hosts to infect, the pathogen dies out.

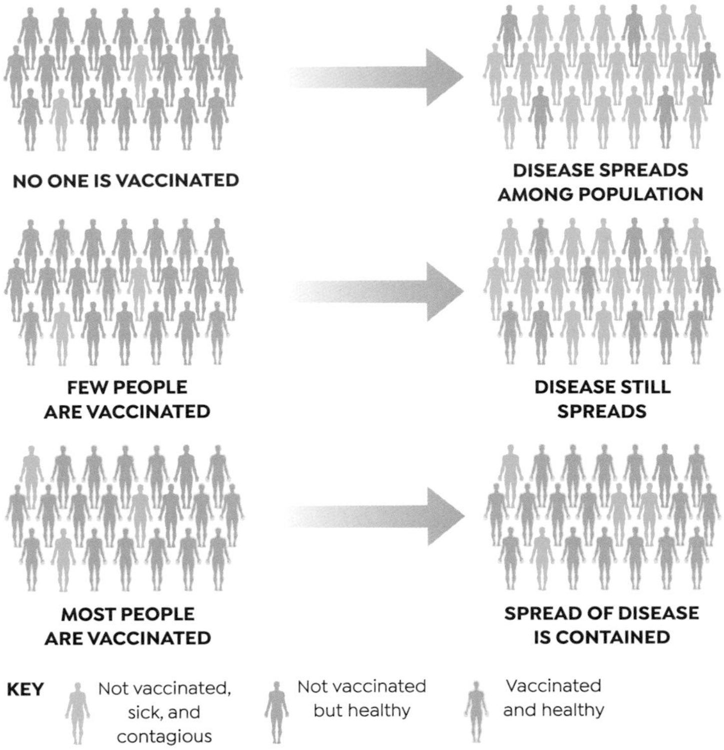

NO ONE IS VACCINATED → **DISEASE SPREADS AMONG POPULATION**

FEW PEOPLE ARE VACCINATED → **DISEASE STILL SPREADS**

MOST PEOPLE ARE VACCINATED → **SPREAD OF DISEASE IS CONTAINED**

KEY
- Not vaccinated, sick, and contagious
- Not vaccinated but healthy
- Vaccinated and healthy

YOU

5 *The antibodies bind to the antigens* to destroy the pathogens before the infection can advance any further.

The antibodies may live in the body for many years to come, ready to attack if the same pathogen infects again.

ANTIBODIES

4 *Antibodies are released* by the plasma B cells, and search the body for the antigens.

Smallpox killed 300 million people in the 20th century before vaccination programmes eradicated it in 1980

The antigens on the pathogen match the antigens presented to the body by the vaccine.

Each plasma B cell will produce a huge number of antibodies.

INFECTION

Sometimes a pathogen you've been vaccinated against enters your body and tries to infect you. When this happens, your body is ready to defend itself.

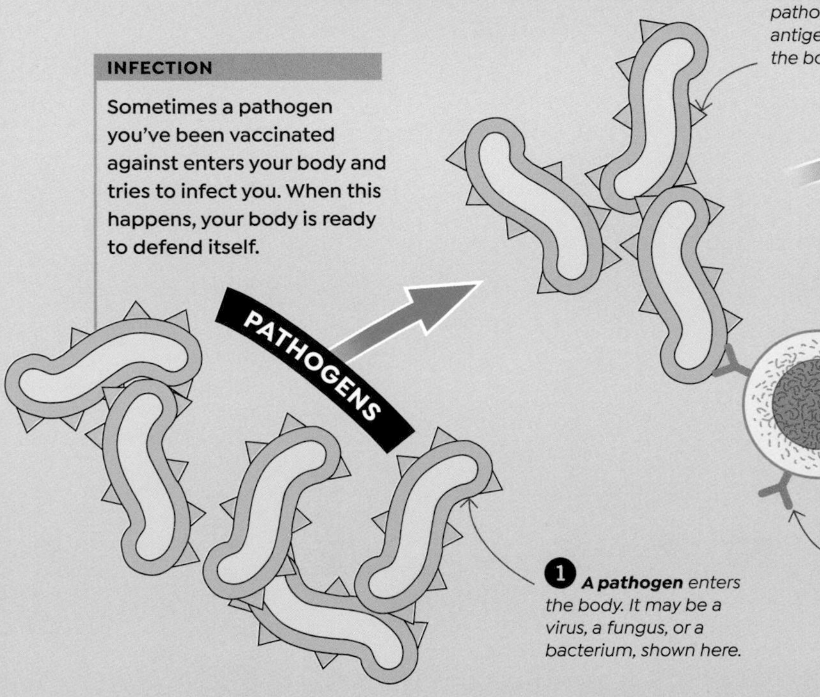

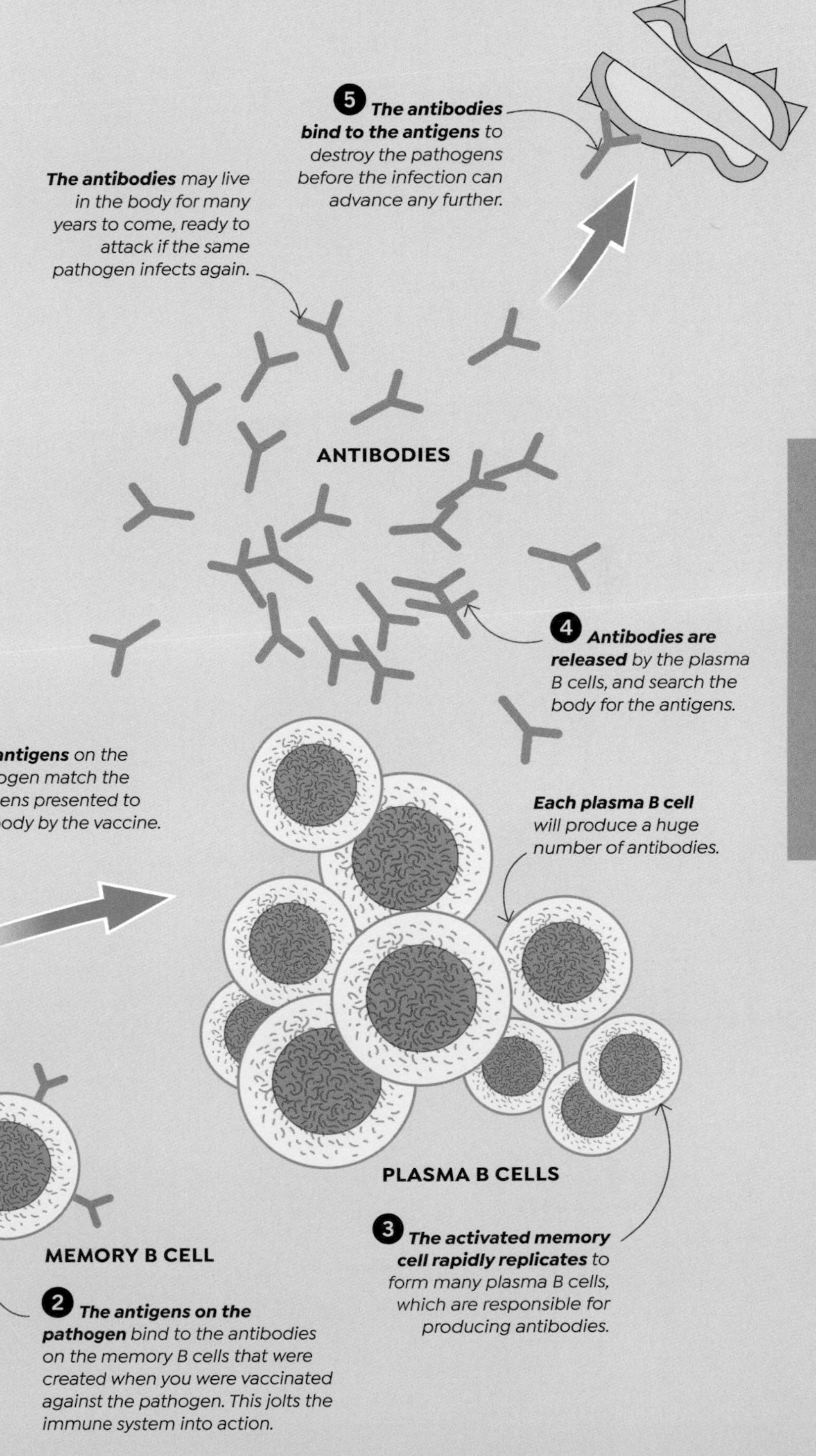

PATHOGENS

PLASMA B CELLS

MEMORY B CELL

3 *The activated memory cell rapidly replicates* to form many plasma B cells, which are responsible for producing antibodies.

1 *A pathogen* enters the body. It may be a virus, a fungus, or a bacterium, shown here.

2 *The antigens on the pathogen* bind to the antibodies on the memory B cells that were created when you were vaccinated against the pathogen. This jolts the immune system into action.

Reproduction

The life of every human that has ever lived began with the process of reproduction, in which an egg cell from a woman fuses with a sperm cell from a man and becomes fertilized. The fertilized egg cell develops in the womb, or uterus, of a woman into a fully formed baby over a period of about 9 months.

3. BALL OF CELLS

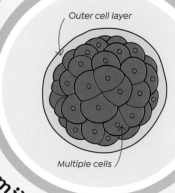

Outer cell layer

Multiple cells

All cells in a morula (a ball of cells) are identical and can develop into any kind of human cell. In 5 days, they start to differentiate into different cell types.

140 million babies are born worldwide each year

3 *A morula* is a ball of about 16 cells that forms 3 days after fertilization by repeated divisions of the cells of the zygote.

1 **Fertilization** occurs when a sperm cell enters an ovum (egg cell).

ZYGOTE

FALLOPIAN TUBE

2 **Cleavage** is when a zygote (a fertilized egg) divides into two identical cells.

MORULA

OVARY

2. TWO-CELL STAGE

Soon after fertilization, the egg cell, now called a zygote, makes its first cell division, making two cells. To achieve fertilization, the sperm cell inside the egg cell was absorbed, leaving just its nucleus, containing its DNA. The nucleus fused with the nucleus of the egg cell. The sperm and egg each contribute half the DNA needed to develop a new human.

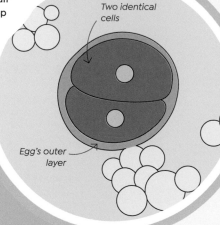

Two identical cells

Egg's outer layer

MALE REPRODUCTIVE SYSTEM

The sperm cell that enters the ovum during fertilization is one of millions, which come from a man's body. Millions of sperm cells develop in a man's testes every day. During sex, they pass along the vas deferens, are mixed with fluid called semen from the seminal vesicle and prostate gland to help them travel more easily, and finally pass out of the body through the ejaculatory duct and urethra in the penis.

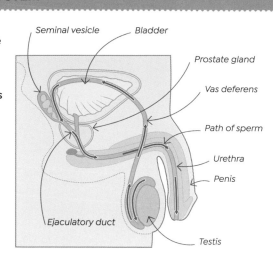

Seminal vesicle

Bladder

Prostate gland

Vas deferens

Path of sperm

Urethra

Penis

Ejaculatory duct

Testis

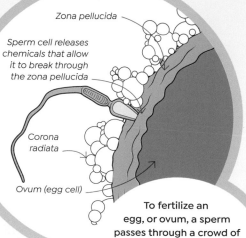

Zona pellucida

Sperm cell releases chemicals that allow it to break through the zona pellucida

Corona radiata

Ovum (egg cell)

To fertilize an egg, or ovum, a sperm passes through a crowd of protective cells called the corona radiata, breaks through a layer known as the zona pellucida, then crosses the ovum's cell membrane. It enters the ovum and loses its tail.

1. FERTILIZATION

GROWING LIFE

The inner ball of cells within a blastocyst becomes an embryo, and after about 9 weeks, the embryo develops into a foetus, such as this 9-week old one. A foetus has all the features of the baby-to-be, but is still smaller than a pear. The foetus grows and matures inside a protective, fluid-filled sac called the amnion until, around 9 months after fertilization, it is ready for birth.

Girls are born with thousands of immature follicles, which mature one by one, beginning in puberty

Ovum starts to mature within the follicle

Follicle is nearly mature

Ovary

Rupturing follicle releases a mature ovum – this is called ovulation

The fallopian tube is where an egg travelling from the ovary meets sperm that have entered through the vagina.

The uterus (or womb) is the organ in which the embryo develops.

UTERUS

BLASTOCYST

myometrium is a scular layer of the uterus wall.

Fimbriae are fingerlike projections that sweep the ovum into the Fallopian tube.

The ovarian ligament connects the ovary to the uterus.

The ovary is the organ in which immature egg cells develop into ova (mature egg cells).

A woman has two ovaries, each with many immature follicles. About once a month, a follicle in one of the ovaries develops and releases a mature egg cell, or ovum.

EGG DEVELOPMENT

42-43

YOU

4 *A blastocyst is a fluid-filled ball of cells that develops from the morula and implants in the uterus wall.*

The endometrium, the innermost layer of the uterus, has a rich supply of blood to nourish the embryo.

The cervix is the neck of the womb. The cylinder-shaped tissue connects the vagina to the uterus.

The birth canal, or vagina, is a flexible muscular cylinder through which a baby is usually born.

CERVIX

BIRTH CANAL

VAGINA

A blastocyst develops about 6 days after fertilization, then settles on the uterus wall, where it nestles and implants. The inner mass of cells develops into an embryo, and generates all the cells of the body. The outer part, called the trophoblast, will interweave with a complex structure grown by the mother to form the placenta, which provides the growing baby with nutrients.

4. IMPLANTED IN THE UTERUS

A newborn baby is made of more than one trillion cells

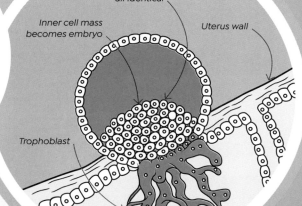

Cells are no longer all identical

Inner cell mass becomes embryo

Uterus wall

Trophoblast

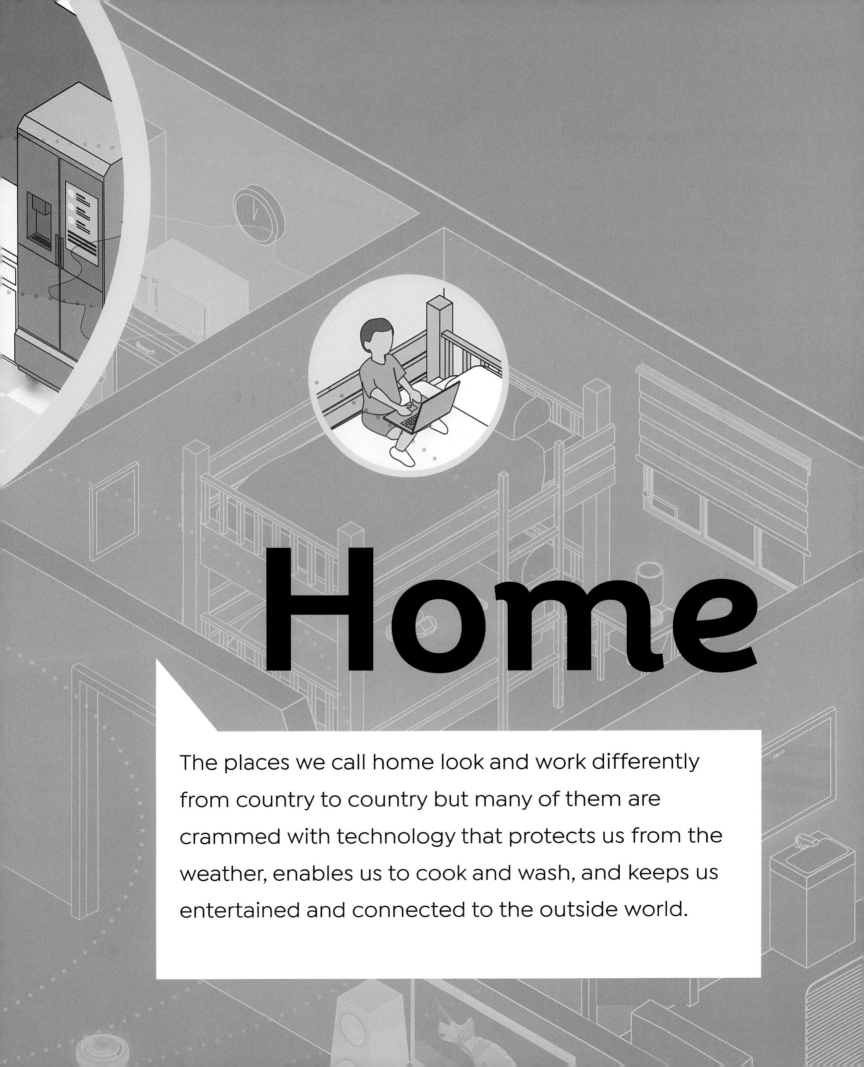

Home

The places we call home look and work differently from country to country but many of them are crammed with technology that protects us from the weather, enables us to cook and wash, and keeps us entertained and connected to the outside world.

Timber houses

Timber – wood from trees – is a relatively lightweight, strong, and plentiful building material that enables fast construction. It is easily cut, shaped, and joined to form sturdy structures that transmit a building's weight to the foundations beneath. Timber is a renewable material, since new trees can be grown, and it can be recycled. Hundreds of thousands of timber-framed houses are built each year.

PREFABRICATED HOUSES

Some houses are put together in factories. Floors and walls are built first, then wiring, plumbing, and windows are installed. Ceilings and insulation are added, and finally the roof and any outer cladding. A finished house is carried by flatbed truck to the site where the building's foundations have already been laid.

Roof joists are sturdy wood or steel girders that support the roof's weight.

A soil stack lets waste water from toilets and bathrooms flow down to the drain and smelly gases to escape from the flue at the top.

Scaffolding forms a rigid steel frame and platform for work on taller parts of the building.

Window openings are left in studwork – the windows themselves will be fitted later.

Workers check that the house matches the building plans at all stages of the project.

The ground-level floor is typically made of concrete slabs and usually covered with tiles, wooden boards, or carpet after most of the construction is complete.

A drainage pipe, passing through the base of the house, carries waste water out to the sewage system.

SCAFFOLDING

ROOF JOISTS

FLOOR JOISTS

TIMBER STUDWORK

GROUNDWORKS

FLOORING

CONCRETE FLOOR

JOISTS

BRICKWORK

GROUNDWORKS

A footings trench is dug in the ground before the brick footings, joists, and other parts of the foundations are then built into the trench.

Utilities, such as electricity, water, and gas, enter via cables and pipes fed into the base of the house.

Foundation joists support the weight of the ground-level flooring and insulation.

A spirit level is used to check that the building's foundations are perfectly level.

Brick footings spread the building's weight over a wide area to prevent subsidence (sinking).

Underfloor insulation, made of timber and plywood (layers of wood stuck together) is suspended beneath the concrete slabs to help reduce draughts and heat loss.

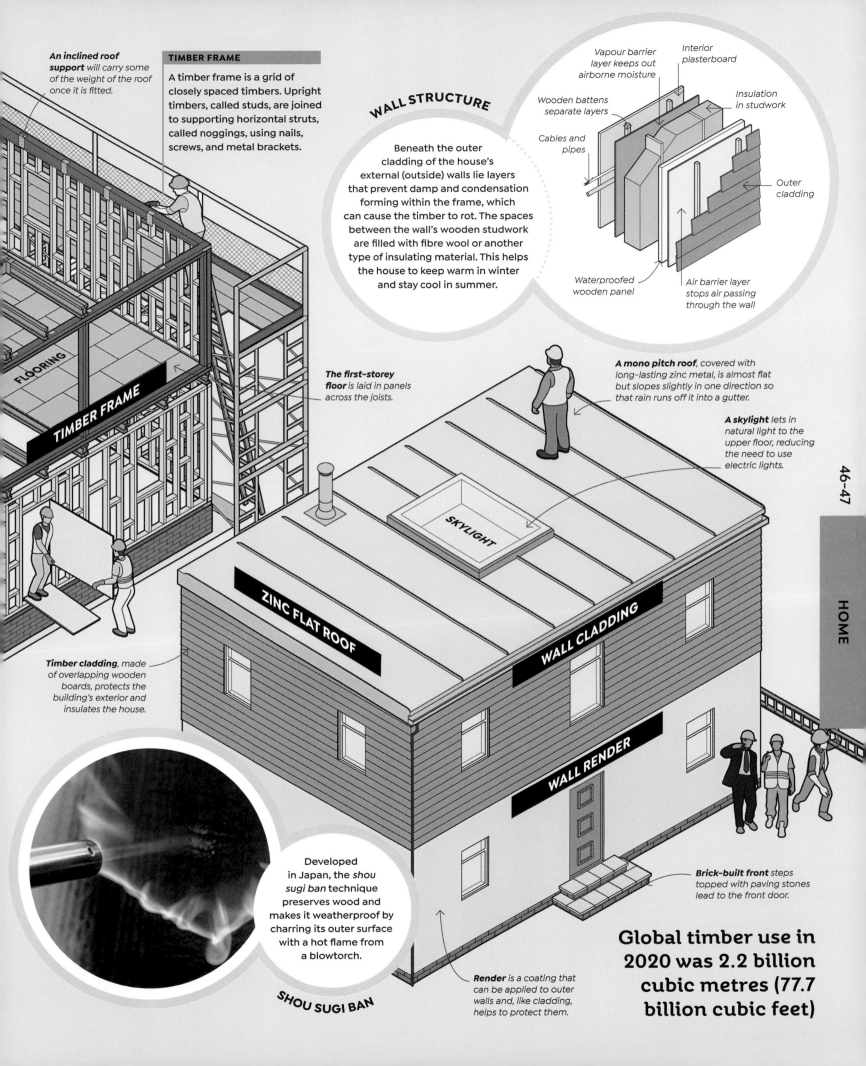

An inclined roof support will carry some of the weight of the roof once it is fitted.

TIMBER FRAME

A timber frame is a grid of closely spaced timbers. Upright timbers, called studs, are joined to supporting horizontal struts, called noggings, using nails, screws, and metal brackets.

WALL STRUCTURE

Beneath the outer cladding of the house's external (outside) walls lie layers that prevent damp and condensation forming within the frame, which can cause the timber to rot. The spaces between the wall's wooden studwork are filled with fibre wool or another type of insulating material. This helps the house to keep warm in winter and stay cool in summer.

Vapour barrier layer keeps out airborne moisture

Interior plasterboard

Wooden battens separate layers

Insulation in studwork

Cables and pipes

Outer cladding

Waterproofed wooden panel

Air barrier layer stops air passing through the wall

FLOORING

TIMBER FRAME

The first-storey floor is laid in panels across the joists.

A mono pitch roof, covered with long-lasting zinc metal, is almost flat but slopes slightly in one direction so that rain runs off it into a gutter.

A skylight lets in natural light to the upper floor, reducing the need to use electric lights.

SKYLIGHT

ZINC FLAT ROOF

WALL CLADDING

Timber cladding, made of overlapping wooden boards, protects the building's exterior and insulates the house.

WALL RENDER

Developed in Japan, the *shou sugi ban* technique preserves wood and makes it weatherproof by charring its outer surface with a hot flame from a blowtorch.

Brick-built front steps topped with paving stones lead to the front door.

SHOU SUGI BAN

Render is a coating that can be applied to outer walls and, like cladding, helps to protect them.

Global timber use in 2020 was 2.2 billion cubic metres (77.7 billion cubic feet)

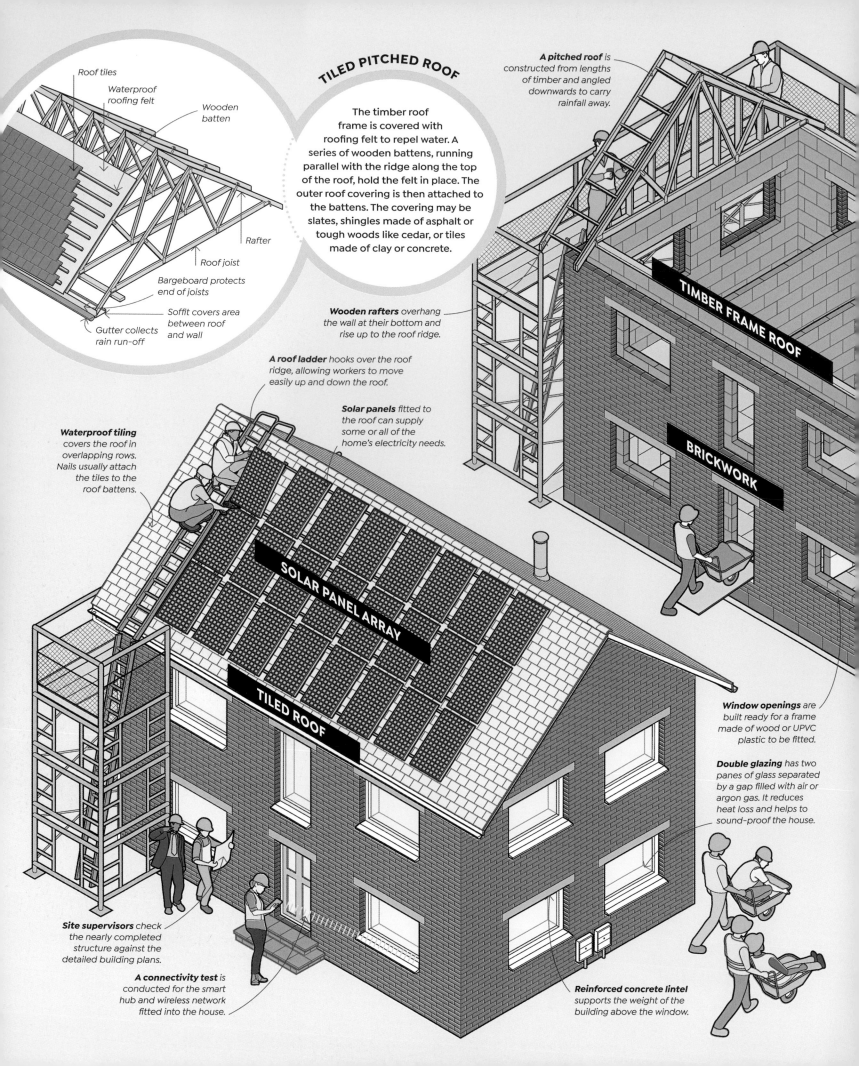

TILED PITCHED ROOF

Roof tiles

Waterproof roofing felt

Wooden batten

Rafter

Roof joist

Bargeboard protects end of joists

Soffit covers area between roof and wall

Gutter collects rain run-off

The timber roof frame is covered with roofing felt to repel water. A series of wooden battens, running parallel with the ridge along the top of the roof, hold the felt in place. The outer roof covering is then attached to the battens. The covering may be slates, shingles made of asphalt or tough woods like cedar, or tiles made of clay or concrete.

A pitched roof is constructed from lengths of timber and angled downwards to carry rainfall away.

TIMBER FRAME ROOF

BRICKWORK

Wooden rafters overhang the wall at their bottom and rise up to the roof ridge.

A roof ladder hooks over the roof ridge, allowing workers to move easily up and down the roof.

Solar panels fitted to the roof can supply some or all of the home's electricity needs.

Waterproof tiling covers the roof in overlapping rows. Nails usually attach the tiles to the roof battens.

SOLAR PANEL ARRAY

TILED ROOF

Window openings are built ready for a frame made of wood or UPVC plastic to be fitted.

Double glazing has two panes of glass separated by a gap filled with air or argon gas. It reduces heat loss and helps to sound-proof the house.

Site supervisors check the nearly completed structure against the detailed building plans.

A connectivity test is conducted for the smart hub and wireless network fitted into the house.

Reinforced concrete lintel supports the weight of the building above the window.

Interior walls between rooms are built from single layers of blocks covered in plasterboard.

The floor of the first storey is constructed using a nail gun to fix panels laid over joists.

SCAFFOLDING

CONSTRUCTION AND THE ENVIRONMENT

To reduce the impact of construction on the environment, many builders are making new houses from recycled wood, bricks, steel, and plastic (seen here). Others are turning to new sustainable materials that rely less on cement or fossil fuels. These include plant-based materials such as hemp, bamboo, and cork. Hemp can be mixed with lime and water and moulded into hemcrete bricks.

Brick houses

Built to last, brick homes are sturdy, durable, and resist mould and rot. Brick houses are constructed on site, their walls rising from strong foundations as bricklayers set bricks into layers of mortar. Many of these homes have two-layer walls. An exterior wall of brick is separated from an inner wall of lightweight breeze blocks by a cavity (space) that is filled with insulation.

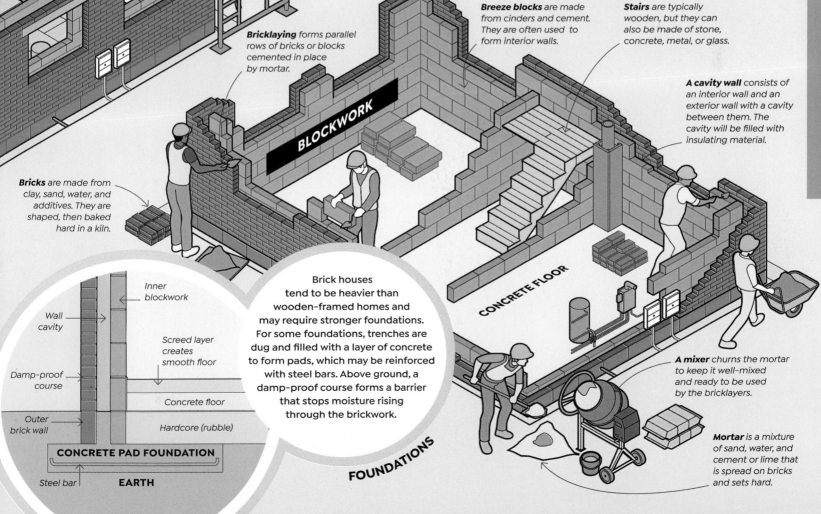

Bricklaying forms parallel rows of bricks or blocks cemented in place by mortar.

Breeze blocks are made from cinders and cement. They are often used to form interior walls.

Stairs are typically wooden, but they can also be made of stone, concrete, metal, or glass.

BLOCKWORK

A cavity wall consists of an interior wall and an exterior wall with a cavity between them. The cavity will be filled with insulating material.

Bricks are made from clay, sand, water, and additives. They are shaped, then baked hard in a kiln.

CONCRETE FLOOR

Brick houses tend to be heavier than wooden-framed homes and may require stronger foundations. For some foundations, trenches are dug and filled with a layer of concrete to form pads, which may be reinforced with steel bars. Above ground, a damp-proof course forms a barrier that stops moisture rising through the brickwork.

A mixer churns the mortar to keep it well-mixed and ready to be used by the bricklayers.

Inner blockwork

Wall cavity

Screed layer creates smooth floor

Damp-proof course

Concrete floor

Outer brick wall

Hardcore (rubble)

CONCRETE PAD FOUNDATION

Steel bar | **EARTH**

FOUNDATIONS

Mortar is a mixture of sand, water, and cement or lime that is spread on bricks and sets hard.

ROCK DWELLERS

The Cappadocia region of Turkey is famous for its more than 2,000-year-old dwellings carved out of the surrounding stone. The rock is a soft volcanic material called ignimbrite that has been eroded by wind and water into tall chimneys. The local people found it easier to cut into the rock than build on it, creating living rooms, storage spaces, animal byres, and even churches. Elsewhere in the region, chambers and passages were dug underground to form small towns. The largest is Derinkuyu, which extends 85 m (279 ft) deep. It was home to as many as 22,000 people.

Modern buildings

Stables

Kitchens

Living quarters

Chapel

Ventilation and well shaft

Reservoir

DERINKUYU UNDERGROUND CITY

Bathroom

Although it is often the smallest room in a house, the bathroom is full of technology. More water flows in and out of this space than any other room in the home. This water supplies devices including a basin, toilet, and a bath or shower. Electric devices in the bathroom follow strict safety codes as water conducts electricity.

Metal heating element warms water

Power switch turns on shower

Showerhead

On/off switch for electricity

Electricity supply to heating element

Cold water flows into shower unit

Temperature control adjusts rate of flow past heating element

Hot water flows out of unit towards showerhead

Cold water flows into the shower unit past an electric heating element. Power showers also feature a pump to increase the water flow out of the shower head. Not all showers are electric, some use the house's hot-water system.

The wall-mounted fan sucks steam out of the room.

A pull cord switches the fan on and off and can also switch the shower electricty supply on.

Water from the shower unit flows up a riser arm and out of the showerhead.

ELECTRIC SHOWER

HEATED RAIL

Hot water flows through pipes inside hollow rails to warm towels.

A waterproof speaker stuck to the shower wall plays music safely while the shower is on.

A shower shelf mounted on the wall holds soap and shampoo.

Water pipes supply the shower with cold water.

SHOWER

HIGH-TECH TOILET

Originating in Japan, high-tech toilets boast several luxury features including a programmable heated seat, automatic lid closure after use, and a bidet function that sprays jets of cleansing water. Some also include an air dryer and purifier to neutralize any odours. The push of a button on the control panel activates these functions.

The drain hole in the shower tray drains away waste water into a waste pipe.

A waste pipe carries waste water away from the home.

An anti-slip mat prevents wet feet sliding on the floor when getting out of the shower.

A U-bend in the shower waste pipe prevents odour rising up into the shower.

Cabinet sliding doors act as mirrors and keep toiletries hidden inside.

Ceramic tiles sealed by grouting protect the wall from water and soap splashes.

An electric socket provides safe power for shavers and electric toothbrushes.

The mixer tap combines hot and cold water.

A moulded sink provides a place to wash hands and faces.

A pedal bin opens via a foot-operated lever.

A U-bend in the waste pipe retains water to seal the drain and prevent sewer gases rising into the sink.

Water flows out from the rim of the toilet into the toilet bowl.

A waste pipe carries flushed water and waste to a soil pipe that flows into local sewage pipes.

SINK

BOWL

CISTERN

TOILET

During flushing, water is sucked through a siphon tube and out into the bowl.

The cistern typically holds 10–15 litres (21–32 pints) of water, replenished by the household water supply.

A piston is drawn up when the toilet is flushed, causing water to flow into the siphon.

Water enters the toilet via a water inlet pipe, flowing into a water storage tank called a cistern.

30 per cent of the water used in the home is flushed down the toilet

Turning handle side to side controls the temperature

Lever handle moves up or down to control flow of water

Ceramic value core releases water from pipes into tap

Water flows from tap spout

Hot water pipe

Cold water pipe

Water flows up pipes from plumbing system

MIXER TAP

A mixer tap combines water from the hot and cold water pipes into a single flow, making it easier to control the temperature of the water coming out of the spout.

THIRSTY ANIMALS

Pets sometimes like to use the toilet too, but for a very different reason to their owner. A cat might leap onto the toilet seat to drink from the bowl because the cool, clean water in a recently flushed toilet tastes fresher than the water in their own dish. When the toilet is flushed, the swirling water also fascinates animals who might dip a paw into the water.

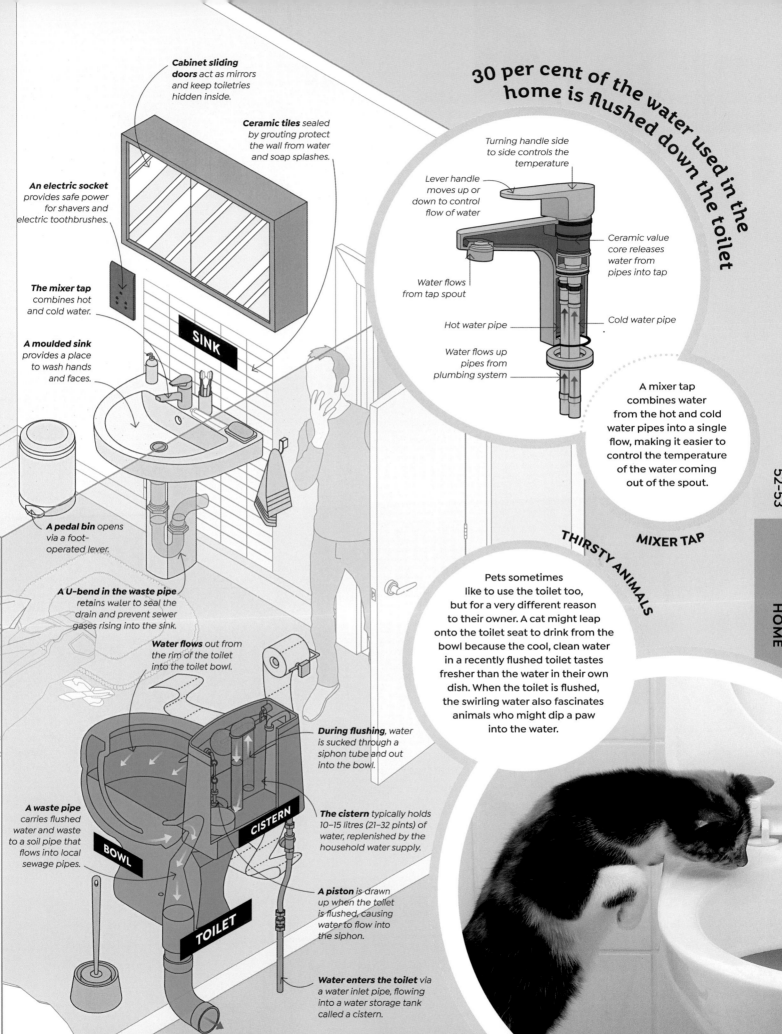

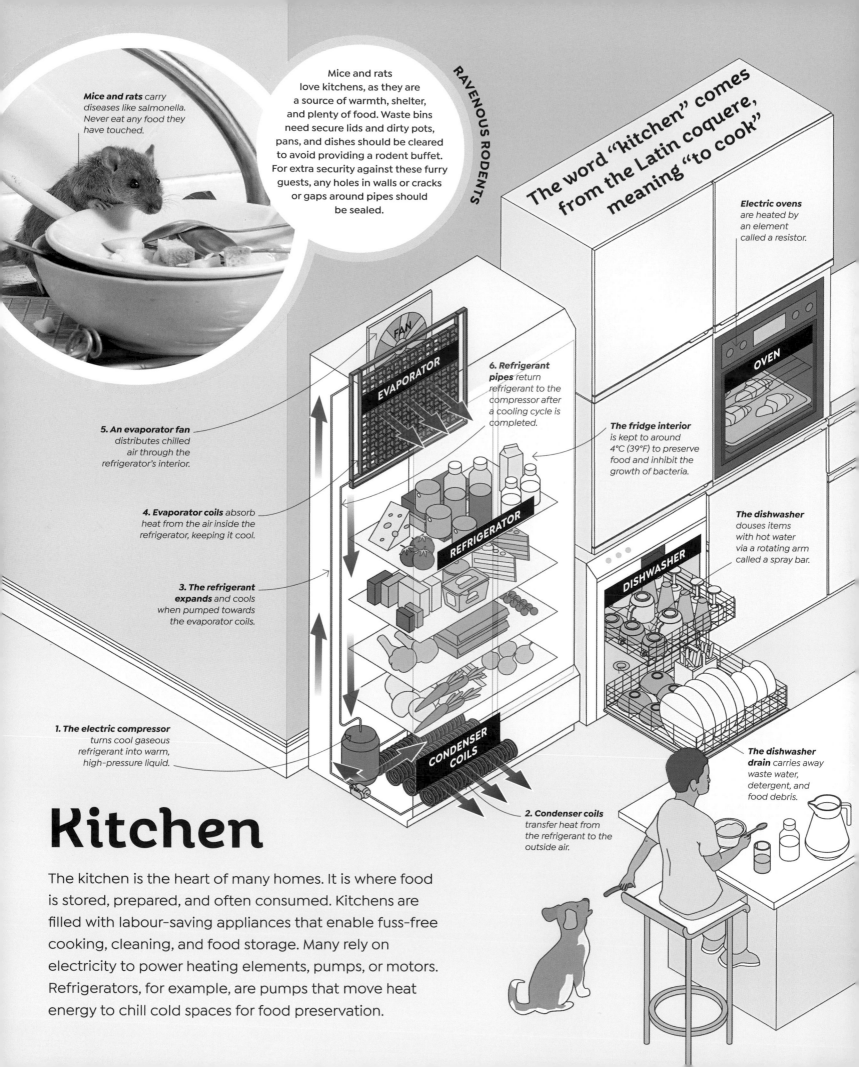

Mice and rats carry diseases like salmonella. Never eat any food they have touched.

Mice and rats love kitchens, as they are a source of warmth, shelter, and plenty of food. Waste bins need secure lids and dirty pots, pans, and dishes should be cleared to avoid providing a rodent buffet. For extra security against these furry guests, any holes in walls or cracks or gaps around pipes should be sealed.

The word "kitchen" comes from the Latin coquere, meaning "to cook"

Electric ovens are heated by an element called a resistor.

FAN

EVAPORATOR

6. Refrigerant pipes return refrigerant to the compressor after a cooling cycle is completed.

5. An evaporator fan distributes chilled air through the refrigerator's interior.

OVEN

The fridge interior is kept to around 4°C (39°F) to preserve food and inhibit the growth of bacteria.

REFRIGERATOR

4. Evaporator coils absorb heat from the air inside the refrigerator, keeping it cool.

The dishwasher douses items with hot water via a rotating arm called a spray bar.

3. The refrigerant expands and cools when pumped towards the evaporator coils.

DISHWASHER

1. The electric compressor turns cool gaseous refrigerant into warm, high-pressure liquid.

CONDENSER COILS

The dishwasher drain carries away waste water, detergent, and food debris.

2. Condenser coils transfer heat from the refrigerant to the outside air.

Kitchen

The kitchen is the heart of many homes. It is where food is stored, prepared, and often consumed. Kitchens are filled with labour-saving appliances that enable fuss-free cooking, cleaning, and food storage. Many rely on electricity to power heating elements, pumps, or motors. Refrigerators, for example, are pumps that move heat energy to chill cold spaces for food preservation.

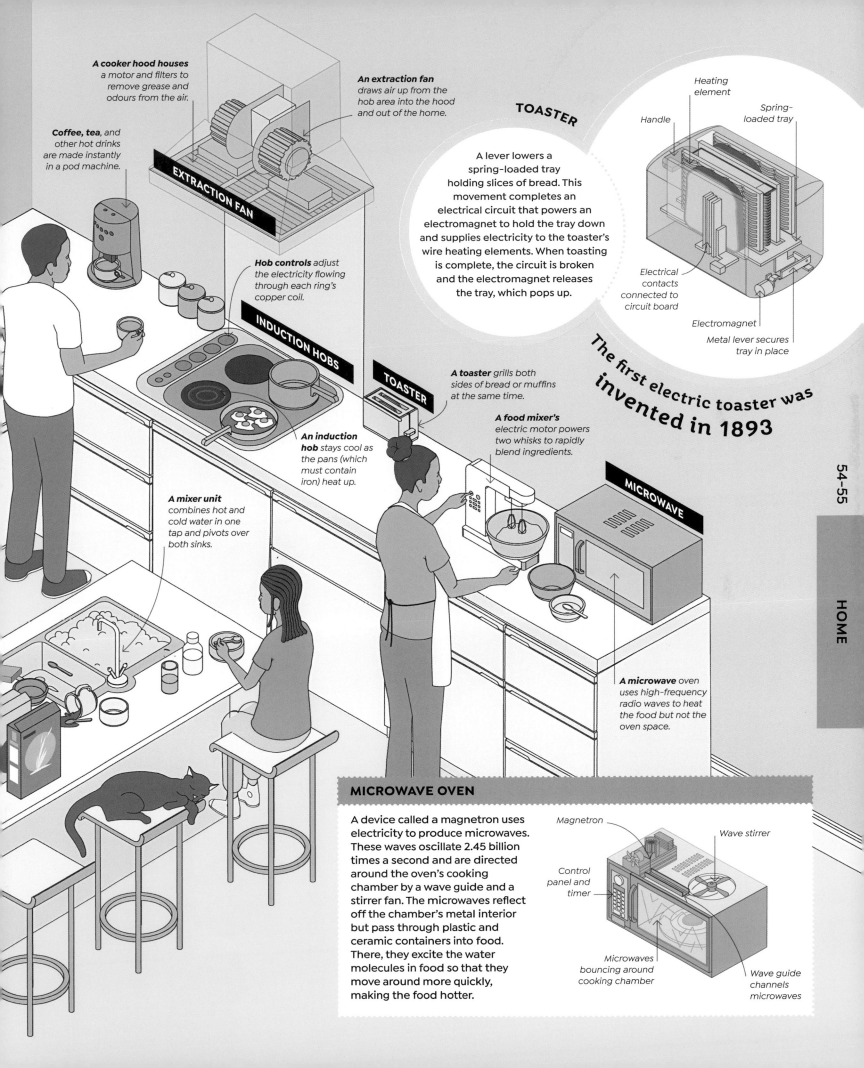

A cooker hood houses a motor and filters to remove grease and odours from the air.

An extraction fan draws air up from the hob area into the hood and out of the home.

Coffee, tea, and other hot drinks are made instantly in a pod machine.

EXTRACTION FAN

TOASTER

A lever lowers a spring-loaded tray holding slices of bread. This movement completes an electrical circuit that powers an electromagnet to hold the tray down and supplies electricity to the toaster's wire heating elements. When toasting is complete, the circuit is broken and the electromagnet releases the tray, which pops up.

Heating element

Handle

Spring-loaded tray

Electrical contacts connected to circuit board

Electromagnet

Metal lever secures tray in place

Hob controls adjust the electricity flowing through each ring's copper coil.

INDUCTION HOBS

The first electric toaster was **invented in 1893**

TOASTER

A toaster grills both sides of bread or muffins at the same time.

An induction hob stays cool as the pans (which must contain iron) heat up.

A food mixer's electric motor powers two whisks to rapidly blend ingredients.

MICROWAVE

A mixer unit combines hot and cold water in one tap and pivots over both sinks.

A microwave oven uses high-frequency radio waves to heat the food but not the oven space.

MICROWAVE OVEN

A device called a magnetron uses electricity to produce microwaves. These waves oscillate 2.45 billion times a second and are directed around the oven's cooking chamber by a wave guide and a stirrer fan. The microwaves reflect off the chamber's metal interior but pass through plastic and ceramic containers into food. There, they excite the water molecules in food so that they move around more quickly, making the food hotter.

Magnetron

Wave stirrer

Control panel and timer

Microwaves bouncing around cooking chamber

Wave guide channels microwaves

HEAT TRANSFER

Heat flows from hot areas to cold. Different cooking methods are chosen for different dishes, sometimes based on one of three ways they can transfer heat to the food.

RADIATION
This form of energy travels in infrared waves, carrying heat from an open fire, barbecue, or a grill or broiler element to the food.

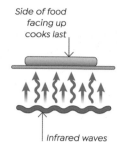

Side of food facing up cooks last

Infrared waves

CONDUCTION
Heat is transferred between materials by direct contact. Cold, raw food is heated and cooked through immersion in the boiling water in a pan.

Water heated through direct contact with hot pan

Boiling water heats food

Pan in direct contact with hot hob

CONVECTION
Heat is transferred through the movement of a liquid or air around the food. In a steamer, steam and heated air rise to cook the food.

Hot steam heats food through convection

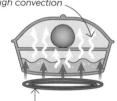

Ring heats water into steam

Cooking

There are lots of ways to cook but they all involve heating food to change its texture, taste, and appearance. Cooking can thicken sauces or soften raw vegetables, making them easier to digest. It can also remove harmful bacteria and prompt chemical reactions that turn unpalatable ingredients into something truly delicious.

HOB COOKING

Electricity is sent through the hob's coil, which contains a resistance wire. The wire resists the electric current, causing the coil to heat up, and transfers heat to the pan.

Temperature controls regulate the electricity, and therefore the heat, passing through the hob coil.

Cooking oil or butter conducts heat from the pan to the food and stops food sticking to the pan.

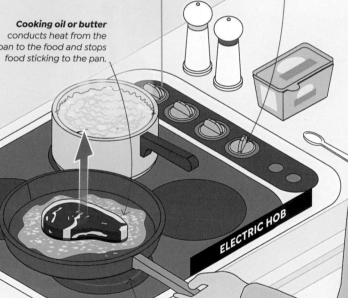

ELECTRIC HOB

The hob's metal coil may be covered by a layer of ceramic or glass that warms the pan base evenly.

COOKING MEAT

Meat is composed mostly of proteins and fats. When it is cooked, these undergo changes. Proteins and muscle fibres break down, water and some juices exit the meat and its texture changes. What is called a Maillard reaction takes place, where amino acids and sugars combine to both give the meat flavour and turn it brown.

Protein chains, made of amino acids, begin to unravel

Amino acids link and form new protein chains

Sugar combines with proteins

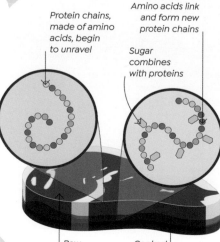

Raw topside

Cooked underside

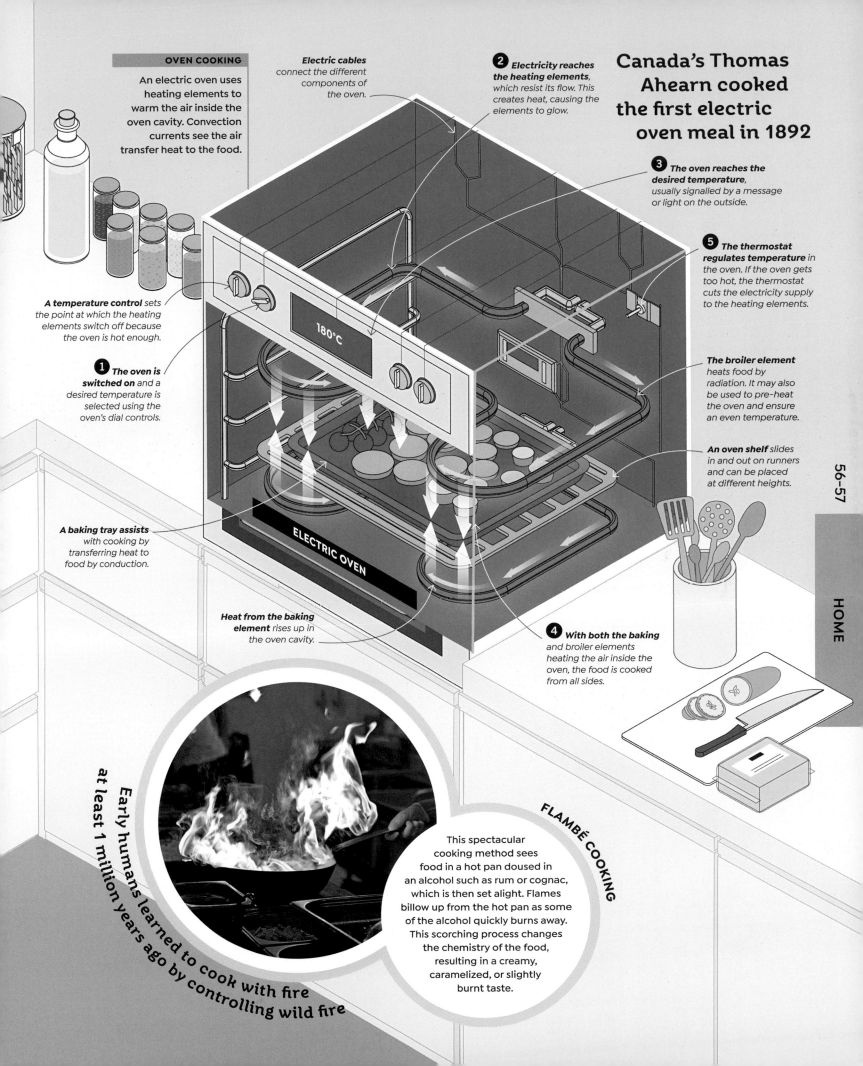

OVEN COOKING

An electric oven uses heating elements to warm the air inside the oven cavity. Convection currents see the air transfer heat to the food.

Electric cables connect the different components of the oven.

2 *Electricity reaches the heating elements*, which resist its flow. This creates heat, causing the elements to glow.

Canada's Thomas Ahearn cooked the first electric oven meal in 1892

3 *The oven reaches the desired temperature,* usually signalled by a message or light on the outside.

5 *The thermostat regulates temperature* in the oven. If the oven gets too hot, the thermostat cuts the electricity supply to the heating elements.

A temperature control sets the point at which the heating elements switch off because the oven is hot enough.

1 *The oven is switched on* and a desired temperature is selected using the oven's dial controls.

180°C

The broiler element heats food by radiation. It may also be used to pre-heat the oven and ensure an even temperature.

An oven shelf slides in and out on runners and can be placed at different heights.

A baking tray assists with cooking by transferring heat to food by conduction.

ELECTRIC OVEN

Heat from the baking element rises up in the oven cavity.

4 *With both the baking* and broiler elements heating the air inside the oven, the food is cooked from all sides.

Early humans learned to cook with fire at least 1 million years ago by controlling wild fire

FLAMBÉ COOKING

This spectacular cooking method sees food in a hot pan doused in an alcohol such as rum or cognac, which is then set alight. Flames billow up from the hot pan as some of the alcohol quickly burns away. This scorching process changes the chemistry of the food, resulting in a creamy, caramelized, or slightly burnt taste.

56-57

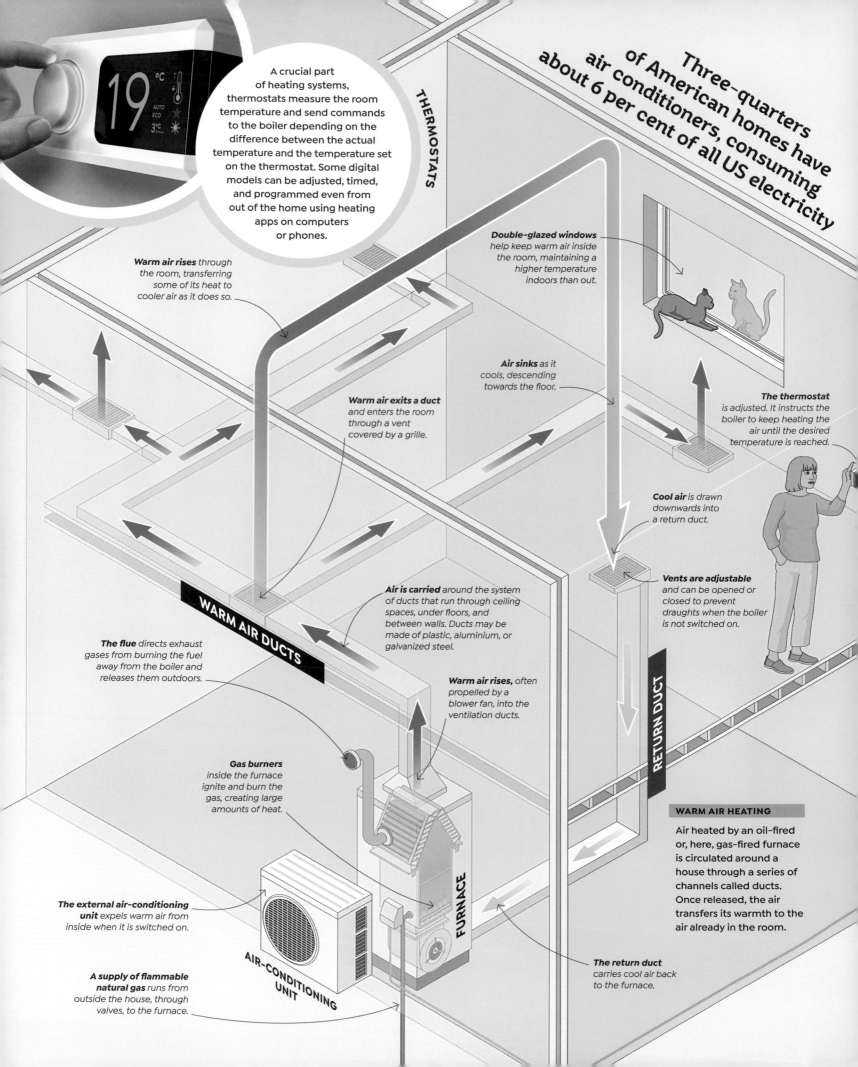

THERMOSTATS

A crucial part of heating systems, thermostats measure the room temperature and send commands to the boiler depending on the difference between the actual temperature and the temperature set on the thermostat. Some digital models can be adjusted, timed, and programmed even from out of the home using heating apps on computers or phones.

Warm air rises through the room, transferring some of its heat to cooler air as it does so.

Double-glazed windows help keep warm air inside the room, maintaining a higher temperature indoors than out.

Warm air exits a duct and enters the room through a vent covered by a grille.

Air sinks as it cools, descending towards the floor.

The thermostat is adjusted. It instructs the boiler to keep heating the air until the desired temperature is reached.

Cool air is drawn downwards into a return duct.

Air is carried around the system of ducts that run through ceiling spaces, under floors, and between walls. Ducts may be made of plastic, aluminium, or galvanized steel.

WARM AIR DUCTS

The flue directs exhaust gases from burning the fuel away from the boiler and releases them outdoors.

Warm air rises, often propelled by a blower fan, into the ventilation ducts.

Vents are adjustable and can be opened or closed to prevent draughts when the boiler is not switched on.

RETURN DUCT

Gas burners inside the furnace ignite and burn the gas, creating large amounts of heat.

FURNACE

The external air-conditioning unit expels warm air from inside when it is switched on.

AIR-CONDITIONING UNIT

A supply of flammable natural gas runs from outside the house, through valves, to the furnace.

WARM AIR HEATING

Air heated by an oil-fired or, here, gas-fired furnace is circulated around a house through a series of channels called ducts. Once released, the air transfers its warmth to the air already in the room.

The return duct carries cool air back to the furnace.

Warm-air heating and air conditioning

Homes, offices, and other buildings control the climate in their internal spaces by heating, cooling, and moving air. Warm-air heating systems can distribute heat throughout a building, while air conditioning can cool room spaces and control airflow and air quality. Both systems can use a lot of energy but they can be made more efficient with the use of thermostats and insulation.

INSULATION

Whenever there's a difference in temperature, heat flows from warmer to cooler areas. Buildings can be made more energy efficient with layers of foam or fibre insulation, which traps heat and stops it escaping through walls or the roof.

Air conditioners don't just make a house cooler, they also make it less humid

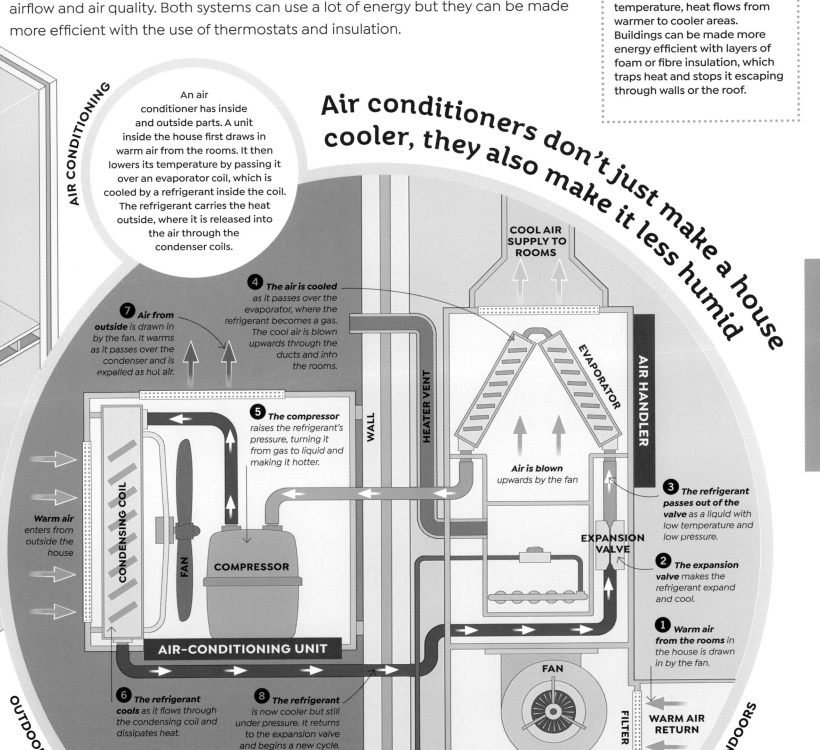

AIR CONDITIONING

An air conditioner has inside and outside parts. A unit inside the house first draws in warm air from the rooms. It then lowers its temperature by passing it over an evaporator coil, which is cooled by a refrigerant inside the coil. The refrigerant carries the heat outside, where it is released into the air through the condenser coils.

7 *Air from outside* is drawn in by the fan. It warms as it passes over the condenser and is expelled as hot air.

4 *The air is cooled* as it passes over the evaporator, where the refrigerant becomes a gas. The cool air is blown upwards through the ducts and into the rooms.

5 *The compressor* raises the refrigerant's pressure, turning it from gas to liquid and making it hotter.

Warm air enters from outside the house

CONDENSING COIL

FAN

COMPRESSOR

AIR-CONDITIONING UNIT

6 *The refrigerant cools* as it flows through the condensing coil and dissipates heat.

8 *The refrigerant* is now cooler but still under pressure. It returns to the expansion valve and begins a new cycle.

WALL

HEATER VENT

COOL AIR SUPPLY TO ROOMS

EVAPORATOR

AIR HANDLER

Air is blown upwards by the fan

3 *The refrigerant passes out of the valve* as a liquid with low temperature and low pressure.

EXPANSION VALVE

2 *The expansion valve* makes the refrigerant expand and cool.

1 *Warm air from the rooms* in the house is drawn in by the fan.

FAN

FILTER

WARM AIR RETURN

OUTDOORS

INDOORS

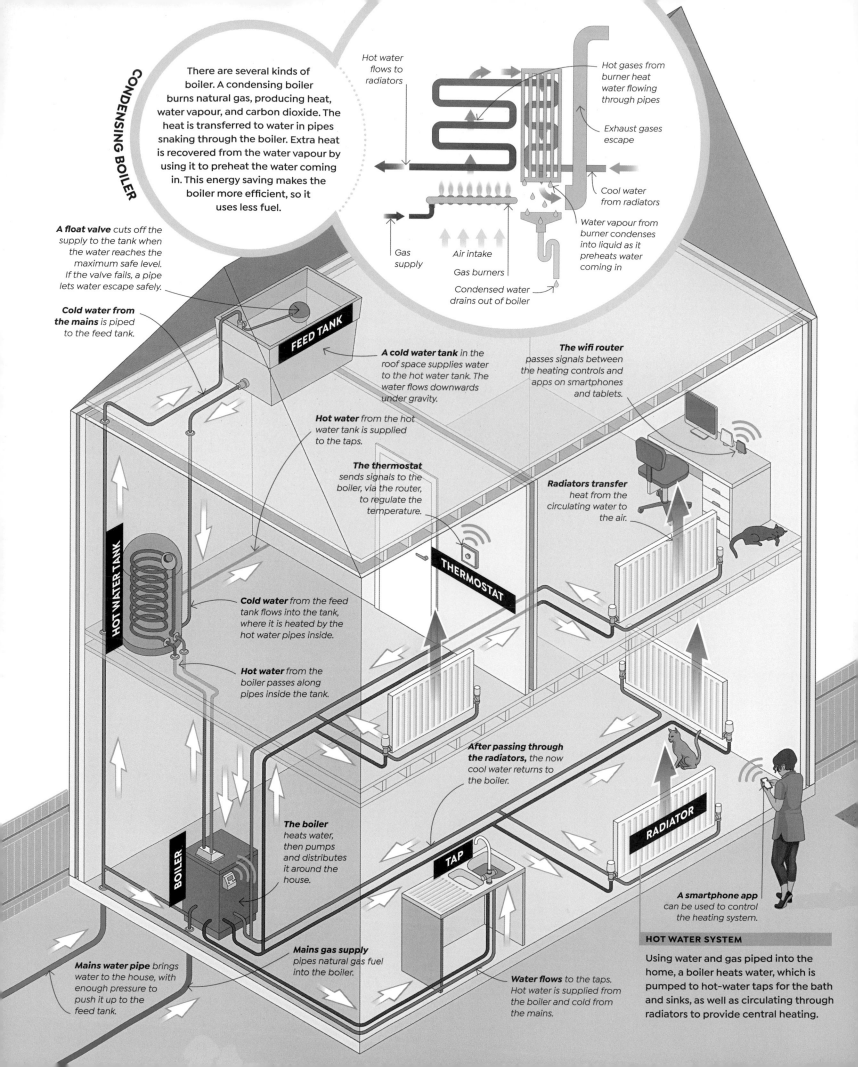

CONDENSING BOILER

There are several kinds of boiler. A condensing boiler burns natural gas, producing heat, water vapour, and carbon dioxide. The heat is transferred to water in pipes snaking through the boiler. Extra heat is recovered from the water vapour by using it to preheat the water coming in. This energy saving makes the boiler more efficient, so it uses less fuel.

Hot water flows to radiators

Hot gases from burner heat water flowing through pipes

Exhaust gases escape

Cool water from radiators

Water vapour from burner condenses into liquid as it preheats water coming in

Gas supply

Air intake

Gas burners

Condensed water drains out of boiler

A float valve cuts off the supply to the tank when the water reaches the maximum safe level. If the valve fails, a pipe lets water escape safely.

Cold water from the mains is piped to the feed tank.

FEED TANK

A cold water tank in the roof space supplies water to the hot water tank. The water flows downwards under gravity.

The wifi router passes signals between the heating controls and apps on smartphones and tablets.

Hot water from the hot water tank is supplied to the taps.

The thermostat sends signals to the boiler, via the router, to regulate the temperature.

Radiators transfer heat from the circulating water to the air.

HOT WATER TANK

Cold water from the feed tank flows into the tank, where it is heated by the hot water pipes inside.

Hot water from the boiler passes along pipes inside the tank.

THERMOSTAT

After passing through the radiators, the now cool water returns to the boiler.

The boiler heats water, then pumps and distributes it around the house.

BOILER

TAP

RADIATOR

A smartphone app can be used to control the heating system.

Mains water pipe brings water to the house, with enough pressure to push it up to the feed tank.

Mains gas supply pipes natural gas fuel into the boiler.

Water flows to the taps. Hot water is supplied from the boiler and cold from the mains.

HOT WATER SYSTEM

Using water and gas piped into the home, a boiler heats water, which is pumped to hot-water taps for the bath and sinks, as well as circulating through radiators to provide central heating.

Hot water and heat pumps

Water is heated in homes for direct use, such as washing in baths and showers, and in some houses to circulate in systems to heat rooms. In response to concerns about the ecological impact of fossil fuels, more renewable energy sources are now being used for heating. They include the sustainable drawing in of heat from the ground and outdoor air using devices called heat pumps.

A heat pump is efficient because it releases more heat energy than the electrical energy it uses

HEAT PUMP SYSTEM

A ground-based heat pump system extracts warmth from underground tubing, which helps to warm fluid that circulates through a circuit of pipes under the floor of the house.

Heat from the pipes radiates out, warming the floor and then the room.

A ground source heat pump sends cool liquid (a mixture of water and antifreeze) under the ground and the returning warmed liquid under the building's floor.

Underfloor heating pipes on top of a bed of insulation carry warm liquid around the circuit.

A network of underground pipes carries liquid, which absorbs heat from the ground.

UNDERGROUND PIPES

GROUND SOURCE HEAT PUMP

UNDERFLOOR HEATING

The fluid in the pipes has cooled by the time it returns to the heat pump.

HEAT PUMP

Inside a ground source heat pump, a refrigerant, such as propane, passes through two devices called heat exchangers. As it does so, it picks up heat from water flowing through pipes under the soil outside the house and changes from liquid to gas. It is then compressed, becoming hot, and changes back to liquid as it heats water flowing through separate pipes under the floor of the house.

1. Liquid is pumped through underground pipes, heating up to the temperature of the soil

2. This liquid goes through a heat exchanger, giving up heat to a refrigerant, which changes from liquid to gas

3. The refrigerant is compressed, making it hotter

4. In a second heat exchanger, refrigerant gives up heat to water flowing under the floor and condenses back to liquid

5. The refrigerant goes through an expansion valve; its temperature drops to below that of the soil so it can capture more heat

6. The cycle starts again.

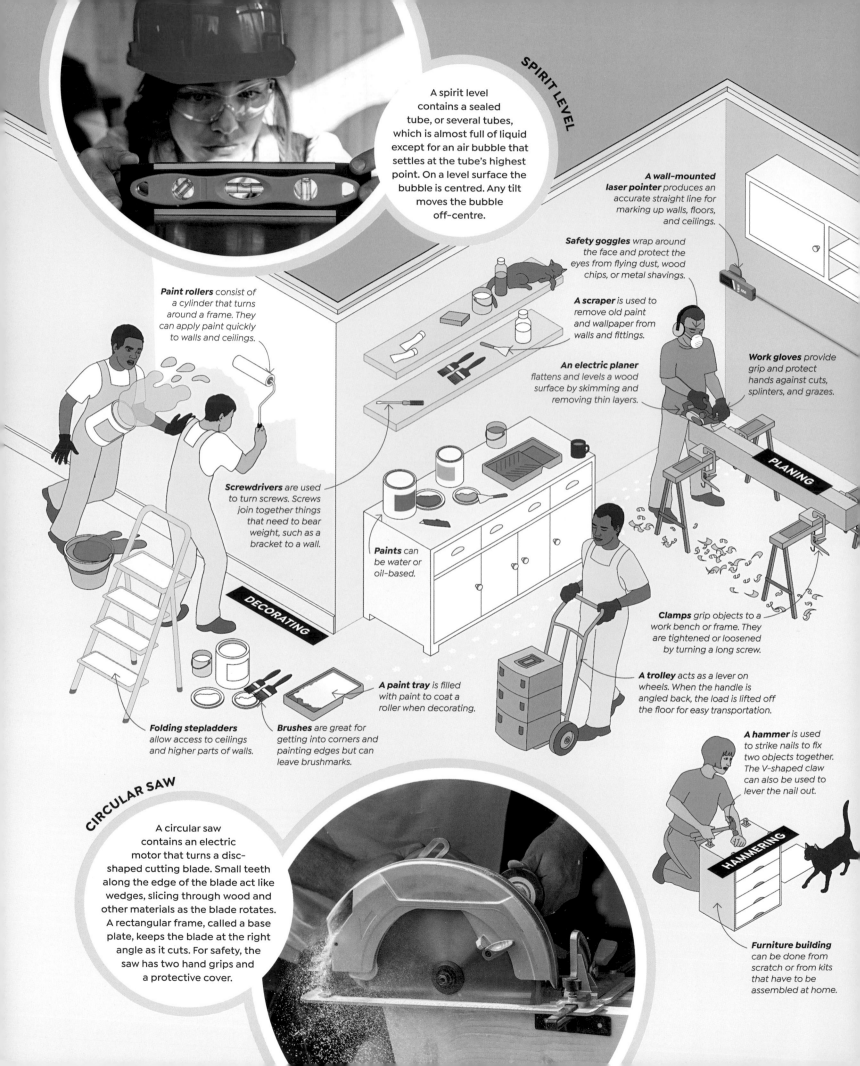

A spirit level contains a sealed tube, or several tubes, which is almost full of liquid except for an air bubble that settles at the tube's highest point. On a level surface the bubble is centred. Any tilt moves the bubble off-centre.

A wall-mounted laser pointer produces an accurate straight line for marking up walls, floors, and ceilings.

Safety goggles wrap around the face and protect the eyes from flying dust, wood chips, or metal shavings.

A scraper is used to remove old paint and wallpaper from walls and fittings.

An electric planer flattens and levels a wood surface by skimming and removing thin layers.

Work gloves provide grip and protect hands against cuts, splinters, and grazes.

PLANING

Paint rollers consist of a cylinder that turns around a frame. They can apply paint quickly to walls and ceilings.

Screwdrivers are used to turn screws. Screws join together things that need to bear weight, such as a bracket to a wall.

Paints can be water or oil-based.

Clamps grip objects to a work bench or frame. They are tightened or loosened by turning a long screw.

A trolley acts as a lever on wheels. When the handle is angled back, the load is lifted off the floor for easy transportation.

DECORATING

Folding stepladders allow access to ceilings and higher parts of walls.

Brushes are great for getting into corners and painting edges but can leave brushmarks.

A paint tray is filled with paint to coat a roller when decorating.

A hammer is used to strike nails to fix two objects together. The V-shaped claw can also be used to lever the nail out.

CIRCULAR SAW

A circular saw contains an electric motor that turns a disc-shaped cutting blade. Small teeth along the edge of the blade act like wedges, slicing through wood and other materials as the blade rotates. A rectangular frame, called a base plate, keeps the blade at the right angle as it cuts. For safety, the saw has two hand grips and a protective cover.

HAMMERING

Furniture building can be done from scratch or from kits that have to be assembled at home.

Home renovation

Renovation can range from simple jobs, such as repainting, to more complicated projects that change a building's layout or make it larger. The tools used include simple devices, such as hammers, which have hardly changed in hundreds of years. Other tools with components such as motors or lasers do the work more quickly or accurately.

Many home renovations now create digital or smart homes. There will be around 500 million smart homes worldwide by 2025

Woodworking projects are the most common cause of DIY injuries

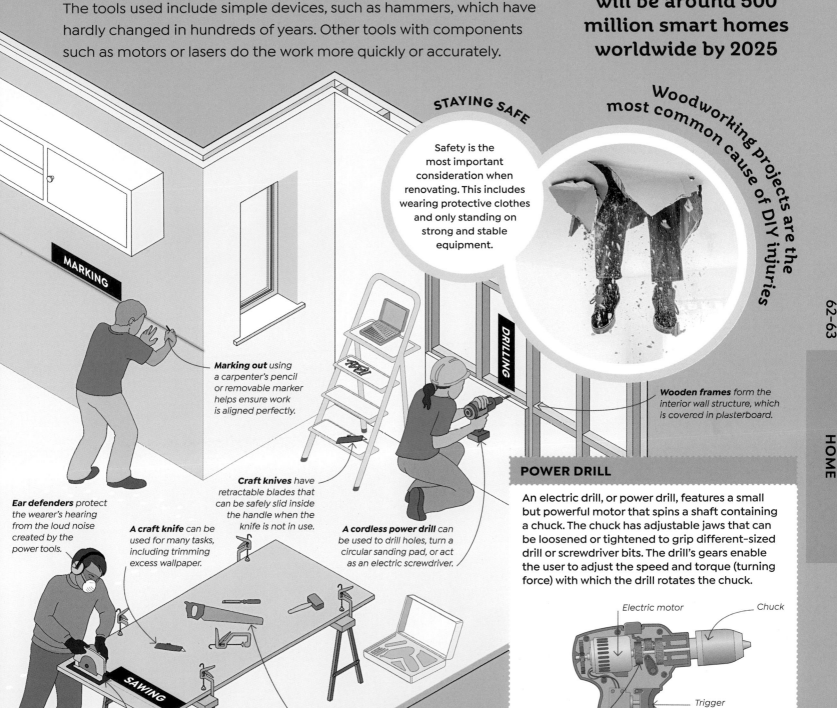

MARKING

STAYING SAFE

Safety is the most important consideration when renovating. This includes wearing protective clothes and only standing on strong and stable equipment.

DRILLING

Marking out using a carpenter's pencil or removable marker helps ensure work is aligned perfectly.

Wooden frames form the interior wall structure, which is covered in plasterboard.

Ear defenders protect the wearer's hearing from the loud noise created by the power tools.

Craft knives have retractable blades that can be safely slid inside the handle when the knife is not in use.

A craft knife can be used for many tasks, including trimming excess wallpaper.

A cordless power drill can be used to drill holes, turn a circular sanding pad, or act as an electric screwdriver.

A circular saw is used to cut through long pieces of wood, plastic, and other materials.

SAWING

A-frame trestles, often used in pairs, support planks, doors, or other parts being worked on.

A hand saw has a long serrated blade which tears into wood to cut pieces in two.

POWER DRILL

An electric drill, or power drill, features a small but powerful motor that spins a shaft containing a chuck. The chuck has adjustable jaws that can be loosened or tightened to grip different-sized drill or screwdriver bits. The drill's gears enable the user to adjust the speed and torque (turning force) with which the drill rotates the chuck.

Electric motor

Chuck

Trigger switch

Gears

Rechargeable battery

ECO-FRIENDLY BUILDINGS

High-rise buildings are often regarded as environmentally unfriendly. Lately, developers have been trying to make buildings that are better at conserving energy and water, use sustainable materials, and even improve biodiversity in the local area through the use of planted balconies.

Sunlight

Tree absorbs carbon dioxide and releases oxygen

Temperature inside

30°C
86°F

Carbon dioxide

Oxygen

21°C
70°F

Temperature outside

Foliage deflects wind and dust

Shade

Recycled water

URBAN OASIS

The Bosco Verticale in Italy features hundreds of trees and plants to improve air quality, and uses recycled water from the building.

Digital home

Homes can contain dozens of devices capable of working by themselves or connecting to a home computer network to share data. With the right apps, these smart devices can be controlled through voice commands or at a touch of a smartphone or tablet screen. They can save us time, effort, and energy.

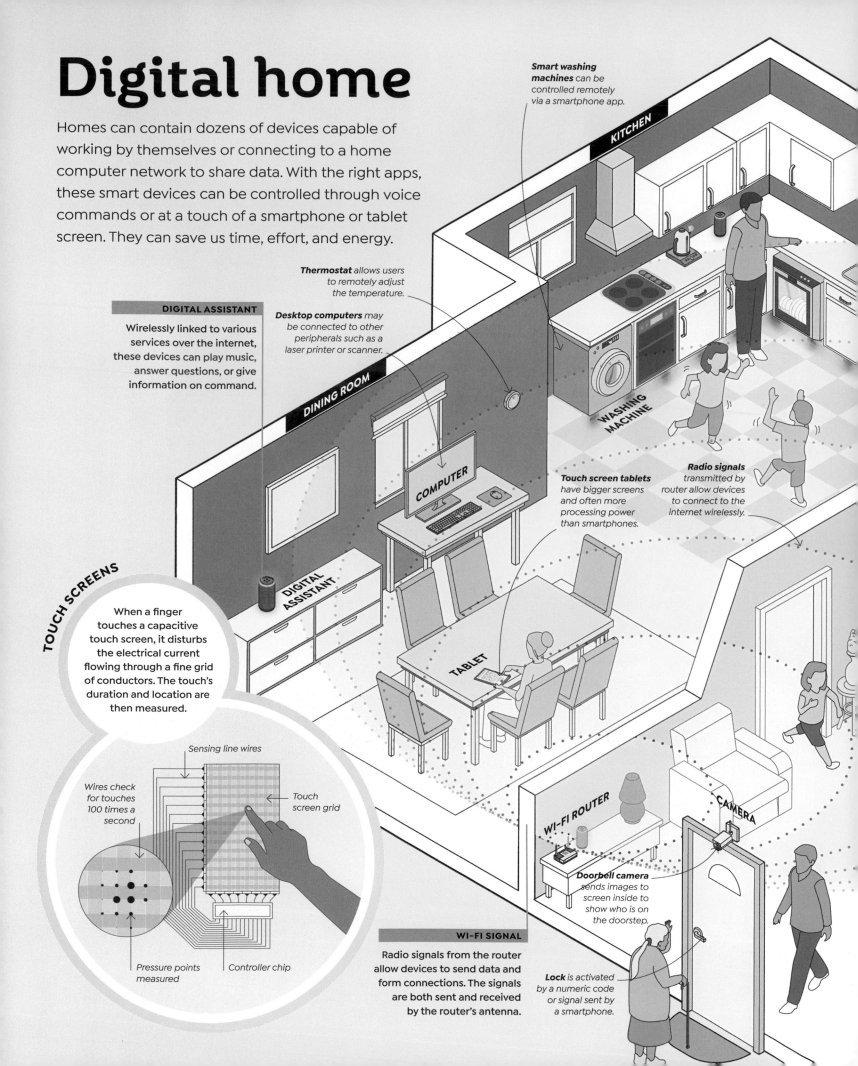

Smart washing machines can be controlled remotely via a smartphone app.

KITCHEN

Thermostat allows users to remotely adjust the temperature.

DIGITAL ASSISTANT

Wirelessly linked to various services over the internet, these devices can play music, answer questions, or give information on command.

Desktop computers may be connected to other peripherals such as a laser printer or scanner.

DINING ROOM

COMPUTER

DIGITAL ASSISTANT

Touch screen tablets have bigger screens and often more processing power than smartphones.

Radio signals transmitted by router allow devices to connect to the internet wirelessly.

WASHING MACHINE

TABLET

TOUCH SCREENS

When a finger touches a capacitive touch screen, it disturbs the electrical current flowing through a fine grid of conductors. The touch's duration and location are then measured.

Sensing line wires

Wires check for touches 100 times a second

Touch screen grid

Pressure points measured

Controller chip

WI-FI ROUTER

CAMERA

Doorbell camera sends images to screen inside to show who is on the doorstep.

WI-FI SIGNAL

Radio signals from the router allow devices to send data and form connections. The signals are both sent and received by the router's antenna.

Lock is activated by a numeric code or signal sent by a smartphone.

Smart fridges have screens that can display what's inside.

Radiation leaking from microwaves can interfere with Wi-Fi.

Smart clocks can display data gathered from the internet, such as outdoor temperature, alerts, or times in other locations.

FRIDGE

CLOCK

BED ROOM

DIGITAL ASSISTANTS

A spoken command to, for example, turn the heating up, is captured by microphones and sent to internet servers, where the speech is analysed and key words extracted. The commands are directed to servers running the heating app, which instruct the user's smartphone to send signals to the smart thermostat.

Speech analyzed

App triggers thermostat's response

Voice command

Digital assistant's microphones

Internet servers

Heating provider's servers

User's smartphone

Powerful portable laptops have a built-in keyboard and can connect to a network and use the internet.

Around 375 million smartphones are sold worldwide every year

LAPTOP

Smart lighting is connected to the network; lights can be customized and scheduled to turn on and off at set times.

LIGHT

Toilet can monitor and adjust flush level and heat its seat on demand.

LIVING ROOM

BATH ROOM

Smart mirrors can connect to the network and display weather and news.

MIRROR

Wi-Fi signal decreases in strength with distance from the router.

Smart speakers can play music through apps on a smartphone.

Heated towel rail sends back current temperature to home heating app.

TOILET

VACUUM

Robot vacuums use lasers to map and navigate a home.

Smart televisions have integrated internet features, such as streaming apps.

TELEVISION

DIGITAL ASSISTANT

CONNECTIVITY

Our homes are connected to the internet by a router. It uses radio waves to send and receive signals carrying data, which enable digital devices, such as laptops, to connect wirelessly both to other devices and the internet.

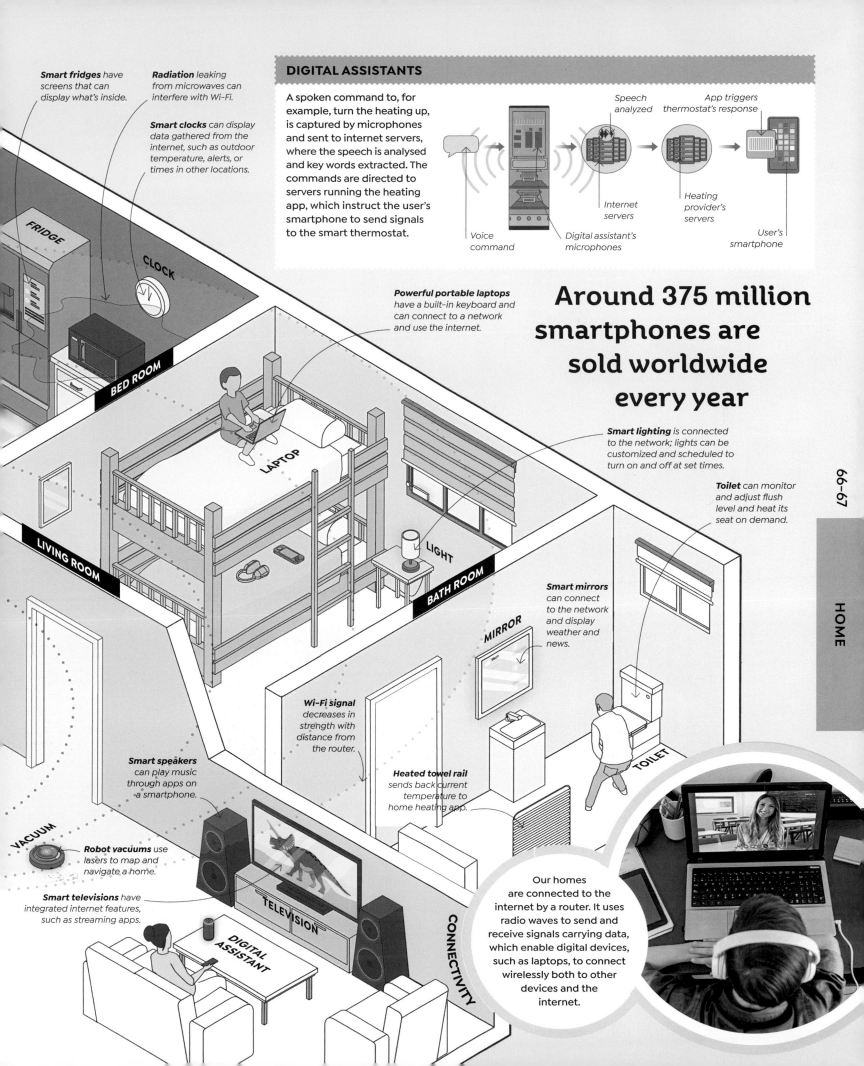

The OLED layers can be 200 times thinner than a human hair

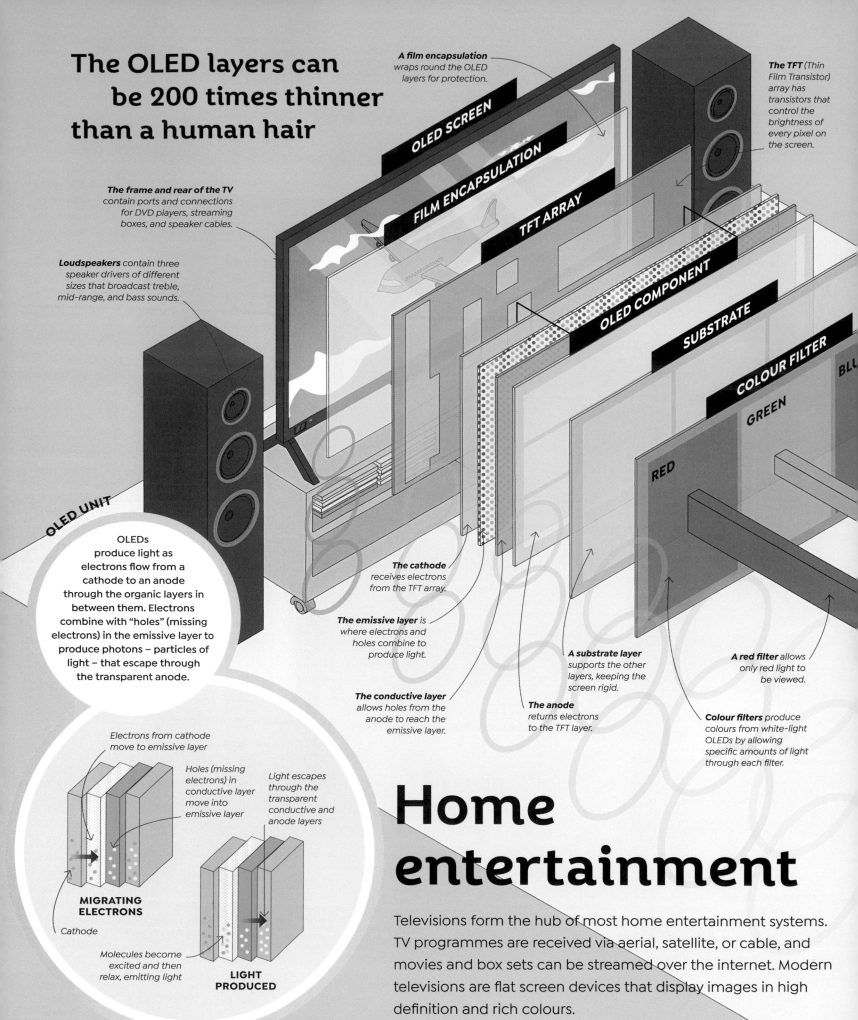

A film encapsulation wraps round the OLED layers for protection.

The TFT (Thin Film Transistor) array has transistors that control the brightness of every pixel on the screen.

OLED SCREEN

FILM ENCAPSULATION

TFT ARRAY

OLED COMPONENT

SUBSTRATE

COLOUR FILTER

BLU

GREEN

RED

The frame and rear of the TV contain ports and connections for DVD players, streaming boxes, and speaker cables.

Loudspeakers contain three speaker drivers of different sizes that broadcast treble, mid-range, and bass sounds.

OLED UNIT

OLEDs produce light as electrons flow from a cathode to an anode through the organic layers in between them. Electrons combine with "holes" (missing electrons) in the emissive layer to produce photons – particles of light – that escape through the transparent anode.

The cathode receives electrons from the TFT array.

The emissive layer is where electrons and holes combine to produce light.

The conductive layer allows holes from the anode to reach the emissive layer.

The anode returns electrons to the TFT layer.

A substrate layer supports the other layers, keeping the screen rigid.

A red filter allows only red light to be viewed.

Colour filters produce colours from white-light OLEDs by allowing specific amounts of light through each filter.

Electrons from cathode move to emissive layer

Holes (missing electrons) in conductive layer move into emissive layer

Light escapes through the transparent conductive and anode layers

MIGRATING ELECTRONS

Cathode

Molecules become excited and then relax, emitting light

LIGHT PRODUCED

Home entertainment

Televisions form the hub of most home entertainment systems. TV programmes are received via aerial, satellite, or cable, and movies and box sets can be streamed over the internet. Modern televisions are flat screen devices that display images in high definition and rich colours.

WIFI ROUTER

The router connects a home network with the internet using a radio transmitter and receiver. Devices within range communicate with the router via radio waves.

No light reaches the blue filter when an orange pixel is being generated on screen.

DIGITAL SOUND

Sounds are analogue signals, but the media and devices we use to listen to them today tend to be digital. An analogue-to-digital converter (ADC) is used to turn analogue signals into digital data, encoded as a long series of binary numbers (zeros and ones). This code can then be manipulated by computer and sent as files. Before the sound can be played, it is converted back into analogue signals.

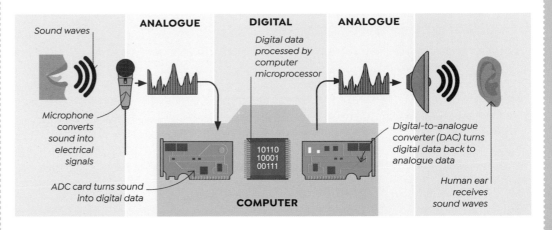

Sound waves

ANALOGUE

DIGITAL

Digital data processed by computer microprocessor

ANALOGUE

Microphone converts sound into electrical signals

ADC card turns sound into digital data

10110
10001
00111

COMPUTER

Digital-to-analogue converter (DAC) turns digital data back to analogue data

Human ear receives sound waves

GLASS LAYER

PIXELS

WHAT IS A PIXEL?

Short for picture element, pixels are individual dots on a screen that make up an image. The number of pixels determines the screen resolution and image clarity.

A remote control commands the TV through transmitted pulses of infrared light.

The filters have let all red light and half green light through, but no blue light creating orange pixels.

Glass protects the delicate OLED screen.

A very high-resolution 8K screen contains 33,177,600 pixels

Gaming

As one of the world's most popular forms of at-home leisure, gaming technology is continuously evolving. Games can be played alone or with others on phones, tablets, personal computers, or on dedicated games consoles. The latest consoles are powerful machines that can produce fast-moving, high-resolution graphics, surround sound, and realistic 3D experiences.

Tablets can be used to play games bought and downloaded from an app store.

TABLET

VR graphics viewed via a headset place the gamer inside a 3D virtual world.

Roll is detected by the headset's accelerometer when the player tilts their head to the side. The accelerometer also monitors the pitch and yaw.

Moving the head forwards and back changes the pitch of the headset, which changes the view in the game.

Yaw is measured by the headset when the player turns their head to the left or right.

Motion controllers convert the physical movement of the player's hands into 3D actions within the game's world.

A Wi-Fi router enables wireless controllers to communicate with the console, or connects some consoles to the internet.

VIRTUAL REALITY

ROUTER

The first computer game with moving graphics, Tennis for Two, was invented in 1958 by American William Higinbotham

A headset contains speakers for a more realistic gaming experience and a microphone for voice commands.

VIRTUAL WORLDS

A Virtual Reality (VR) headset displays slightly different views for each eye, creating the illusion of depth. When the headset detects head movements, the console adjusts the views so the player feels as though they are inside the 3D virtual world and able to explore. When coupled with motion controllers that convert hand movements to in-game actions, games can feel incredibly realistic.

Headset contains stereo speakers that play virtual sounds seemingly from different directions

Left eyepiece displays one view of virtual world

Right eyepiece shows slightly different view to left eye, creating a 3D scene

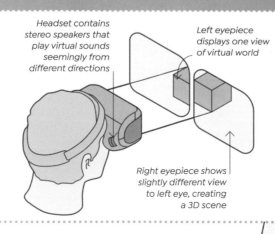

GAMING HEADSET

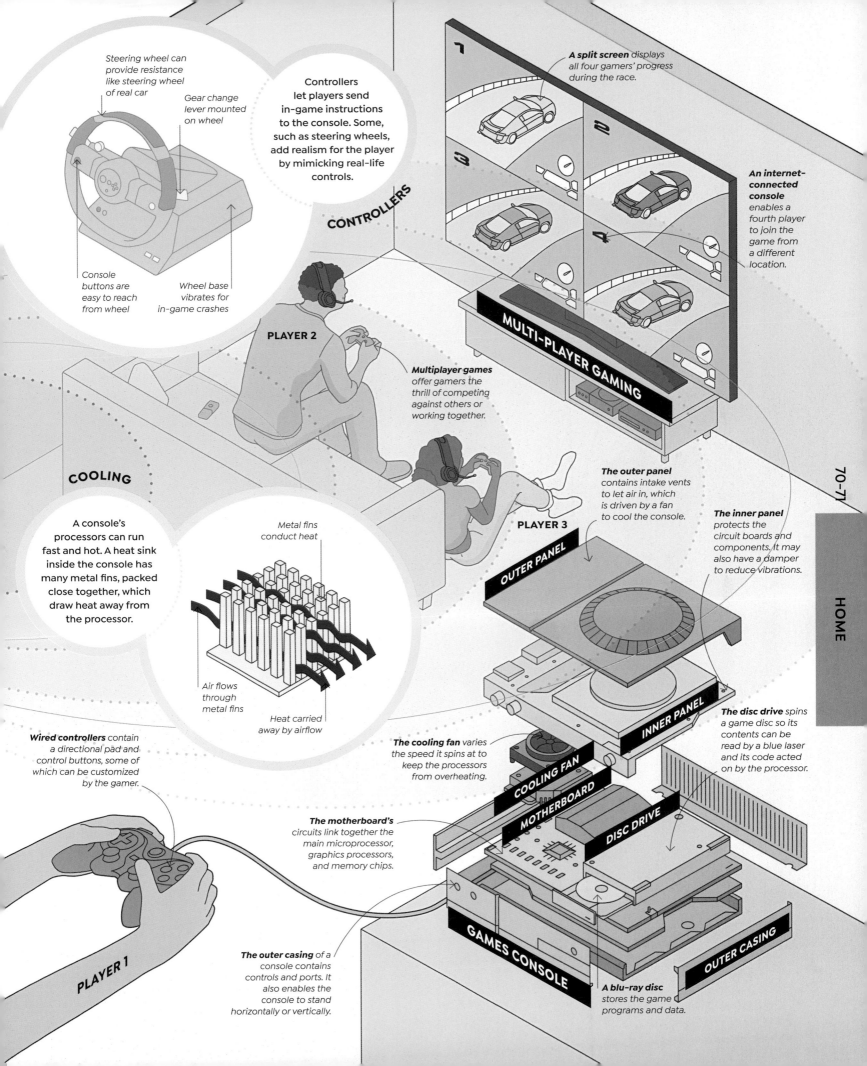

Steering wheel can provide resistance like steering wheel of real car

Gear change lever mounted on wheel

Console buttons are easy to reach from wheel

Wheel base vibrates for in-game crashes

Controllers let players send in-game instructions to the console. Some, such as steering wheels, add realism for the player by mimicking real-life controls.

CONTROLLERS

1

2

3

4

A split screen displays all four gamers' progress during the race.

An internet-connected console enables a fourth player to join the game from a different location.

MULTI-PLAYER GAMING

PLAYER 2

Multiplayer games offer gamers the thrill of competing against others or working together.

COOLING

A console's processors can run fast and hot. A heat sink inside the console has many metal fins, packed close together, which draw heat away from the processor.

Metal fins conduct heat

Air flows through metal fins

Heat carried away by airflow

PLAYER 3

The outer panel contains intake vents to let air in, which is driven by a fan to cool the console.

The inner panel protects the circuit boards and components. It may also have a damper to reduce vibrations.

OUTER PANEL

INNER PANEL

The disc drive spins a game disc so its contents can be read by a blue laser and its code acted on by the processor.

The cooling fan varies the speed it spins at to keep the processors from overheating.

Wired controllers contain a directional pad and control buttons, some of which can be customized by the gamer.

The motherboard's circuits link together the main microprocessor, graphics processors, and memory chips.

COOLING FAN

MOTHERBOARD

DISC DRIVE

GAMES CONSOLE

OUTER CASING

PLAYER 1

The outer casing of a console contains controls and ports. It also enables the console to stand horizontally or vertically.

A blu-ray disc stores the game programs and data.

City
and
Industry

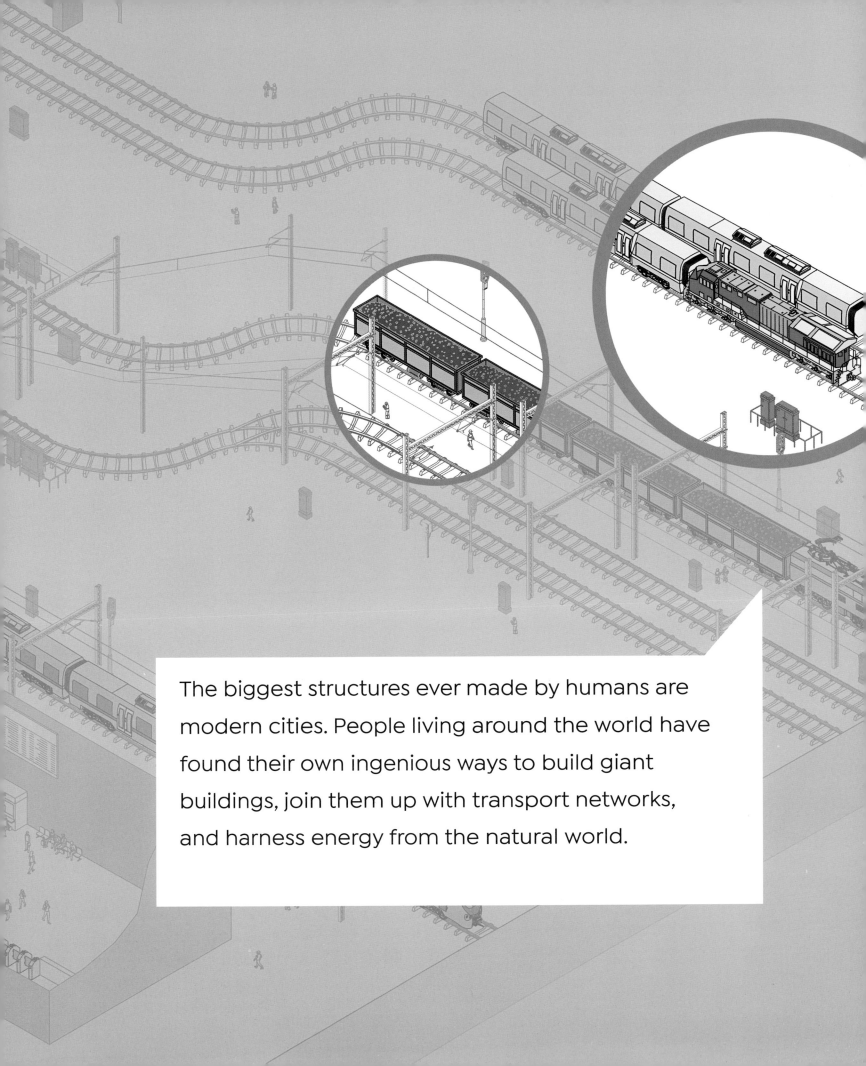

The biggest structures ever made by humans are modern cities. People living around the world have found their own ingenious ways to build giant buildings, join them up with transport networks, and harness energy from the natural world.

Construction site

Constructing a new building or a structure such as a bridge, road, or tunnel demands precision, teamwork, and specialized machinery. Construction projects vary in size from individual homes to giant shopping complexes and towering skyscrapers. Some parts of the structure are built on the site, but others are made elsewhere and brought to the site to be fitted together.

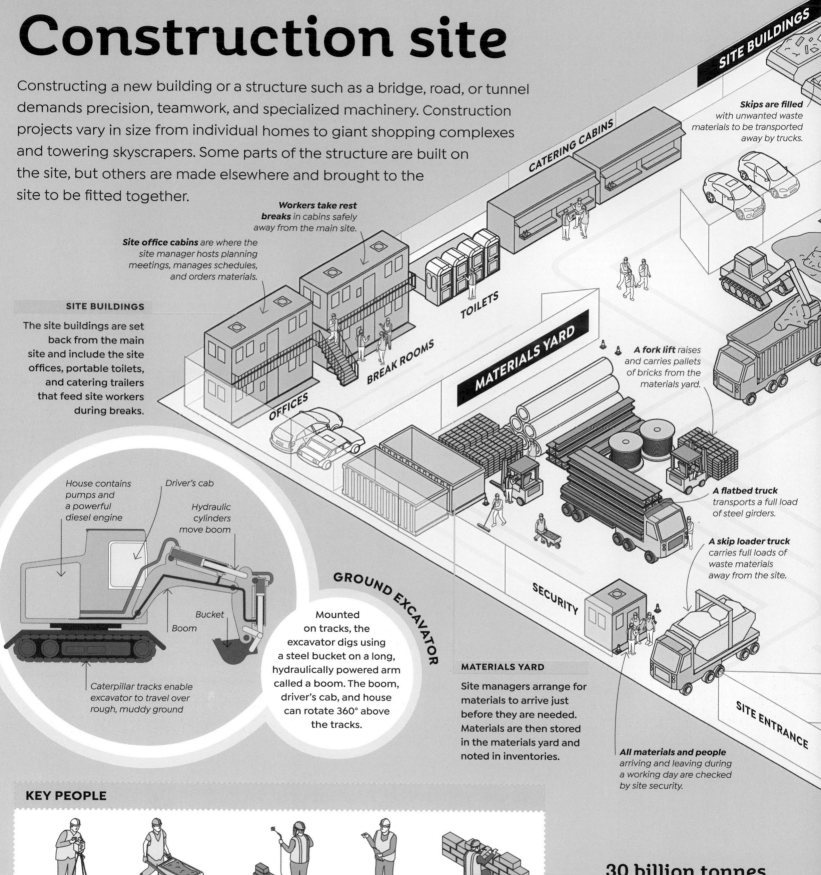

SITE BUILDINGS

Skips are filled with unwanted waste materials to be transported away by trucks.

CATERING CABINS

Workers take rest breaks in cabins safely away from the main site.

Site office cabins are where the site manager hosts planning meetings, manages schedules, and orders materials.

SITE BUILDINGS

The site buildings are set back from the main site and include the site offices, portable toilets, and catering trailers that feed site workers during breaks.

TOILETS

BREAK ROOMS

OFFICES

MATERIALS YARD

A fork lift raises and carries pallets of bricks from the materials yard.

A flatbed truck transports a full load of steel girders.

A skip loader truck carries full loads of waste materials away from the site.

House contains pumps and a powerful diesel engine

Driver's cab

Hydraulic cylinders move boom

Bucket

Boom

Caterpillar tracks enable excavator to travel over rough, muddy ground

GROUND EXCAVATOR

Mounted on tracks, the excavator digs using a steel bucket on a long, hydraulically powered arm called a boom. The boom, driver's cab, and house can rotate 360° above the tracks.

SECURITY

MATERIALS YARD

Site managers arrange for materials to arrive just before they are needed. Materials are then stored in the materials yard and noted in inventories.

SITE ENTRANCE

All materials and people arriving and leaving during a working day are checked by site security.

KEY PEOPLE

Surveyor
Measures and marks out land, so the building matches the plans.

Labourer
Does physical work on site like moving materials and digging trenches.

Welder
Uses tools to cut and join steel on the frameworks of buildings.

Foreman
An experienced builder who supervises the workers on site.

Bricklayer
Builds walls using bricks, blocks, and stone cemented with mortar.

30 billion tonnes of concrete is used worldwide every year – the weight of 91,000 Empire State buildings

1 **An excavator** digs up earth to level the site before footings and foundations are created. The earth may be used for landscaping or is transported off-site.

EXCAVATION

BAMBOO SCAFFOLDING

Light and fast to assemble, bamboo is often used for scaffolding in Hong Kong. As a fast-growing plant, bamboo is a sustainable material to build with.

Pulley cables running over the crane's arm raise and lower loads.

The tower crane has modular sections that can be added to raise the crane's height as the building rises.

FOOTINGS

2 **Footings** help support the exterior wall of the building. To create them, concrete is poured into a trench around the edge of the site and steel rods are fixed inside.

6 **Materials** are lifted to higher levels by the tower crane as the building gets taller.

3 **A concrete slab** forms the building's foundations. It is made by laying down a mesh made of criss-crossing steel rods and pouring concrete over the top. The mesh reinforces the concrete and helps to distribute loads evenly.

FOUNDATIONS

A concrete mixer pours concrete over the steel mesh to form a firm base.

Pre-cast concrete wall sections are stacked ready to be lifted by the tower crane.

5 **Steel girders** are riveted, bolted, or welded together to form the building's frame.

4 **A framework** known as scaffolding, commonly made of steel tubing clamped together, is built to enable workers to reach a building's upper levels.

CONSTRUCTION

CONCRETE MIXER

Concrete is a mixture of cement, aggregate (gravel or sand), and water. The rotating drum mixes the concrete, while a turning screw pumps the mixture out.

Large drum holds ready-mixed concrete

Powerful motor turns mixer drum

Exit chute

Twin axles (two sets of wheels) help support weight of truck

Screw

Driver's cab

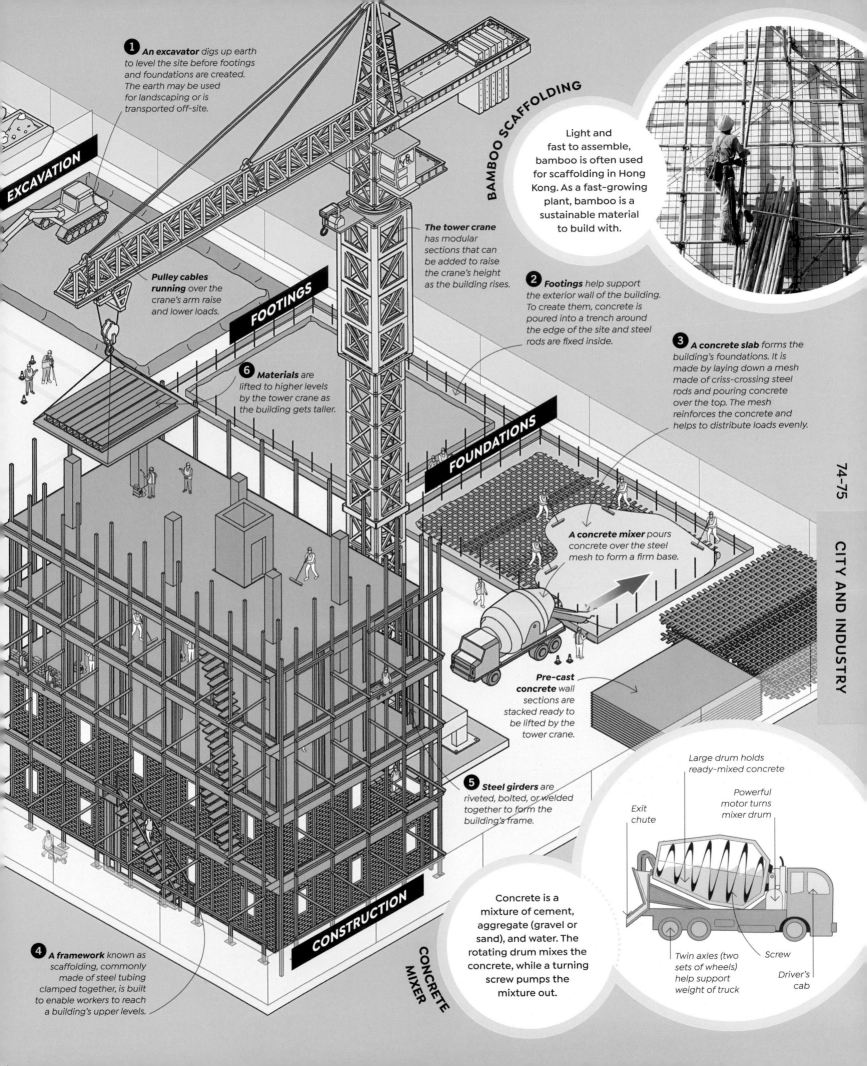

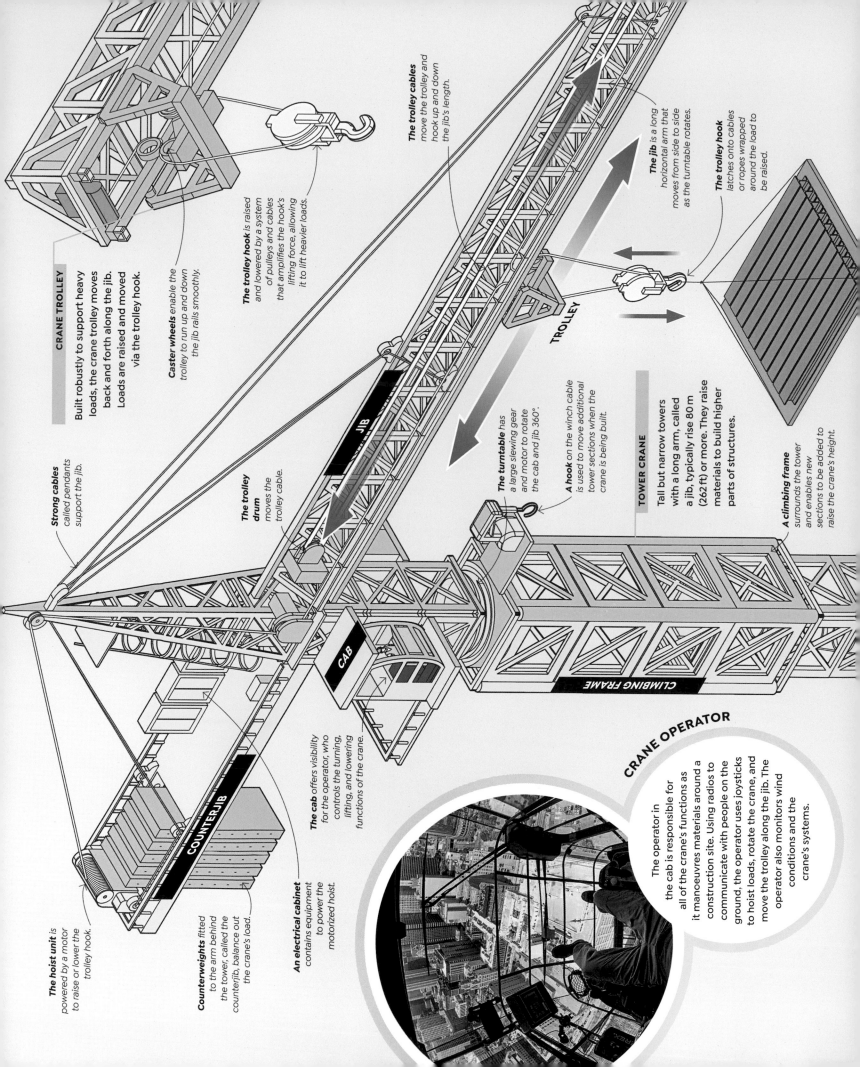

CRANE TROLLEY

Built robustly to support heavy loads, the crane trolley moves back and forth along the jib. Loads are raised and moved via the trolley hook.

Caster wheels enable the trolley to run up and down the jib rails smoothly.

The trolley hook is raised and lowered by a system of pulleys and cables that amplifies the hook's lifting force, allowing it to lift heavier loads.

The trolley cables move the trolley and hook up and down the jib's length.

The jib is a long horizontal arm that moves from side to side as the turntable rotates.

The trolley hook latches onto cables or ropes wrapped around the load to be raised.

TROLLEY

Strong cables called pendants support the jib.

The trolley drum moves the trolley cable.

JIB

The turntable has a large slewing gear and motor to rotate the cab and jib 360°.

A hook on the winch cable is used to move additional tower sections when the crane is being built.

TOWER CRANE

Tall but narrow towers with a long arm, called a jib, typically rise 80 m (262 ft) or more. They raise materials to build higher parts of structures.

A climbing frame surrounds the tower and enables new sections to be added to raise the crane's height.

The hoist unit is powered by a motor to raise or lower the trolley hook.

Counterweights fitted to the arm behind the tower, called the counterjib, balance out the crane's load.

An electrical cabinet contains equipment to power the motorized hoist.

The cab offers visibility for the operator, who controls the turning, lifting, and lowering functions of the crane.

COUNTERJIB

CAB

CLIMBING FRAME

CRANE OPERATOR

The operator in the cab is responsible for all of the crane's functions as it manoeuvres materials around a construction site. Using radios to communicate with people on the ground, the operator uses joysticks to hoist loads, rotate the crane, and move the trolley along the jib. The operator also monitors wind conditions and the crane's systems.

Crane

Cranes are complex machines that utilize pulleys and cables to lift heavy loads to great heights. There are many types of crane, which can be found at ports, factories, and especially on construction sites. At these sites, large tower cranes enable soaring multi-floored hotels, apartment blocks, and office buildings to be built quickly and safely.

HOW CRANES ARE BUILT

Tower cranes are initially assembled on the ground or using a mobile crane. When the crane has to be made taller, a climbing frame, powered by hydraulics, is used to lift up the jib and the upper crane. A new section of the tower is assembled on the ground then hoisted up into place by the crane's hook.

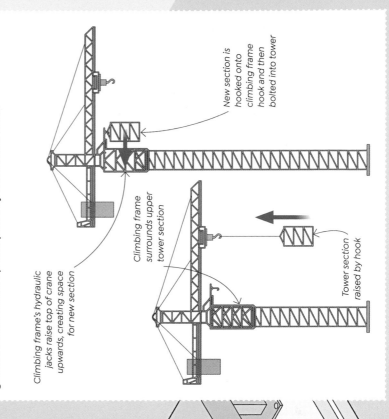

New section is hooked onto climbing frame hook and then bolted into tower

Climbing frame surrounds upper tower section

Climbing frame's hydraulic jacks raise top of crane upwards, creating space for new section

Tower section raised by hook

The world's tallest crane, Big Carl, can reach a huge 250 m (820 ft) high

TOWER

Ladders running inside the tower give workers access from the ground to the crane cab.

Tower sections are made of a sturdy steel framework and fitted together to form the tower.

MOBILE CRANE

Smaller, mobile cranes have telescopic arms that raise loads with hydraulics and use stabilizers for balance.

A mobile crane on a truck provides portable lifting power.

MOBILE CRANE

Hydraulics drive the crane's arm and hook upwards to raise a large concrete panel.

Footings secure the crane to deep foundations made of concrete, giving the crane a solid base.

TOWER BASE

FOUNDATIONS

FOOTINGS

The tower base is bolted securely to the footings.

Skyscraper

The world's cities are not just sprawling outwards, they're also growing upwards. Skyscrapers are their tallest buildings, soaring at least 150 m (490 ft) into the sky with most of their height taken up with floors of offices, hotels, or apartments. Advances in design, materials, and construction techniques have led to skyscrapers becoming taller and more being built.

Rooftop swimming pools feature on skyscrapers that house hotels and luxury apartments.

Skylights made of glass or transparent plastics allow daylight into upper floors.

Solar glass contains photovoltaic cells that enable the skyscraper windows to generate electricity from sunlight.

Steel frames are common in skyscrapers as they can be rapidly assembled to form tall structures.

Window cleaners working at dizzying heights operate from a lifting gondola, raised and lowered by rooftop cranes.

A suspended walkway or skybridge links two buildings, making it easy to move from one building to another.

Some skyscrapers have concrete frames, making it possible to build unusual shapes. Concrete may also be cheaper than steel.

Vertical gardens built on exterior walls help to absorb some air pollution.

CONCRETE FRAME

STEEL FRAME

LIVING WALLS

SOLAR GLASS

STEEL FRAMES

Steel column

Steel girder

Concrete flooring laid over steel deck

Utility pipes run under flooring

Filler beam adds further support

Many skyscrapers have a central concrete core but the rest of their structure is a skeleton of steel. Sturdy steel beams that are strong under tension are bolted together to form columns that transfer the structure's weight to its foundations. Horizontal girders are connected to the columns with filler beams fitted between girders for additional support.

A twisted design reduces vortex shedding – the creation of suction forces by high winds, which can cause the building to sway and shake.

An outer glass covering of a building, called a curtain wall, protects the structure from the weather.

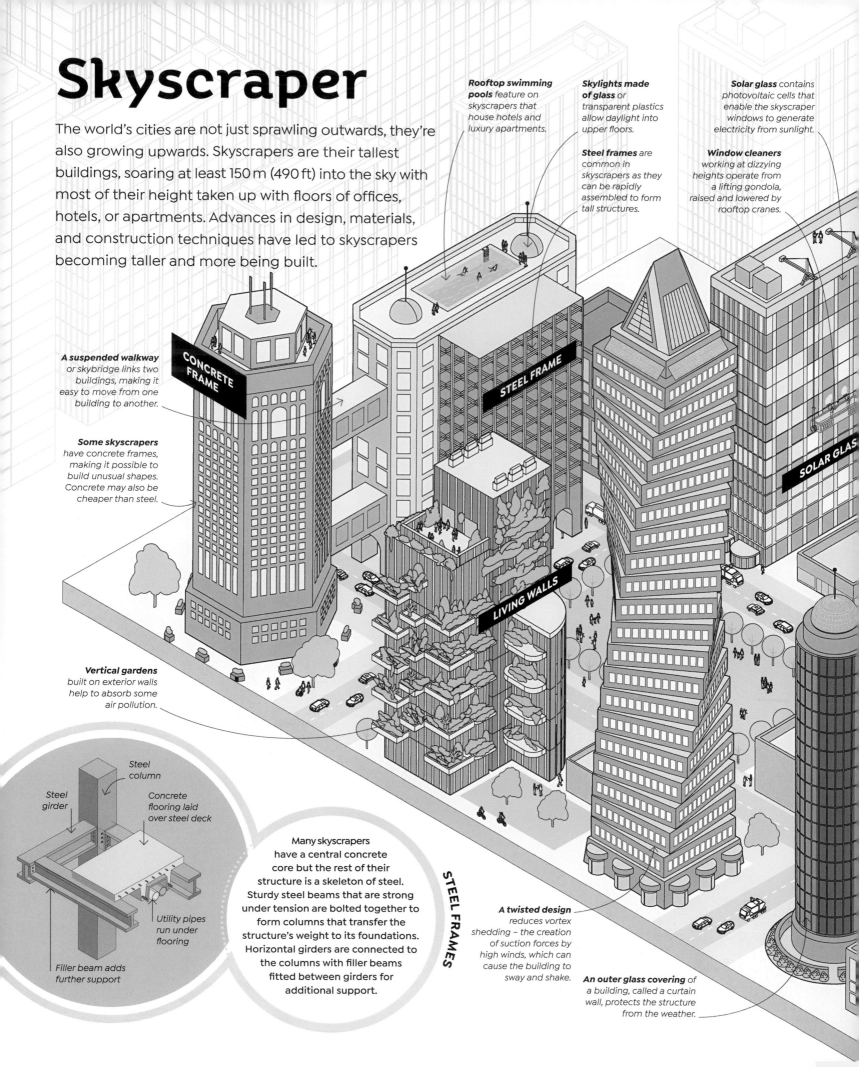

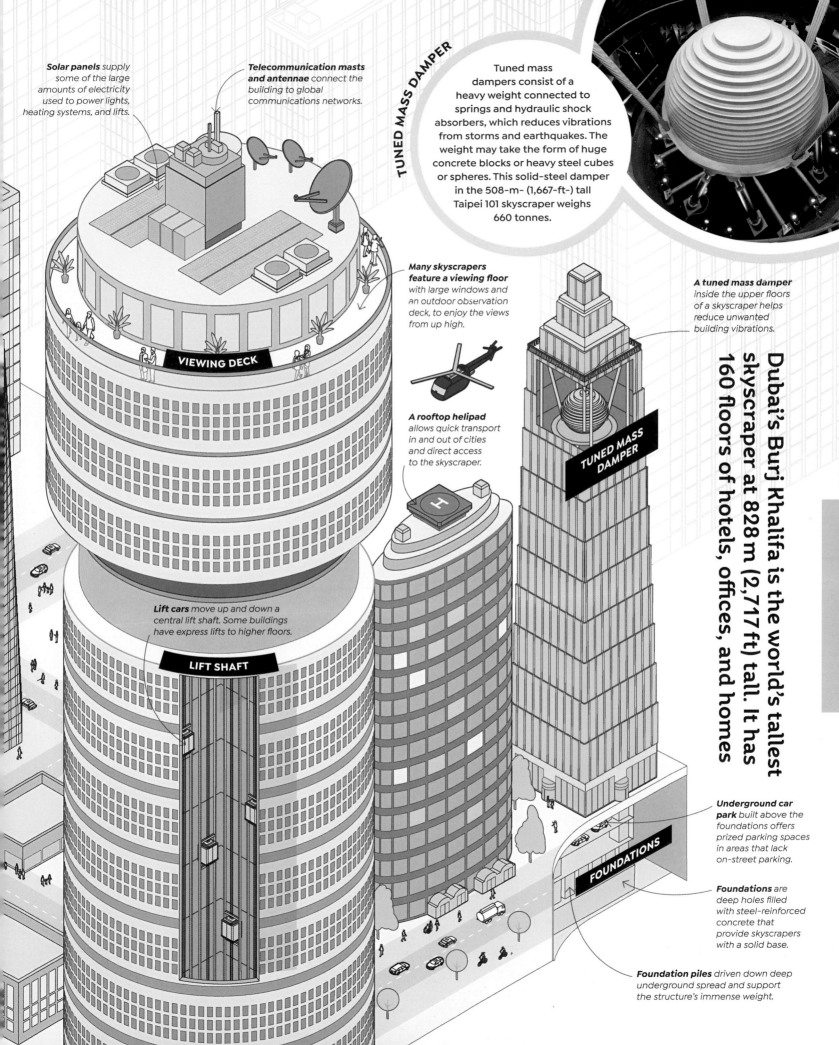

Solar panels supply some of the large amounts of electricity used to power lights, heating systems, and lifts.

Telecommunication masts and antennae connect the building to global communications networks.

Tuned mass dampers consist of a heavy weight connected to springs and hydraulic shock absorbers, which reduces vibrations from storms and earthquakes. The weight may take the form of huge concrete blocks or heavy steel cubes or spheres. This solid-steel damper in the 508-m- (1,667-ft-) tall Taipei 101 skyscraper weighs 660 tonnes.

Many skyscrapers feature a viewing floor with large windows and an outdoor observation deck, to enjoy the views from up high.

VIEWING DECK

A tuned mass damper inside the upper floors of a skyscraper helps reduce unwanted building vibrations.

A rooftop helipad allows quick transport in and out of cities and direct access to the skyscraper.

TUNED MASS DAMPER

Lift cars move up and down a central lift shaft. Some buildings have express lifts to higher floors.

LIFT SHAFT

Dubai's Burj Khalifa is the world's tallest skyscraper at 828 m (2,717 ft) tall. It has 160 floors of hotels, offices, and homes

Underground car park built above the foundations offers prized parking spaces in areas that lack on-street parking.

FOUNDATIONS

Foundations are deep holes filled with steel-reinforced concrete that provide skyscrapers with a solid base.

Foundation piles driven down deep underground spread and support the structure's immense weight.

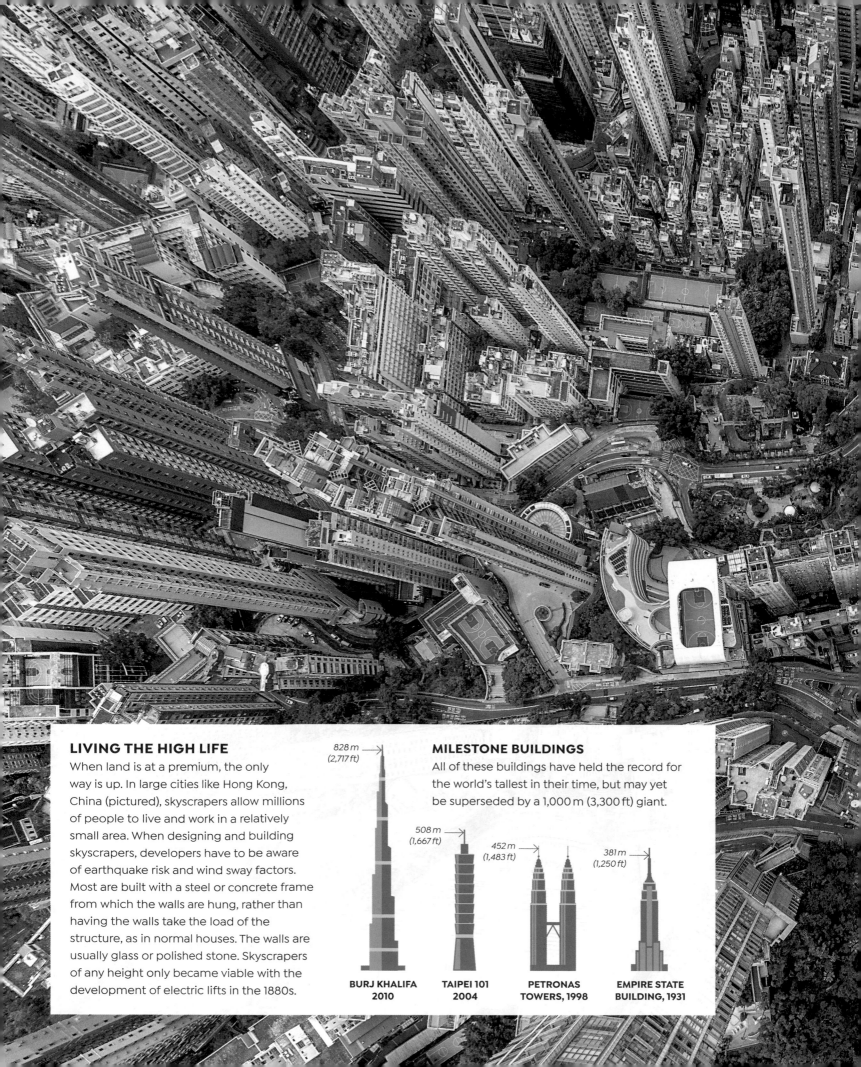

LIVING THE HIGH LIFE

When land is at a premium, the only way is up. In large cities like Hong Kong, China (pictured), skyscrapers allow millions of people to live and work in a relatively small area. When designing and building skyscrapers, developers have to be aware of earthquake risk and wind sway factors. Most are built with a steel or concrete frame from which the walls are hung, rather than having the walls take the load of the structure, as in normal houses. The walls are usually glass or polished stone. Skyscrapers of any height only became viable with the development of electric lifts in the 1880s.

MILESTONE BUILDINGS

All of these buildings have held the record for the world's tallest in their time, but may yet be superseded by a 1,000 m (3,300 ft) giant.

828 m
(2,717 ft)

508 m
(1,667 ft)

452 m
(1,483 ft)

381 m
(1,250 ft)

**BURJ KHALIFA
2010**

**TAIPEI 101
2004**

**PETRONAS
TOWERS, 1998**

**EMPIRE STATE
BUILDING, 1931**

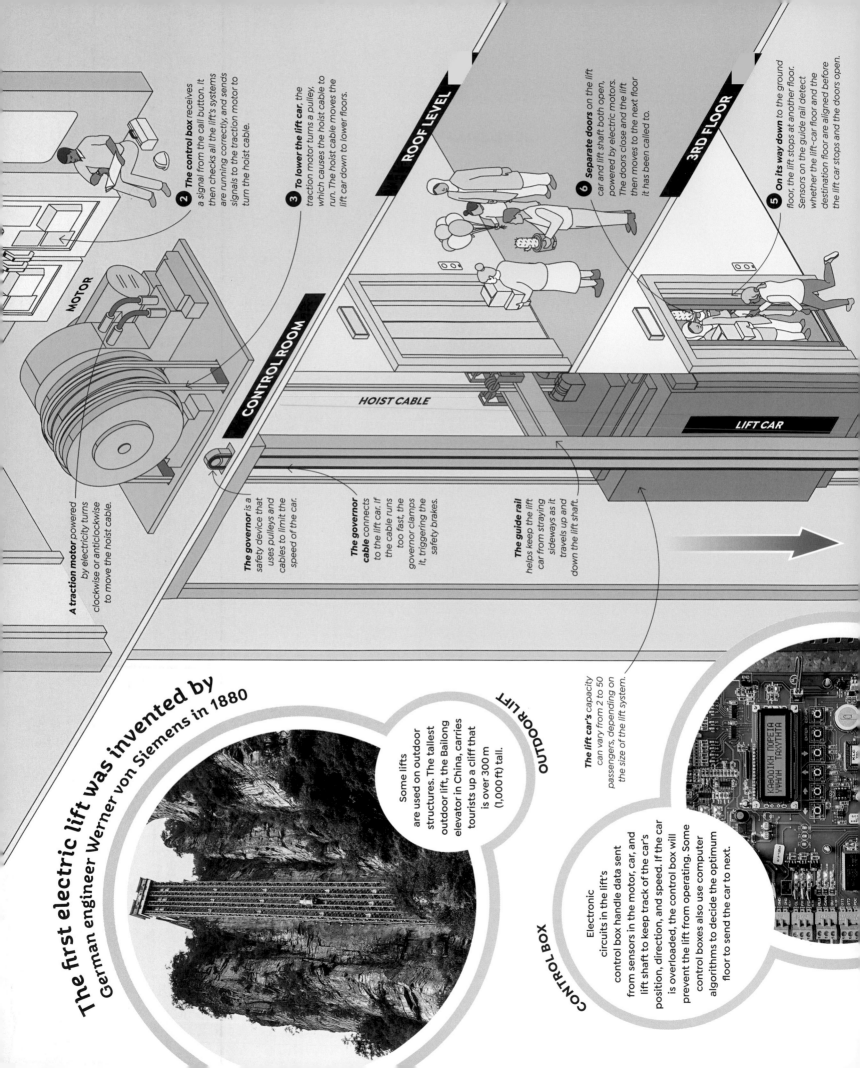

The first electric lift was invented by German engineer Werner von Siemens in 1880

2 The control box receives a signal from the call button. It then checks all the lift's systems are running correctly, and sends signals to the traction motor to turn the hoist cable.

3 To lower the lift car, the traction motor turns a pulley, which causes the hoist cable to run. The hoist cable moves the lift car down to lower floors.

MOTOR

A traction motor powered by electricity turns clockwise or anticlockwise to move the hoist cable.

ROOF LEVEL

CONTROL ROOM

HOIST CABLE

6 Separate doors on the lift car and lift shaft both open, powered by electric motors. The doors close and the lift then moves to the next floor it has been called to.

3RD FLOOR

5 On its way down to the ground floor, the lift stops at another floor. Sensors on the guide rail detect whether the lift-car floor and the destination floor are aligned before the lift car stops and the doors open.

The governor is a safety device that uses pulleys and cables to limit the speed of the car.

The governor cable connects to the lift car. If the cable runs too fast, the governor clamps it, triggering the safety brakes.

The guide rail helps keep the lift car from straying sideways as it travels up and down the lift shaft.

LIFT CAR

The lift car's capacity can vary from 2 to 50 passengers, depending on the size of the lift system.

OUTDOOR LIFT

Some lifts are used on outdoor structures. The tallest outdoor lift, the Bailong elevator in China, carries tourists up a cliff that is over 300 m (1,000 ft) tall.

CONTROL BOX

Electronic circuits in the lift's control box handle data sent from sensors in the motor, car, and lift shaft to keep track of the car's position, direction, and speed. If the car is overloaded, the control box will prevent the lift from operating. Some control boxes also use computer algorithms to decide the optimum floor to send the car to next.

Lifts

Lifts raise and lower loads, carrying people or goods up and down between the floors of a building. While some lifts are powered by hydraulics, most use a roped system with a lift car suspended from cables running over a pulley. Rapid safety lifts have enabled the construction of ever-taller buildings and skyscrapers.

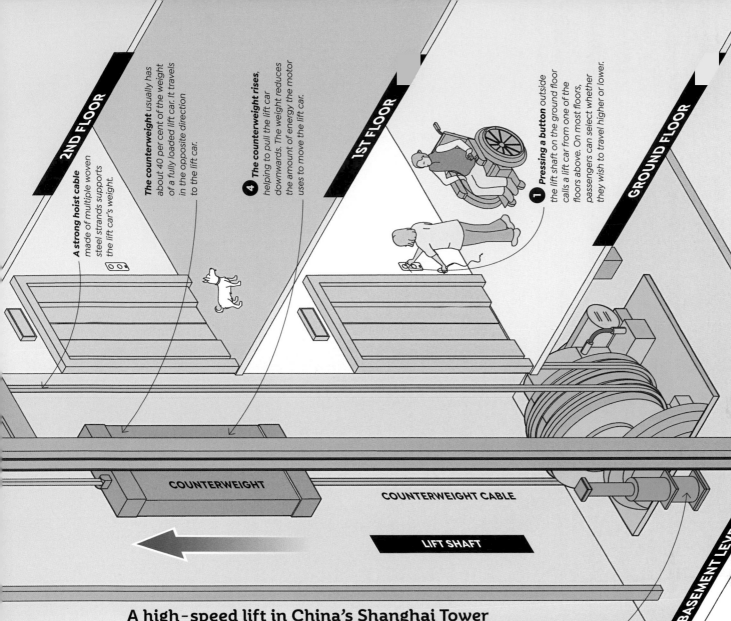

2ND FLOOR

A strong hoist cable made of multiple woven steel strands supports the lift car's weight.

The counterweight usually has about 40 per cent of the weight of a fully loaded lift car. It travels in the opposite direction to the lift car.

4 The counterweight rises, helping to pull the lift car downwards. The weight reduces the amount of energy the motor uses to move the lift car.

1ST FLOOR

1 Pressing a button outside the lift shaft on the ground floor calls a lift car from one of the floors above. On most floors, passengers can select whether they wish to travel higher or lower.

GROUND FLOOR

The governor tension sheave keeps the governor cable at the correct level of tautness as the lift car moves.

COUNTERWEIGHT

COUNTERWEIGHT CABLE

LIFT SHAFT

BASEMENT LEVEL

A high-speed lift in China's Shanghai Tower travels 121 floors in just 53 seconds!

Safety buffers fitted to a suspension system cushion the lift car's impact should other safety systems fail.

HORIZONTAL LIFTS

New lift systems without hoist cables enable lift cars to travel not only vertically but also horizontally. They adopt the electromagnetic track technology used in maglev trains (see p. 113) to propel lift cars along steel tracks. This system can house many lift cars in a single shaft, making lift journeys even more efficient.

Hospital

A hospital gives people a complete range of healthcare services, ranging from investigation and diagnosis to complex surgery. People with a medical emergency will also be taken to a hospital, where staff will start by working out what they need, a process called triage. Many patients go back home the same day, but others stay for days or weeks to be cared for on a ward.

PHARMACY

Staff in this department manage, test, and supply medicines. Pharmacists advise doctors on the medicines and doses that most suit a patient.

Cleaning regularly helps to restrict the spread of diseases and infections.

OUTPATIENTS

People with health problems who are not admitted for overnight stays in the hospital are diagnosed and treated in outpatients clinics.

ACCIDENT AND EMERGENCY

This department offers immediate treatment to people who are seriously ill or have had a severe accident.

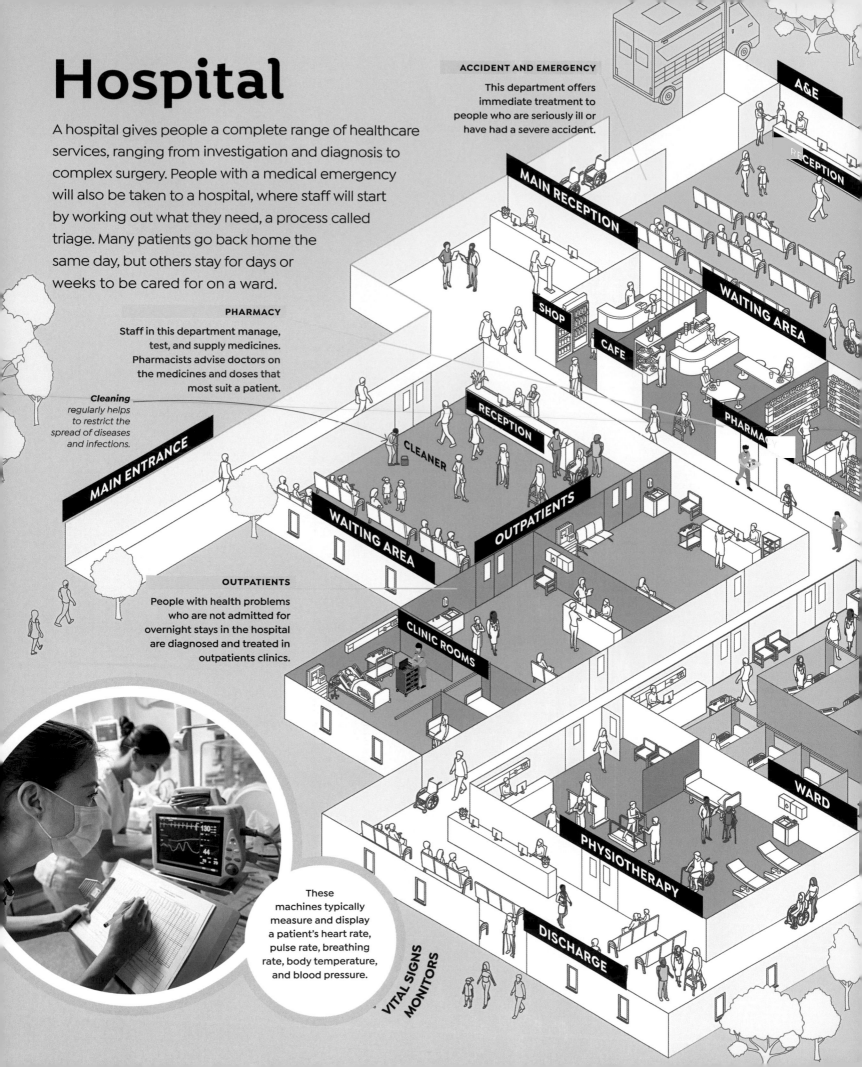

These machines typically measure and display a patient's heart rate, pulse rate, breathing rate, body temperature, and blood pressure.

A&E

RECEPTION

MAIN RECEPTION

SHOP

CAFE

WAITING AREA

PHARMACY

RECEPTION

CLEANER

OUTPATIENTS

MAIN ENTRANCE

WAITING AREA

CLINIC ROOMS

WARD

PHYSIOTHERAPY

DISCHARGE

VITAL SIGNS MONITORS

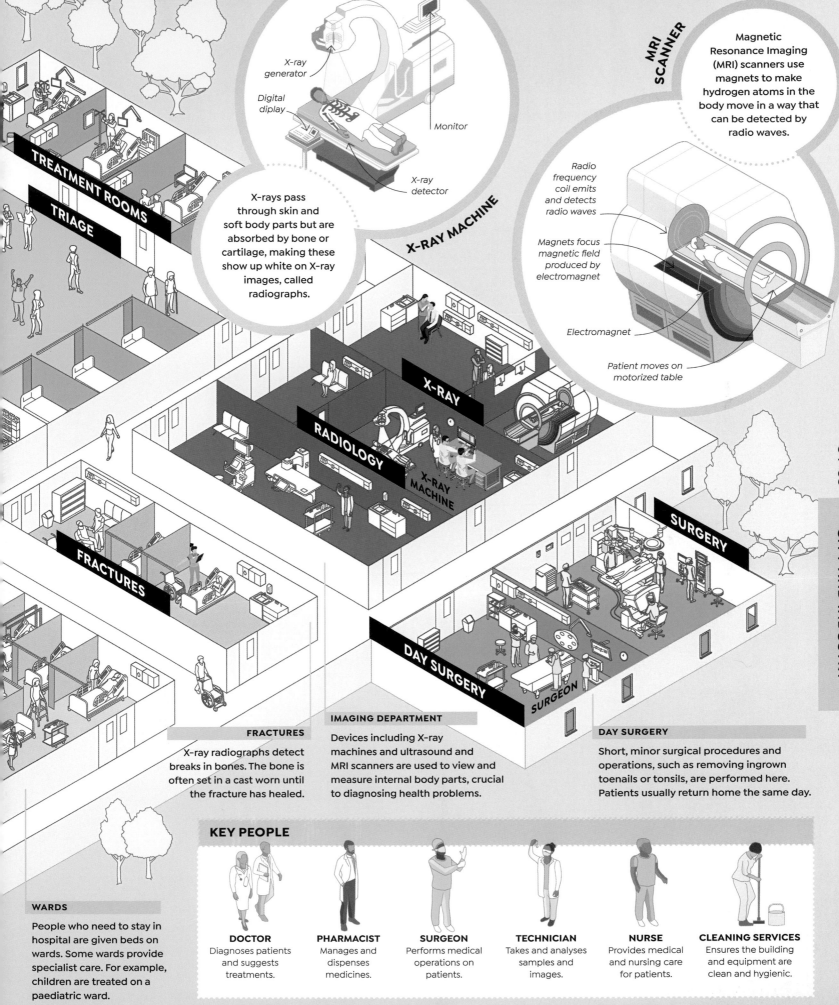

TREATMENT ROOMS

TRIAGE

X-ray generator

Digital display

Monitor

X-ray detector

X-rays pass through skin and soft body parts but are absorbed by bone or cartilage, making these show up white on X-ray images, called radiographs.

X-RAY MACHINE

MRI SCANNER

Magnetic Resonance Imaging (MRI) scanners use magnets to make hydrogen atoms in the body move in a way that can be detected by radio waves.

Radio frequency coil emits and detects radio waves

Magnets focus magnetic field produced by electromagnet

Electromagnet

Patient moves on motorized table

X-RAY

RADIOLOGY

X-RAY MACHINE

FRACTURES

SURGERY

DAY SURGERY

SURGEON

FRACTURES

X-ray radiographs detect breaks in bones. The bone is often set in a cast worn until the fracture has healed.

IMAGING DEPARTMENT

Devices including X-ray machines and ultrasound and MRI scanners are used to view and measure internal body parts, crucial to diagnosing health problems.

DAY SURGERY

Short, minor surgical procedures and operations, such as removing ingrown toenails or tonsils, are performed here. Patients usually return home the same day.

KEY PEOPLE

DOCTOR
Diagnoses patients and suggests treatments.

PHARMACIST
Manages and dispenses medicines.

SURGEON
Performs medical operations on patients.

TECHNICIAN
Takes and analyses samples and images.

NURSE
Provides medical and nursing care for patients.

CLEANING SERVICES
Ensures the building and equipment are clean and hygienic.

WARDS

People who need to stay in hospital are given beds on wards. Some wards provide specialist care. For example, children are treated on a paediatric ward.

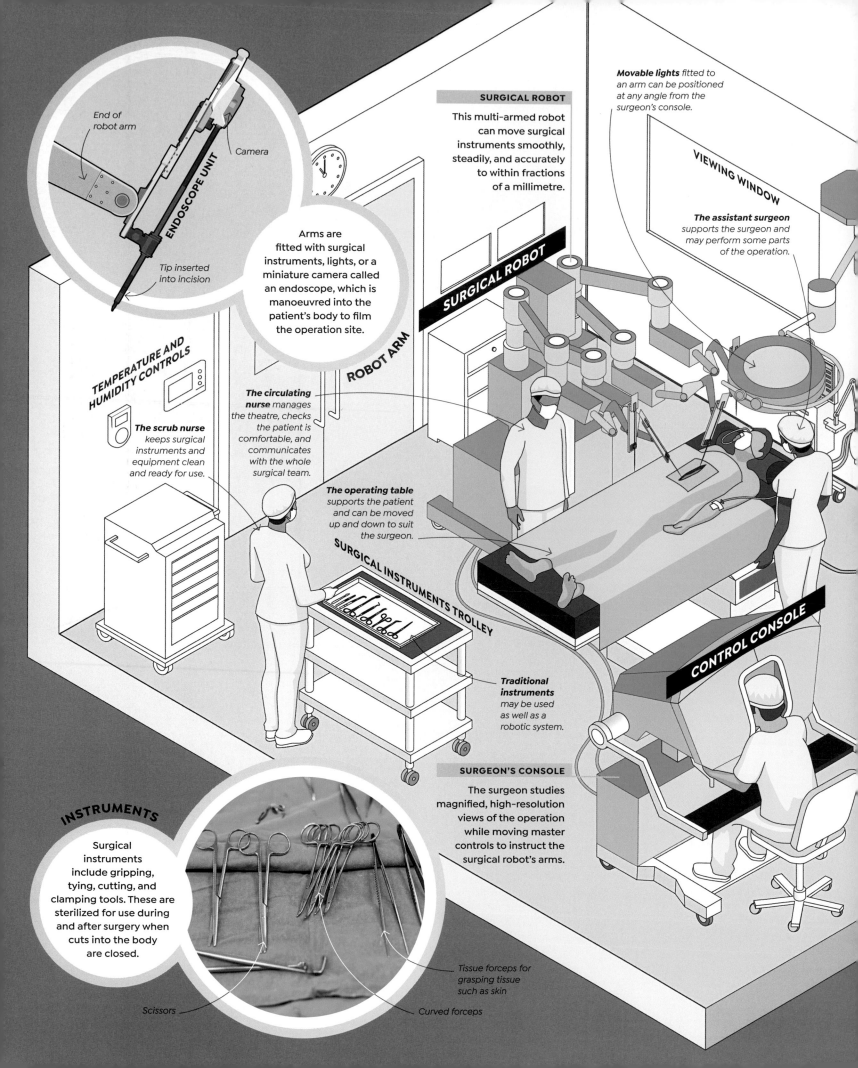

END OF ROBOT ARM

End of robot arm

Camera

ENDOSCOPE UNIT

Tip inserted into incision

SURGICAL ROBOT

This multi-armed robot can move surgical instruments smoothly, steadily, and accurately to within fractions of a millimetre.

Movable lights fitted to an arm can be positioned at any angle from the surgeon's console.

VIEWING WINDOW

The assistant surgeon supports the surgeon and may perform some parts of the operation.

Arms are fitted with surgical instruments, lights, or a miniature camera called an endoscope, which is manoeuvred into the patient's body to film the operation site.

ROBOT ARM

SURGICAL ROBOT

TEMPERATURE AND HUMIDITY CONTROLS

The scrub nurse keeps surgical instruments and equipment clean and ready for use.

The circulating nurse manages the theatre, checks the patient is comfortable, and communicates with the whole surgical team.

The operating table supports the patient and can be moved up and down to suit the surgeon.

SURGICAL INSTRUMENTS TROLLEY

Traditional instruments may be used as well as a robotic system.

CONTROL CONSOLE

SURGEON'S CONSOLE

The surgeon studies magnified, high-resolution views of the operation while moving master controls to instruct the surgical robot's arms.

INSTRUMENTS

Surgical instruments include gripping, tying, cutting, and clamping tools. These are sterilized for use during and after surgery when cuts into the body are closed.

Tissue forceps for grasping tissue such as skin

Scissors

Curved forceps

SCRUB ROOM

Theatre staff wash thoroughly before putting on sterile caps, gowns, masks, and gloves. This helps reduce the risk of patient infection.

crubbing for surgery, theatre nurse ensures is hands and forearms are spotlessly clean.

SCRUB ROOM

OPERATING BY HAND

Most operations are still performed by people without assistance from robots. Highly trained surgeons and their assistants handle surgical instruments and must operate accurately and with as steady a hand as possible. For especially long operations, lasting 8–10 hours or more, an additional surgical team may scrub up and take over.

A monitor shows the patient's heart rate, breathing rate, and other vital signs.

ANAESTHETICS TROLLEY

The anaesthetist calculates the right amount of anaesthetic and monitors the patient's vital signs.

MONITOR SCREEN

Theatre staff can get a close-up view of how the operation is progressing. This can include views captured inside the body using the endoscope.

Incision (or cut) can be just 1 cm (½ in) long

Scalpel on end of robot arm

Surgical robots can correct a surgeon's hand tremors

ANAESTHETICS

An anaesthetic is a substance that produces a loss of feeling. A general anaesthetic makes a patient unconscious so they cannot feel pain during the operation.

Operating theatre

An operating theatre or room is where invasive surgery is performed. Helped by a skilled team, surgeons cut into a patient's body and work inside with instruments to repair, remove, or replace body parts. Increasing numbers of routine operations are performed with the aid of surgical robots that move instruments precisely but always under the command of a human surgeon.

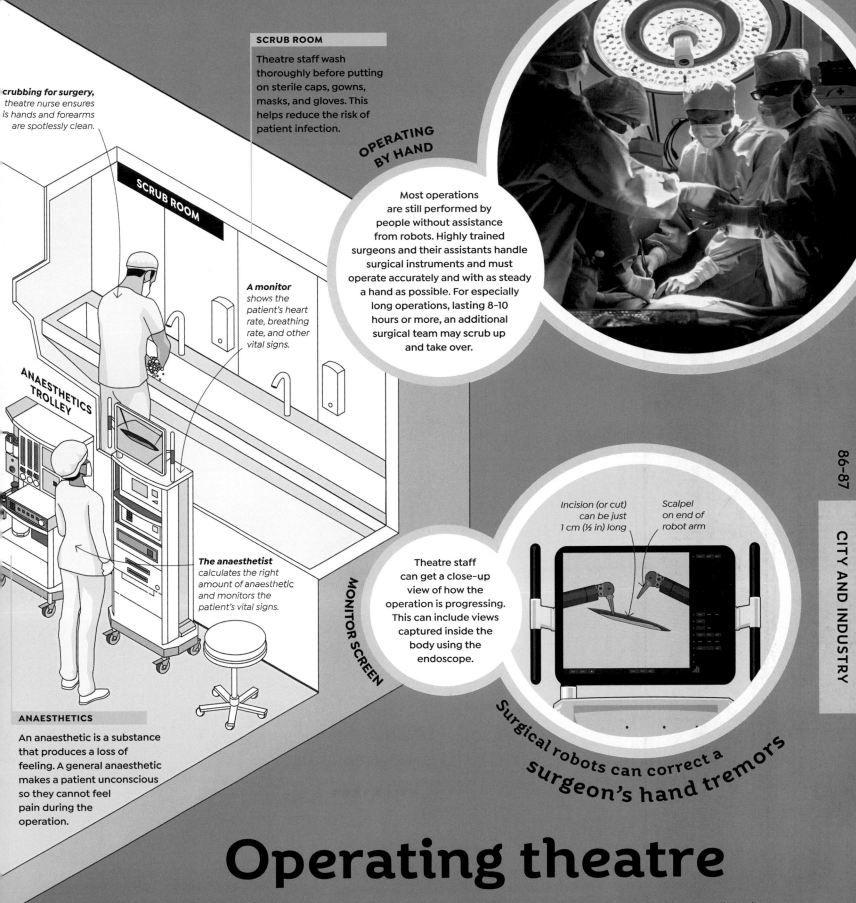

Cinema

Millions of people around the world are thrilled by the action and drama shown on big cinema screens. Movies are a collection of individual still images, called frames, that create the illusion of movement when replayed at high speeds. Movies are stored by cinemas as computer files on hard disks and played via digital projectors.

SURROUND SOUND

Many speakers are positioned around the theatre. Sound processors send signals to different speakers to create a 3D soundscape, placing the audience in the middle of the movie.

Theatre lighting is adjustable and dimmed to a minimum when a movie is playing.

Rear speakers provide ambient or background sound

Side speakers often play sound effects

Screen speakers often play dialogue

Right side speakers receive different signals from left side speakers

SPEAKER

Surround sound speakers on the wall help create exciting soundscapes to enhance the customer's enjoyment of a movie.

Speaker enclosures hold the loudspeakers that direct sound from behind the screen into the theatre.

A cafe serves a wide range of hot and cold drinks and snacks.

POPCORN

Popcorn is one of the world's most popular cinema snacks. When heated, the water inside corn kernels turns to steam, causing the kernels to explode or "pop".

A snack bar serves drinks, popcorn, hot dogs, and other snacks to take into the theatre.

The theatre is signposted as a cinema may have many theatres.

CAFE

POPCORN

THEATRE 1

Social spaces are used by cinema-goers to relax or wait for friends to arrive.

Popcorn is made and kept warm in a machine. Buttered, salted, and sweetened popcorn are often offered as options.

Rope barriers are used to guide customers to the box office before entering the cinema foyer.

ENTRANCE

BOX OFFICE

Tickets are purchased from the box office. Tickets booked online can also be collected from here.

Tickets are checked by an attendant.

Sound insulation absorbs loud sounds from the theatre and quietens sound from outside.

The cinema projector receives and processes data from a movie's files, which are held on computers.

The projector beam travels at the speed of light to be displayed on the projection screen.

EXIT

STAFF

2. Prism splits light into red, blue, and green

3. Each DMD produces image in one colour

1. Light directed to prism

6. Adjustable projection lens ensures movie appears sharp on screen

5. Lens combines images from three DMDs

4. Red, green and blue light reflects from each DMD back through prism

DLP PROJECTORS

Digital Light Processing (DLP) projectors use digital micro-mirror devices, or DMDs, to project movies. DMDs have millions of microscopic mirrors that tilt away or towards light thousands of times a second. Each mirror produces one pixel of an image, creating detailed images that are focused through lenses and then projected onto the screen.

The projector room is where the projectionist works, ensuring the smooth running of a movie.

Cinema seats are designed to be comfortable for people of all sizes. Premium seating may tilt back and have drinks holders, USB chargers, and foot rests.

Illuminated exit signs show the theatre's main and emergency exits. Many theatres also have floor-level lighting to help guide audience members out while the movie is playing.

Seat rows are set at a steep angle, known as raked seating, so the audience all gain a clear view of the screen.

Snacks can be taken into the theatre. Cinemas make a lot of money from selling food and drink to their audiences.

The corridors leading to the theatres often have toilets, posters, and displays advertising future releases coming to the cinema.

Kinepolis Madrid, Spain, is the largest cinema complex in the world, seating up to 9,200 visitors

HOME CINEMA

Audio-visual technology has advanced to the point that people can recreate the cinema experience in their own homes. Large widescreen televisions display ultra high-resolution images. Multiple speakers connected to an amplifier and a sound processor can also be used to split and direct sound, creating surround sound.

CHANGING PITCHES

Some stadiums have the ability to switch pitches or playing surfaces. At the Sapporo Dome in Japan (below), a football pitch can be slid over the stadium's baseball field. At the Tottenham Hotspur Stadium in England, a grass pitch can be rolled away in three sections, each running on 300 wheels and weighing 3,000 tonnes, revealing an artificial pitch beneath.

Stadium

Large venues host the world's leading sports events watched by thousands of spectators sitting in banked tiers of seats. These towering sports facilities may also hold other live events such as concerts and shows. Some like the Camp Nou in Spain, Wembley Stadium in England, and Fenway Park in the US are global landmarks.

Roof supports and tension cables support the permanent roof, which shields most spectators when the retractable roof is open.

Corporate boxes offer dining and hospitality with a view of the pitch for businesses and their clients.

Stadium seating is arranged in stands and sections that may include family-only areas.

MATCH DAY ATMOSPHERE

The noise and spectacle of a large stadium crowd can be a stirring experience. Fans cheer their side to victory, boo or whistle fouls and poor decisions by officials, and rise out of their seats in anticipation of a win. To celebrate, fans may stand in sequence to perform spectacular waves that ripple around the stadium.

Large event rooms are used by the club, or hired by businesses or fans for special occasions.

The Hall of Fame features trophies, photos, and memorabilia of star sports people from the team's past and present.

Walkways inside the stadium keep crowds moving, and make it easier and safer for fans to get to their seats.

❸ Food outlets provide fans with refreshments. Inside the stadium, fans can also purchase programmes from vendors.

CORPORATE ENTERTAINMENT

FOOD OUTLETS

FAN STORE

❶ Fans use cars, shuttle buses, or public transport, to get to the ground.

Coach transportation is sometimes provided by clubs to help fans get to matches far from their home ground.

❷ Tickets are checked at electronic turnstile gates before fans are allowed to pass into the ground. There are often separate turnstiles for home and away fans.

Merchandise including team shirts and books is sold in shops around the stadium.

❹ Fans are seated in the numbered seat allocated on their ticket. Stadium staff, called stewards, direct fans to the correct seat.

The Narendra Modi cricket stadium in India is the world's largest stadium, seating up to 132,000 spectators

CLOSING ROOF

Retractable roofs allow sunlight and the elements in for outdoor sports but can be closed if the weather is particularly poor. Some stadiums also close the retractable roof to hold noisy indoor events such as concerts. The roof is often in segments that are pulled open and shut by electric motors pulling winch cables.

The retractable roof can slide open or closed depending on the event and weather conditions.

LED lights around the roof edge illuminate the seating and pitch for evening matches.

Giant TV screens on all four sides of this cube relay the action on the pitch to fans.

8 **In-stadium screens** show highlights of the match as it happens. The whole match may also be broadcast on TV or the internet.

7 **Footage from the cameras** is mixed and combined with commentary and interviews in the media suite.

The player's lounge is a private area where players can eat a pre-match meal and socialize after a game.

The gym and fitness centre is used by players for training and when recovering from injuries.

A press box gives radio and TV commentators an excellent view.

Changing rooms for the home and away teams are used by players to change into their kit, and also for motivational talks ahead of the match.

RETRACTABLE ROOF

THIRD TIER

MEDIA SUITE

SECOND TIER

SCREENS

LOUNGE

GYM

PRESS BOX

SEATING

FIRST TIER

CHANGING ROOMS

6 **Cameras** film the action both at pitch level and from positions higher up in the stadium.

The first sports stadiums with seating were often built by the ancient Greeks built into the side of a hill

5 **Only players**, medical staff, and match officials are allowed on the pitch. Stewards guard the pitch from invasions from fans – and occasionally animals.

PITCH TECHNOLOGY

Grass pitches are often reinforced with woven-in plastic fibres. Wembley Stadium's pitch contains 75,000 km (46,600 miles) of fibre. The living grass and plastic sit on supporting layers that contain networks of drainage pipes and under-soil heating tubes. The latter carry warm water to stop the pitch from freezing.

Pitch surface

Plastic fibres make pitch more hard wearing

Layer of sand beneath soil

Soil layer

Binding layer

Drainage pipes carry excess water and rainfall away

Base layer

Under-soil heating tubes

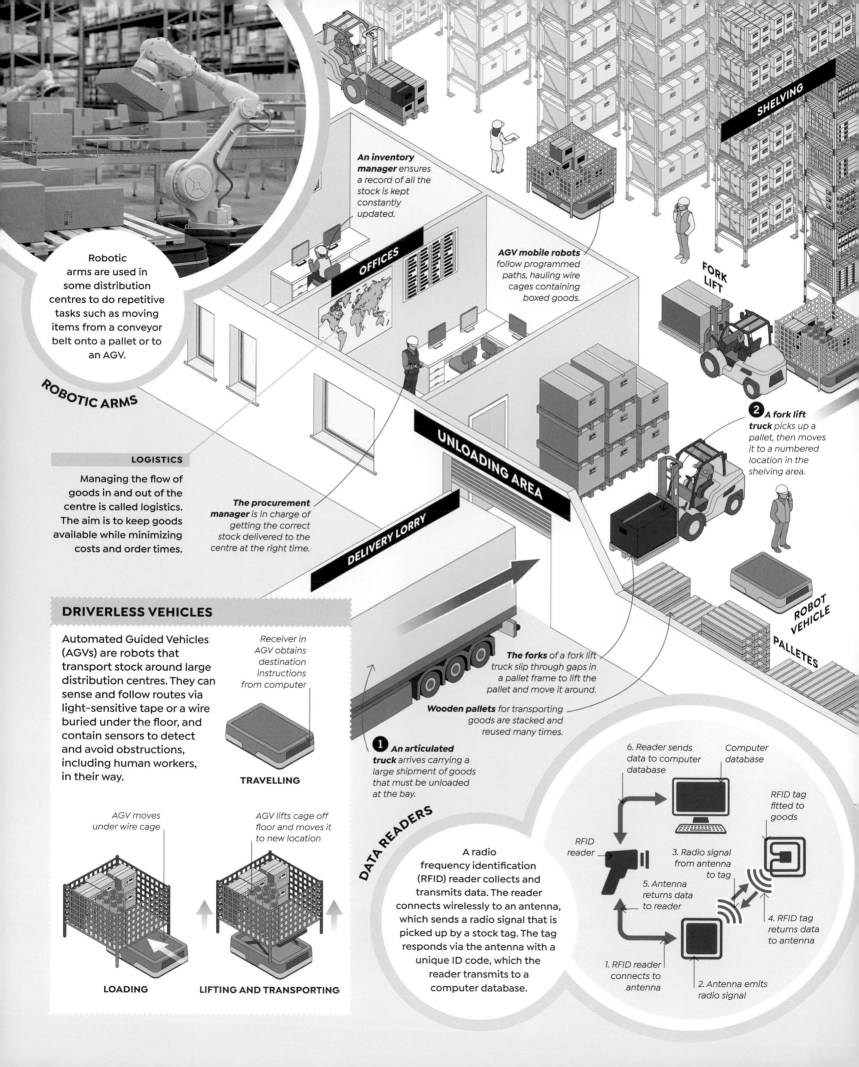

Robotic arms are used in some distribution centres to do repetitive tasks such as moving items from a conveyor belt onto a pallet or to an AGV.

ROBOTIC ARMS

An inventory manager ensures a record of all the stock is kept constantly updated.

OFFICES

AGV mobile robots follow programmed paths, hauling wire cages containing boxed goods.

SHELVING

FORK LIFT

LOGISTICS

Managing the flow of goods in and out of the centre is called logistics. The aim is to keep goods available while minimizing costs and order times.

The procurement manager is in charge of getting the correct stock delivered to the centre at the right time.

UNLOADING AREA

DELIVERY LORRY

2 A fork lift truck picks up a pallet, then moves it to a numbered location in the shelving area.

ROBOT VEHICLE

PALLETES

DRIVERLESS VEHICLES

Automated Guided Vehicles (AGVs) are robots that transport stock around large distribution centres. They can sense and follow routes via light-sensitive tape or a wire buried under the floor, and contain sensors to detect and avoid obstructions, including human workers, in their way.

Receiver in AGV obtains destination instructions from computer

TRAVELLING

The forks of a fork lift truck slip through gaps in a pallet frame to lift the pallet and move it around.

Wooden pallets for transporting goods are stacked and reused many times.

1 An articulated truck arrives carrying a large shipment of goods that must be unloaded at the bay.

AGV moves under wire cage

AGV lifts cage off floor and moves it to new location

LOADING

LIFTING AND TRANSPORTING

DATA READERS

A radio frequency identification (RFID) reader collects and transmits data. The reader connects wirelessly to an antenna, which sends a radio signal that is picked up by a stock tag. The tag responds via the antenna with a unique ID code, which the reader transmits to a computer database.

6. Reader sends data to computer database

Computer database

RFID tag fitted to goods

RFID reader

3. Radio signal from antenna to tag

5. Antenna returns data to reader

4. RFID tag returns data to antenna

1. RFID reader connects to antenna

2. Antenna emits radio signal

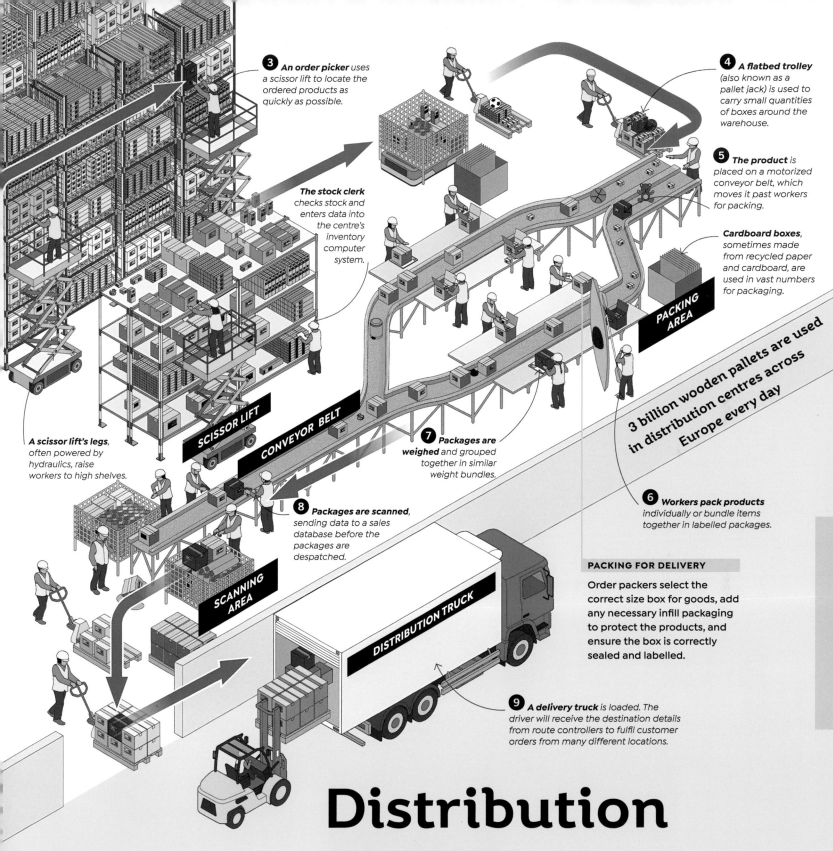

3 *An order picker* uses a scissor lift to locate the ordered products as quickly as possible.

The stock clerk checks stock and enters data into the centre's inventory computer system.

4 *A flatbed trolley* (also known as a pallet jack) is used to carry small quantities of boxes around the warehouse.

5 *The product* is placed on a motorized conveyor belt, which moves it past workers for packing.

Cardboard boxes, sometimes made from recycled paper and cardboard, are used in vast numbers for packaging.

PACKING AREA

A scissor lift's legs, often powered by hydraulics, raise workers to high shelves.

SCISSOR LIFT

CONVEYOR BELT

7 *Packages are weighed* and grouped together in similar weight bundles.

3 billion wooden pallets are used in distribution centres across Europe every day

6 *Workers pack products* individually or bundle items together in labelled packages.

8 *Packages are scanned*, sending data to a sales database before the packages are despatched.

SCANNING AREA

DISTRIBUTION TRUCK

PACKING FOR DELIVERY

Order packers select the correct size box for goods, add any necessary infill packaging to protect the products, and ensure the box is correctly sealed and labelled.

9 *A delivery truck* is loaded. The driver will receive the destination details from route controllers to fulfil customer orders from many different locations.

Distribution centre

Amazon's MQY1 fulfilment **centre in Tennessee, US is the size of 48 football pitches**

Whether ordered online, by phone, or in store, products often travel through at least one distribution centre on their way to the customer. These large warehouses receive and store bulk quantities of goods, known as stock, from manufacturers, then workers pick, pack, and despatch orders directly to customers or to retail outlets.

Supermarket

A family's big weekly shop is most likely done at a supermarket. These large self-service stores hold thousands of different food, drink, and household goods for sale. The first supermarkets opened in the 1920s, but most now use modern technologies such as apps, inventory scanners, and smart checkouts to keep fresh produce stocked on shelves and allow customers to pay quickly for goods.

WAREHOUSE

STOCK

The warehouse holds supplies of quick-selling goods used to restock the store shelves. The inventory tracks whether products are in date to ensure there is no waste.

WAREHOUSE COLD ROOM

The security office monitors CCTV footage from in-store cameras for shoplifting and other incidents.

MANAGER'S OFFICE

WAREHOUSE OFFICE

TOILETS

SECURITY

MEAT COUNTER

CHANGING ROOMS

BUTCHER

FISH COUNTER

The bakery heats pre- or part-baked bread products for sale.

BAKERY OVENS

FISHMONGER

DAIRY SECTION

SECURITY CAMERA

Barcode

Light sensor reads barcode

Interior circuit converts code into binary digits and sends them to computer

FREEZERS

ZERO WASTE

A zero waste aisle offers cereals, nuts, and other unpackaged goods for customers' own containers.

Red light shines on barcode

DRINKS SECTION

Scanners capture light reflected from a barcode to identify an item's Universal Product Code (UPC). A computer then finds its price and updates the stock database.

BARCODE SCANNER

Supermarkets employ **4.8 million people** in the US – twice the population of Panama

Some supermarkets now have zero waste aisles to reduce packaging waste. These hold bulk containers of stock that customers can use to fill their own jars and bags.

ZERO WASTE AISLES

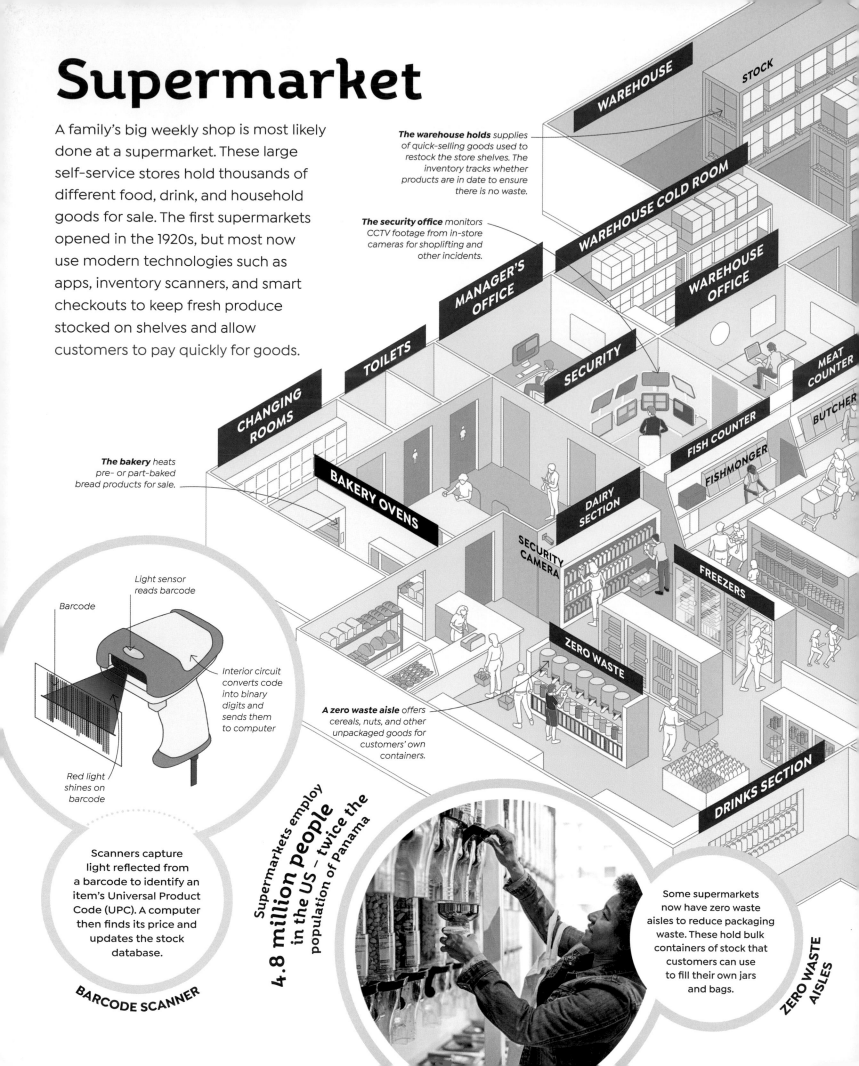

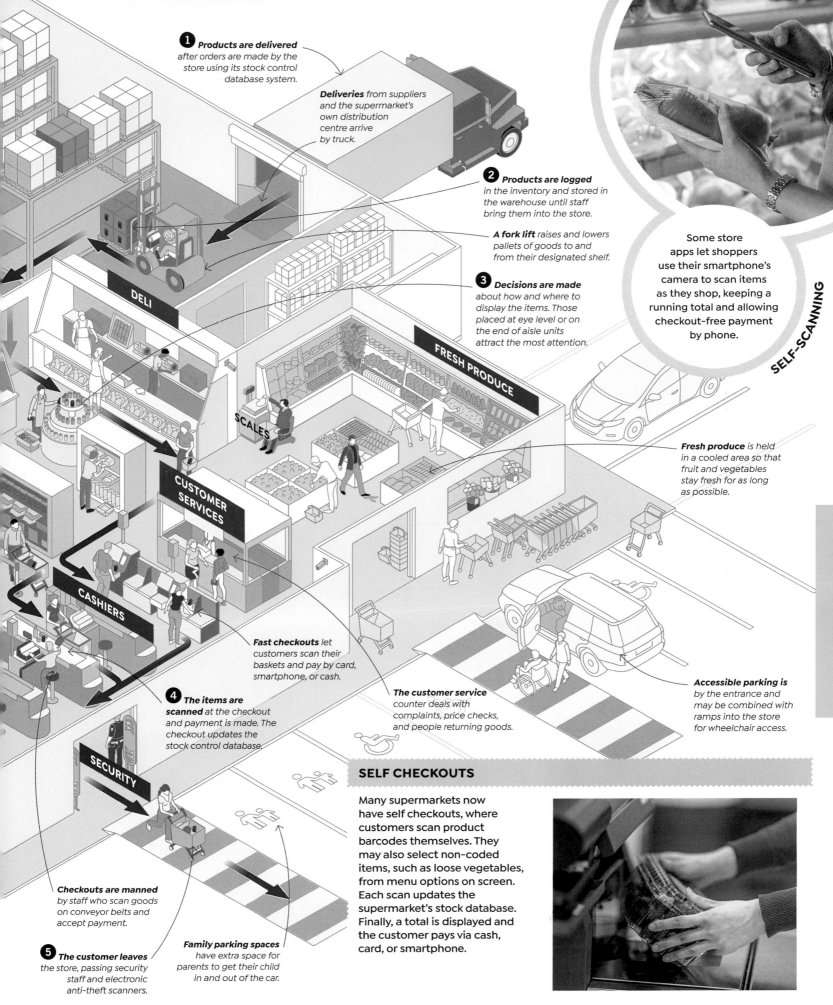

1 **Products are delivered** after orders are made by the store using its stock control database system.

Deliveries from suppliers and the supermarket's own distribution centre arrive by truck.

2 **Products are logged** in the inventory and stored in the warehouse until staff bring them into the store.

A fork lift raises and lowers pallets of goods to and from their designated shelf.

3 **Decisions are made** about how and where to display the items. Those placed at eye level or on the end of aisle units attract the most attention.

DELI

SCALES

FRESH PRODUCE

CUSTOMER SERVICES

CASHIERS

SECURITY

Fresh produce is held in a cooled area so that fruit and vegetables stay fresh for as long as possible.

Some store apps let shoppers use their smartphone's camera to scan items as they shop, keeping a running total and allowing checkout-free payment by phone.

Fast checkouts let customers scan their baskets and pay by card, smartphone, or cash.

The customer service counter deals with complaints, price checks, and people returning goods.

4 **The items are scanned** at the checkout and payment is made. The checkout updates the stock control database.

Accessible parking is by the entrance and may be combined with ramps into the store for wheelchair access.

Checkouts are manned by staff who scan goods on conveyor belts and accept payment.

5 **The customer leaves** the store, passing security staff and electronic anti-theft scanners.

Family parking spaces have extra space for parents to get their child in and out of the car.

SELF CHECKOUTS

Many supermarkets now have self checkouts, where customers scan product barcodes themselves. They may also select non-coded items, such as loose vegetables, from menu options on screen. Each scan updates the supermarket's stock database. Finally, a total is displayed and the customer pays via cash, card, or smartphone.

Payment system

Having coins jingling in a pocket was common until the arrival of electronic payment systems in the late 20th century. Banknotes and coins are still used to pay for some goods and services, but payments using a swipe or tap of a plastic card or smartphone are increasingly common. Stores, restaurants, and other businesses now offer multiple ways for customers to pay.

Barcodes fixed to products track the sale, and security tags trigger alarms if the item leaves the store with them on.

COINS

Coins of different value are made in different weights and sizes. Ridges and raised patterns and letters help visually impaired people to tell the different coins apart.

Cash payments (banknotes and coins) are still accepted in most stores.

The first coins were made by the Greeks **2,600 years ago** in the kingdom of Lydia

CASH PAYMENT

A PIN card needs buyers to key in their Personal Identification Number.

CHIP AND PIN PAYMENT

A cash drawer stores notes and coins. Some cash drawers identify and weigh each type of coin or note to calculate exactly how much money is in the drawer.

A small printer produces a paper receipt for the customer.

ANTI-COUNTERFEIT DESIGN

To deter forgers from producing counterfeits (fakes), banknotes are made using special inks, papers, and plastics. Each note also contains security features, such as woven 3D strips or threads, watermarks (images embedded in the paper when it is made), or holograms that are hard for forgers to copy accurately.

Hologram shows a different image when tilted

A plastic window reveals an image when tilted in light

COUNTRY

100

100

123257456

Each note has its own serial number that can be tracked on a database

Foil strip woven into banknote

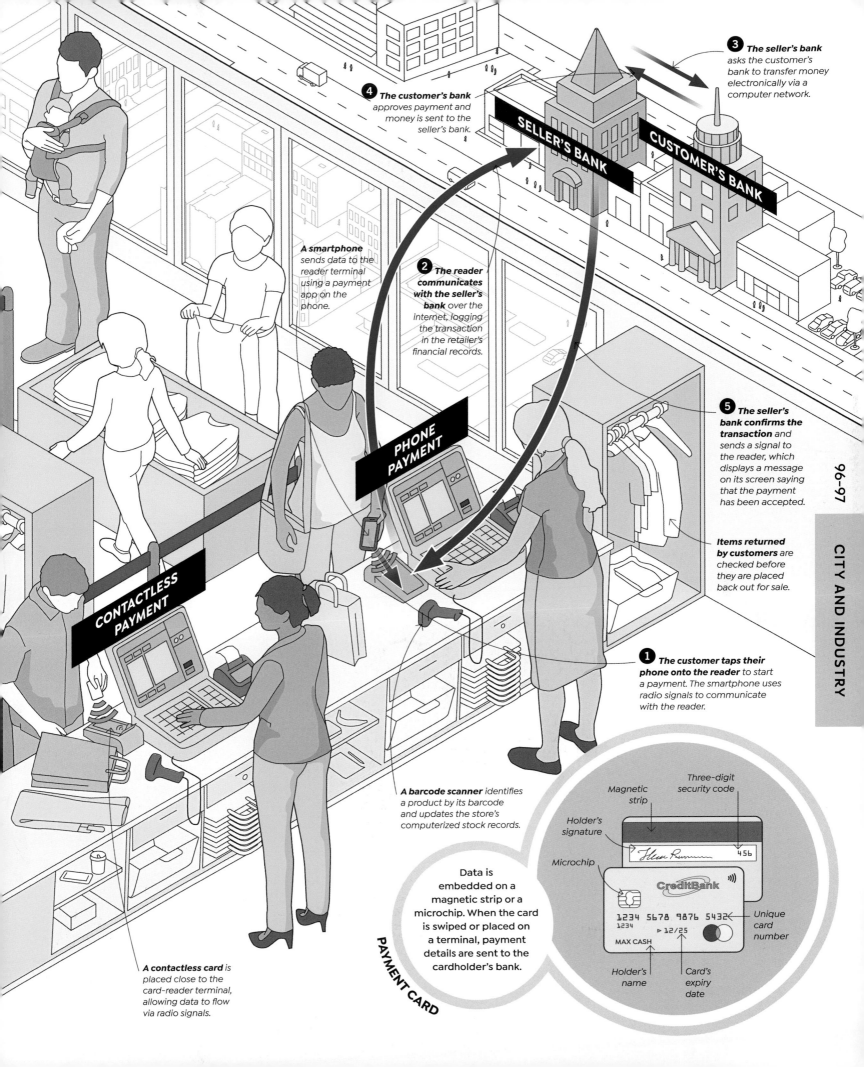

③ The seller's bank asks the customer's bank to transfer money electronically via a computer network.

④ The customer's bank approves payment and money is sent to the seller's bank.

SELLER'S BANK

CUSTOMER'S BANK

A smartphone sends data to the reader terminal using a payment app on the phone.

② The reader communicates with the seller's bank over the internet, logging the transaction in the retailer's financial records.

PHONE PAYMENT

⑤ The seller's bank confirms the transaction and sends a signal to the reader, which displays a message on its screen saying that the payment has been accepted.

Items returned by customers are checked before they are placed back out for sale.

① The customer taps their phone onto the reader to start a payment. The smartphone uses radio signals to communicate with the reader.

CONTACTLESS PAYMENT

A barcode scanner identifies a product by its barcode and updates the store's computerized stock records.

Magnetic strip

Three-digit security code

Holder's signature

456

Microchip

CreditBank

Data is embedded on a magnetic strip or a microchip. When the card is swiped or placed on a terminal, payment details are sent to the cardholder's bank.

PAYMENT CARD

1234 5678 9876 5432
1234
▶ 12/25
MAX CASH

Unique card number

Holder's name

Card's expiry date

A contactless card is placed close to the card-reader terminal, allowing data to flow via radio signals.

GPS satellite obtains car's location and road speed limit

Driver can override limiter by pressing foot pedal accelerator

60

Speed limiter warns driver and may slow engine and car down

Speed limit signs detected by car's onboard camera

These safety devices detect the speed limit on the road a vehicle is travelling on and control the engine power to keep the vehicle's speed below that limit.

SPEED LIMITERS

Speed cameras reduce road accidents by up to 49 per cent

Speed cameras calculate the speed a vehicle is travelling at by recording the time it takes to travel between two fixed points.

Warning lights signal to drivers the presence of a pedestrian crossing.

Roundabouts are used in some countries to keep traffic flowing from different directions.

BUS LANE

A bus lane is used only by public transport and emergency vehicles.

A bus stop layby allows buses to pick up passengers without halting road traffic.

ROUNDABOUT

Vehicles drive on the right in most countries around the world.

Pedestrian crossings stop road traffic, offering a safe place for people to cross a road on foot.

Street lighting illuminates the road, cycle lane, and pavement.

Overpasses or flyovers are elevated sections of road that travel above another road or a railway track.

Slip roads enable drivers to join and exit a motorway.

A hard shoulder is a narrow lane alongside a motorway for vehicles to move onto in an emergency.

OVERPASS

MOTORWAY

Major highways, known as expressways or A-roads in some countries, often have multiple lanes of traffic travelling in both directions.

TRAFFIC LIGHTS

Many traffic light systems use inductive loops to detect vehicles. The loop is made of electrical wires embedded in the road surface that create an electromagnetic field. When a car drives over a loop, it disturbs the electromagnetic field, which is detected by a computer that controls the traffic light timings. The computer may give one particularly busy road a longer period under the green "go" light to clear a build-up of traffic.

Traffic light computer

Car disturbs electromagnetic field

Electromagnetic field

Electric current flows through underground wire loop

At busy junctions, tangles of roads bend around and overlap each other on different levels. Curved roads and slip roads let vehicles change to other roads.

TANGLED JUNCTIONS

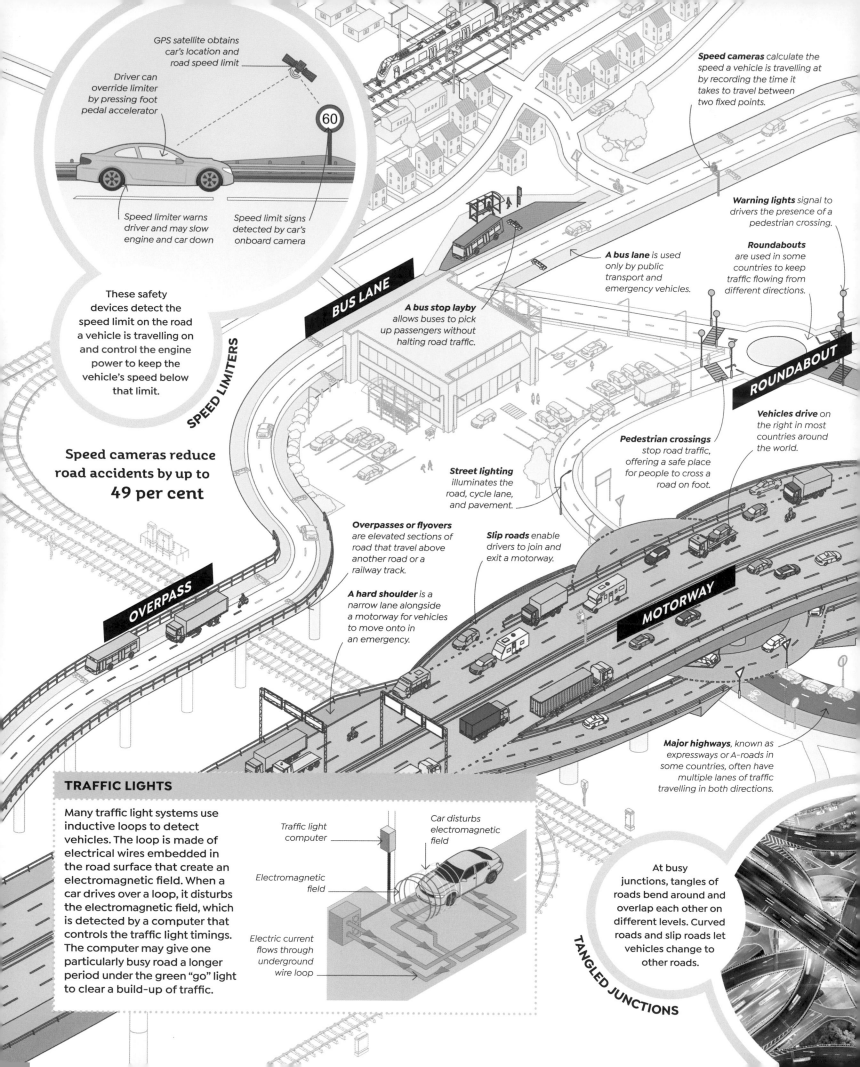

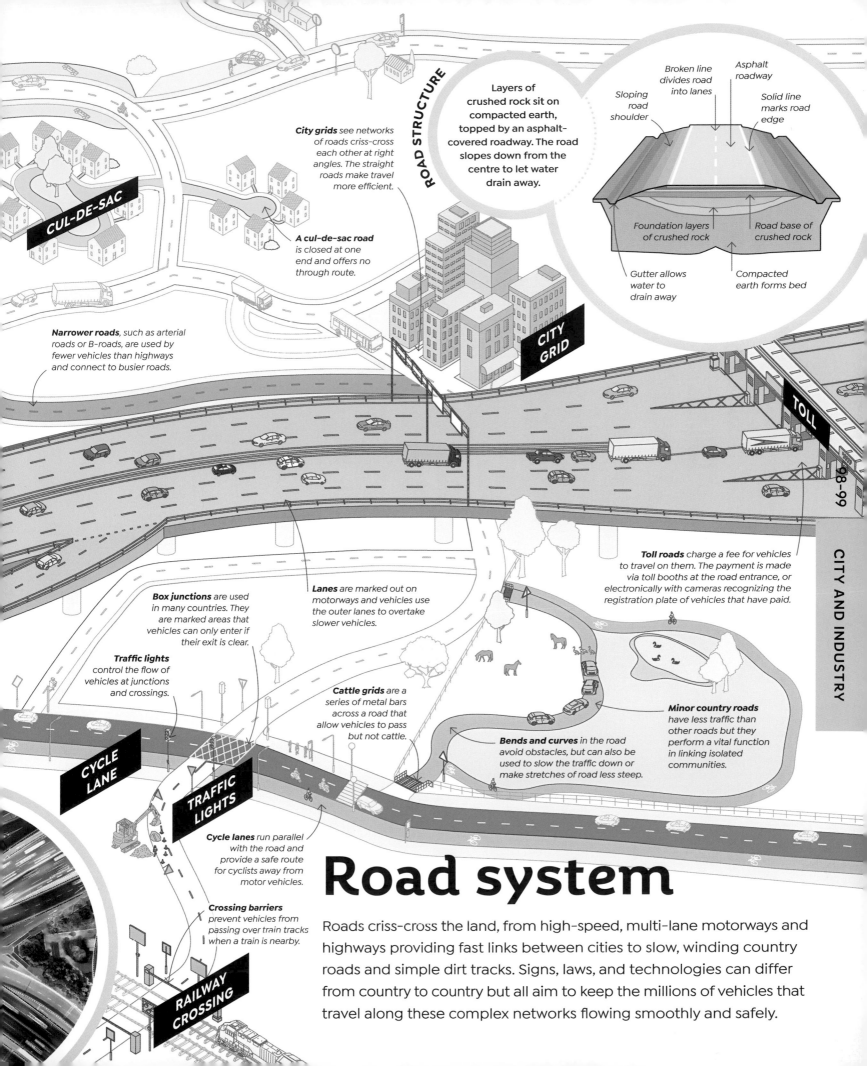

City grids see networks of roads criss-cross each other at right angles. The straight roads make travel more efficient.

Layers of crushed rock sit on compacted earth, topped by an asphalt-covered roadway. The road slopes down from the centre to let water drain away.

Broken line divides road into lanes

Sloping road shoulder

Asphalt roadway

Solid line marks road edge

Foundation layers of crushed rock

Road base of crushed rock

Gutter allows water to drain away

Compacted earth forms bed

CUL-DE-SAC

A cul-de-sac road is closed at one end and offers no through route.

Narrower roads, such as arterial roads or B-roads, are used by fewer vehicles than highways and connect to busier roads.

CITY GRID

TOLL

Toll roads charge a fee for vehicles to travel on them. The payment is made via toll booths at the road entrance, or electronically with cameras recognizing the registration plate of vehicles that have paid.

Box junctions are used in many countries. They are marked areas that vehicles can only enter if their exit is clear.

Lanes are marked out on motorways and vehicles use the outer lanes to overtake slower vehicles.

Traffic lights control the flow of vehicles at junctions and crossings.

Cattle grids are a series of metal bars across a road that allow vehicles to pass but not cattle.

Minor country roads have less traffic than other roads but they perform a vital function in linking isolated communities.

Bends and curves in the road avoid obstacles, but can also be used to slow the traffic down or make stretches of road less steep.

CYCLE LANE

TRAFFIC LIGHTS

Cycle lanes run parallel with the road and provide a safe route for cyclists away from motor vehicles.

Crossing barriers prevent vehicles from passing over train tracks when a train is nearby.

RAILWAY CROSSING

Road system

Roads criss-cross the land, from high-speed, multi-lane motorways and highways providing fast links between cities to slow, winding country roads and simple dirt tracks. Signs, laws, and technologies can differ from country to country but all aim to keep the millions of vehicles that travel along these complex networks flowing smoothly and safely.

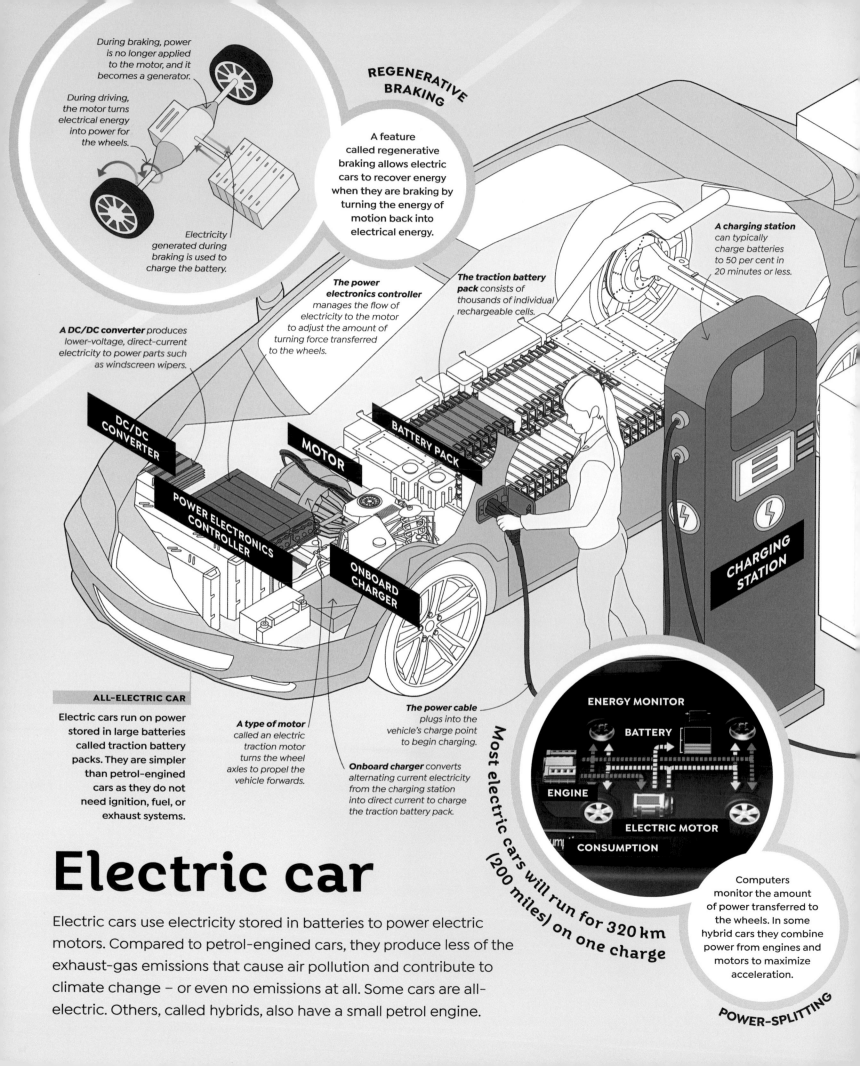

During braking, power is no longer applied to the motor, and it becomes a generator.

During driving, the motor turns electrical energy into power for the wheels.

Electricity generated during braking is used to charge the battery.

REGENERATIVE BRAKING

A feature called regenerative braking allows electric cars to recover energy when they are braking by turning the energy of motion back into electrical energy.

A charging station can typically charge batteries to 50 per cent in 20 minutes or less.

The power electronics controller manages the flow of electricity to the motor to adjust the amount of turning force transferred to the wheels.

The traction battery pack consists of thousands of individual rechargeable cells.

A DC/DC converter produces lower-voltage, direct-current electricity to power parts such as windscreen wipers.

DC/DC CONVERTER

POWER ELECTRONICS CONTROLLER

MOTOR

BATTERY PACK

ONBOARD CHARGER

CHARGING STATION

ALL-ELECTRIC CAR

Electric cars run on power stored in large batteries called traction battery packs. They are simpler than petrol-engined cars as they do not need ignition, fuel, or exhaust systems.

A type of motor called an electric traction motor turns the wheel axles to propel the vehicle forwards.

The power cable plugs into the vehicle's charge point to begin charging.

Onboard charger converts alternating current electricity from the charging station into direct current to charge the traction battery pack.

Most electric cars will run for 320 km (200 miles) on one charge

ENERGY MONITOR

BATTERY

ENGINE

ELECTRIC MOTOR

CONSUMPTION

Computers monitor the amount of power transferred to the wheels. In some hybrid cars they combine power from engines and motors to maximize acceleration.

POWER-SPLITTING

Electric car

Electric cars use electricity stored in batteries to power electric motors. Compared to petrol-engined cars, they produce less of the exhaust-gas emissions that cause air pollution and contribute to climate change – or even no emissions at all. Some cars are all-electric. Others, called hybrids, also have a small petrol engine.

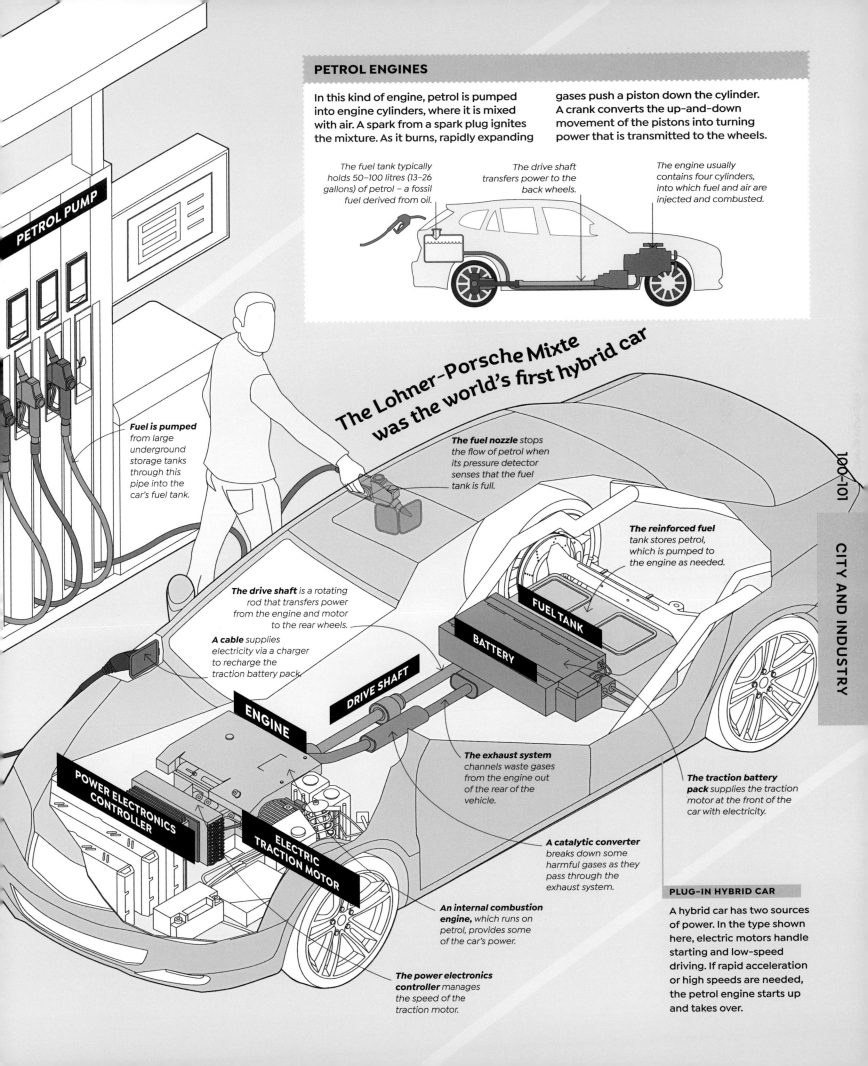

PETROL ENGINES

In this kind of engine, petrol is pumped into engine cylinders, where it is mixed with air. A spark from a spark plug ignites the mixture. As it burns, rapidly expanding gases push a piston down the cylinder. A crank converts the up-and-down movement of the pistons into turning power that is transmitted to the wheels.

The fuel tank typically holds 50–100 litres (13–26 gallons) of petrol – a fossil fuel derived from oil.

The drive shaft transfers power to the back wheels.

The engine usually contains four cylinders, into which fuel and air are injected and combusted.

PETROL PUMP

Fuel is pumped from large underground storage tanks through this pipe into the car's fuel tank.

The Lohner-Porsche Mixte was the world's first hybrid car

The fuel nozzle stops the flow of petrol when its pressure detector senses that the fuel tank is full.

The reinforced fuel tank stores petrol, which is pumped to the engine as needed.

The drive shaft is a rotating rod that transfers power from the engine and motor to the rear wheels.

A cable supplies electricity via a charger to recharge the traction battery pack.

FUEL TANK

BATTERY

DRIVE SHAFT

ENGINE

The exhaust system channels waste gases from the engine out of the rear of the vehicle.

The traction battery pack supplies the traction motor at the front of the car with electricity.

POWER ELECTRONICS CONTROLLER

ELECTRIC TRACTION MOTOR

A catalytic converter breaks down some harmful gases as they pass through the exhaust system.

An internal combustion engine, which runs on petrol, provides some of the car's power.

The power electronics controller manages the speed of the traction motor.

PLUG-IN HYBRID CAR

A hybrid car has two sources of power. In the type shown here, electric motors handle starting and low-speed driving. If rapid acceleration or high speeds are needed, the petrol engine starts up and takes over.

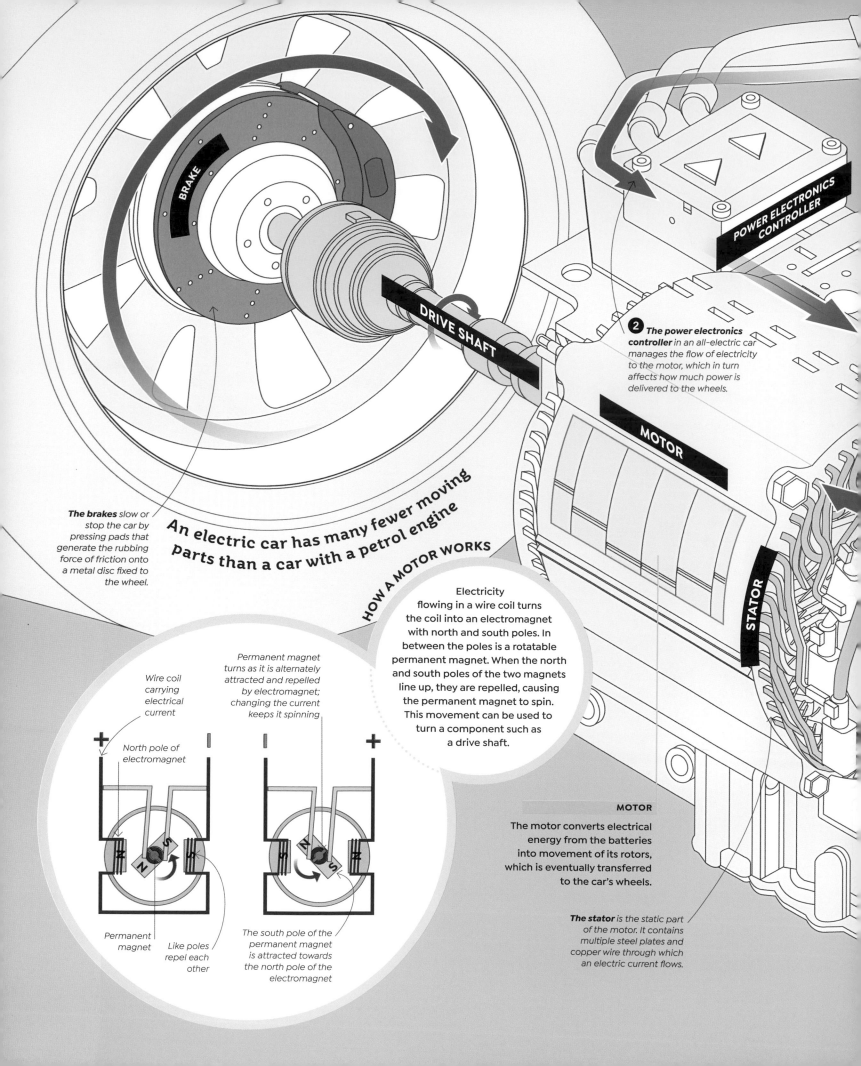

BRAKE

POWER ELECTRONICS CONTROLLER

DRIVE SHAFT

2 *The power electronics controller* in an all-electric car manages the flow of electricity to the motor, which in turn affects how much power is delivered to the wheels.

MOTOR

STATOR

The brakes slow or stop the car by pressing pads that generate the rubbing force of friction onto a metal disc fixed to the wheel.

An electric car has many fewer moving parts than a car with a petrol engine

HOW A MOTOR WORKS

Electricity flowing in a wire coil turns the coil into an electromagnet with north and south poles. In between the poles is a rotatable permanent magnet. When the north and south poles of the two magnets line up, they are repelled, causing the permanent magnet to spin. This movement can be used to turn a component such as a drive shaft.

Wire coil carrying electrical current

North pole of electromagnet

Permanent magnet turns as it is alternately attracted and repelled by electromagnet; changing the current keeps it spinning

Permanent magnet

Like poles repel each other

The south pole of the permanent magnet is attracted towards the north pole of the electromagnet

MOTOR

The motor converts electrical energy from the batteries into movement of its rotors, which is eventually transferred to the car's wheels.

The stator is the static part of the motor. It contains multiple steel plates and copper wire through which an electric current flows.

Electric motor

Electric motors are found everywhere, from tiny motors that vibrate a smartphone to giant power plants that propel heavy ships. A car or truck may have 80 or more small motors, which power fans, windscreen wipers, and door locks. Electric vehicles make use of one or more powerful motors, called traction motors, to turn their wheels, providing transport without the harmful gas emissions that come from vehicles with petrol engines.

1 *The electric power connector* carries electricity to the motor from the vehicle's lithium-ion batteries.

3 *A rotor* containing permanent magnets spins in a rotating magnetic field created by the stator.

4 *The rotor* connects to a central gear called a sun gear, which turns four smaller planet gears as it spins.

DIFFERENTIAL

When a vehicle turns, its outside wheels have to travel farther than the inside wheels. A differential is a gearing system that enables the two wheels to turn at different speeds.

5 *The planetary output carrier* transfers power from the sun and planet gears to the drive shaft.

6 *The drive shaft* transfers power to the front wheels.

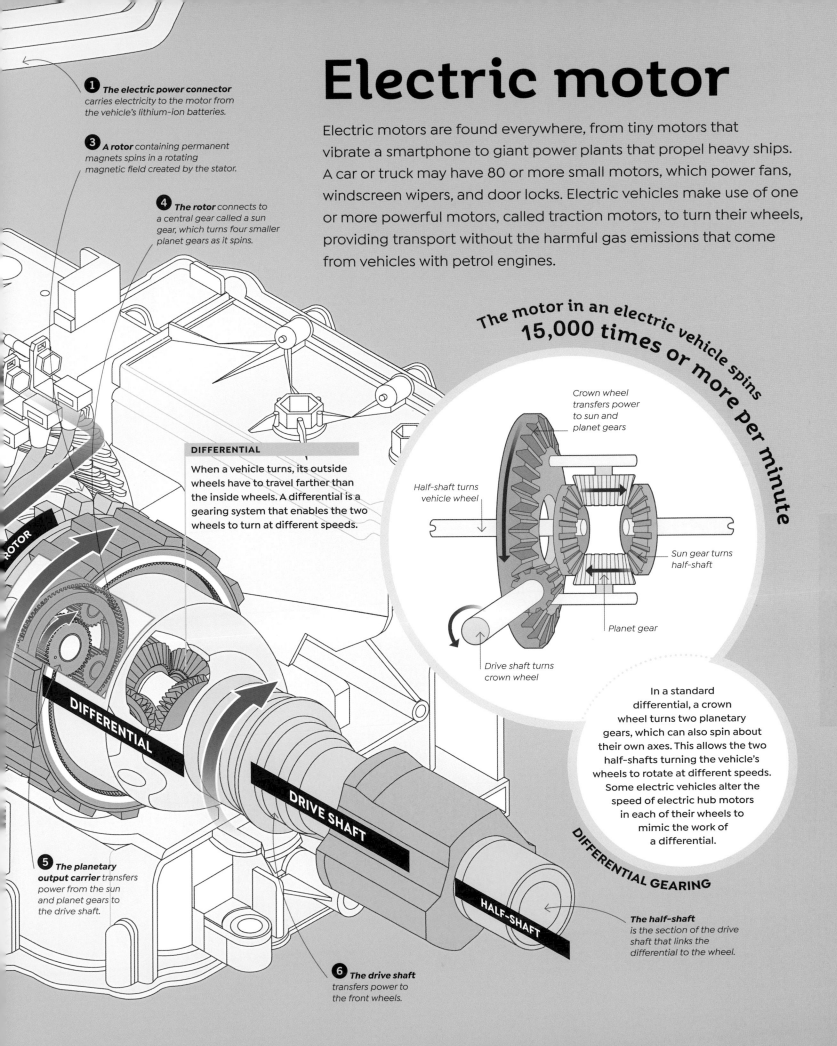

ROTOR

DIFFERENTIAL

DRIVE SHAFT

HALF-SHAFT

The motor in an electric vehicle spins **15,000 times or more per minute**

Crown wheel transfers power to sun and planet gears

Half-shaft turns vehicle wheel

Sun gear turns half-shaft

Planet gear

Drive shaft turns crown wheel

In a standard differential, a crown wheel turns two planetary gears, which can also spin about their own axes. This allows the two half-shafts turning the vehicle's wheels to rotate at different speeds. Some electric vehicles alter the speed of electric hub motors in each of their wheels to mimic the work of a differential.

DIFFERENTIAL GEARING

The half-shaft is the section of the drive shaft that links the differential to the wheel.

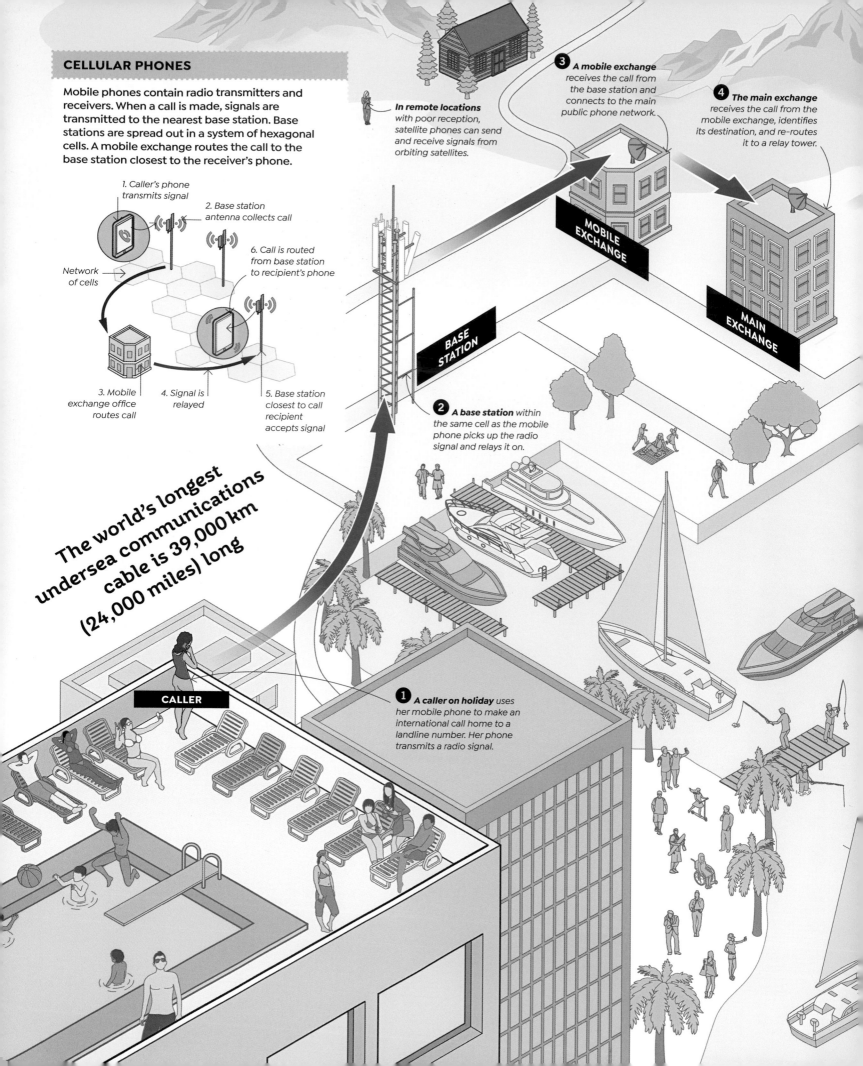

CELLULAR PHONES

Mobile phones contain radio transmitters and receivers. When a call is made, signals are transmitted to the nearest base station. Base stations are spread out in a system of hexagonal cells. A mobile exchange routes the call to the base station closest to the receiver's phone.

1. Caller's phone transmits signal

2. Base station antenna collects call

6. Call is routed from base station to recipient's phone

Network of cells

3. Mobile exchange office routes call

4. Signal is relayed

5. Base station closest to call recipient accepts signal

In remote locations with poor reception, satellite phones can send and receive signals from orbiting satellites.

3 *A mobile exchange* receives the call from the base station and connects to the main public phone network.

4 *The main exchange* receives the call from the mobile exchange, identifies its destination, and re-routes it to a relay tower.

MOBILE EXCHANGE

MAIN EXCHANGE

BASE STATION

2 *A base station* within the same cell as the mobile phone picks up the radio signal and relays it on.

The world's longest undersea communications cable is 39,000 km (24,000 miles) long

CALLER

1 *A caller on holiday* uses her mobile phone to make an international call home to a landline number. Her phone transmits a radio signal.

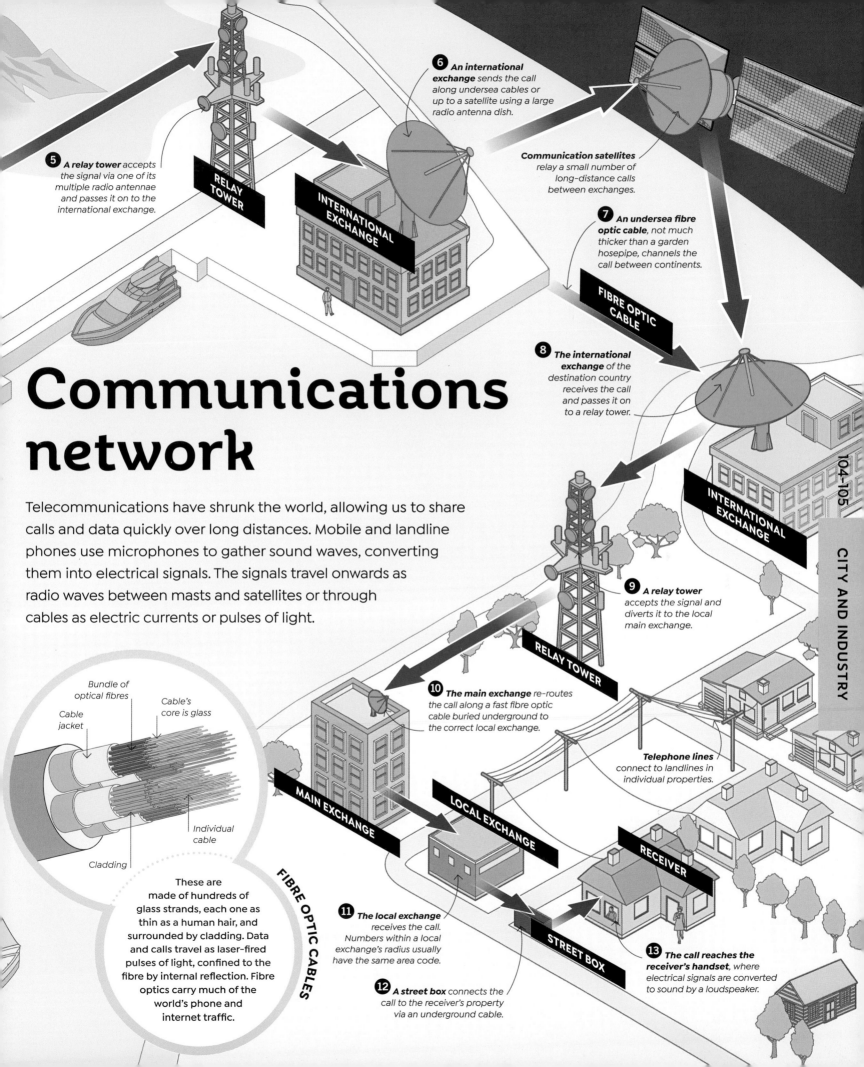

Communications network

Telecommunications have shrunk the world, allowing us to share calls and data quickly over long distances. Mobile and landline phones use microphones to gather sound waves, converting them into electrical signals. The signals travel onwards as radio waves between masts and satellites or through cables as electric currents or pulses of light.

5 *A relay tower* accepts the signal via one of its multiple radio antennae and passes it on to the international exchange.

RELAY TOWER

INTERNATIONAL EXCHANGE

6 *An international exchange* sends the call along undersea cables or up to a satellite using a large radio antenna dish.

Communication satellites relay a small number of long-distance calls between exchanges.

7 *An undersea fibre optic cable*, not much thicker than a garden hosepipe, channels the call between continents.

FIBRE OPTIC CABLE

8 *The international exchange* of the destination country receives the call and passes it on to a relay tower.

INTERNATIONAL EXCHANGE

9 *A relay tower* accepts the signal and diverts it to the local main exchange.

RELAY TOWER

Telephone lines connect to landlines in individual properties.

10 *The main exchange* re-routes the call along a fast fibre optic cable buried underground to the correct local exchange.

MAIN EXCHANGE

LOCAL EXCHANGE

RECEIVER

Fibre optic cable detail

Bundle of optical fibres

Cable jacket

Cable's core is glass

Individual cable

Cladding

FIBRE OPTIC CABLES

These are made of hundreds of glass strands, each one as thin as a human hair, and surrounded by cladding. Data and calls travel as laser-fired pulses of light, confined to the fibre by internal reflection. Fibre optics carry much of the world's phone and internet traffic.

11 *The local exchange* receives the call. Numbers within a local exchange's radius usually have the same area code.

12 *A street box* connects the call to the receiver's property via an underground cable.

STREET BOX

13 *The call reaches the receiver's handset*, where electrical signals are converted to sound by a loudspeaker.

Smartphone

A smartphone is a handheld computer and communications device. Utilizing a powerful set of microprocessor chips and internal memory, it can run multiple programs or apps simultaneously while receiving voice calls, emails, messages, and data, and streaming audio and video. Most smartphones use GPS (see pp.108–09) for navigation and all use radio waves to connect with their mobile network as well as to other devices via Bluetooth or Near Field Communications (NFC) signals.

A smartphone CPU can perform up to 2.8 billion instructions per second

CENTRAL PROCESSING UNIT

A CPU (central processing unit) controls the smartphone's functions. It is grouped with other chips such as graphics processors and memory chips.

Apps are computer programs for games, social media, or video streaming that can be run on the smartphone.

A small opening is provided for a front-facing camera lens.

The top enclosure helps stiffen the phone and contains a grille for the loudspeaker.

The screen display assembly strengthens the narrow space between the touchscreen and the other components.

The daughterboard is a secondary circuit board that supports the motherboard.

A miniature motor causes the phone to vibrate when alerts or calls arrive.

SCREEN

TOUCHSCREEN

The touchscreen registers swipes and presses, converting them into commands sent as signals to the phone's CPU.

DAUGHTERBOARD

MOTOR

A ribbon cable links the motherboard and daughterboard together.

Tiny cones inside the loudspeaker vibrate to transmit sound through the air.

LOUDSPEAKER

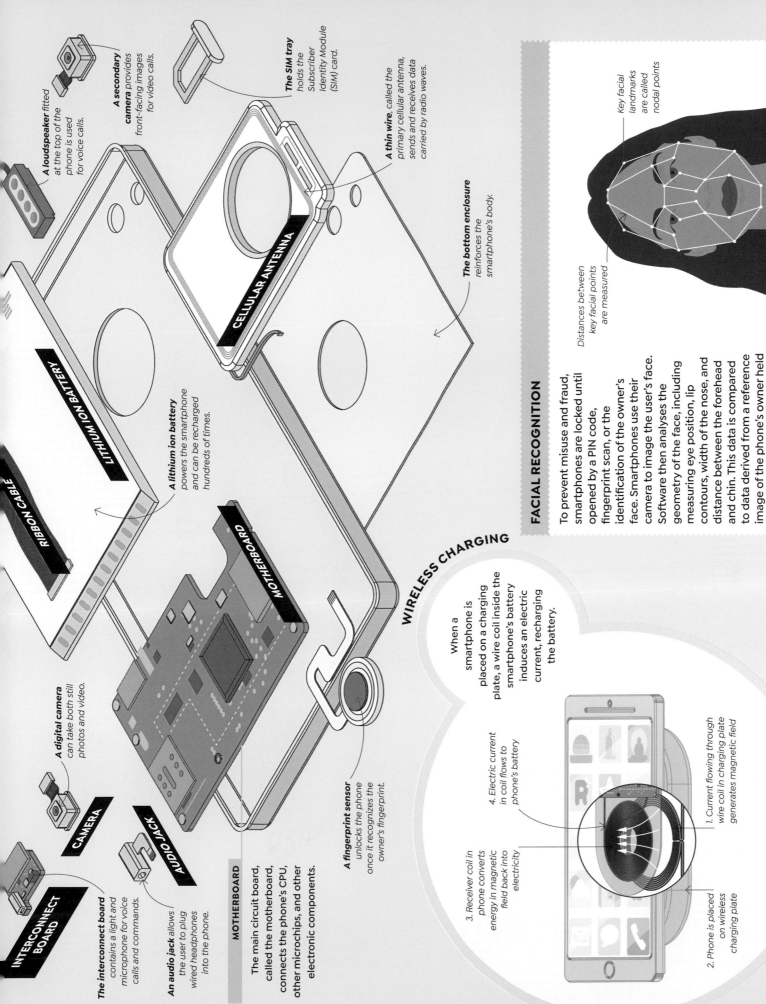

A loudspeaker fitted at the top of the phone is used for voice calls.

A secondary camera provides front-facing images for video calls.

The SIM tray holds the Subscriber Identity Module (SIM) card.

A thin wire, called the primary cellular antenna, sends and receives data carried by radio waves.

The bottom enclosure reinforces the smartphone's body.

CELLULAR ANTENNA

LITHIUM ION BATTERY

A lithium ion battery powers the smartphone and can be recharged hundreds of times.

RIBBON CABLE

MOTHERBOARD

A digital camera can take both still photos and video.

CAMERA

AUDIO JACK

An audio jack allows the user to plug wired headphones into the phone.

MOTHERBOARD
The main circuit board, called the motherboard, connects the phone's CPU, and other microchips, and other electronic components.

A fingerprint sensor unlocks the phone once it recognizes the owner's fingerprint.

INTERCONNECT BOARD

The interconnect board contains a light and microphone for voice calls and commands.

FACIAL RECOGNITION

To prevent misuse and fraud, smartphones are locked until opened by a PIN code, fingerprint scan, or the identification of the owner's face. Smartphones use their camera to image the user's face. Software then analyses the geometry of the face, including measuring eye position, lip contours, width of the nose, and distance between the forehead and chin. This data is compared to data derived from a reference image of the phone's owner held in memory or online. If there's a match, the phone is unlocked.

key facial landmarks are called nodal points

Distances between key facial points are measured

WIRELESS CHARGING

When a smartphone is placed on a charging plate, a wire coil inside the smartphone's battery induces an electric current, recharging the battery.

4. Electric current in coil flows to phone's battery

3. Receiver coil in phone converts energy in magnetic field back into electricity

1. Current flowing through wire coil in charging plate generates magnetic field

2. Phone is placed on wireless charging plate

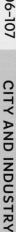

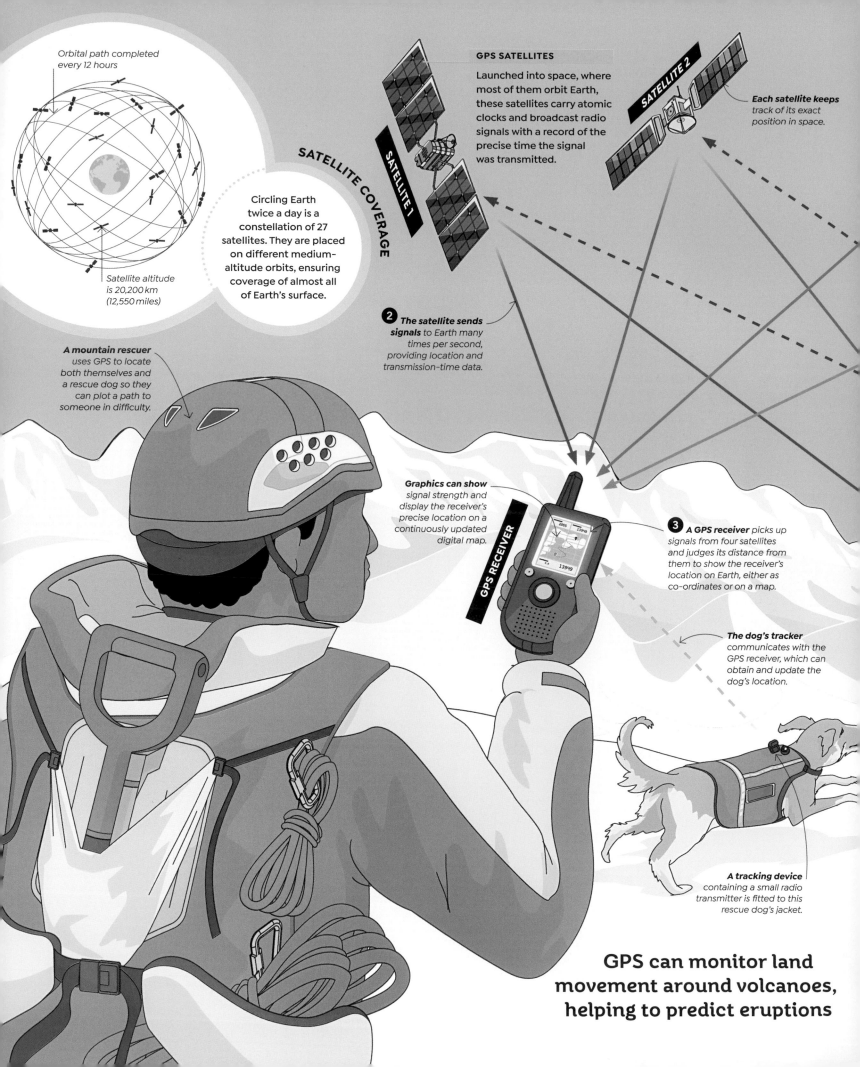

Orbital path completed every 12 hours

Satellite altitude is 20,200 km (12,550 miles)

Circling Earth twice a day is a constellation of 27 satellites. They are placed on different medium-altitude orbits, ensuring coverage of almost all of Earth's surface.

GPS SATELLITES

Launched into space, where most of them orbit Earth, these satellites carry atomic clocks and broadcast radio signals with a record of the precise time the signal was transmitted.

SATELLITE 2

Each satellite keeps track of its exact position in space.

SATELLITE COVERAGE

SATELLITE 1

2 *The satellite sends signals* to Earth many times per second, providing location and transmission-time data.

A mountain rescuer uses GPS to locate both themselves and a rescue dog so they can plot a path to someone in difficulty.

Graphics can show signal strength and display the receiver's precise location on a continuously updated digital map.

GPS RECEIVER

3 *A GPS receiver* picks up signals from four satellites and judges its distance from them to show the receiver's location on Earth, either as co-ordinates or on a map.

The dog's tracker communicates with the GPS receiver, which can obtain and update the dog's location.

A tracking device containing a small radio transmitter is fitted to this rescue dog's jacket.

GPS can monitor land movement around volcanoes, helping to predict eruptions

SATELLITE 3

SATELLITE 4

Satellites transmit data about their altitude, speed, and position to the monitor station.

Wild animals fitted with a GPS collar can be tracked to learn more about their movements, feeding habits, territory, and to help protect them from poaching.

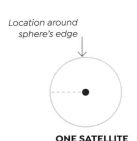

GPS

The Global Positioning System (GPS) uses satellites orbiting Earth to fix a person's or machine's location on the planet's surface to within a handful of metres. GPS provides in-car route planning and mapping, and is used in smartwatches and phones to measure speeds or distances travelled. It's also part of the navigation systems used by ships, planes, and mobile robots.

❶ *A satellite dish* sends data and programs to satellites using radio waves.

Large, weatherproof radomes protect the sensitive radio antenna housed inside.

GROUND STATIONS

Located around the world, these facilities upload programs and commands to the GPS satellites and collect performance data, or telemetry, from them.

The monitor station checks for atomic clock errors or issues with the satellites' orbit or performance.

The monitor station communicates with the ground station and a master control station.

MONITOR STATION

GROUND STATION

FIXING A LOCATION

A GPS receiver relies on simultaneous signals from multiple satellites in the network. The time it takes a satellite's signal to reach the receiver can be converted into its distance away. When the distance of one satellite is known, the receiver could be at any point on a sphere whose radius equals the satellite's distance. But when the distances to at least three satellites are known, the receiver can be at only one point on the planet's surface.

Location around sphere's edge

ONE SATELLITE
The distance from one satellite places the receiver somewhere around the edge of a sphere.

Distance from Earth to satellite

Intersection points show two possible locations

TWO SATELLITES
With two satellites, the location is narrowed down to where the two spheres intersect.

Exact location of GPS receiver

THREE OR MORE SATELLITES
A third satellite gives a precise position. A fourth satellite is used to synchronize the receiver and satellites' clocks.

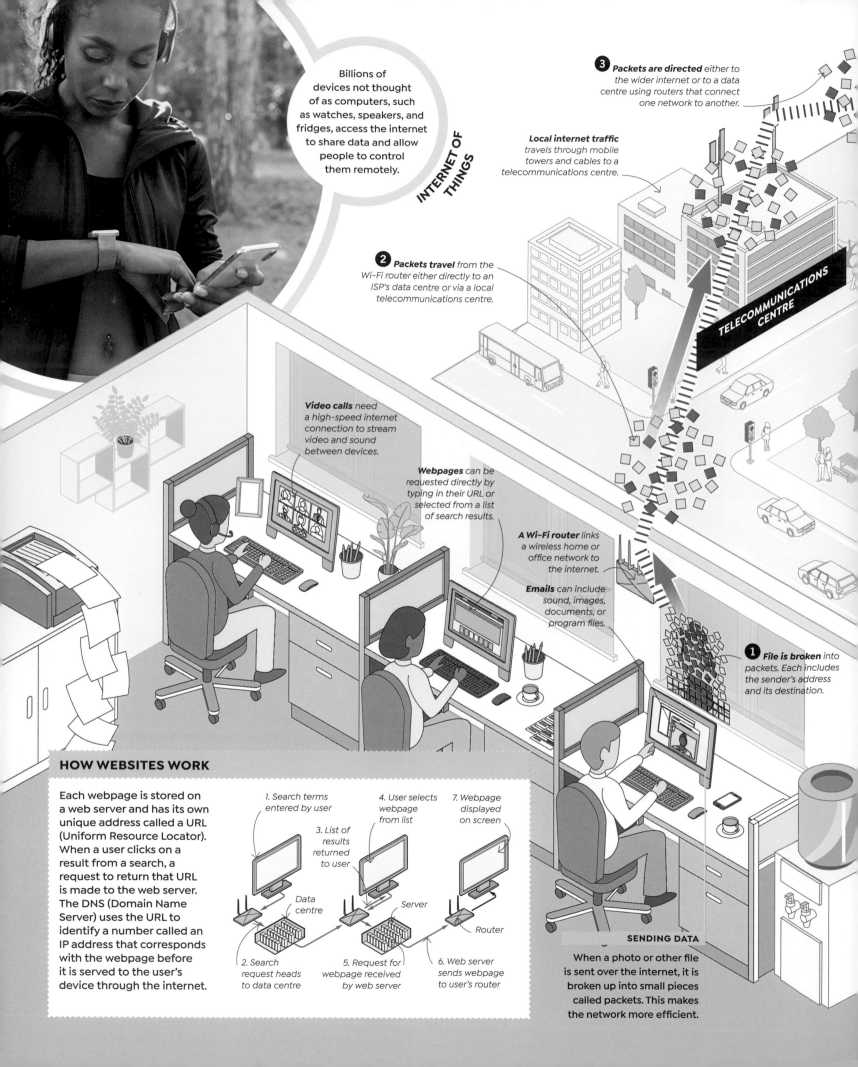

Billions of devices not thought of as computers, such as watches, speakers, and fridges, access the internet to share data and allow people to control them remotely.

INTERNET OF THINGS

3 *Packets are directed* either to the wider internet or to a data centre using routers that connect one network to another.

Local internet traffic travels through mobile towers and cables to a telecommunications centre.

2 *Packets travel* from the Wi-Fi router either directly to an ISP's data centre or via a local telecommunications centre.

TELECOMMUNICATIONS CENTRE

Video calls need a high-speed internet connection to stream video and sound between devices.

Webpages can be requested directly by typing in their URL or selected from a list of search results.

A Wi-Fi router links a wireless home or office network to the internet.

Emails can include sound, images, documents, or program files.

1 *File is broken* into packets. Each includes the sender's address and its destination.

HOW WEBSITES WORK

Each webpage is stored on a web server and has its own unique address called a URL (Uniform Resource Locator). When a user clicks on a result from a search, a request to return that URL is made to the web server. The DNS (Domain Name Server) uses the URL to identify a number called an IP address that corresponds with the webpage before it is served to the user's device through the internet.

1. Search terms entered by user

3. List of results returned to user

4. User selects webpage from list

7. Webpage displayed on screen

Data centre

Server

Router

2. Search request heads to data centre

5. Request for webpage received by web server

6. Web server sends webpage to user's router

SENDING DATA

When a photo or other file is sent over the internet, it is broken up into small pieces called packets. This makes the network more efficient.

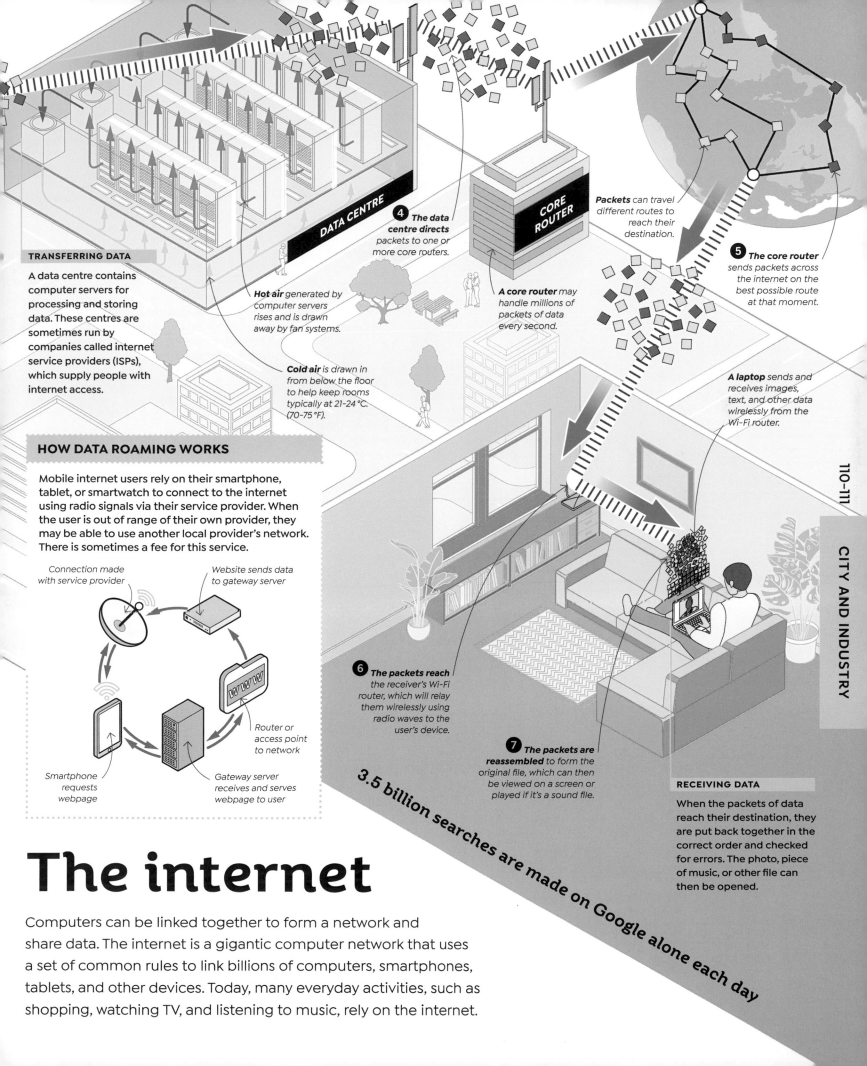

TRANSFERRING DATA

A data centre contains computer servers for processing and storing data. These centres are sometimes run by companies called internet service providers (ISPs), which supply people with internet access.

4 *The data centre directs* packets to one or more core routers.

Hot air generated by computer servers rises and is drawn away by fan systems.

Cold air is drawn in from below the floor to help keep rooms typically at 21-24 °C. (70-75 °F).

CORE ROUTER

DATA CENTRE

A core router may handle millions of packets of data every second.

Packets can travel different routes to reach their destination.

5 *The core router* sends packets across the internet on the best possible route at that moment.

A laptop sends and receives images, text, and other data wirelessly from the Wi-Fi router.

HOW DATA ROAMING WORKS

Mobile internet users rely on their smartphone, tablet, or smartwatch to connect to the internet using radio signals via their service provider. When the user is out of range of their own provider, they may be able to use another local provider's network. There is sometimes a fee for this service.

Connection made with service provider

Website sends data to gateway server

Router or access point to network

Gateway server receives and serves webpage to user

Smartphone requests webpage

6 *The packets reach* the receiver's Wi-Fi router, which will relay them wirelessly using radio waves to the user's device.

7 *The packets are reassembled* to form the original file, which can then be viewed on a screen or played if it's a sound file.

RECEIVING DATA

When the packets of data reach their destination, they are put back together in the correct order and checked for errors. The photo, piece of music, or other file can then be opened.

3.5 billion searches are made on Google alone each day

The internet

Computers can be linked together to form a network and share data. The internet is a gigantic computer network that uses a set of common rules to link billions of computers, smartphones, tablets, and other devices. Today, many everyday activities, such as shopping, watching TV, and listening to music, rely on the internet.

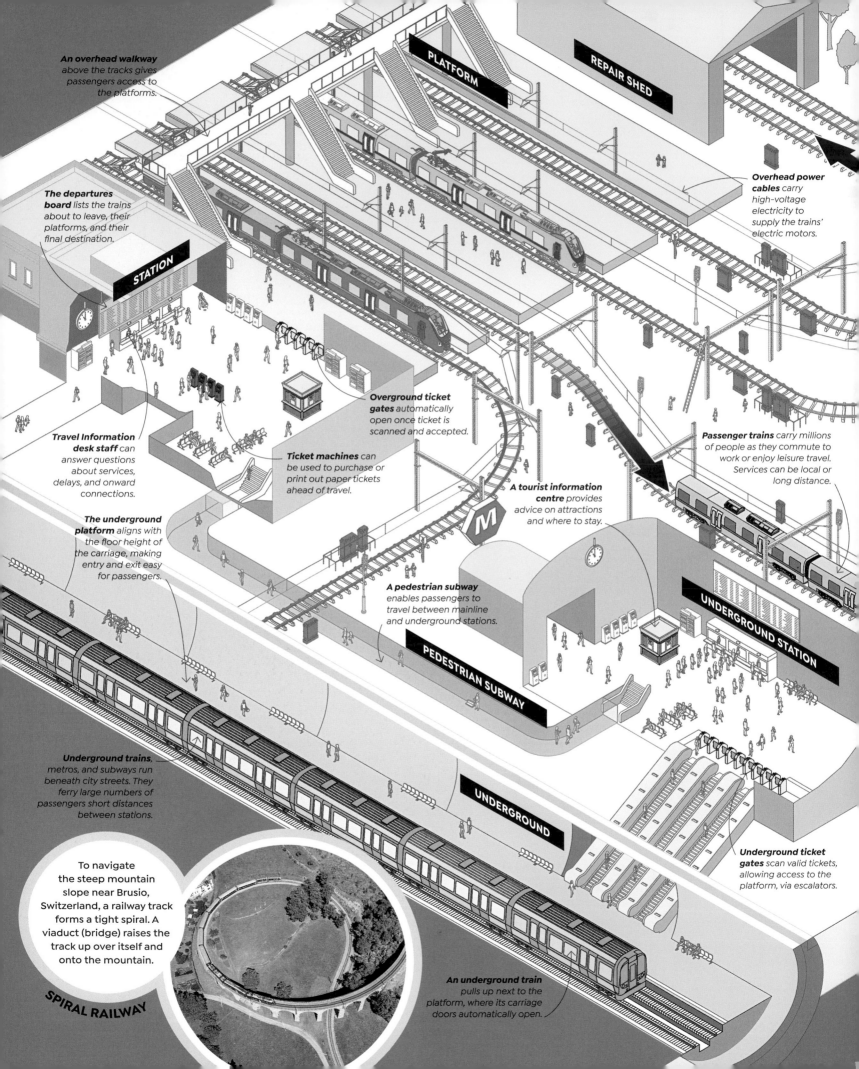

An overhead walkway above the tracks gives passengers access to the platforms.

PLATFORM

REPAIR SHED

Overhead power cables carry high-voltage electricity to supply the trains' electric motors.

The departures board lists the trains about to leave, their platforms, and their final destination.

STATION

Travel Information desk staff can answer questions about services, delays, and onward connections.

Overground ticket gates automatically open once ticket is scanned and accepted.

Ticket machines can be used to purchase or print out paper tickets ahead of travel.

Passenger trains carry millions of people as they commute to work or enjoy leisure travel. Services can be local or long distance.

The underground platform aligns with the floor height of the carriage, making entry and exit easy for passengers.

A tourist information centre provides advice on attractions and where to stay.

A pedestrian subway enables passengers to travel between mainline and underground stations.

M

UNDERGROUND STATION

PEDESTRIAN SUBWAY

Underground trains, metros, and subways run beneath city streets. They ferry large numbers of passengers short distances between stations.

UNDERGROUND

Underground ticket gates scan valid tickets, allowing access to the platform, via escalators.

To navigate the steep mountain slope near Brusio, Switzerland, a railway track forms a tight spiral. A viaduct (bridge) raises the track up over itself and onto the mountain.

SPIRAL RAILWAY

An underground train pulls up next to the platform, where its carriage doors automatically open.

Every day 3.6 million people travel through Shinjuku station, Japan, making it the world's busiest station

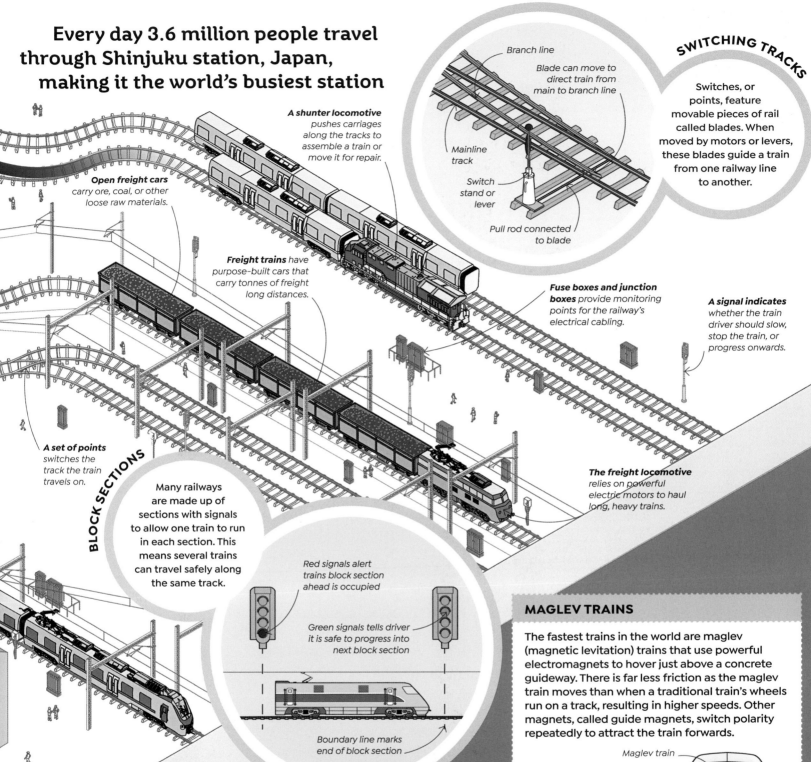

A shunter locomotive pushes carriages along the tracks to assemble a train or move it for repair.

Open freight cars carry ore, coal, or other loose raw materials.

Freight trains have purpose-built cars that carry tonnes of freight long distances.

Branch line

Blade can move to direct train from main to branch line

Mainline track

Switch stand or lever

Pull rod connected to blade

Switches, or points, feature movable pieces of rail called blades. When moved by motors or levers, these blades guide a train from one railway line to another.

Fuse boxes and junction boxes provide monitoring points for the railway's electrical cabling.

A signal indicates whether the train driver should slow, stop the train, or progress onwards.

A set of points switches the track the train travels on.

BLOCK SECTIONS

Many railways are made up of sections with signals to allow one train to run in each section. This means several trains can travel safely along the same track.

Red signals alert trains block section ahead is occupied

Green signals tells driver it is safe to progress into next block section

Boundary line marks end of block section

The freight locomotive relies on powerful electric motors to haul long, heavy trains.

MAGLEV TRAINS

The fastest trains in the world are maglev (magnetic levitation) trains that use powerful electromagnets to hover just above a concrete guideway. There is far less friction as the maglev train moves than when a traditional train's wheels run on a track, resulting in higher speeds. Other magnets, called guide magnets, switch polarity repeatedly to attract the train forwards.

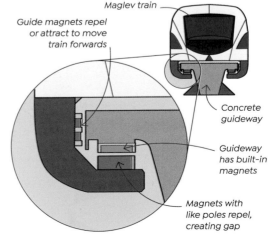

Maglev train

Guide magnets repel or attract to move train forwards

Concrete guideway

Guideway has built-in magnets

Magnets with like poles repel, creating gap

Railway

Railways act as the backbone of many nations' transport systems. Trains travel along networks, totalling 1.4 million km (870,000 miles) across the world. They deliver people or goods (also known as freight) between depots or stations. A large railway station in a city is often a major transport hub with links to other transport networks such as an underground or metro system.

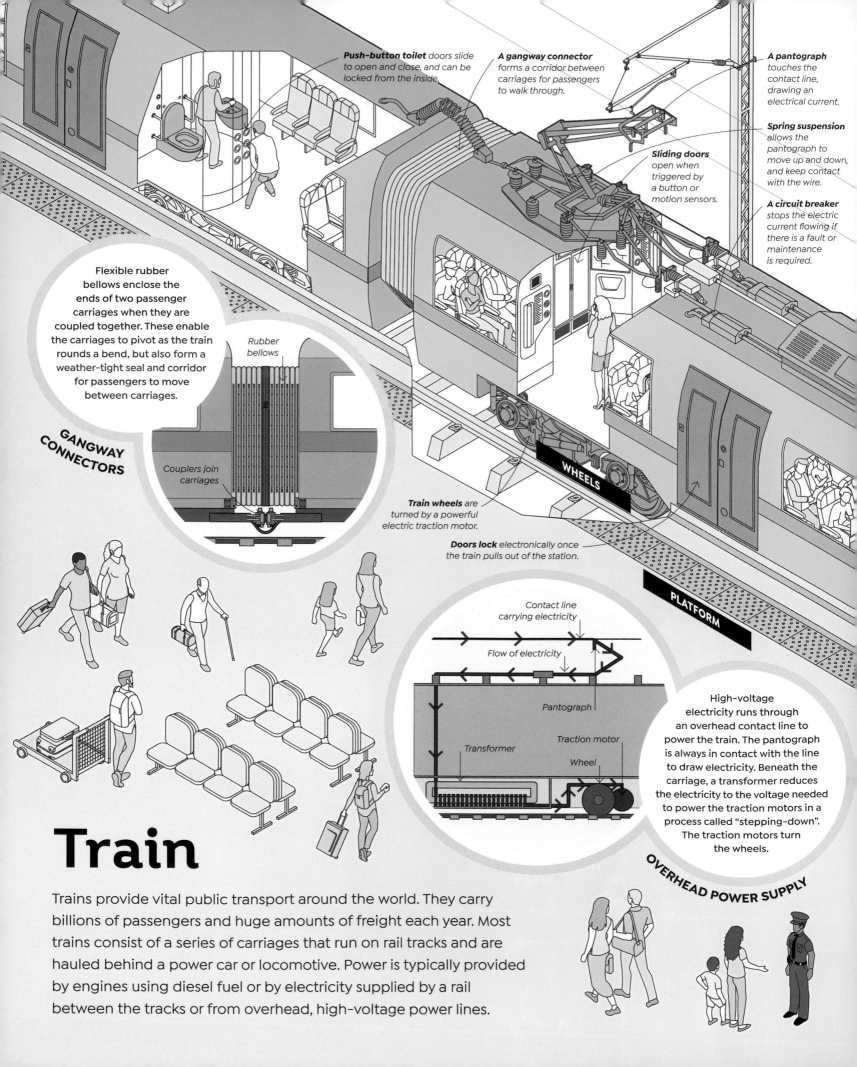

Push-button toilet doors slide to open and close, and can be locked from the inside.

A gangway connector forms a corridor between carriages for passengers to walk through.

A pantograph touches the contact line, drawing an electrical current.

Spring suspension allows the pantograph to move up and down, and keep contact with the wire.

Sliding doors open when triggered by a button or motion sensors.

A circuit breaker stops the electric current flowing if there is a fault or maintenance is required.

Flexible rubber bellows enclose the ends of two passenger carriages when they are coupled together. These enable the carriages to pivot as the train rounds a bend, but also form a weather-tight seal and corridor for passengers to move between carriages.

Rubber bellows

Couplers join carriages

GANGWAY CONNECTORS

Train wheels are turned by a powerful electric traction motor.

Doors lock electronically once the train pulls out of the station.

WHEELS

PLATFORM

Contact line carrying electricity

Flow of electricity

Pantograph

Traction motor

Transformer

Wheel

High-voltage electricity runs through an overhead contact line to power the train. The pantograph is always in contact with the line to draw electricity. Beneath the carriage, a transformer reduces the electricity to the voltage needed to power the traction motors in a process called "stepping-down". The traction motors turn the wheels.

OVERHEAD POWER SUPPLY

Train

Trains provide vital public transport around the world. They carry billions of passengers and huge amounts of freight each year. Most trains consist of a series of carriages that run on rail tracks and are hauled behind a power car or locomotive. Power is typically provided by engines using diesel fuel or by electricity supplied by a rail between the tracks or from overhead, high-voltage power lines.

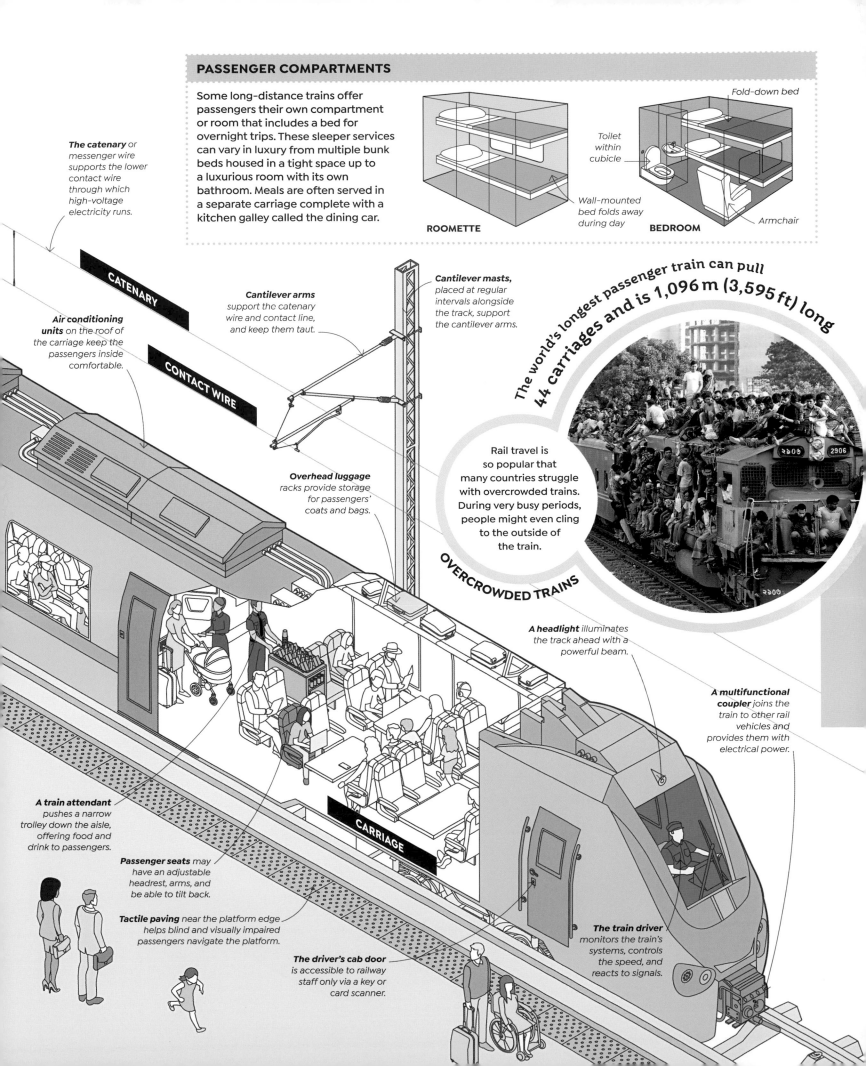

PASSENGER COMPARTMENTS

Some long-distance trains offer passengers their own compartment or room that includes a bed for overnight trips. These sleeper services can vary in luxury from multiple bunk beds housed in a tight space up to a luxurious room with its own bathroom. Meals are often served in a separate carriage complete with a kitchen galley called the dining car.

Fold-down bed

Toilet within cubicle

Wall-mounted bed folds away during day

ROOMETTE

BEDROOM

Armchair

The catenary or messenger wire supports the lower contact wire through which high-voltage electricity runs.

CATENARY

Cantilever arms support the catenary wire and contact line, and keep them taut.

Cantilever masts, placed at regular intervals alongside the track, support the cantilever arms.

Air conditioning units on the roof of the carriage keep the passengers inside comfortable.

CONTACT WIRE

Overhead luggage racks provide storage for passengers' coats and bags.

The world's longest passenger train can pull 44 carriages and is 1,096 m (3,595 ft) long

Rail travel is so popular that many countries struggle with overcrowded trains. During very busy periods, people might even cling to the outside of the train.

OVERCROWDED TRAINS

A headlight illuminates the track ahead with a powerful beam.

A multifunctional coupler joins the train to other rail vehicles and provides them with electrical power.

A train attendant pushes a narrow trolley down the aisle, offering food and drink to passengers.

Passenger seats may have an adjustable headrest, arms, and be able to tilt back.

Tactile paving near the platform edge helps blind and visually impaired passengers navigate the platform.

CARRIAGE

The driver's cab door is accessible to railway staff only via a key or card scanner.

The train driver monitors the train's systems, controls the speed, and reacts to signals.

DETECTING WHALES

Many whales are tragically killed each year after being struck by massive ships. Mapping whale movements can help ships to avoid collisions. Buoys fitted with underwater microphones scan the waters for whales, using artificial intelligence (AI) to identify the species. Ship captains are then warned so that they can slow down their vessels or change course if necessary.

The world's largest cruise ship, the Wonder of the Seas, is over
360 m (1,180 ft) long
and 64 m (210 ft) wide

GUEST CABINS

Cabins provide guests with a place to sleep, wash, and store their luggage. Some cruise ships offer balconies and luxury facilities for relaxation.

ENTERTAINMENT

Leisure activities range from cooking and craft classes to live shows, sports, and swimming. Many guests prefer to just take it easy and soak up the cruise views.

Crazy golf, along with tennis and shuffleboard, are common deck sports.

Flotation devices can be thrown into the water to help anyone who falls overboard stay afloat.

Mis-hit golf balls made from lobster shells biodegrade (rot) in the water.

Pools are filled with sea water that has been chemically treated and filtered. There may be a wave machine to simulate open-sea surfing conditions.

CRAZY GOLF

Large slides can run from higher decks to pools on lower decks, giving passengers a thrilling ride.

Safety rails around the edge of each deck prevent people from falling into the water.

Outdoor cinemas and theatres allow passengers to enjoy films and other performances alongside the ocean views.

POOL

CAFE

TENNIS

SURFING POOL

Restaurants serve thousands of meals to guests each day.

SLIDE POOL

The hull is the main body of the ship. It is divided horizontally by decks, and vertically into compartments by strong walls called bulkheads.

OUTDOOR CINEMA

BAR

RESTAURANT

CABINS

SIDE THRUSTERS

Diesel-electric or gas turbine engines provide the power that drives the propeller.

PROPULSION

Engines rotate a shaft that drives the spinning blades of a propeller. Water is pushed backwards by the blades to create an opposing force, called thrust, that propels the ship forwards.

RUDDER

PROPELLER

Side thrusters turn the stern (rear) or bow (front) of the ship to make small manoeuvres at ports.

KEEL

The rudder deflects water in one direction, turning the ship.

The propeller may be many metres in diameter.

The keel is the deepest part of the ship and runs from the bow to the stern like a backbone.

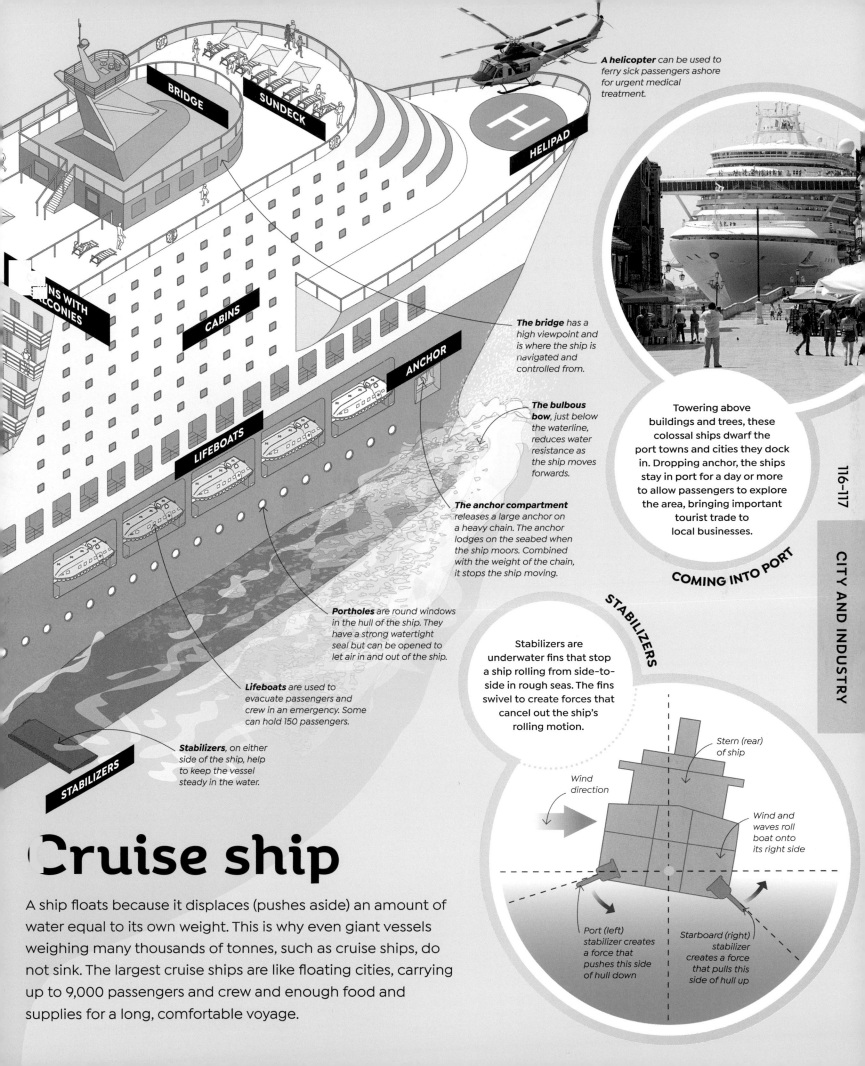

BRIDGE

SUNDECK

HELIPAD

A helicopter can be used to ferry sick passengers ashore for urgent medical treatment.

NS WITH BALCONIES

CABINS

ANCHOR

LIFEBOATS

STABILIZERS

STABILIZERS

The bridge has a high viewpoint and is where the ship is navigated and controlled from.

The bulbous bow, just below the waterline, reduces water resistance as the ship moves forwards.

The anchor compartment releases a large anchor on a heavy chain. The anchor lodges on the seabed when the ship moors. Combined with the weight of the chain, it stops the ship moving.

Portholes are round windows in the hull of the ship. They have a strong watertight seal but can be opened to let air in and out of the ship.

Lifeboats are used to evacuate passengers and crew in an emergency. Some can hold 150 passengers.

Stabilizers, on either side of the ship, help to keep the vessel steady in the water.

Towering above buildings and trees, these colossal ships dwarf the port towns and cities they dock in. Dropping anchor, the ships stay in port for a day or more to allow passengers to explore the area, bringing important tourist trade to local businesses.

COMING INTO PORT

STABILIZERS

Stabilizers are underwater fins that stop a ship rolling from side-to-side in rough seas. The fins swivel to create forces that cancel out the ship's rolling motion.

Stern (rear) of ship

Wind direction

Wind and waves roll boat onto its right side

Port (left) stabilizer creates a force that pushes this side of hull down

Starboard (right) stabilizer creates a force that pulls this side of hull up

Cruise ship

A ship floats because it displaces (pushes aside) an amount of water equal to its own weight. This is why even giant vessels weighing many thousands of tonnes, such as cruise ships, do not sink. The largest cruise ships are like floating cities, carrying up to 9,000 passengers and crew and enough food and supplies for a long, comfortable voyage.

Yacht

Yachts are sailing vessels with accommodation, built for spending days out on the water. Fast, light yachts with sails are used for pleasure cruising or racing, while larger leisure vessels are powered by engines. Some of the largest motor yachts – known as super yachts – are enormous and cost many millions to build before they can set sail.

The fastest sailing boat, piloted by Australian sailor Paul Larsen, reached a speed of 121 kph (75 mph)

The triangular jib sail is mounted ahead of the mast, increasing the yacht's stability and speed.

The mast is a tall, vertical pole, rising from the deck, that supports the yacht's sails.

The main sail is the yacht's largest sail. It is rigged behind the mast and catches the wind to propel the vessel.

SAILING YACHT

MAST

MAIN SAIL

JIB SAIL

A pole hinged to the mast, called the boom, runs horizontally along the bottom of the main sail.

Steering is achieved via this wheel, which controls the rudder. On some yachts a lever, called the tiller, is used instead.

The helmsperson steers and navigates the yacht. They may instruct the crew to change and trim sails.

Living quarters include a galley (the kitchen), beds, a living area, and a bathroom.

The angle of the sail can be altered by "trimming" – adjusting how tightly lines called sheets hold the sail.

HULL

KEEL

The watertight body of a boat is called the hull. It is filled with air, making the boat less dense than water, which keeps it afloat.

The keel helps balance forces to prevent the yacht capsizing or winds pushing the yacht sideways.

RUDDER

A rudder is a hinged, vertical panel that can be angled to deflect water and turn the yacht.

STEERING A SAILING YACHT

Sailing yachts can be skilfully manoeuvred to sail into the wind (upwind) by a technique called tacking. This sees the sails angled so the bow (front) of the yacht turns first one way and then the other through the wind. By repeating the manoeuvre, the yacht can sail a zig-zagging course forwards despite the wind direction.

5. Yacht moves through wind, starting on new course

4. Sails are moved across to port (left) side

3. Sails are moved across to centre as yacht straightens

Direction of wind

2. Sails are moved to starboard (right) side of yacht

Path taken by boat

1. Boat begins manoeuvre with wind on left, called a port tack

The world's longest super yacht, the Azzam, measures 180 m (590 ft) long

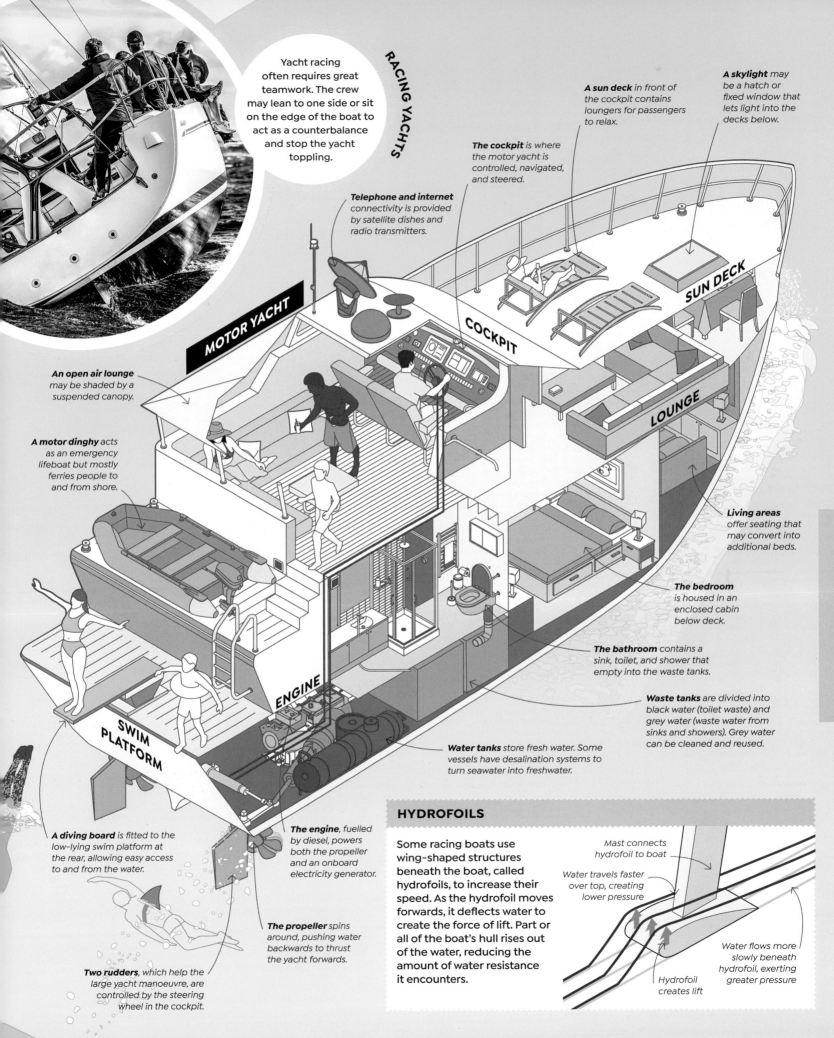

Yacht racing often requires great teamwork. The crew may lean to one side or sit on the edge of the boat to act as a counterbalance and stop the yacht toppling.

A sun deck in front of the cockpit contains loungers for passengers to relax.

A skylight may be a hatch or fixed window that lets light into the decks below.

The cockpit is where the motor yacht is controlled, navigated, and steered.

Telephone and internet connectivity is provided by satellite dishes and radio transmitters.

SUN DECK

COCKPIT

MOTOR YACHT

LOUNGE

An open air lounge may be shaded by a suspended canopy.

A motor dinghy acts as an emergency lifeboat but mostly ferries people to and from shore.

Living areas offer seating that may convert into additional beds.

The bedroom is housed in an enclosed cabin below deck.

The bathroom contains a sink, toilet, and shower that empty into the waste tanks.

ENGINE

SWIM PLATFORM

Waste tanks are divided into black water (toilet waste) and grey water (waste water from sinks and showers). Grey water can be cleaned and reused.

Water tanks store fresh water. Some vessels have desalination systems to turn seawater into freshwater.

A diving board is fitted to the low-lying swim platform at the rear, allowing easy access to and from the water.

The engine, fuelled by diesel, powers both the propeller and an onboard electricity generator.

The propeller spins around, pushing water backwards to thrust the yacht forwards.

Two rudders, which help the large yacht manoeuvre, are controlled by the steering wheel in the cockpit.

HYDROFOILS

Some racing boats use wing-shaped structures beneath the boat, called hydrofoils, to increase their speed. As the hydrofoil moves forwards, it deflects water to create the force of lift. Part or all of the boat's hull rises out of the water, reducing the amount of water resistance it encounters.

Mast connects hydrofoil to boat

Water travels faster over top, creating lower pressure

Water flows more slowly beneath hydrofoil, exerting greater pressure

Hydrofoil creates lift

Multi-bladed propeller *is turned by engines, powering the submarine forwards.*

BALLAST TANKS

The submarine crew, also known as submariners, work six- or eight-hour shifts. When not working, they rest in cramped bunk beds with just a curtain drawn across for privacy and their few possessions stored in a small locker. Further beds are often laid out in the torpedo room, which may also be used as a gym for the crew to stay fit.

ENGINE ROOM

NUCLEAR REACTOR

Diving planes *are wing-like devices whose angle can be altered to help the submarine dive and rise.*

Ballast tanks *wrap around the submarine hull and hold vast amounts of either air or water.*

A turbine generator *produces electricity to power the submarine's systems and engines.*

The engine room *is largely taken up by the submarine's engines and turbine generator.*

Air purification machines *recycle air inside the submarine to produce fresh, breathable air.*

A nuclear reactor *produces heat to turn water into steam. This steam is used to drive electricity generators.*

Bunks *stacked two or three beds high provide limited space for the crew to rest.*

Sonar array *scans waters below and to the side for hazards including other submarines.*

Submarine

Unlike other ships, submarines can control how buoyant they are, using large ballast tanks to adjust their depth underwater and to dive or rise to the surface. A large military submarine can be longer than a football pitch, carry a crew of more than 100, and cruise underwater on missions lasting many months.

BALLAST TANKS

Submarines feature an inner hull and an outer hull. Between the two lie giant ballast tanks. They can be flooded with seawater to push out air and increase the submarine's weight, causing it to dive. To rise, compressed air is pumped into the ballast tanks, pushing the water out and reducing the submarine's weight.

Fully flooded tanks cause submarine to dive deep underwater

Ballast tanks full of air keep submarine floating on surface

Valves open, flooding ballast tanks with water

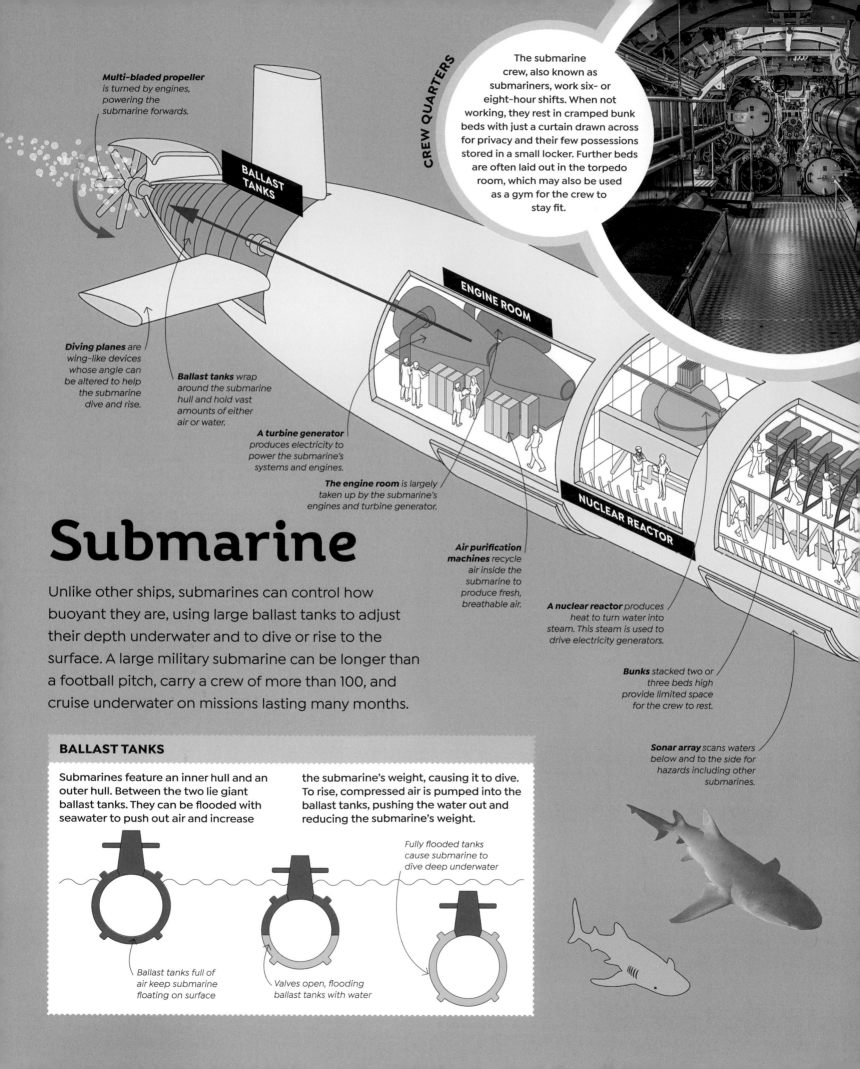

SONAR

Sound Navigation And Ranging (SONAR) enables submarines to map the waters they move through. Active sonar systems send out a constant series of sound waves that reflect off objects and return to the submarine. The time taken for the sounds to bounce back can be converted into distances. This tells the submarine crew how far away the submarine is from obstacles, hazards, and targets such as enemy ships or other submarines.

Side-mounted sonar array seeks out threats and targets

Sonar signals overlap to ensure all areas are covered

Sail sonar array operates over shorter distances so submarine can avoid ships

Passive sonar listens for distant sounds ahead of submarine

Chin array searches forwards and down, to detect anti-submarine mines below

Masts include a radar system and antennae for transmitting and receiving radio signals.

A global positioning system antenna receives satellite signals to plot the submarine's precise position.

The vessel is navigated from the command centre. This is also where weapons are deployed.

CONNING TOWER

COMMAND CENTRE

SONAR ARRAY

CRUISE MISSILE

Launched vertically from the upper hull of the submarine, cruise missiles quickly rise out of the water, aided by a small solid rocket booster. Once in the air, small, stubby wings fold out and a turbofan jet engine takes over. It propels the missile to its target up to 1,600 km (1,000 miles) away, directed by guidance systems in the nose of the missile.

The Russian Typhoon class nuclear submarine is the longest in the world at 175 m (570 ft)

MISSILE TUBES

Missile tubes are covered with watertight hatches until missiles are ready to be fired.

SONAR SPHERE

A bow diving plane tilts to help the submarine's nose rise or fall.

Missiles are launched vertically underwater and guide themselves to their target.

The sonar sphere can detect sounds many kilometres away, coming from any direction.

CRANE OPERATOR

CRANE OPERATOR

An operator controls the crane either directly from a cab high up on the crane itself or remotely from a port building, using cameras to view the containers.

2 *A gantry crane,* which stands over the railway and moves on wheels or rails, unloads the container from the train.

3 *A long-reach stacker* moves the container quickly to the storage area and places it in a stack.

1 *A container arrives* at the port transported by train.

RAIL TERMINAL

Some containers arrive or leave the port carried on trains with flat, standard-sized wagons.

Some container ships are big enough to carry 860 million bananas

GANTRY CRANE

REACH STACKER

Refrigerated containers are fitted with cooling systems that work like fridges to keep food cold.

Power supply

Double stacking makes it possible for some trains to carry extra large loads.

WINDING GEAR

RAIL

ROAD

TERMINAL ENTRANCE

CONTROL CENTRE

STORAGE

TERMINAL ENTRANCE

CAR PARK

Road trucks carry containers on standard-sized metal frames called skeletal trailers.

Port operations are coordinated from the control centre.

ROAD TERMINAL

Most container ports are linked to a road network. Truck drivers arrive at port and show their entry permits. Their trucks are loaded up with containers. The drivers leave the port and take the containers to their next destination.

STORAGE AREA

Containers are stored in numbered locations to identify them. They are stacked carefully so they can be moved easily when it is time to leave port.

QUAYSIDE

STACKED CONTAINERS

RAIL-MOUNTED GANTRY CRANE

TROLLEY

HARBOUR

SEA HIGHWAYS

Shipping lanes are like major roads at sea. They are direct routes for large ships to follow in safety. The Suez and Panama canals are among the world's busiest shipping lanes. In 2021 this container ship, named Ever Given, got stuck in the Suez Canal for almost a week. The transportation of global goods was badly affected by this obstruction.

HARBOUR

Huge container ships can dock only in ports with deep water. They must stay balanced while loading and unloading. Water is pumped in and out of chambers called ballast tanks to stop ships tilting.

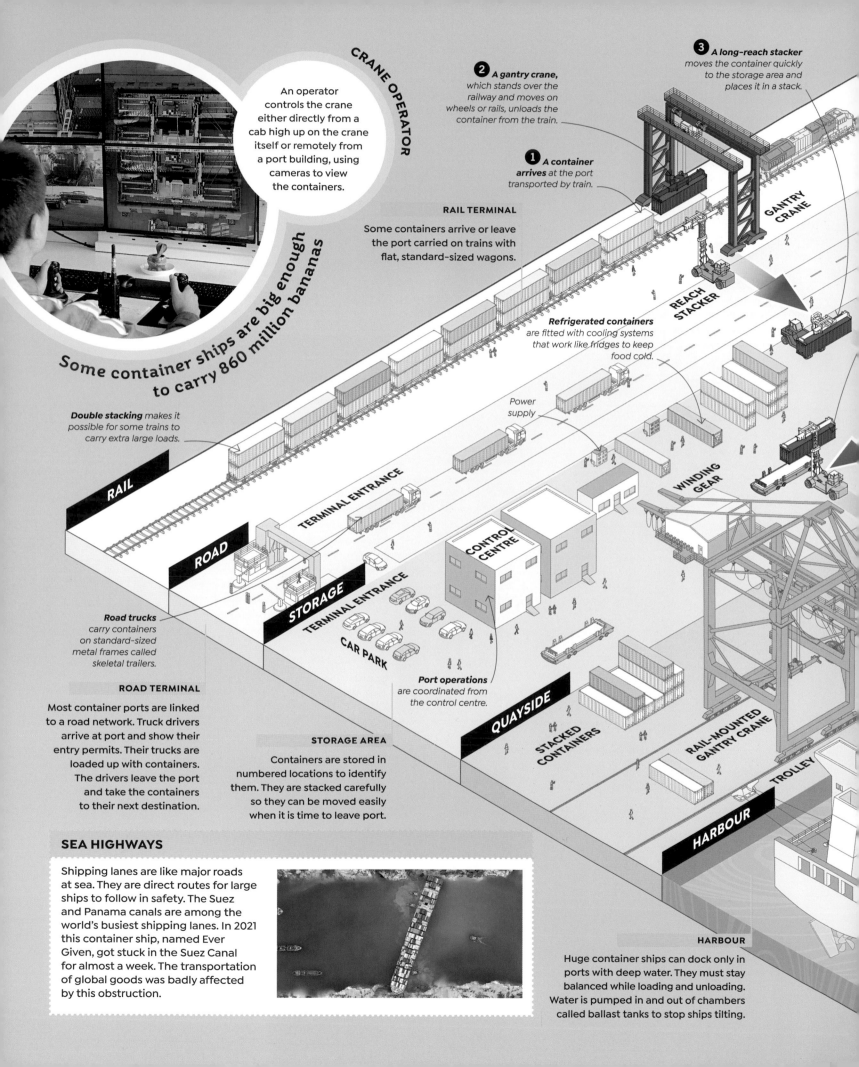

Container port

Most of the world's goods are transported by ship, many of them in giant steel boxes. Called containers, these boxes come in standard sizes, making it easy to stack them, lift them with a crane, and carry them on trucks, trains, and ships. At ports around the world, they are moved on and off huge container ships.

4 *At loading time,* the container is taken from the stack and carried to the quayside by a driverless truck.

STORED CONTAINERS

DRIVERLESS TRUCK

QUAYSIDE

The area of the port closest to the water is called the quayside. Gantry cranes at the quayside can work 24 hours a day, loading and unloading more than 50 containers an hour.

Old shipping containers have been adapted to make offices, shops, hotels, and cafes. Before being reused, they must first be given a thorough clean.

CONTAINER LIVING

5 *A quayside crane* lowers the container onto the ship. Containers are loaded in a careful arrangement to spread their weight out evenly across the ship.

The hull of the ship is divided into sections called cells. Containers are lifted and lowered along upright rails, called cell guides, to keep them stacked in position.

CELLULAR HULL

Containers on deck can be piled up to 10 boxes high

Containers stored in hold

Tanks between hulls

Containers are piled high above and below deck. Most ships have separate inner and outer hulls. In between, there are tanks for ballast, fuel, and drinking water.

CONTAINER SHIPS

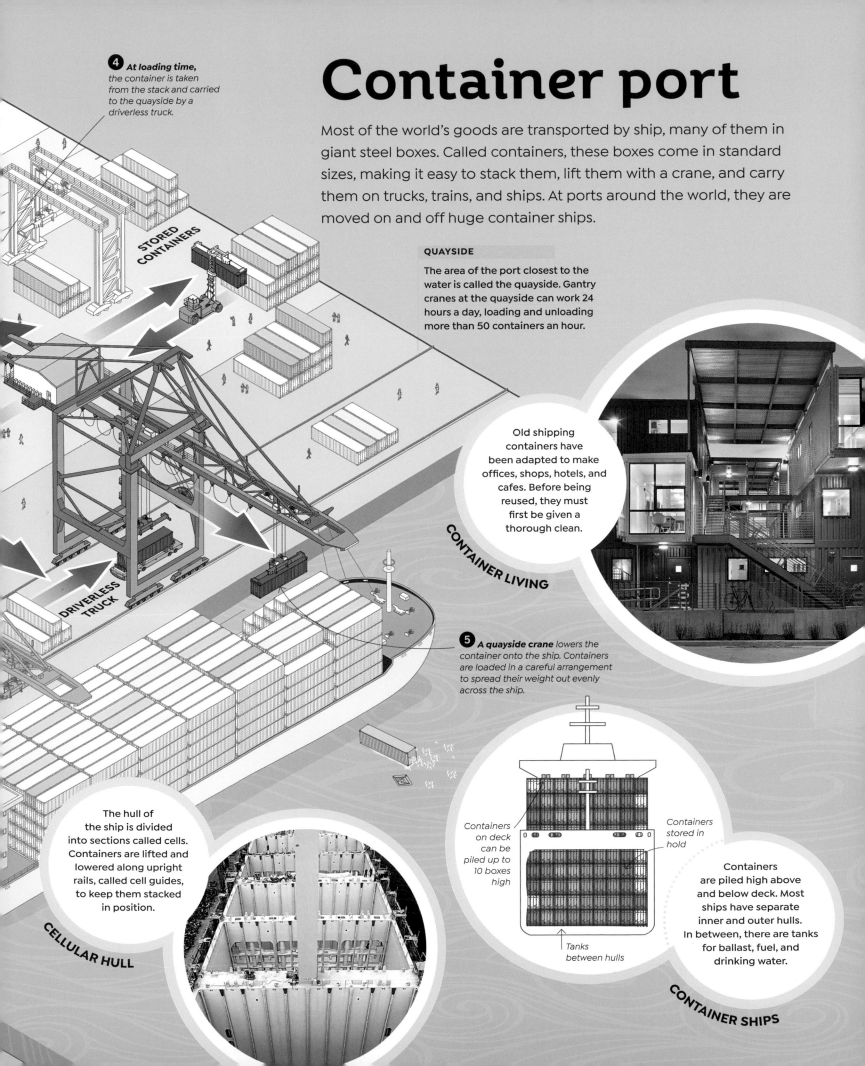

X-RAY BAGGAGE MACHINE

These machines take X-ray images of luggage, enabling security officers to view their contents without having to open the bags. X-rays pass through some objects but not others, forming an image on a detector plate that is sent to a screen. Any suspicious items spotted result in a thorough bag search and possible police action.

Conveyor belt

Second screen shows inside of bag from different angle

Luggage

Luggage shelf

Viewscreen image shows baggage contents

Emergency stop button

ARRIVALS

Passengers arriving at the airport exit the aircraft and pass through security before they can leave.

ARRIVALS

8 *Retractable skybridge* allows passengers to board the aircraft.

3 *Metal detector* checks passengers for possible dangerous materials.

4 *Security officer* views bag contents using the X-ray baggage scanner. In some airports, this follows the passport or ID check.

Bags must be removed for security screening.

DEPARTURES

People on outgoing journeys check in, then wait in the departures lounge for their flight. The security process can vary from country to country.

DEPARTURES

5 *A passport officer* checks that passengers have valid passports or ID.

SECURITY

PASSPORT CONTROL

7 *Airline staff* check boarding passes before passengers board.

WAITING AREA

6 *At the gate,* passengers await their turn to board their flight.

Electronic devices must be put in flight mode.

Airport

Airports are far more than a runway where aircraft takeoff or make landings. Passengers take complex routes through an airport's terminal buildings as they start and end their journeys. An airport also provides facilities for aircraft maintenance, refuelling, cleaning, and freight handling. Major airports are busy places, handling more than 2,000 flights a day.

Chip embedded between pages of passport

PASSPORT

Biometric passports can be scanned electronically. They contain a chip encoded with key identifying data, such as a digital face map, fingerprints, or an iris scan.

Antenna used for communication

Chip contains biometric data

BIOMETRIC PASSPORTS

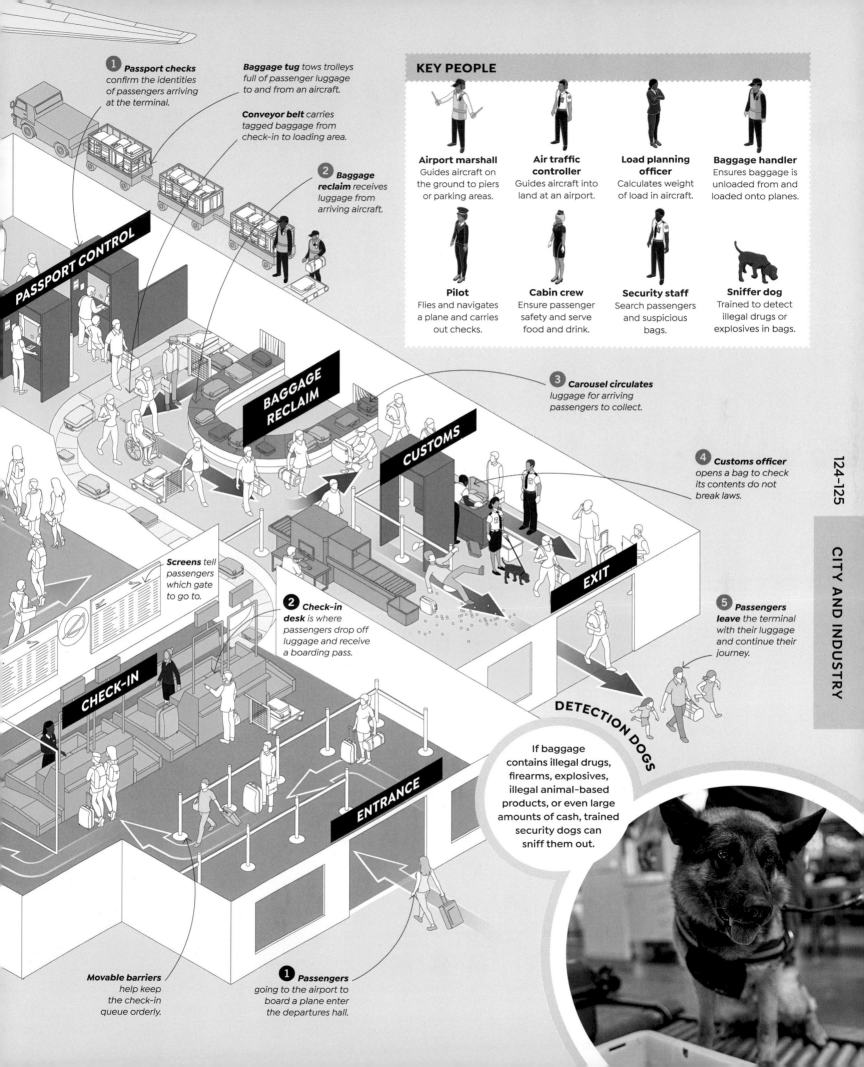

① *Passport checks* confirm the identities of passengers arriving at the terminal.

Baggage tug tows trolleys full of passenger luggage to and from an aircraft.

Conveyor belt carries tagged baggage from check-in to loading area.

② *Baggage reclaim* receives luggage from arriving aircraft.

PASSPORT CONTROL

BAGGAGE RECLAIM

③ *Carousel circulates* luggage for arriving passengers to collect.

CUSTOMS

④ *Customs officer* opens a bag to check its contents do not break laws.

Screens tell passengers which gate to go to.

② *Check-in desk* is where passengers drop off luggage and receive a boarding pass.

EXIT

⑤ *Passengers leave* the terminal with their luggage and continue their journey.

CHECK-IN

DETECTION DOGS

If baggage contains illegal drugs, firearms, explosives, illegal animal-based products, or even large amounts of cash, trained security dogs can sniff them out.

ENTRANCE

Movable barriers help keep the check-in queue orderly.

① *Passengers* going to the airport to board a plane enter the departures hall.

KEY PEOPLE

Airport marshall
Guides aircraft on the ground to piers or parking areas.

Air traffic controller
Guides aircraft into land at an airport.

Load planning officer
Calculates weight of load in aircraft.

Baggage handler
Ensures baggage is unloaded from and loaded onto planes.

Pilot
Flies and navigates a plane and carries out checks.

Cabin crew
Ensure passenger safety and serve food and drink.

Security staff
Search passengers and suspicious bags.

Sniffer dog
Trained to detect illegal drugs or explosives in bags.

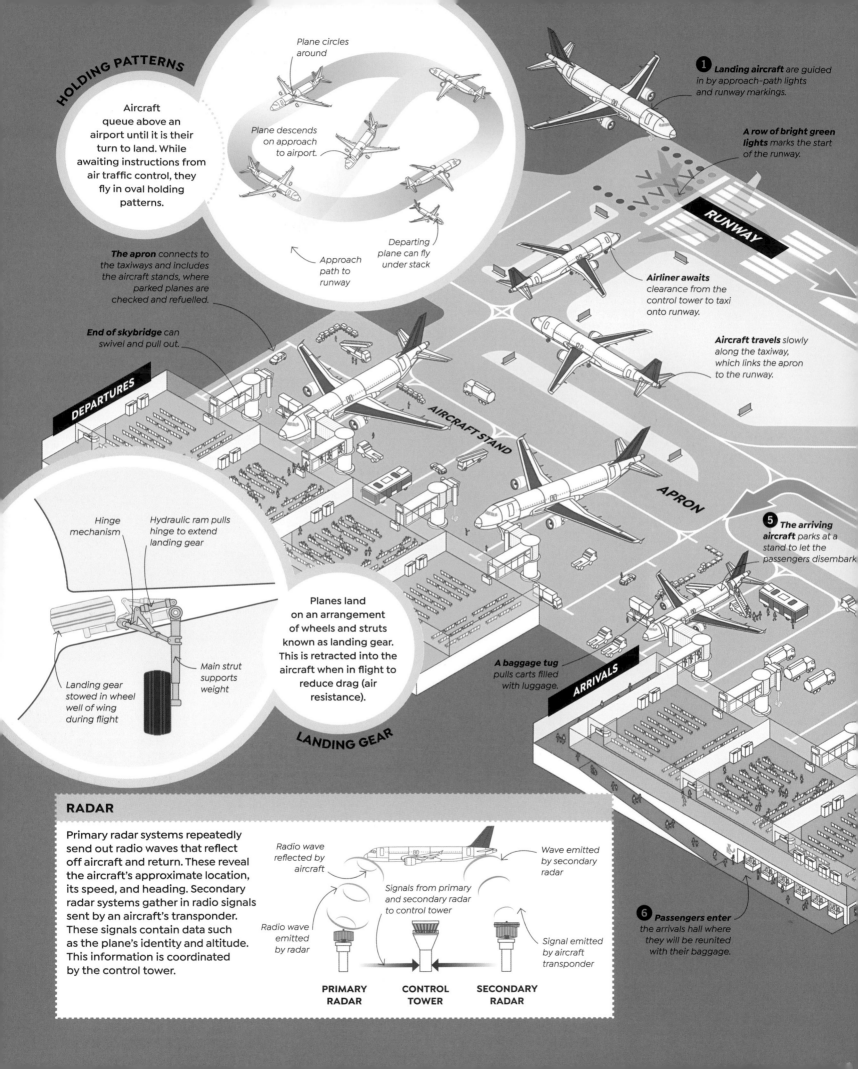

HOLDING PATTERNS

Aircraft queue above an airport until it is their turn to land. While awaiting instructions from air traffic control, they fly in oval holding patterns.

Plane circles around

Plane descends on approach to airport.

Departing plane can fly under stack

Approach path to runway

The apron connects to the taxiways and includes the aircraft stands, where parked planes are checked and refuelled.

End of skybridge can swivel and pull out.

DEPARTURES

1 **Landing aircraft** are guided in by approach-path lights and runway markings.

A row of bright green lights marks the start of the runway.

RUNWAY

Airliner awaits clearance from the control tower to taxi onto runway.

Aircraft travels slowly along the taxiway, which links the apron to the runway.

AIRCRAFT STAND

APRON

5 **The arriving aircraft** parks at a stand to let the passengers disembark.

A baggage tug pulls carts filled with luggage.

ARRIVALS

LANDING GEAR

Hinge mechanism

Hydraulic ram pulls hinge to extend landing gear

Main strut supports weight

Landing gear stowed in wheel well of wing during flight

Planes land on an arrangement of wheels and struts known as landing gear. This is retracted into the aircraft when in flight to reduce drag (air resistance).

6 **Passengers enter** the arrivals hall where they will be reunited with their baggage.

RADAR

Primary radar systems repeatedly send out radio waves that reflect off aircraft and return. These reveal the aircraft's approximate location, its speed, and heading. Secondary radar systems gather in radio signals sent by an aircraft's transponder. These signals contain data such as the plane's identity and altitude. This information is coordinated by the control tower.

Radio wave reflected by aircraft

Wave emitted by secondary radar

Signals from primary and secondary radar to control tower

Radio wave emitted by radar

Signal emitted by aircraft transponder

PRIMARY RADAR

CONTROL TOWER

SECONDARY RADAR

Airport runway

A busy airport's runways may see an aircraft take off or land every one or two minutes. With potentially thousands of aircraft movements a day, great coordination is required to keep air traffic moving efficiently and safely. Controllers organize an aircraft's movements in the air and on the ground from the apron to taxiways and runways. Other ground staff clean, refuel, load, and maintain an aircraft so it can quickly turn around and begin its next flight.

RUNWAY MARKINGS

A runway centre line, the runway's compass heading in degrees, and other markings provide visual aids for pilots during take-off and landing.

2 *Double lines* mark out touchdown zone where pilots aim their aircraft's wheels to land.

The shortest paved runway is just 400 m (¹/₄ mile) long

REFUELLING

Airliners usually refuel at the airport, with fuel for each journey held in tanks in the wings. Small planes, like military aircraft, may use tanker planes to refuel in mid-air.

3 *After touching down* the aircraft brakes hard and reverses thrust to decelerate.

Runway barriers indicate runway boundaries for pilots and crew.

Long-range radar can see aircraft at very high altitudes.

TAXIWAY

AIRCRAFT STAND

Tanker trucks carry thousands of litres of aviation fuel to planes preparing for take-off.

Controllers track aircraft and instruct pilots on the ground and in the air.

Large windows provide a clear view of the runways and surrounding skies.

CONTROL TOWER

The control tower houses the computer servers and approach control rooms, where the staff coordinate information about aircraft and weather forecasts.

CONTROL TOWER

Runway numbers show which way the runway points on the compass in degrees.

4 *After landing* an aircraft taxies off the runway towards the apron.

A chevron-patterned area at the end of the runway provides extra space should a plane abort take-off.

Aircraft

On a typical day, more than 100,000 flights are made by aircraft criss-crossing the globe. They vary in size from single-seater light aircraft to giant jet airliners capable of carrying 500 or more passengers long distances between continents. All aircraft rely on lift from their wings and thrust from their engines to take off from the ground and soar into the air.

Large wings provide the lift a heavy airliner needs to stay in the air.

The biggest passenger plane in the world, the Airbus A380, can carry up to 850 people

Business class features fewer seats per row and more legroom, meaning passengers enjoy more comfort.

Toilets use a vacuum to flush waste, which is stored in a tank at the rear of the aircraft.

Hinged panels are found on the rear of the wings, tailplane, and tail. They deflect the air flowing past them, changing the direction the plane is travelling.

Rudder turns plane side-to-side

Elevator makes nose point up or down

Ailerons bank aircraft left or right

STEERING

FUSELAGE

BUSINESS CLASS

FIRST CLASS

HOLD

COCKPIT

ENGINE

The flight deck is where the pilot and co-pilot control and fly the plane from.

Jet engines propel the aircraft at cruising speeds of up to 1,050 kph (652 mph).

Passengers' luggage, plus additional cargo and air mail, are stored in the hold.

First class passengers pay a premium to enjoy fine dining, more space, and large, reclining seats.

A sleeping area is provided on long-haul airliners for the plane's crew.

The nose wheel is stored in flight but can be lowered and rotated to steer the plane on the ground.

The world's fastest jet aircraft, the SR-71 Blackbird, can fly at over 3,500 kph (2,100 mph)

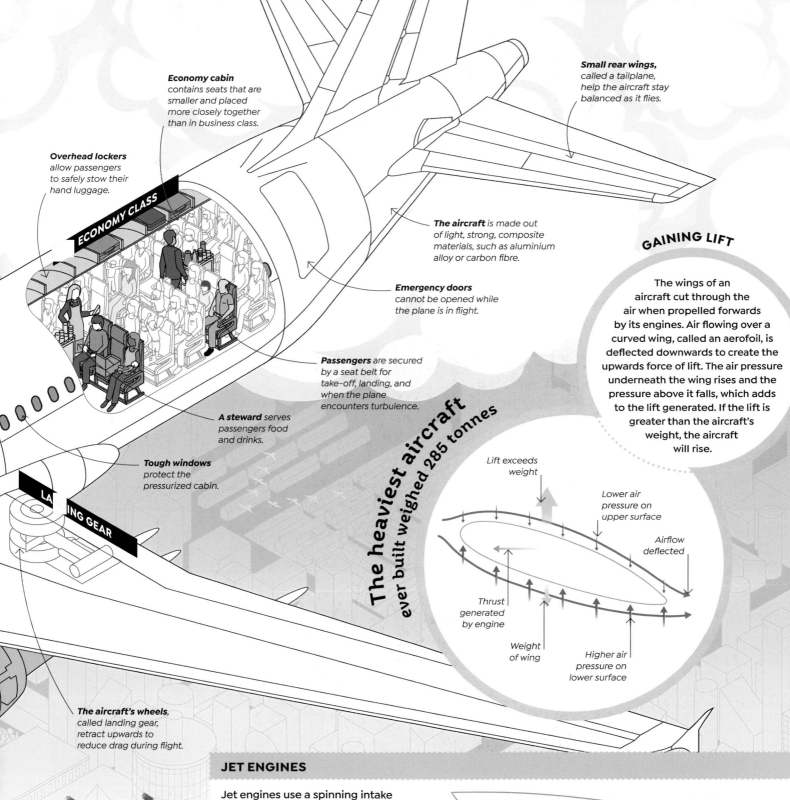

Economy cabin
contains seats that are smaller and placed more closely together than in business class.

Overhead lockers
allow passengers to safely stow their hand luggage.

ECONOMY CLASS

Small rear wings,
called a tailplane, help the aircraft stay balanced as it flies.

The aircraft is made out of light, strong, composite materials, such as aluminium alloy or carbon fibre.

Emergency doors
cannot be opened while the plane is in flight.

Passengers are secured by a seat belt for take-off, landing, and when the plane encounters turbulence.

A steward serves passengers food and drinks.

Tough windows
protect the pressurized cabin.

LANDING GEAR

The aircraft's wheels,
called landing gear, retract upwards to reduce drag during flight.

The heaviest aircraft ever built weighed 285 tonnes

GAINING LIFT

The wings of an aircraft cut through the air when propelled forwards by its engines. Air flowing over a curved wing, called an aerofoil, is deflected downwards to create the upwards force of lift. The air pressure underneath the wing rises and the pressure above it falls, which adds to the lift generated. If the lift is greater than the aircraft's weight, the aircraft will rise.

Lift exceeds weight

Lower air pressure on upper surface

Airflow deflected

Thrust generated by engine

Weight of wing

Higher air pressure on lower surface

JET ENGINES

Jet engines use a spinning intake fan to draw air into the engine. The air enters the combustion chamber, where it is mixed with fuel and burned, creating large amounts of hot gases. These gases expand rapidly out of the exhaust nozzle at the rear of the engine, through a turbine that keeps the intake fan spinning. The backward expulsion of gases causes an opposite reaction, thrusting the aircraft forwards at enough speed to create lift.

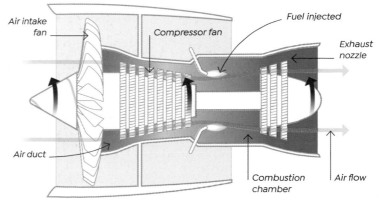

Air intake fan

Compressor fan

Fuel injected

Exhaust nozzle

Air duct

Combustion chamber

Air flow

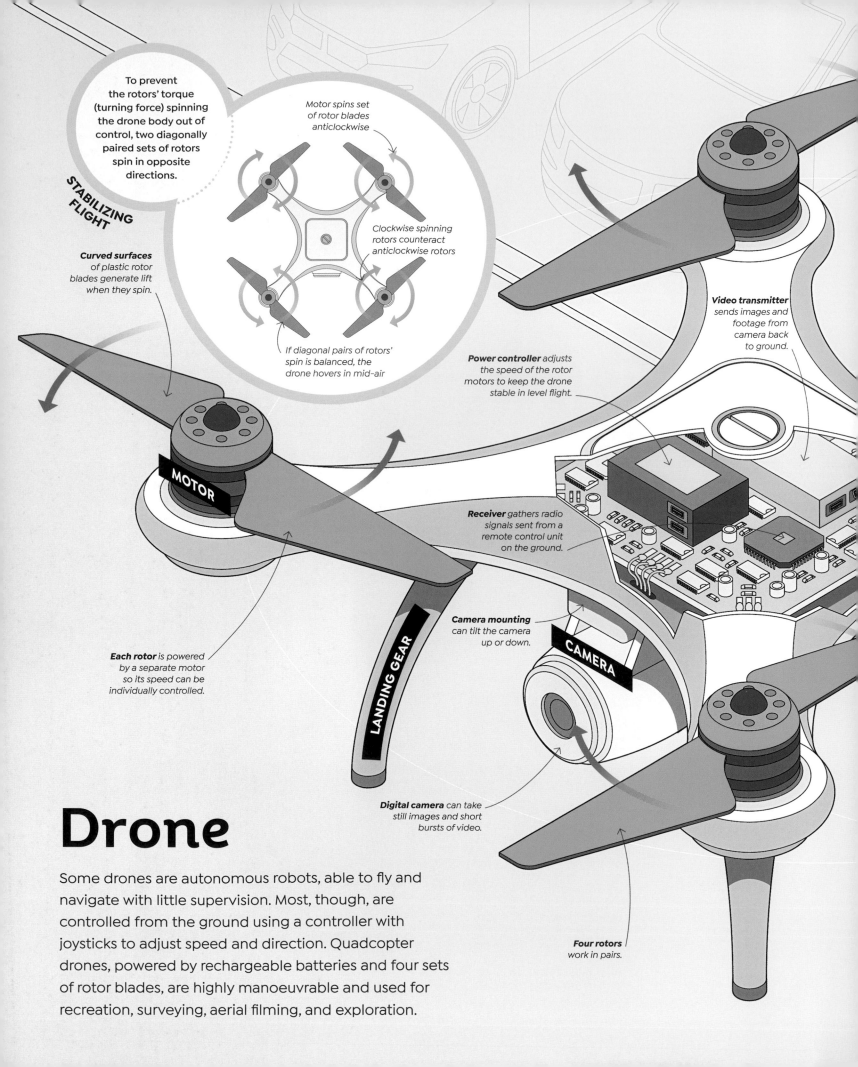

STABILIZING FLIGHT

To prevent the rotors' torque (turning force) spinning the drone body out of control, two diagonally paired sets of rotors spin in opposite directions.

Motor spins set of rotor blades anticlockwise

Clockwise spinning rotors counteract anticlockwise rotors

Curved surfaces of plastic rotor blades generate lift when they spin.

If diagonal pairs of rotors' spin is balanced, the drone hovers in mid-air

Power controller adjusts the speed of the rotor motors to keep the drone stable in level flight.

Video transmitter sends images and footage from camera back to ground.

Receiver gathers radio signals sent from a remote control unit on the ground.

MOTOR

LANDING GEAR

CAMERA

Camera mounting can tilt the camera up or down.

Each rotor is powered by a separate motor so its speed can be individually controlled.

Digital camera can take still images and short bursts of video.

Four rotors work in pairs.

Drone

Some drones are autonomous robots, able to fly and navigate with little supervision. Most, though, are controlled from the ground using a controller with joysticks to adjust speed and direction. Quadcopter drones, powered by rechargeable batteries and four sets of rotor blades, are highly manoeuvrable and used for recreation, surveying, aerial filming, and exploration.

MOVING FORWARDS

When the operator instructs the drone to move forwards, the front pair of rotors spin slightly more slowly, producing less thrust and tilting the front of the drone downwards. This angles all four of the quadcopter's rotors diagonally down and back, allowing them to produce both lift and forward thrust at the same time.

Lift generated by spinning rotor blades

Thrust propels drone forwards

Drag, or air resistance, slows drone down

Gravity pulls drone down to Earth

Slower rotor speed causes drone to dip

HOW HELICOPTERS FLY

Most helicopters have one set of main rotors that provide both lift and thrust. The angle of each blade can be altered by the pilot to steer left and right. The pilot can also tilt the swashplates (a pair of discs on the main rotor shaft), which alters the angle of all blades. Raising the rear of the swashplate upwards, for example, tilts the helicopter forwards.

Main rotor shaft spins, powered by engine

Rotor blade

Control rod moves rotor blade up or down

Swashplates separated by ball bearings

The fastest racing drone has a top speed of 262 kph (163 mph)

BLADE

Electric motor, inside housing, can vary the speed of the rotor's rotation to generate more or less lift.

Remote control contains a transmitter, which sends commands to the drone via radio waves.

Leg forms part of landing gear. Some drones land on long runners called skids.

AERIAL EXPLOITS

Drone light shows feature lightweight drones carrying bright LED lights. A computer program controls the choreography, so the lights and formations can be synchronized.

In 2019, a kidney was delivered by drone to a hospital for transplant

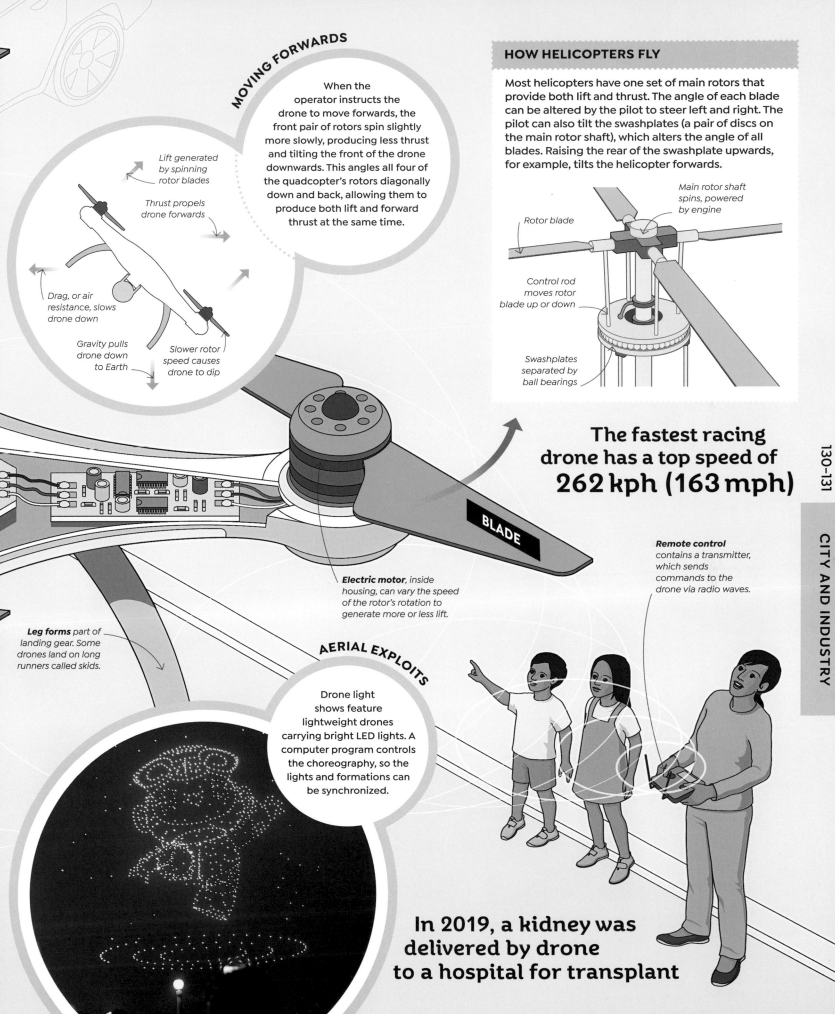

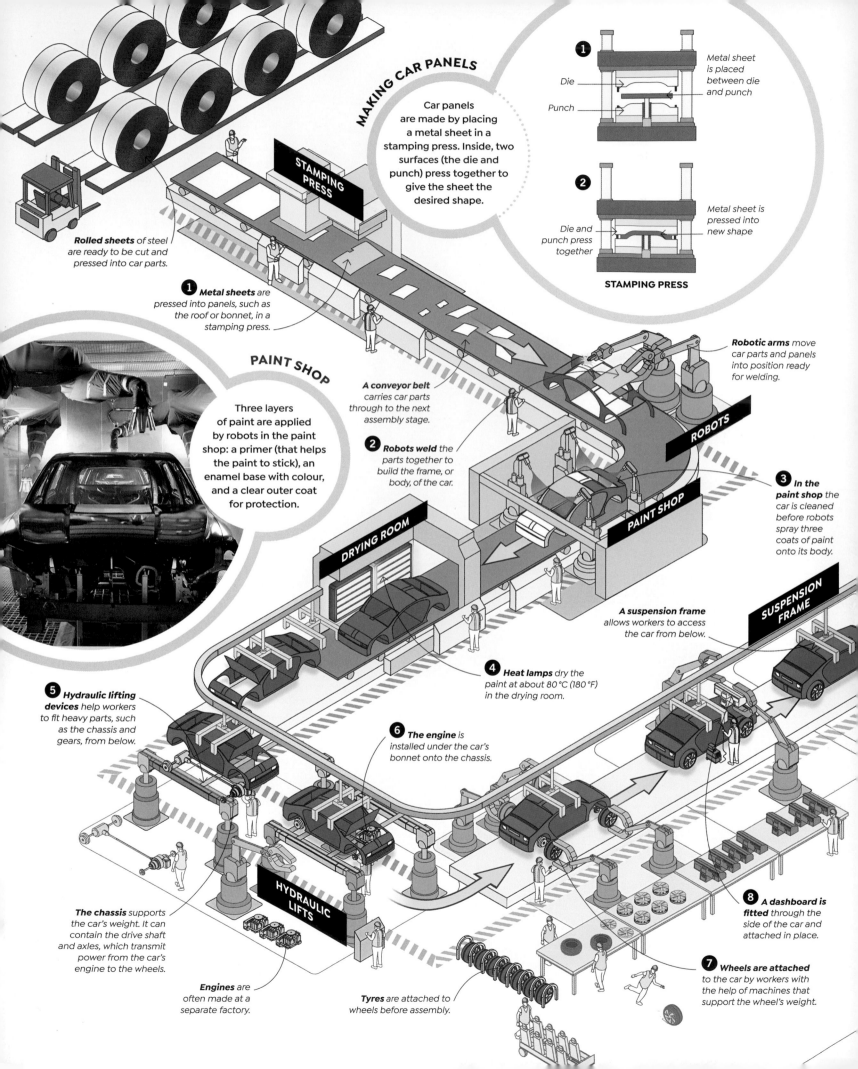

MAKING CAR PANELS

Car panels are made by placing a metal sheet in a stamping press. Inside, two surfaces (the die and punch) press together to give the sheet the desired shape.

1 Metal sheet is placed between die and punch

Die

Punch

2 Metal sheet is pressed into new shape

Die and punch press together

STAMPING PRESS

STAMPING PRESS

Rolled sheets of steel are ready to be cut and pressed into car parts.

1 *Metal sheets* are pressed into panels, such as the roof or bonnet, in a stamping press.

Robotic arms move car parts and panels into position ready for welding.

A conveyor belt carries car parts through to the next assembly stage.

2 *Robots weld* the parts together to build the frame, or body, of the car.

ROBOTS

PAINT SHOP

Three layers of paint are applied by robots in the paint shop: a primer (that helps the paint to stick), an enamel base with colour, and a clear outer coat for protection.

3 *In the paint shop* the car is cleaned before robots spray three coats of paint onto its body.

PAINT SHOP

DRYING ROOM

A suspension frame allows workers to access the car from below.

SUSPENSION FRAME

5 *Hydraulic lifting devices* help workers to fit heavy parts, such as the chassis and gears, from below.

6 *The engine* is installed under the car's bonnet onto the chassis.

4 *Heat lamps* dry the paint at about 80 °C (180 °F) in the drying room.

HYDRAULIC LIFTS

The chassis supports the car's weight. It can contain the drive shaft and axles, which transmit power from the car's engine to the wheels.

Engines are often made at a separate factory.

Tyres are attached to wheels before assembly.

8 *A dashboard is fitted* through the side of the car and attached in place.

7 *Wheels are attached* to the car by workers with the help of machines that support the wheel's weight.

Assembly line

Cars are complicated machines, made up of around 30,000 parts, ranging from tiny nuts and bolts to large components such as the windscreen. An assembly line is a quick and efficient way of putting these parts together, breaking down the building of the car into steps. Workers and robots work together to complete each step as the car moves along on a conveyor belt between assembly stages.

HYDRAULICS

Hydraulic tools allow heavy objects to be moved easily. Inside each tool is a fluid (usually oil) and two movable cylinders called pistons. Pushing the small piston down with a little force puts pressure on the fluid. Because the fluid used cannot be compressed, it creates a larger force to push the large piston up a short distance, lifting heavy loads with ease.

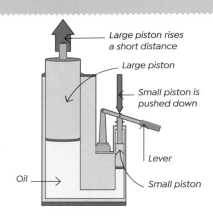

Large piston rises a short distance

Large piston

Small piston is pushed down

Lever

Oil

Small piston

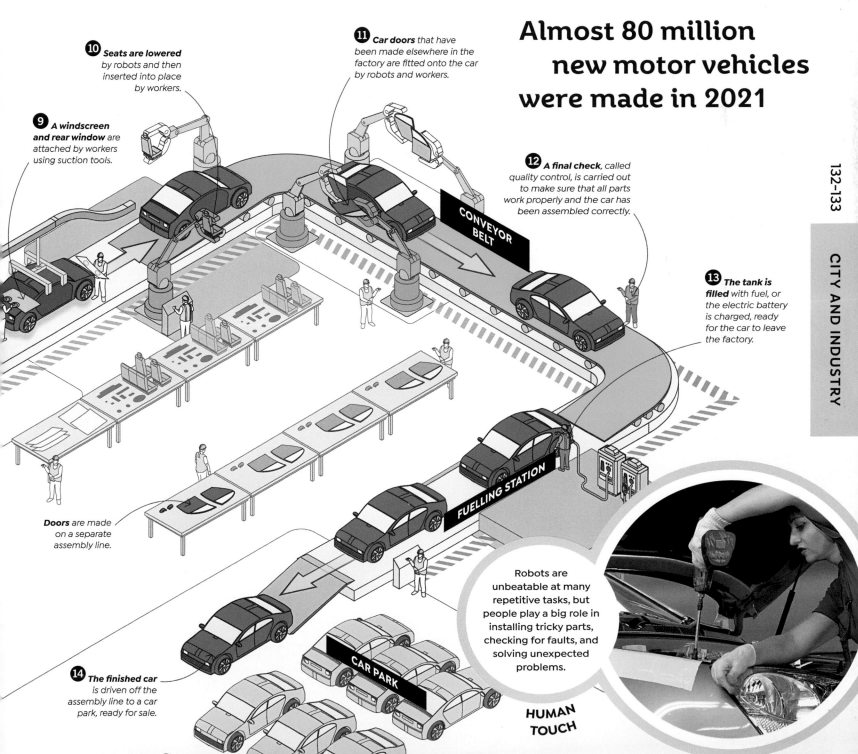

10 *Seats are lowered* by robots and then inserted into place by workers.

11 *Car doors* that have been made elsewhere in the factory are fitted onto the car by robots and workers.

9 *A windscreen and rear window* are attached by workers using suction tools.

Almost 80 million new motor vehicles were made in 2021

12 *A final check*, called quality control, is carried out to make sure that all parts work properly and the car has been assembled correctly.

CONVEYOR BELT

13 *The tank is filled* with fuel, or the electric battery is charged, ready for the car to leave the factory.

Doors are made on a separate assembly line.

FUELLING STATION

Robots are unbeatable at many repetitive tasks, but people play a big role in installing tricky parts, checking for faults, and solving unexpected problems.

CAR PARK

14 *The finished car* is driven off the assembly line to a car park, ready for sale.

HUMAN TOUCH

FULLY AUTOMATIC

Robots have speeded up manufacturing so much that a car can be made in an hour and a half. Most are used for repetitive tasks or heavy lifting because they are more precise, accurate, and faster than humans. They can perform a variety of tasks including welding and painting.

SIX-AXIS ROBOTIC ARM

Robotic arms are highly flexible. They can bend in many directions, making them ideal for fixing things in hard-to-reach places.

Axis 3
Axis 4
Axis 5
Axis 6
Interchangeable tool
Axis 1
Axis 2

Animal farming

The animals raised on farms, called livestock, are reared for meat and other products such as eggs, milk, and wool. Some smaller farms may keep a few different animals but most large farms specialize in one type of livestock, such as cattle, sheep, or poultry. Factors like the climate, landscape, and the amount of space available all affect this specialization.

Livestock may eat foods grown on the farm, such as grass or hay, but this food supply often needs to be topped up by manufactured animal feed. These feeds are usually supplied as concentrated pellets or blocks. Some are made from wheat and other grains with vitamins and other nutrients added.

ANIMAL FEEDS

Concentrated pellets

Corn and dried fruit

Grain and shredded hay

Hay is dried grass that is cut in summer and kept as food for cattle and sheep in winter.

Mucking out is cleaning dung from animal pens. The dung can be used to fertilize crops.

Toys may be provided to entertain the animals, and to reduce stress and conflict in the pen.

HAY BARN

Caged barn hens are kept inside, cannot walk or fly, and must poke their heads out of their cage to reach food.

Goat huts provide shelter and a sleeping place at night. The grassy pen has food and water troughs as well as objects for the goats to climb on.

CAGED HEN BARN

CAGE-FREE HENS

Laying hens produce an egg every day or so. The eggs roll onto a shelf ready for collection.

Chicken coops are little houses for outdoor hens. The hens are free to roam around.

GOAT PEN

A feed trough is a long, open container where many animals can eat together.

UNCAGED HEN BARN

A cow in Brazil called Marília produced 123 litres (27 gallons) of milk in 24 hours. That's enough to half-fill a bathtub!

Outside space lets hens scratch around for seeds to eat, like their wild relatives do.

Uncaged barn hens are able to move around inside the barn but they can never go outside.

Feeders hang from the ceiling so that the hens can peck at seeds.

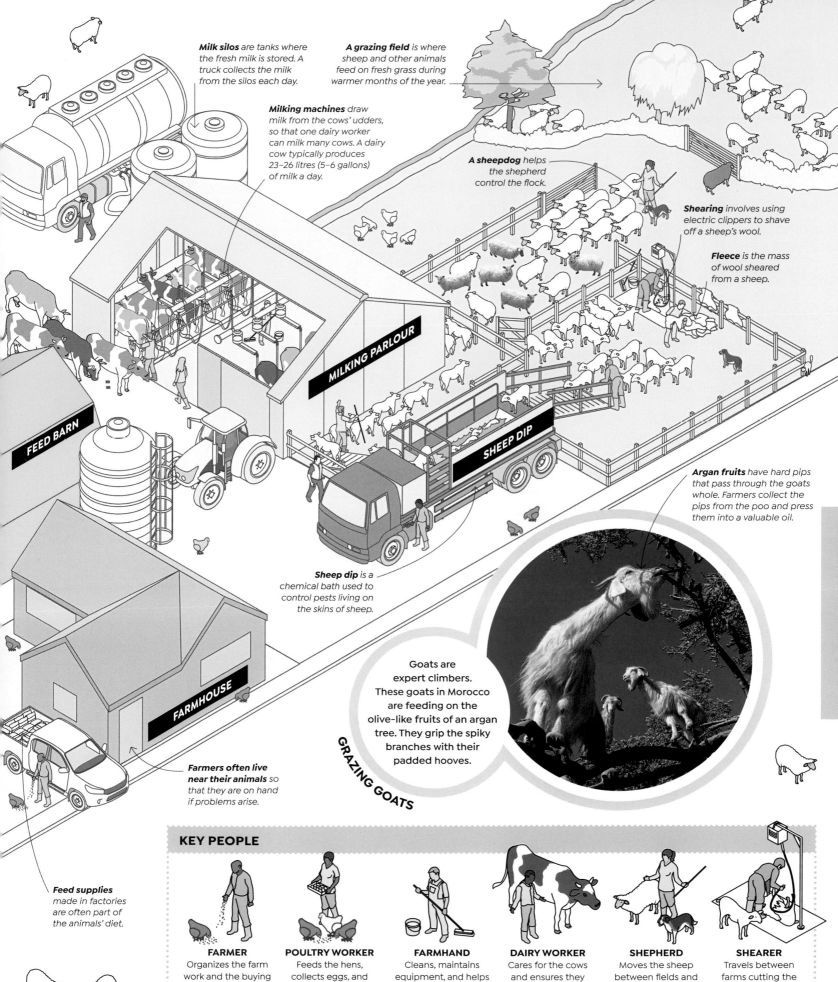

Milk silos are tanks where the fresh milk is stored. A truck collects the milk from the silos each day.

A grazing field is where sheep and other animals feed on fresh grass during warmer months of the year.

Milking machines draw milk from the cows' udders, so that one dairy worker can milk many cows. A dairy cow typically produces 23–26 litres (5–6 gallons) of milk a day.

A sheepdog helps the shepherd control the flock.

Shearing involves using electric clippers to shave off a sheep's wool.

Fleece is the mass of wool sheared from a sheep.

MILKING PARLOUR

FEED BARN

SHEEP DIP

Argan fruits have hard pips that pass through the goats whole. Farmers collect the pips from the poo and press them into a valuable oil.

Sheep dip is a chemical bath used to control pests living on the skins of sheep.

FARMHOUSE

Goats are expert climbers. These goats in Morocco are feeding on the olive-like fruits of an argan tree. They grip the spiky branches with their padded hooves.

GRAZING GOATS

Farmers often live near their animals so that they are on hand if problems arise.

Feed supplies made in factories are often part of the animals' diet.

KEY PEOPLE

FARMER
Organizes the farm work and the buying and selling of animals.

POULTRY WORKER
Feeds the hens, collects eggs, and cleans the coops.

FARMHAND
Cleans, maintains equipment, and helps the other farm workers.

DAIRY WORKER
Cares for the cows and ensures they are milked daily.

SHEPHERD
Moves the sheep between fields and checks their health.

SHEARER
Travels between farms cutting the wool from sheep.

Growing crops

Crop farming was invented at least 10,000 years ago as an alternative to collecting food plants from the wild. Instead, food plants, or crops, were grown in one place to maximize the amount being produced and to make it easier to harvest. Modern crop farming does the same thing but it is aided by a range of inventions and technologies.

RICE TERRACES

Rice is grown in flooded fields, called paddy fields, which help the young plants grow and prevent weeds. Earthen walled terraces are used on sloping fields.

KEY CROPS

Four of the world's major crops are grasses. Of these, maize (corn), rice, and wheat are grown for their seeds, which can be eaten whole or ground into flour.

Sugar cane stems are used for sugar and maize can also be made into corn syrup. The fifth largest crop, potato, is a tuber and a staple of many people's diets.

SUGAR CANE (1.9 billion metric tonnes)	MAIZE (1.1 billion metric tonnes)	RICE (782 million metric tonnes)	WHEAT (734 million metric tonnes)	POTATO (368 million metric tonnes)

4 *Fertilizers* containing chemicals, or natural fertilizers such as manure, are spread over the fields to help the crops grow.

Growing the same crop year after year on the same soil is called monocropping. It depletes the nutrients in the soil, which means more fertilizer needs to be used. Rotating crops keeps the soil healthy.

CROP CYCLE

Farmers grow crops according to a cycle of steps. This starts with preparing the ground and planting seeds, and ends with harvesting.

3 *Water sprinklers* provide young, sprouting crops with extra water, especially when there is little rainfall. This is called irrigation.

2 *A seed drill* places seeds into the furrows at a fixed distance apart. It then pushes the soil over the top, burying the seeds.

1 *A plough* breaks the top layer of soil, ready for planting. Disc ploughs are particularly good at preparing new, stony fields.

FERTILIZING

IRRIGATION

SPRINKLER

SEED DRILL

DISC PLOUGH

LAND PREPARATION

SOWING SEEDS

Tractors often use GPS and may have touchscreens for the farmer to monitor the equipment. In the future, some may even become driverless.

Birds may get to the seeds before they can sprout. To scare them away, farmers use scarecrows, recordings of bird distress calls, or devices that make loud noises.

5 **Liquid pesticides**, either chemical or organic pesticides made from plants and minerals, are sprayed over the crops to stop pests such as beetles and flies eating them.

Drones carrying pesticides can be used to spray crops in areas that are hard to reach.

Grains are collected in a tractor trailer, which is pulled alongside the combine harvester.

The stalks, or straw, are cut up and dropped behind the vehicle to be collected later.

6 **A combine harvester** cuts the crop, known as reaping, and then scrapes the grains from the stalks with spiked wheels in a process called threshing.

Only 7 per cent of Earth's land is used to grow crops

A header cuts the crops and pulls them into the combine harvester.

TRAILER

COMBINE HARVESTER

CROP SPRAYER

MUCK SPREADER

HARVEST

PEST CONTROL

The chemicals in pesticides are designed to kill insects and then break down into harmless substances. When they don't break down properly, pesticide residues can damage the environment.

Birds can help to control pests naturally by eating insects.

A muck spreader releases animal dung or other organic matter from the back of a trailer as it moves.

Good farming soil will have a good balance of clay, silt, and sand that will hold some water but also drain it away. This stops the soil becoming waterlogged and drowning the crop roots.

Sprinklers can be switched on and off manually, with automatic timers, or remotely via apps. They pump water from the mains water supply, nearby rivers, or underground water stores.

SILO STORAGE

After harvesting, grains are kept safe and dry in storage silos, which keep out pests, such as rodents and insects. The natural moisture must be removed from the crop to prevent mould from taking hold. Silos have fans and ventilation that keep air moving through the crop to dry it out.

Ventilation reduces condensation inside silo

Crop at top of silo is last to dry

Air moves through silo, drying crop

Air circulates around crop

Fans circulate air

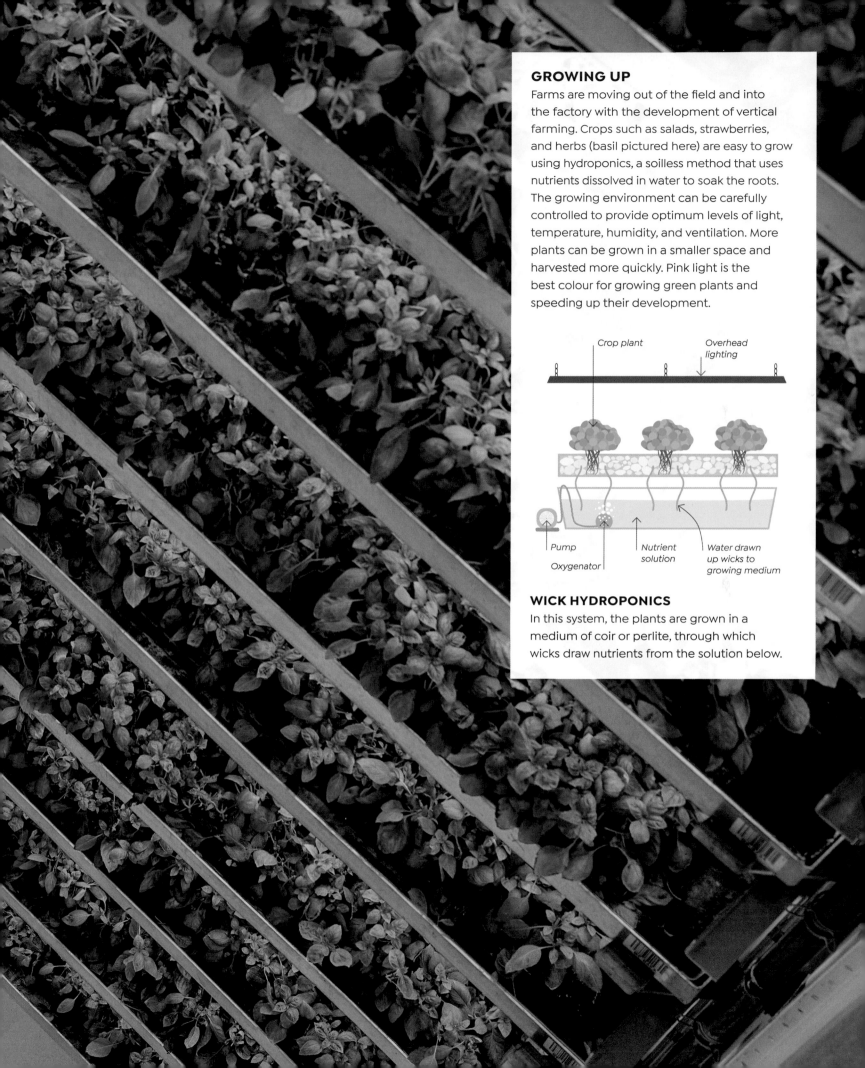

GROWING UP

Farms are moving out of the field and into the factory with the development of vertical farming. Crops such as salads, strawberries, and herbs (basil pictured here) are easy to grow using hydroponics, a soilless method that uses nutrients dissolved in water to soak the roots. The growing environment can be carefully controlled to provide optimum levels of light, temperature, humidity, and ventilation. More plants can be grown in a smaller space and harvested more quickly. Pink light is the best colour for growing green plants and speeding up their development.

Crop plant

Overhead lighting

Pump

Oxygenator

Nutrient solution

Water drawn up wicks to growing medium

WICK HYDROPONICS

In this system, the plants are grown in a medium of coir or perlite, through which wicks draw nutrients from the solution below.

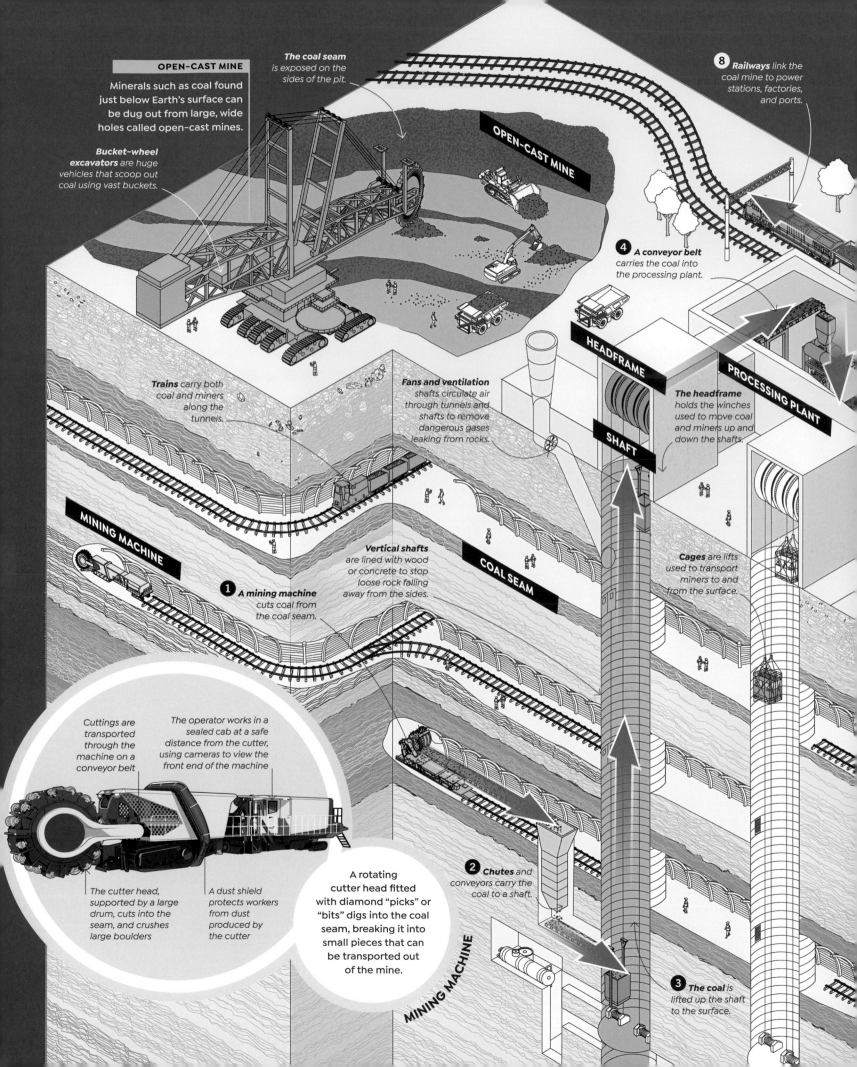

OPEN-CAST MINE

Minerals such as coal found just below Earth's surface can be dug out from large, wide holes called open-cast mines.

The coal seam is exposed on the sides of the pit.

Bucket-wheel excavators are huge vehicles that scoop out coal using vast buckets.

OPEN-CAST MINE

8 *Railways* link the coal mine to power stations, factories, and ports.

4 *A conveyor belt* carries the coal into the processing plant.

HEADFRAME

PROCESSING PLANT

Trains carry both coal and miners along the tunnels.

Fans and ventilation shafts circulate air through tunnels and shafts to remove dangerous gases leaking from rocks.

The headframe holds the winches used to move coal and miners up and down the shafts.

SHAFT

MINING MACHINE

Vertical shafts are lined with wood or concrete to stop loose rock falling away from the sides.

COAL SEAM

1 *A mining machine* cuts coal from the coal seam.

Cages are lifts used to transport miners to and from the surface.

Cuttings are transported through the machine on a conveyor belt

The operator works in a sealed cab at a safe distance from the cutter, using cameras to view the front end of the machine

The cutter head, supported by a large drum, cuts into the seam, and crushes large boulders

A dust shield protects workers from dust produced by the cutter

A rotating cutter head fitted with diamond "picks" or "bits" digs into the coal seam, breaking it into small pieces that can be transported out of the mine.

2 *Chutes* and conveyors carry the coal to a shaft.

MINING MACHINE

3 *The coal* is lifted up the shaft to the surface.

Mine

Many of the raw materials used in industry – such as coal, metals, clays, and sand – are located deep underground. To dig them out, a complex network of shafts and tunnels called an underground mine has to be constructed. If the materials are not deeply buried, they can simply be dug up from the surface, often using enormous machines.

5 *A crusher* breaks the coal into smaller pieces that will pack closely together.

6 *Screening and washing machines* sort the coal into similar-sized pieces and remove grit and dust.

7 *Processed coal* is loaded onto specialized carriages called hoppers.

A rechargeable light mounted on a hard hat provides working light.

A mask and goggles protect the miner's lungs and eyes from dust and chemicals.

Reflective clothing makes the miner visible to other workers operating machines and vehicles.

Coal-carrying hoppers are loaded from the top but unloaded through doors underneath.

PROCESSING PLANT

The mined material, in this case coal, is filtered, washed, and dried out to remove unwanted substances that will stop the fuel from burning well.

Narrow railways connect the coal faces to the vertical shafts.

Unwanted rock and earth above and between coal seams is called overburden.

COAL SEAM

Coal exists in seams sandwiched between unwanted rocks. Miners dig down to a seam to extract as much coal as they can from it.

PROTECTIVE EQUIPMENT

Miners wear tough clothing, including helmets with powerful lights. They also carry gas detectors that pick up poisonous or flammable gases.

ROOF SUPPORTS

A tunnel collapse that blocks the way to the surface is one of the biggest risks in mining. A tunnel's roof is reinforced with steel arches and beams.

The world's deepest mine extends to almost 4 km (2.5 miles) below ground

RIP IT UP

Surface, or strip, mining is a large-scale process that needs equipment to match. This huge bucket excavator is used to mine coal. Fully extended, the excavator stretches to nearly 230 m (755 ft) in length and 96 m (315 ft) tall. It can excavate nearly a quarter of a million cubic metres (approx. 8.5 million cu ft) of coal per day with its enormous buckets. As the wheel rotates it tips the contents of the buckets onto a conveyor, which dumps it onto another external conveyor or into a truck. The biggest excavators run day and night, and are the largest vehicles ever built.

= 1,000 dump truck loads

BIG LOAD

The quantity excavated by the digger can fill the equivalent of 10,000 dump trucks, each holding 24 cubic metres (850 cu ft).

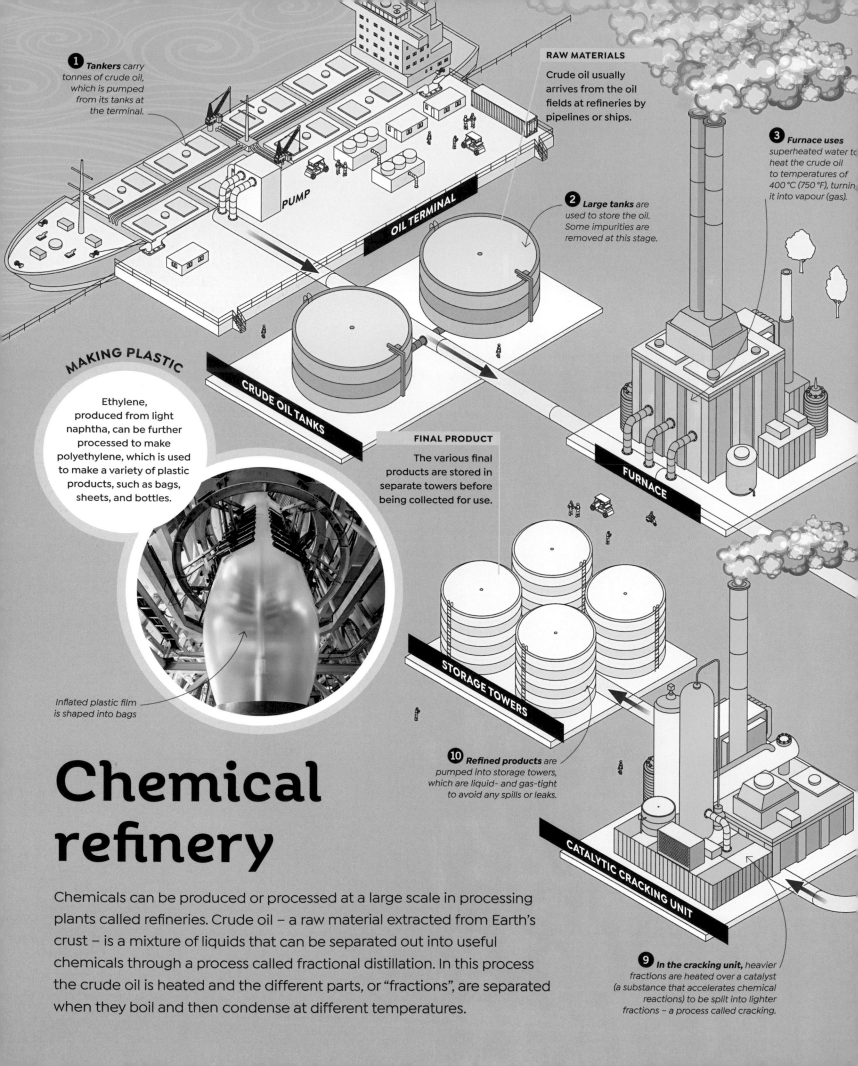

1 *Tankers* carry tonnes of crude oil, which is pumped from its tanks at the terminal.

RAW MATERIALS

Crude oil usually arrives from the oil fields at refineries by pipelines or ships.

3 *Furnace uses* superheated water to heat the crude oil to temperatures of 400 °C (750 °F), turning it into vapour (gas).

PUMP

OIL TERMINAL

2 *Large tanks* are used to store the oil. Some impurities are removed at this stage.

MAKING PLASTIC

Ethylene, produced from light naphtha, can be further processed to make polyethylene, which is used to make a variety of plastic products, such as bags, sheets, and bottles.

CRUDE OIL TANKS

FINAL PRODUCT

The various final products are stored in separate towers before being collected for use.

FURNACE

Inflated plastic film is shaped into bags

STORAGE TOWERS

10 *Refined products* are pumped into storage towers, which are liquid- and gas-tight to avoid any spills or leaks.

Chemical refinery

Chemicals can be produced or processed at a large scale in processing plants called refineries. Crude oil – a raw material extracted from Earth's crust – is a mixture of liquids that can be separated out into useful chemicals through a process called fractional distillation. In this process the crude oil is heated and the different parts, or "fractions", are separated when they boil and then condense at different temperatures.

CATALYTIC CRACKING UNIT

9 *In the cracking unit,* heavier fractions are heated over a catalyst (a substance that accelerates chemical reactions) to be split into lighter fractions – a process called cracking.

TREATING OIL SPILLS

Accidental oil spills damage the environment. These spills can be cleaned up by burning the oil at the site of the spill, skimming the oil on the surface with long floating barriers called booms, or by chemical treatments.

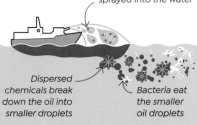

Chemicals are sprayed into the water

Dispersed chemicals break down the oil into smaller droplets

Bacteria eat the smaller oil droplets

CHEMICAL TREATMENT

Gases, including propane and butane, do not condense. They are processed into bottled gases and used for heating and cooking.

Light naphtha is used to produce ethylene, which is then used to make plastics.

LIGHT NAPHTHA

PETROL

Straight-run petrol is not processed further and makes up almost half of the refined crude oil.

HEAVY NAPHTHA

Heavy naphtha is usually processed further by cracking to produce petrol.

Downcomer pipes carry excess liquid down.

5 At a certain height and temperature, a fraction condenses into liquid. The lighter oils have the lowest boiling point, boil quickest, and rise highest in the column.

KEROSENE

Kerosene can be used to fuel lamps and heaters or further refined to produce jet fuel.

4 Pipeline feeds the heated oil vapour from the furnace to the distillation tower.

A distillation tower is a high column divided into levels, each with a tray to collect a different fraction.

DIESEL

Diesel is used to fuel generators, which in turn produce electricity, and vehicle engines.

DISTILLATION

Once boiled, different chemicals are produced by evaporating the oil and condensing the gases in the distillation tower.

6 A flare burns excess gases that cannot be recovered or recycled by pollution control devices.

GAS OIL

Gas oil condenses at this level. It includes oil lubricants and heavy fuel oils that are used in power stations and ship engines.

RESIDUE

Residue, or oil that does not boil, is collected in the bottom tray and used to make asphalt – a substance used to make roads.

8 Heavier fractions have higher boiling points and are sent to the catalytic cracking unit to be "cracked" into lighter and more useful products.

DISTILLATION TOWER

FLARE

7 Heavier fractions cool quickly and turn into liquid, which is collected at the bottom of the column.

Remaining vapour passes through the slot and continues to rise up

Riser directs the flow of vapour

CAP

Slot

TRAY

VAPOUR

Tray collects condensed liquid

Trays at different levels of the distillation tower collect the condensed liquid. Each tray has holes fitted with floating caps. These caps allow the vapour to pass through but keep the liquid from flowing back down.

BUBBLE CAP TRAY

Steelworks

A mixture of iron and carbon, steel is used to make a variety of products – from nuts and bolts to bridges and skyscrapers. It can be produced in two main ways – in a basic oxygen converter that makes steel from iron, or in an electric arc furnace that recycles scrap steel.

PROCESSING INGREDIENTS

The materials necessary for steelmaking are coke, sinter, and limestone. They are processed in separate plants.

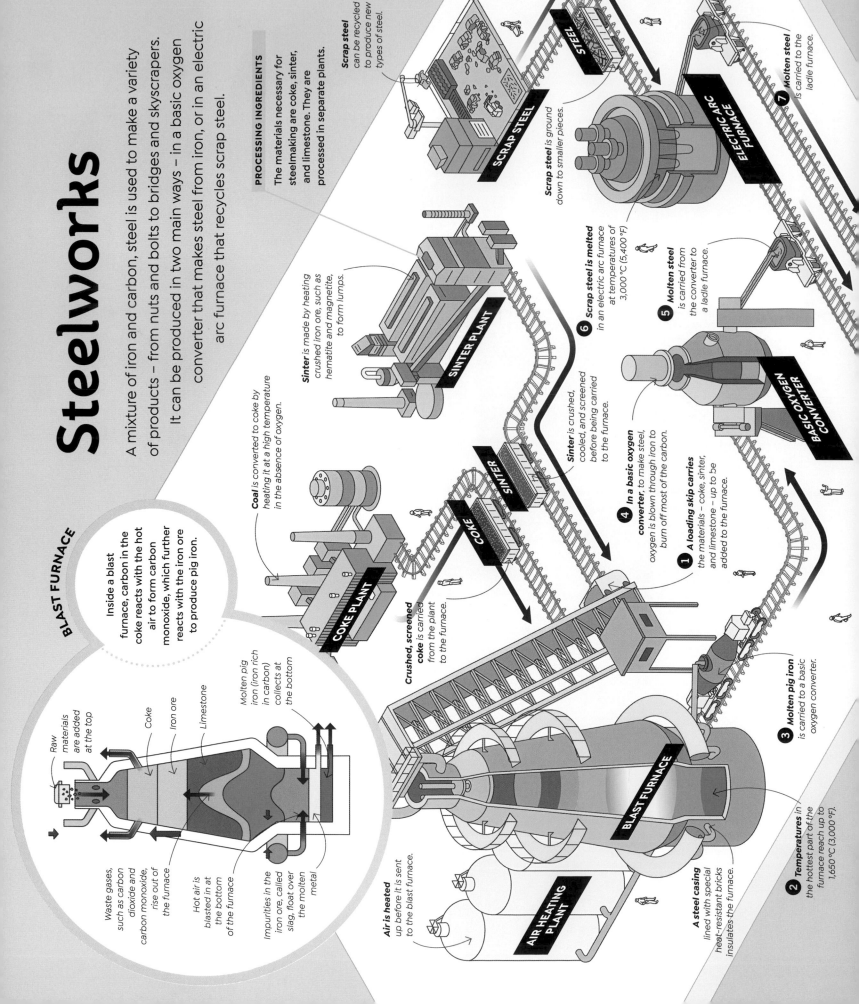

BLAST FURNACE

Inside a blast furnace, carbon in the coke reacts with the hot air to form carbon monoxide, which further reacts with the iron ore to produce pig iron.

Raw materials are added at the top

Coke

Iron ore

Limestone

Molten pig iron (iron rich in carbon) collects at the bottom

Waste gases, such as carbon dioxide and carbon monoxide, rise out of the furnace

Hot air is blasted in at the bottom of the furnace

Impurities in the iron ore, called slag, float over the molten metal

Coal is converted to coke by heating it at a high temperature in the absence of oxygen.

Sinter is made by heating crushed iron ore, such as hematite and magnetite, to form lumps.

Sinter is crushed, cooled, and screened before being carried to the furnace.

Crushed, screened coke is carried from the plant to the furnace.

Scrap steel can be recycled to produce new types of steel.

Scrap steel is ground down to smaller pieces.

7 Molten steel is carried to the ladle furnace.

6 Scrap steel is melted in an electric arc furnace at temperatures of 3,000°C (5,400°F).

5 Molten steel is carried from the converter to a ladle furnace.

4 In a basic oxygen converter, to make steel, oxygen is blown through iron to burn off most of the carbon.

1 A loading skip carries the materials – coke, sinter, and limestone – up to be added to the furnace.

3 Molten pig iron is carried to a basic oxygen converter.

2 Temperatures in the hottest part of the furnace reach up to 1,650°C (3,000°F).

A steel casing lined with special heat-resistant bricks insulates the furnace.

Air is heated up before it is sent to the blast furnace.

STEEL

SCRAP STEEL

ELECTRIC ARC FURNACE

SINTER PLANT

COKE PLANT

COKE

SINTER

BASIC OXYGEN CONVERTER

BLAST FURNACE

AIR HEATING PLANT

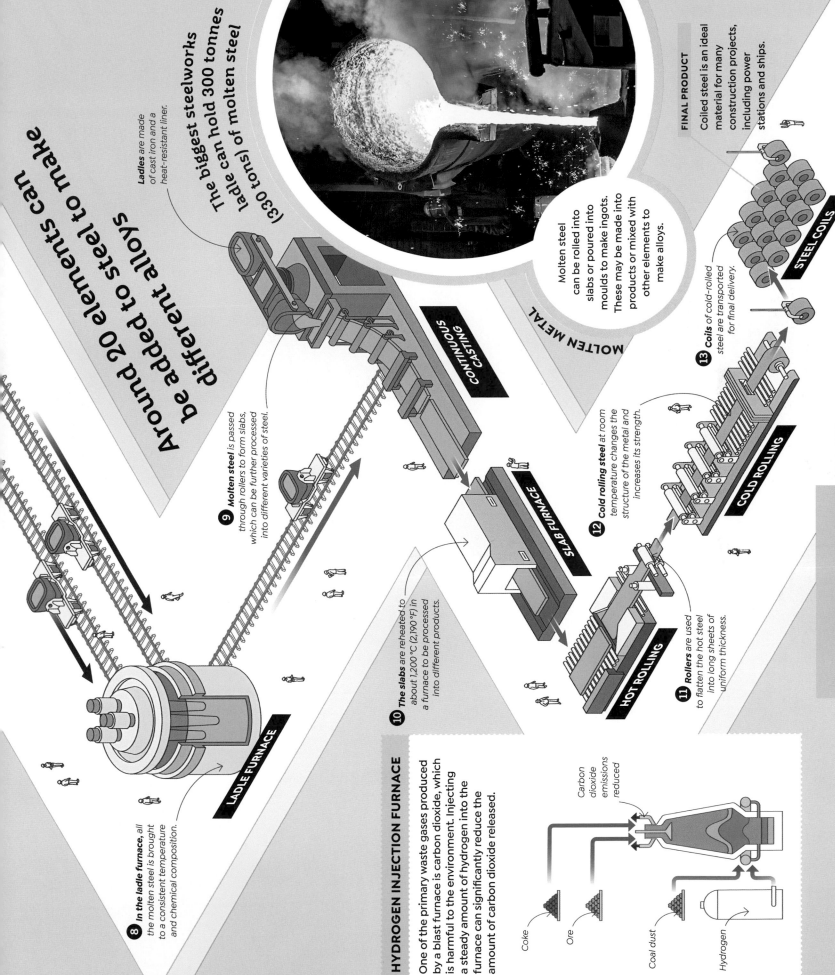

Around 20 elements can be added to steel to make different alloys

Ladles are made of cast iron and a heat-resistant liner.

The biggest steelworks ladle can hold 300 tonnes (330 tons) of molten steel

8 In the ladle furnace, all the molten steel is brought to a consistent temperature and chemical composition.

LADLE FURNACE

9 Molten steel is passed through rollers to form slabs, which can be further processed into different varieties of steel.

CONTINUOUS CASTING

Molten steel can be rolled into slabs or poured into moulds to make ingots. These may be made into products or mixed with other elements to make alloys.

MOLTEN METAL

10 The slabs are reheated to about 1,200 °C (2,190 °F) in a furnace to be processed into different products.

SLAB FURNACE

11 Rollers are used to flatten the hot steel into long sheets of uniform thickness.

HOT ROLLING

12 Cold rolling steel at room temperature changes the structure of the metal and increases its strength.

COLD ROLLING

13 Coils of cold-rolled steel are transported for final delivery.

STEEL COILS

FINAL PRODUCT
Coiled steel is an ideal material for many construction projects, including power stations and ships.

HYDROGEN INJECTION FURNACE

One of the primary waste gases produced by a blast furnace is carbon dioxide, which is harmful to the environment. Injecting a steady amount of hydrogen into the furnace can significantly reduce the amount of carbon dioxide released.

Coke

Ore

Coal dust

Hydrogen

Carbon dioxide emissions reduced

HOT METAL

There are many different types of steel. Its main constituent is iron, but other metals can be added to give the steel particular properties, such as strength, flexibility, and resistance to corrosion. Such mixtures are called alloys. Carbon steel contains small amounts of carbon and is extremely strong, but corrodes over time. Alloy steel contains nickel, copper, and aluminium and corrodes less. Tool steel is durable and heat resistant from the addition of tungsten and cobalt. Chromium in stainless steel makes it shiny and corrosion-free.

Kitchen utensils →
← Surgical equipment

STAINLESS STEEL

Construction ↓
Ship building ↓

ALLOY STEEL

Breaking and driving tools →
← Cutting equipment

TOOL STEEL

Fencing →

CARBON STEEL

FUNCTIONS OF STEEL

The uses of steel are widespread, ranging from corrosion-free kitchen equipment and tools to strong structural girders and reinforcing rods.

Oil well

Petroleum, or crude oil, is a naturally occurring liquid that is found in underground reservoirs. The oil can be refined to make many useful substances, such as fuels, and so it is extracted through a well that is drilled down to the reservoir. Oil wells can be drilled from land or from platforms above the seabed.

A tower, called the derrick, holds the well pipe and other equipment.

A helicopter is one of the best ways to get to an oil platform.

A helipad provides a safe landing spot for helicopters.

Used drilling mud is circulated back up to be cleaned and re-used.

MUD STORAGE

Drilling mud is pumped down to the drill.

A hook holds up the drillstring, which is lifted up and down by a winch.

Supports help the platform withstand gales and massive waves.

DERRICK TOWER

A crane loads cargo on and off supply ships.

CRANE

The buildings on the platform contain offices, sleeping quarters, and machinery.

Sleeping quarters are provided, as workers live on the platform for several weeks at a time.

Self-launching lifeboats drop from the deck into the sea.

LIFEBOATS

Oil is flammable and can cause serious fires and explosions around the oil well. In the event of an emergency, the crew can escape into the sea using lifeboats.

Some lifeboats can safely drop 60m (200ft) in order to launch.

EMERGENCIES

A gas flare will burn away the flammable gases that rise up the well with the oil.

GAS FLARE

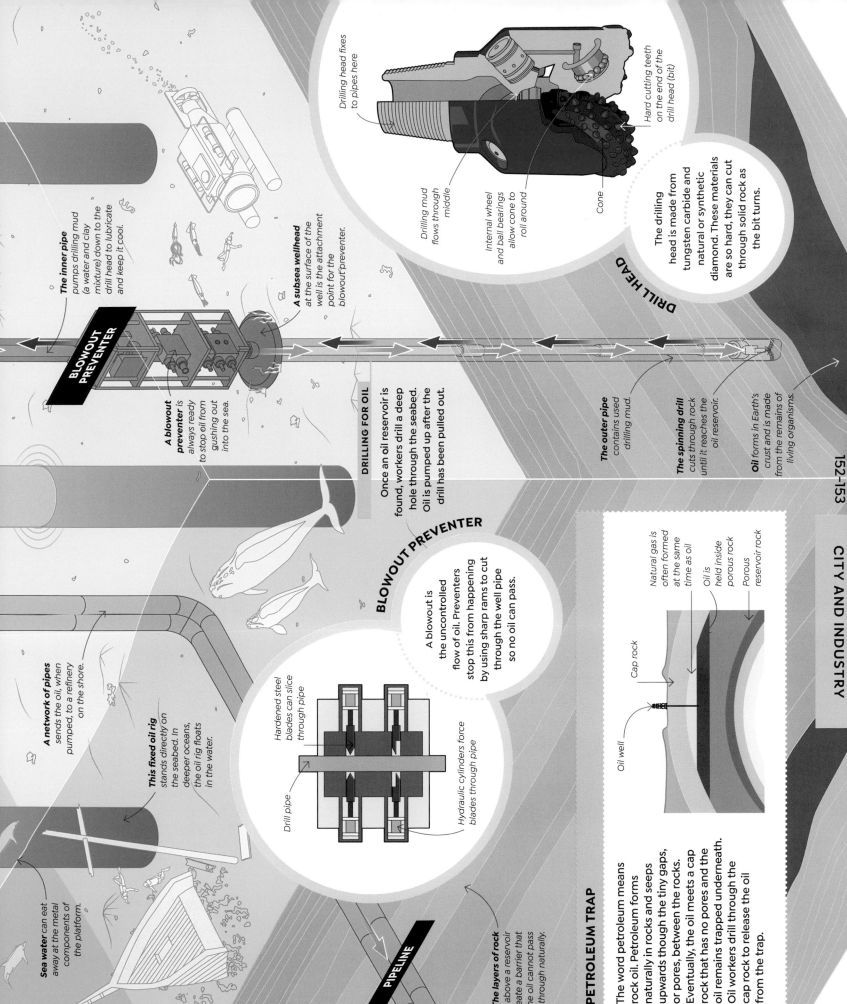

DRILL HEAD

Drilling head fixes to pipes here

Hard cutting teeth on the end of the drill head (bit)

Drilling mud flows though middle

Internal wheel and ball bearings allow cone to roll around

Cone

The drilling head is made from tungsten carbide and natural or synthetic diamond. These materials are so hard, they can cut through solid rock as the bit turns.

The inner pipe pumps drilling mud (a water and clay mixture) down to the drill head to lubricate and keep it cool.

A subsea wellhead at the surface of the well is the attachment point for the blowout preventer.

BLOWOUT PREVENTER

A blowout preventer is always ready to stop oil from gushing out into the sea.

DRILLING FOR OIL

Once an oil reservoir is found, workers drill a deep hole through the seabed. Oil is pumped up after the drill has been pulled out.

The outer pipe contains used drilling mud.

The spinning drill cuts through rock until it reaches the oil reservoir.

Oil forms in Earth's crust and is made from the remains of living organisms.

BLOWOUT PREVENTER

A blowout is the uncontrolled flow of oil. Preventers stop this from happening by using sharp rams to cut through the well pipe so no oil can pass.

Hardened steel blades can slice through pipe

Drill pipe

Hydraulic cylinders force blades through pipe

A network of pipes sends the oil, when pumped, to a refinery on the shore.

This fixed oil rig stands directly on the seabed. In deeper oceans, the oil rig floats in the water.

Sea water can eat away at the metal components of the platform.

The layers of rock above a reservoir create a barrier that the oil cannot pass through naturally.

PIPELINE

PETROLEUM TRAP

Natural gas is often formed at the same time as oil

Cap rock

Oil well

Oil is held inside porous rock

Porous reservoir rock

The word petroleum means rock oil. Petroleum forms naturally in rocks and seeps upwards though the tiny gaps, or pores, between the rocks. Eventually, the oil meets a cap rock that has no pores and the oil remains trapped underneath. Oil workers drill through the cap rock to release the oil from the trap.

GEOTHERMAL POWER STATION

This power plant generates electricity using the heat from volcanic activity deep underground. At the surface there is a turbine and generator as in any power station but instead of a furnace and boiler, water is heated by pumping it into an area of hot rocks and then bringing it back to the surface as high-pressure steam.

Steam turns turbine

Flash tank converts water to steam

Water cooled in cooling tower

Hot water pumped from underground

Cool water pumped back to reservoir

Underground reservoir in area of hot rocks

Generator

STACK

PYLONS

The precipitator electrifies gases released by the furnace and pulls out particles of soot using a strong electric field.

PRECIPITATOR

⑤ High-pressure steam pushes on the turbine, making it spin around.

A steam drum keeps steam and liquid water separate from each other.

BOILER

SCRUBBER

The scrubber washes out polluting chemicals, such as sulphur dioxide, in the gas and smoke from the furnace.

The smokestack is often very tall so that it releases smoke into fast-flowing wind high above ground level.

① A tall bunker contains the coal, which enters at the top and exits through a chute below.

WATER TANK

④ Water passing through pipes is heated by the burning coal and becomes a stream of superheated steam.

COAL CONVEYOR

CRUSHER

③ Coal is burned and releases its heat. Smoke and gases are diverted to be cleaned.

② The crusher, or pulverizing mill, turns the coal into a fine powder so that it burns faster and hotter.

COAL STORAGE

BURNING FOSSIL FUELS

To generate electricity, most thermal power plants burn fossil fuels, such as coal, natural gas, and oil. This releases harmful carbon dioxide into the environment.

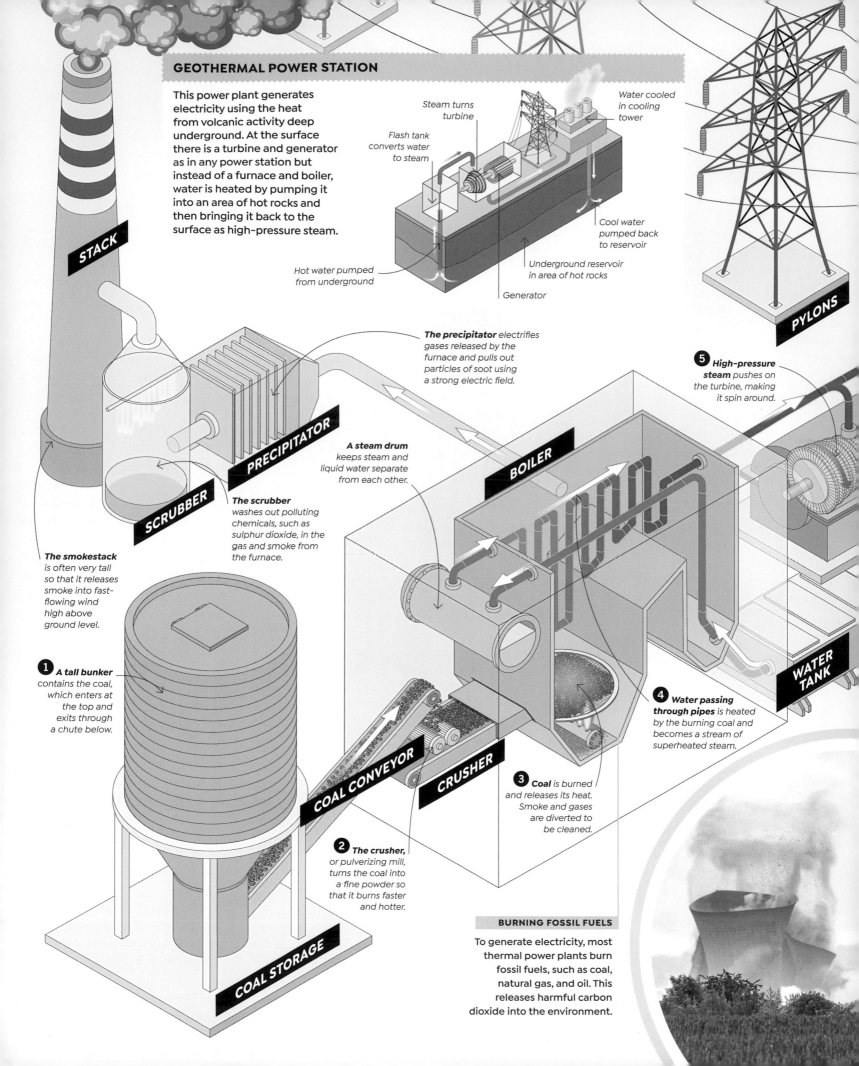

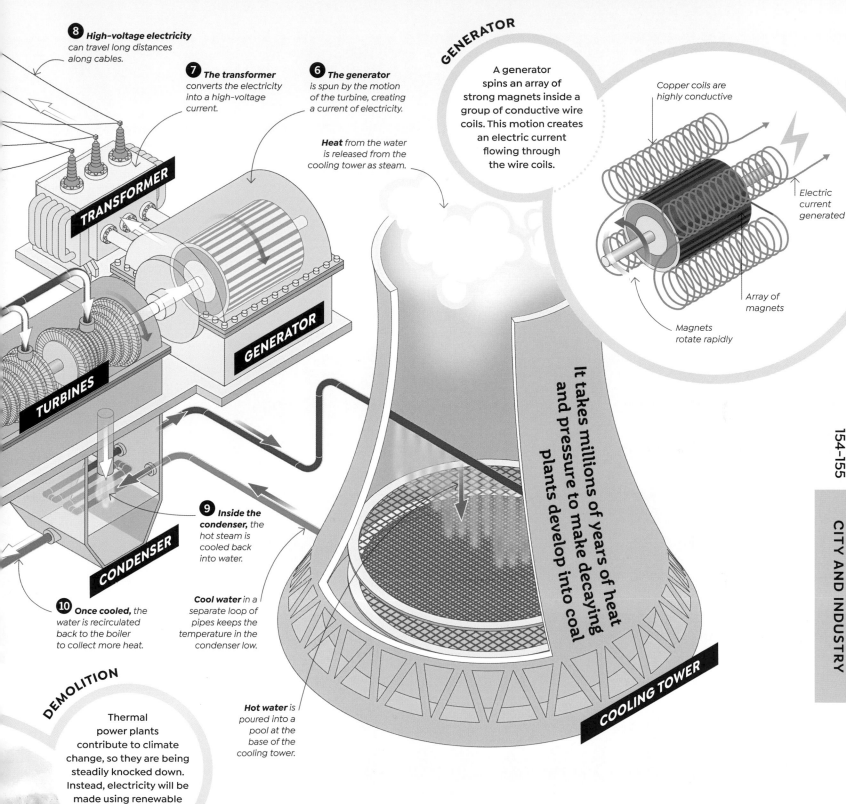

8 **High-voltage electricity** can travel long distances along cables.

7 **The transformer** converts the electricity into a high-voltage current.

6 **The generator** is spun by the motion of the turbine, creating a current of electricity.

Heat from the water is released from the cooling tower as steam.

GENERATOR

A generator spins an array of strong magnets inside a group of conductive wire coils. This motion creates an electric current flowing through the wire coils.

Copper coils are highly conductive

Electric current generated

Array of magnets

Magnets rotate rapidly

TRANSFORMER

GENERATOR

TURBINES

CONDENSER

9 **Inside the condenser,** the hot steam is cooled back into water.

Cool water in a separate loop of pipes keeps the temperature in the condenser low.

10 **Once cooled,** the water is recirculated back to the boiler to collect more heat.

DEMOLITION

Thermal power plants contribute to climate change, so they are being steadily knocked down. Instead, electricity will be made using renewable energy sources.

It takes millions of years of heat and pressure to make decaying plants develop into coal

Hot water is poured into a pool at the base of the cooling tower.

COOLING TOWER

Thermal power plant

Electricity is generated in a thermal power plant using the heat energy produced by burning a fuel – usually a fossil fuel such as coal. The heat energy is converted into motion energy. The plant's generator then converts that motion into electrical energy. Burning fuels is very polluting, so thermal power plants are being phased out.

Nuclear power

Instead of burning, nuclear fuel gives out heat due to a reaction called nuclear fission. That heat can be used to generate electricity in the same way as power stations that burn coal or gas fuels. However, unlike these fuels, nuclear power does not produce the greenhouse gas carbon dioxide.

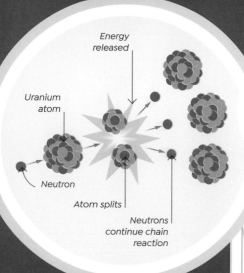

Energy released

Uranium atom

Neutron

Atom splits

Neutrons continue chain reaction

NUCLEAR FISSION

Hitting a uranium atom with a neutron makes it split in two in a process called nuclear fission. Fission releases energy and more neutrons, creating a chain reaction.

Staff in a power station's control room monitor both the reactor and the generator and ensure that both are working well together.

A reinforced concrete dome can contain explosions, fires, and radiation leaks.

3 **Hot steam** under high pressure is piped to turbines.

2 **Heat** generated by fission in the reactor boils water inside the heat exchanger, creating steam.

Protective shield absorbs dangerous radiation – rays caused by fission, which can harm living cells.

NUCLEAR REACTION

The chain reactions triggered by nuclear fission produce heat. This heat turns water inside the reactor into steam, which is harnessed to spin turbines.

CONTROL ROOM

REACTOR

HEAT EXCHANGER

Nuclear power makes up to 15 per cent of the world's electricity

Raised control rod accelerates reaction

Lowered control rod slows reaction

Fuel rod

PUMP

CONTROL RODS

Nuclear fission reactions happen so fast that they can produce a powerful explosion. Boron control rods in the reactor soak up free neutrons and slow the reaction.

Cool water returns to the reactor to start the process again.

1 **Nuclear fuel** is packed into rods that are lowered into the reactor, a structure in which fission takes place.

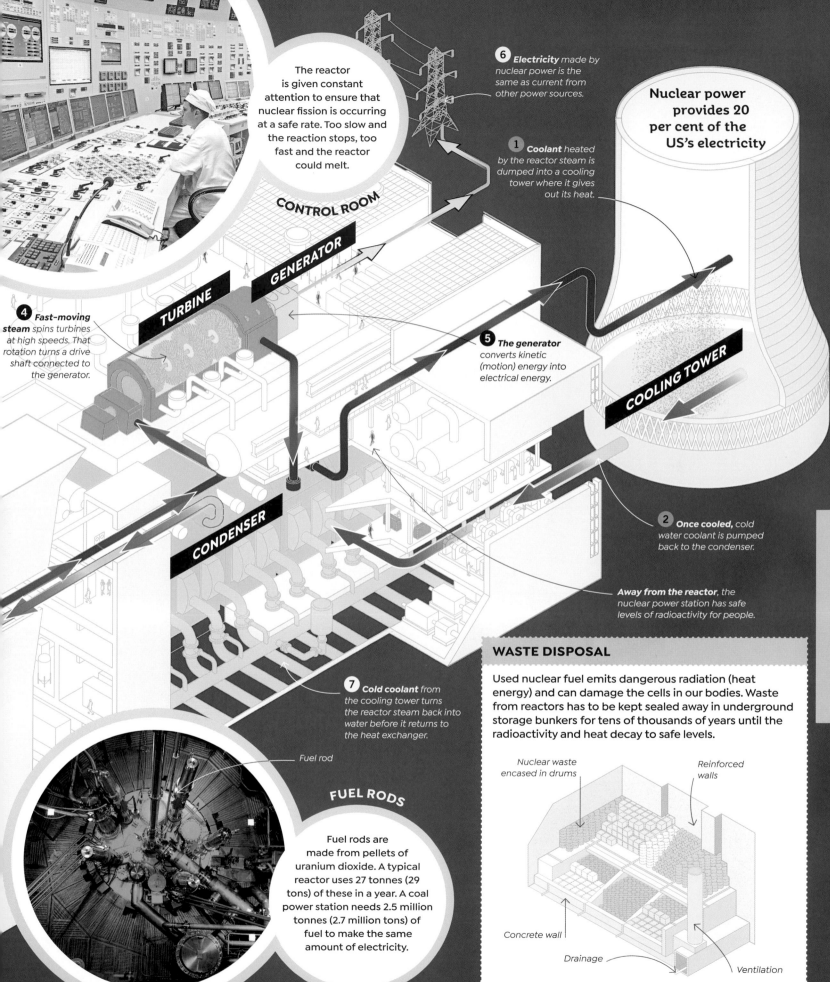

The reactor is given constant attention to ensure that nuclear fission is occurring at a safe rate. Too slow and the reaction stops, too fast and the reactor could melt.

CONTROL ROOM

6 Electricity made by nuclear power is the same as current from other power sources.

1 Coolant heated by the reactor steam is dumped into a cooling tower where it gives out its heat.

Nuclear power provides 20 per cent of the US's electricity

TURBINE

GENERATOR

4 Fast-moving steam spins turbines at high speeds. That rotation turns a drive shaft connected to the generator.

5 The generator converts kinetic (motion) energy into electrical energy.

COOLING TOWER

CONDENSER

2 Once cooled, cold water coolant is pumped back to the condenser.

Away from the reactor, the nuclear power station has safe levels of radioactivity for people.

7 Cold coolant from the cooling tower turns the reactor steam back into water before it returns to the heat exchanger.

Fuel rod

FUEL RODS

Fuel rods are made from pellets of uranium dioxide. A typical reactor uses 27 tonnes (29 tons) of these in a year. A coal power station needs 2.5 million tonnes (2.7 million tons) of fuel to make the same amount of electricity.

WASTE DISPOSAL

Used nuclear fuel emits dangerous radiation (heat energy) and can damage the cells in our bodies. Waste from reactors has to be kept sealed away in underground storage bunkers for tens of thousands of years until the radioactivity and heat decay to safe levels.

Nuclear waste encased in drums

Reinforced walls

Concrete wall

Drainage

Ventilation

WASTE STORAGE BUNKER

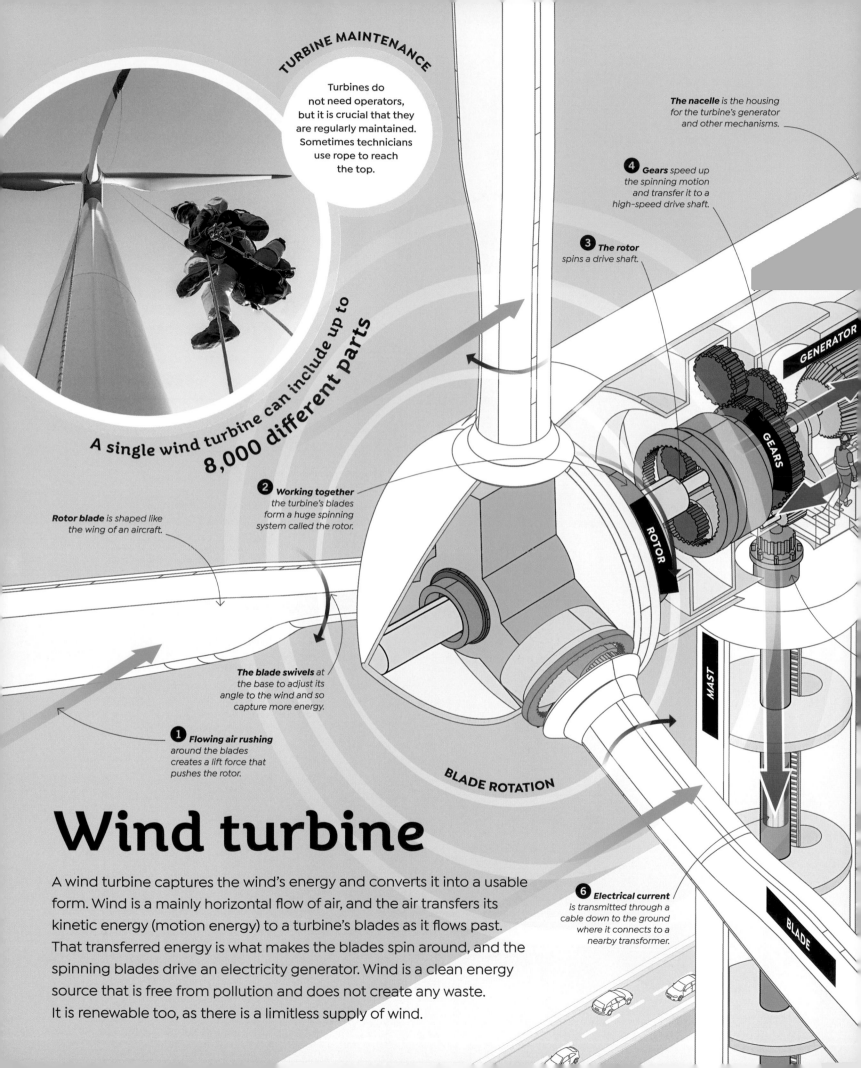

Turbines do not need operators, but it is crucial that they are regularly maintained. Sometimes technicians use rope to reach the top.

The nacelle is the housing for the turbine's generator and other mechanisms.

4 *Gears* speed up the spinning motion and transfer it to a high-speed drive shaft.

3 *The rotor* spins a drive shaft.

A single wind turbine can include up to 8,000 different parts

2 *Working together* the turbine's blades form a huge spinning system called the rotor.

GENERATOR

GEARS

ROTOR

Rotor blade is shaped like the wing of an aircraft.

The blade swivels at the base to adjust its angle to the wind and so capture more energy.

1 *Flowing air rushing* around the blades creates a lift force that pushes the rotor.

MAST

BLADE ROTATION

Wind turbine

A wind turbine captures the wind's energy and converts it into a usable form. Wind is a mainly horizontal flow of air, and the air transfers its kinetic energy (motion energy) to a turbine's blades as it flows past. That transferred energy is what makes the blades spin around, and the spinning blades drive an electricity generator. Wind is a clean energy source that is free from pollution and does not create any waste. It is renewable too, as there is a limitless supply of wind.

6 *Electrical current* is transmitted through a cable down to the ground where it connects to a nearby transformer.

BLADE

At maximum speed, blade tips can spin at up to 290 kph (180 mph)

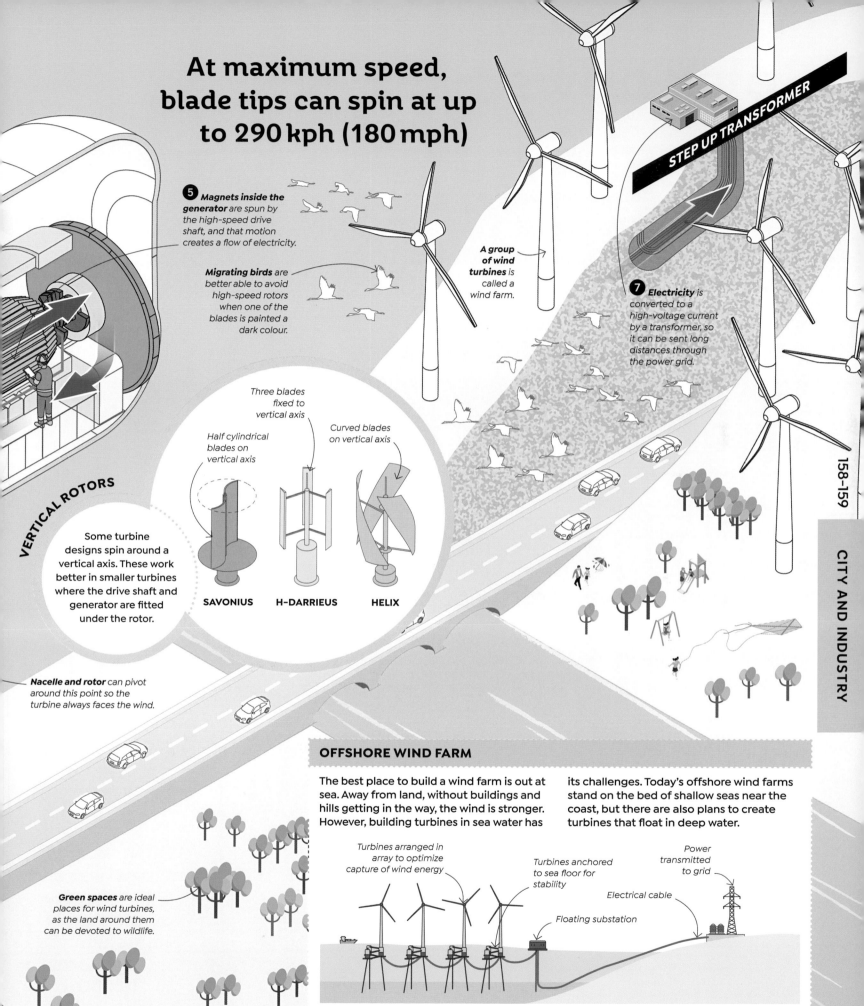

5 *Magnets inside the generator* are spun by the high-speed drive shaft, and that motion creates a flow of electricity.

Migrating birds are better able to avoid high-speed rotors when one of the blades is painted a dark colour.

A group of wind turbines is called a wind farm.

STEP UP TRANSFORMER

7 *Electricity* is converted to a high-voltage current by a transformer, so it can be sent long distances through the power grid.

VERTICAL ROTORS

Some turbine designs spin around a vertical axis. These work better in smaller turbines where the drive shaft and generator are fitted under the rotor.

Three blades fixed to vertical axis

Half cylindrical blades on vertical axis

Curved blades on vertical axis

SAVONIUS **H-DARRIEUS** **HELIX**

Nacelle and rotor can pivot around this point so the turbine always faces the wind.

Green spaces are ideal places for wind turbines, as the land around them can be devoted to wildlife.

OFFSHORE WIND FARM

The best place to build a wind farm is out at sea. Away from land, without buildings and hills getting in the way, the wind is stronger. However, building turbines in sea water has its challenges. Today's offshore wind farms stand on the bed of shallow seas near the coast, but there are also plans to create turbines that float in deep water.

Turbines arranged in array to optimize capture of wind energy

Turbines anchored to sea floor for stability

Power transmitted to grid

Electrical cable

Floating substation

Solar power

The light and heat from the Sun reaching Earth can be captured and put to work. This is called solar power. Unlike most other forms of power generation, which have to be built on a large scale, solar power systems can be made small enough to install in individual houses. They provide supplies of hot water and electricity and create far less carbon dioxide pollution.

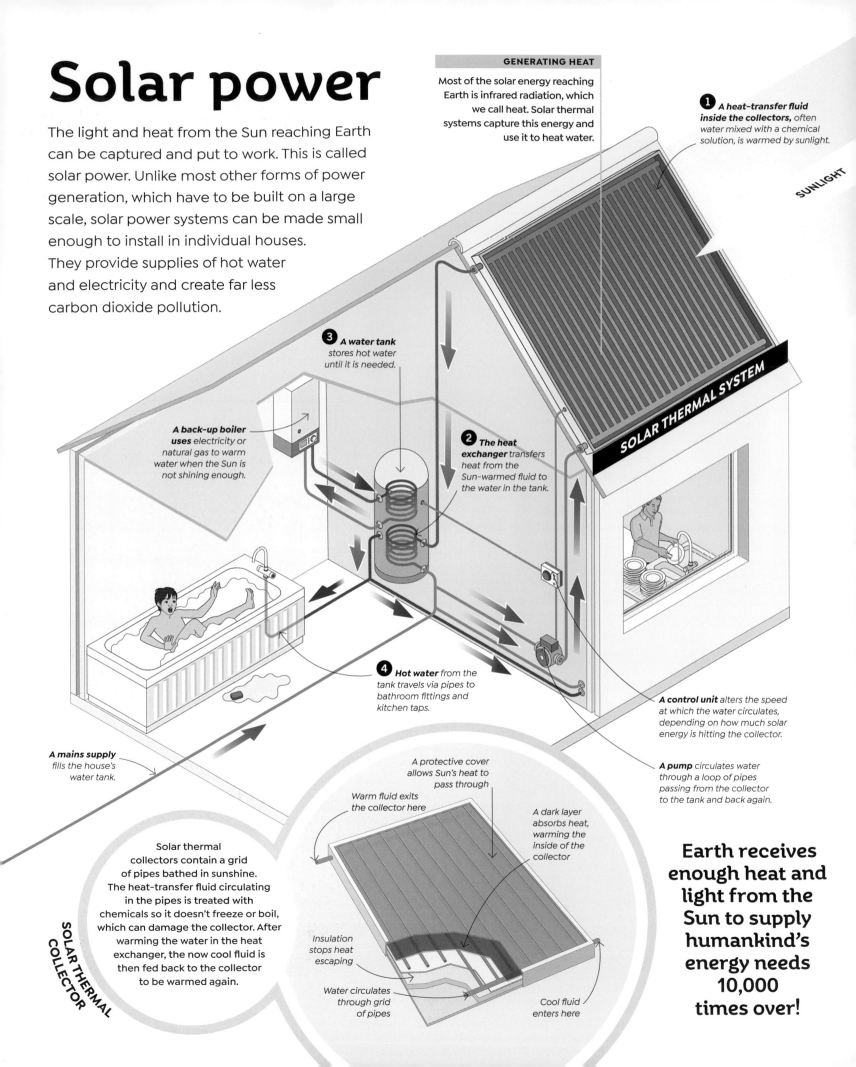

GENERATING HEAT

Most of the solar energy reaching Earth is infrared radiation, which we call heat. Solar thermal systems capture this energy and use it to heat water.

1 *A heat-transfer fluid inside the collectors,* often water mixed with a chemical solution, is warmed by sunlight.

SUNLIGHT

SOLAR THERMAL SYSTEM

3 *A water tank* stores hot water until it is needed.

A back-up boiler uses electricity or natural gas to warm water when the Sun is not shining enough.

2 *The heat exchanger* transfers heat from the Sun-warmed fluid to the water in the tank.

4 *Hot water* from the tank travels via pipes to bathroom fittings and kitchen taps.

A control unit alters the speed at which the water circulates, depending on how much solar energy is hitting the collector.

A mains supply fills the house's water tank.

A pump circulates water through a loop of pipes passing from the collector to the tank and back again.

A protective cover allows Sun's heat to pass through

Warm fluid exits the collector here

A dark layer absorbs heat, warming the inside of the collector

SOLAR THERMAL COLLECTOR

Solar thermal collectors contain a grid of pipes bathed in sunshine. The heat-transfer fluid circulating in the pipes is treated with chemicals so it doesn't freeze or boil, which can damage the collector. After warming the water in the heat exchanger, the now cool fluid is then fed back to the collector to be warmed again.

Insulation stops heat escaping

Water circulates through grid of pipes

Cool fluid enters here

Earth receives enough heat and light from the Sun to supply humankind's energy needs 10,000 times over!

SOLAR CELLS

Solar panels are made of solar cells, each with two layers of semiconductor material. The top layer has extra electrons, which are negatively charged. The bottom layer has positively charged spaces for electrons, called holes. Sunlight knocks electrons free from their atoms. They move to the holes through a conductor, creating a current.

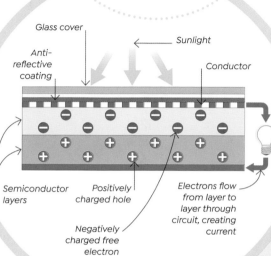

Glass cover

Anti-reflective coating

Sunlight

Conductor

Semiconductor layers

Positively charged hole

Negatively charged free electron

Electrons flow from layer to layer through circuit, creating current

CONCENTRATED SOLAR POWER

This solar power system works best in sunny, desert regions. Curved mirrors focus sunlight into an intensely hot beam. The beam's heat can be used to melt or burn materials in a furnace. It can also boil water and create high-pressure steam to drive a turbine linked to an electricity generator.

GENERATING ELECTRICITY

Solar panels use materials called semiconductors to harness the energy of sunlight and generate electricity.

1 *Solar panels* are best set at an angle, so they face the Sun throughout the day.

SUNLIGHT

SOLAR PANEL SYSTEM

2 *Electricity made by the panels* is direct current (DC), which always flows in one direction.

3 *An inverter* changes the DC into AC.

The consumer unit has safety switches that shut off the power if the current rises dangerously high.

4 *The generation meter* logs the amount of electricity produced by the panels.

5 *Cables* linked to sockets and light fittings carry electricity produced by the solar panels all over the house.

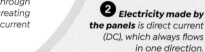

6 *Current* powers lights and electrical devices, including this band's equipment. Houses can have batteries installed to store electricity until it is needed.

A smart meter adds up how much electricity the house uses and how much it sends to the public grid.

Water can also be heated using electricity from solar panels.

Electricity used by homes is alternating current (AC), which reverses direction many times each second.

The isolator switch can disconnect the solar panels from the network.

7 *Unused electricity* can be fed into the public grid for other people to use. If the Sun isn't shining, the grid can supply the house with electricity.

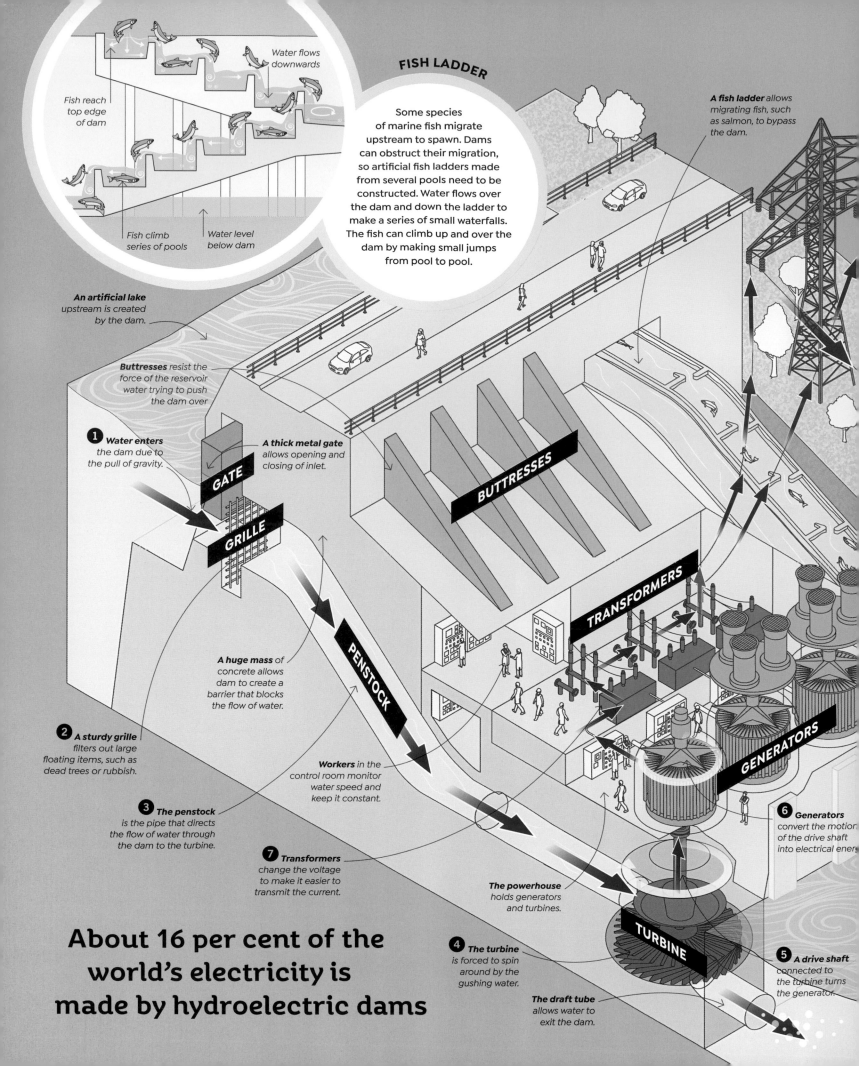

FISH LADDER

Fish reach top edge of dam

Water flows downwards

Fish climb series of pools

Water level below dam

Some species of marine fish migrate upstream to spawn. Dams can obstruct their migration, so artificial fish ladders made from several pools need to be constructed. Water flows over the dam and down the ladder to make a series of small waterfalls. The fish can climb up and over the dam by making small jumps from pool to pool.

A fish ladder allows migrating fish, such as salmon, to bypass the dam.

An artificial lake upstream is created by the dam.

Buttresses resist the force of the reservoir water trying to push the dam over

1 *Water enters* the dam due to the pull of gravity.

A thick metal gate allows opening and closing of inlet.

GATE

GRILLE

BUTTRESSES

TRANSFORMERS

GENERATORS

A huge mass of concrete allows dam to create a barrier that blocks the flow of water.

PENSTOCK

2 *A sturdy grille* filters out large floating items, such as dead trees or rubbish.

3 *The penstock* is the pipe that directs the flow of water through the dam to the turbine.

Workers in the control room monitor water speed and keep it constant.

7 *Transformers* change the voltage to make it easier to transmit the current.

The powerhouse holds generators and turbines.

6 *Generators* convert the motion of the drive shaft into electrical energy

TURBINE

About 16 per cent of the world's electricity is made by hydroelectric dams

4 *The turbine* is forced to spin around by the gushing water.

The draft tube allows water to exit the dam.

5 *A drive shaft* connected to the turbine turns the generator.

Hydroelectric power station

The flow of a river downstream is a source of renewable energy and is harnessed and turned into electricity by a hydroelectric dam. A dam is a barrier built across a river to control the flow of the water. Dams create a reservoir that can extend far upstream. When the reservoir is deep enough, its water is funnelled through the dam's powerhouse. The high-speed flow of water drives generators.

Pylons support the transmission of electricity to the grid.

8 **Electricity** from the dam is carried along high-voltage cables.

PYLON

The spillway carries water through dam when reservoir levels are too high.

Three Gorges Dam in China backs up water in the river for 600 km (370 miles)

Water flows downstream as normal when leaving the dam.

PUMPED STORAGE

A pumped storage hydropower system can go into reverse, using electricity to pump water uphill. When there is too much electricity being generated, the left-over power is used to pump water up to an extra storage reservoir at a higher level. When there is greater demand for electricity, the water is released from that reservoir and is used to generate hydroelectricity in the normal way.

Transmission network

Upper reservoir

Electricity cables

Turbine and pump

Lower reservoir

Pump mode consumes power

Flow mode generates power

The world's tallest dam is 305 m (1,000 ft) tall

A penstock can only carry a certain amount of water. If too much water enters the reservoir, the excess needs somewhere to go, so that it does not flood or spill over the top of the dam. To combat this, dams have a spillway down which excess water can flow away. Sometimes spillways are in the centre of the reservoir, and look like giant plugholes.

SPILLWAY

HOLDING IT ALL BACK

Dams are built to control the flow of a river. The type of dam built depends on its use, usually to prevent flooding or to generate electricity. The Hoover Dam pictured here is a hybrid concrete arch-gravity dam, designed to fit between the steep walls of the Colorado River valley. It stands 221 m (726 ft) tall and measures 380 m (1,244 ft) along its crest.

Crest or walkway

Water pressure

Concrete or stone masonry

Bedrock foundation

Force of water deflected down

GRAVITY DAM

Gravity dams transfer the water load downward. They are usually built across narrow valleys and have bedrock foundations.

Load spread to walls of canyon

Concrete arch

Water pressure

Bedrock or excavated foundation

ARCH DAM

The thin, curved shape of these dams is designed to transfer some of the water load to the rock walls of the canyon.

Power grid

Electricity is transmitted from the power stations, where it is generated, through a network called the power grid, to the homes and factories where it is used. High-voltage electricity, where the current is pushed along with great force, is used for long-distance transmission. The supply used in homes is converted to a much lower and safer voltage.

③ *A substation* houses transformers, which change the electricity's voltage. This one is stepping up to a high voltage.

④ *Stepping up the voltage* makes transmission more efficient, because the electricity loses less energy as it flows.

DISTRIBUTION SUBSTATION

⑤ *Transmission lines* carry current at a voltage of around 500,000 volts.

GENERATION

Electric current is generated by an energy source. This energy can come from many sources, such as heat contained in sunlight.

① *Visible sunlight* carries energy that is transferred to electrons in the solar panels.

SOLAR PANELS

② *Solar panels* convert the energy in sunlight directly into a flow of electricity.

The power grid needs frequent maintenance to keep it working and safe. Engineers need a head for heights as they carry out repairs high up in the pylons.

⑦ *A further step-down transformer* reduces the voltage of the power supply to make it more suitable for use in homes.

Birds can perch safely on power lines because there is no route for the electric current to pass through their bodies to the ground.

PYLONS

STEP-DOWN TRANSFORMER

Lattice frameworks let the wind through so the pylons do not blow over.

Weather and damp resistant outer layer

Aluminium sheath

Only buried cable is sheathed by many layers of protection to insulate and strengthen it. Overhead cable is too high for direct contact, so it has no insulation.

Plastic insulation

Copper conductor

BURIED CABLES

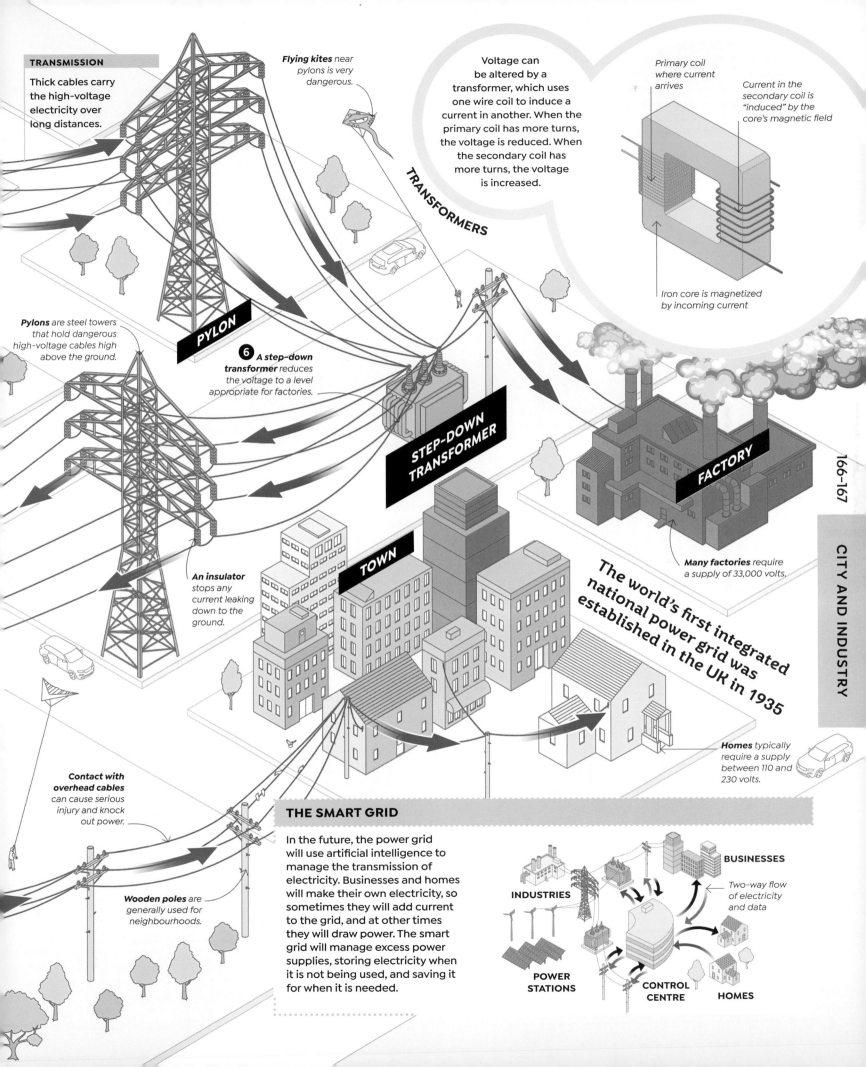

TRANSMISSION

Thick cables carry the high-voltage electricity over long distances.

Flying kites near pylons is very dangerous.

Voltage can be altered by a transformer, which uses one wire coil to induce a current in another. When the primary coil has more turns, the voltage is reduced. When the secondary coil has more turns, the voltage is increased.

Primary coil where current arrives

Current in the secondary coil is "induced" by the core's magnetic field

Iron core is magnetized by incoming current

TRANSFORMERS

PYLON

Pylons are steel towers that hold dangerous high-voltage cables high above the ground.

6 *A step-down transformer* reduces the voltage to a level appropriate for factories.

An insulator stops any current leaking down to the ground.

STEP-DOWN TRANSFORMER

FACTORY

Many factories require a supply of 33,000 volts.

The world's first integrated national power grid was established in the UK in 1935

TOWN

Homes typically require a supply between 110 and 230 volts.

Contact with overhead cables can cause serious injury and knock out power.

Wooden poles are generally used for neighbourhoods.

THE SMART GRID

In the future, the power grid will use artificial intelligence to manage the transmission of electricity. Businesses and homes will make their own electricity, so sometimes they will add current to the grid, and at other times they will draw power. The smart grid will manage excess power supplies, storing electricity when it is not being used, and saving it for when it is needed.

BUSINESSES

INDUSTRIES

Two-way flow of electricity and data

POWER STATIONS

CONTROL CENTRE

HOMES

CARBON CAPTURE

Unlike fossil fuels, biofuels can be grown as a renewable source. As they grow, plants extract carbon dioxide (CO_2) from the air and convert it into carbon in their tissue. If a thermal power plant burned only biofuels, then captured and stored the CO_2 underground, the process would be carbon negative. Carbon capture is still a new technology, but it could make a huge positive difference.

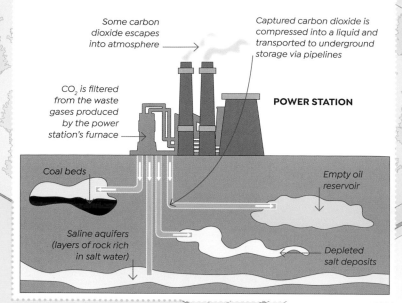

Some carbon dioxide escapes into atmosphere

Captured carbon dioxide is compressed into a liquid and transported to underground storage via pipelines

CO_2 is filtered from the waste gases produced by the power station's furnace

POWER STATION

Coal beds

Empty oil reservoir

Saline aquifers (layers of rock rich in salt water)

Depleted salt deposits

CORN

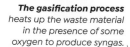

WOOD CHIP

The gasification process heats up the waste material in the presence of some oxygen to produce syngas.

Non-recyclable waste, such as carbon-rich plastics, is a raw material for making gas fuels.

GASIFICATION PLANT

1 *Biomass* – carbon-rich material made from dried wood chips and unwanted plant materials – is brought for processing.

BIOMASS PLANT

2 *Biomass is heated* in a reactor to convert it into syngas and biochar through the process of pyrolysis.

3 *Biochar* is either removed to be used as a fertilizer, or carried to a power plant.

BIOCHAR

MAKING SYNGAS

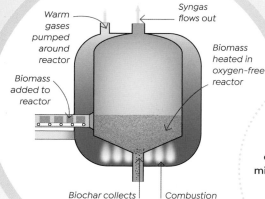

Warm gases pumped around reactor

Syngas flows out

Biomass heated in oxygen-free reactor

Biomass added to reactor

Biochar collects at bottom

Combustion chamber

PYROLYSIS

Pyrolysis is the process by which biomass is heated in an oxygen-free environment in order to convert it into a useful mixture of synthetic gases (syngas) and a solid fuel called biochar. Pyrolysis breaks up the raw materials into simpler, more flammable chemicals.

Biofuels

Fossil fuels, such as natural gas, coal, and oil, are made from the remains of long-dead organisms. Biofuels, including bioethanol and biodiesel, are made using renewable biomass, such as plant materials, which remove carbon dioxide (CO_2) from the air as they grow. When burned, they also release less CO_2 per unit of energy generated.

BIOCHAR

Biochar is a pure carbon fuel made by roasting wood. It can be burned at thermal power plants, but a more environmentally friendly use is to add it to soil. This not only helps plant growth, but also avoids further CO_2 emissions.

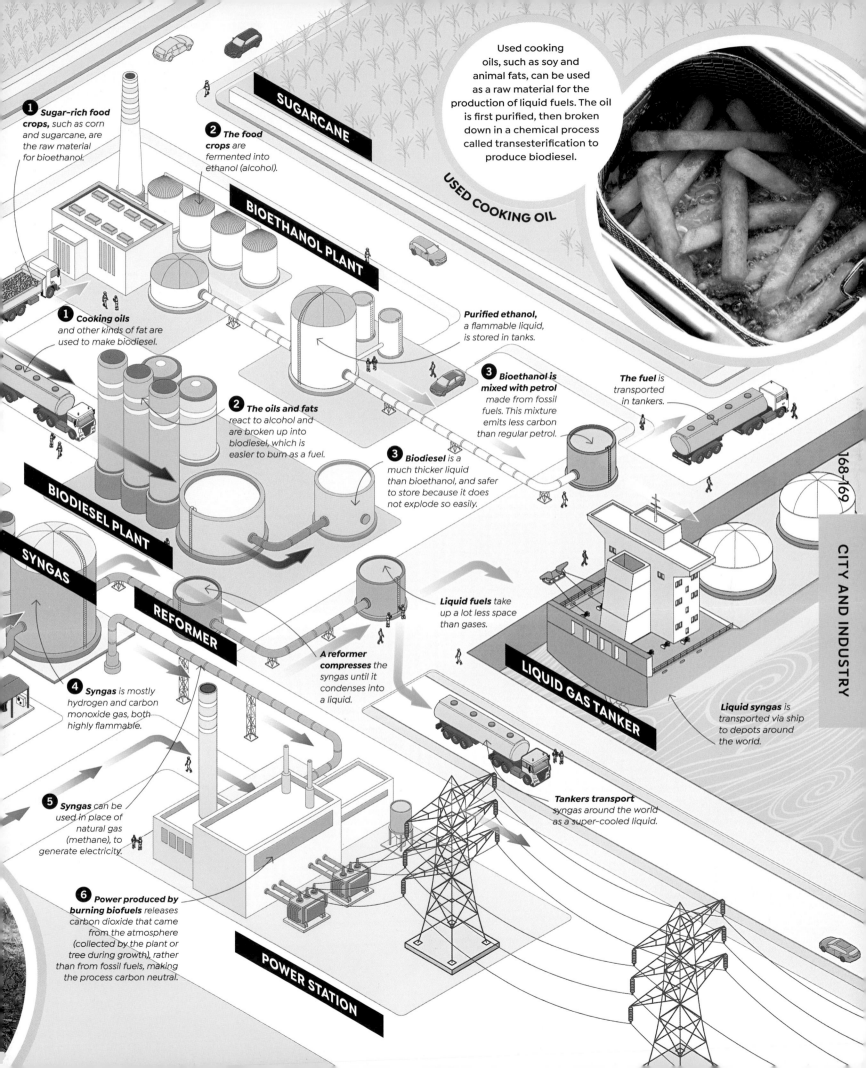

1 **Sugar-rich food crops,** such as corn and sugarcane, are the raw material for bioethanol.

2 **The food crops are** fermented into ethanol (alcohol).

SUGARCANE

Used cooking oils, such as soy and animal fats, can be used as a raw material for the production of liquid fuels. The oil is first purified, then broken down in a chemical process called transesterification to produce biodiesel.

USED COOKING OIL

BIOETHANOL PLANT

1 **Cooking oils** and other kinds of fat are used to make biodiesel.

Purified ethanol, a flammable liquid, is stored in tanks.

3 **Bioethanol is mixed with petrol** made from fossil fuels. This mixture emits less carbon than regular petrol.

The fuel is transported in tankers.

2 **The oils and fats** react to alcohol and are broken up into biodiesel, which is easier to burn as a fuel.

3 **Biodiesel** is a much thicker liquid than bioethanol, and safer to store because it does not explode so easily.

BIODIESEL PLANT

SYNGAS

Liquid fuels take up a lot less space than gases.

REFORMER

A reformer compresses the syngas until it condenses into a liquid.

LIQUID GAS TANKER

Liquid syngas is transported via ship to depots around the world.

4 **Syngas** is mostly hydrogen and carbon monoxide gas, both highly flammable.

Tankers transport syngas around the world as a super-cooled liquid.

5 **Syngas** can be used in place of natural gas (methane), to generate electricity.

6 **Power produced by burning biofuels** releases carbon dioxide that came from the atmosphere (collected by the plant or tree during growth), rather than from fossil fuels, making the process carbon neutral.

POWER STATION

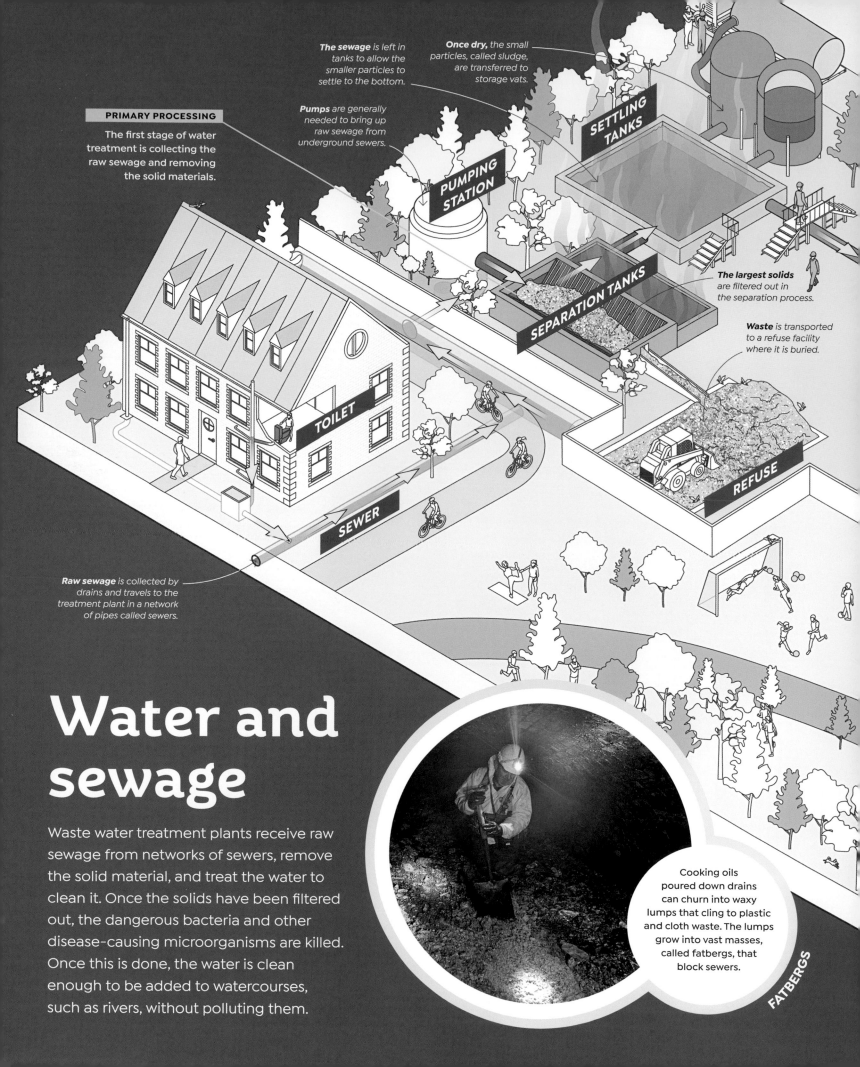

The first stage of water treatment is collecting the raw sewage and removing the solid materials.

The sewage is left in tanks to allow the smaller particles to settle to the bottom.

Once dry, the small particles, called sludge, are transferred to storage vats.

Pumps are generally needed to bring up raw sewage from underground sewers.

PUMPING STATION

SETTLING TANKS

SEPARATION TANKS

The largest solids are filtered out in the separation process.

Waste is transported to a refuse facility where it is buried.

TOILET

SEWER

REFUSE

Raw sewage is collected by drains and travels to the treatment plant in a network of pipes called sewers.

Water and sewage

Waste water treatment plants receive raw sewage from networks of sewers, remove the solid material, and treat the water to clean it. Once the solids have been filtered out, the dangerous bacteria and other disease-causing microorganisms are killed. Once this is done, the water is clean enough to be added to watercourses, such as rivers, without polluting them.

Cooking oils poured down drains can churn into waxy lumps that cling to plastic and cloth waste. The lumps grow into vast masses, called fatbergs, that block sewers.

FATBERGS

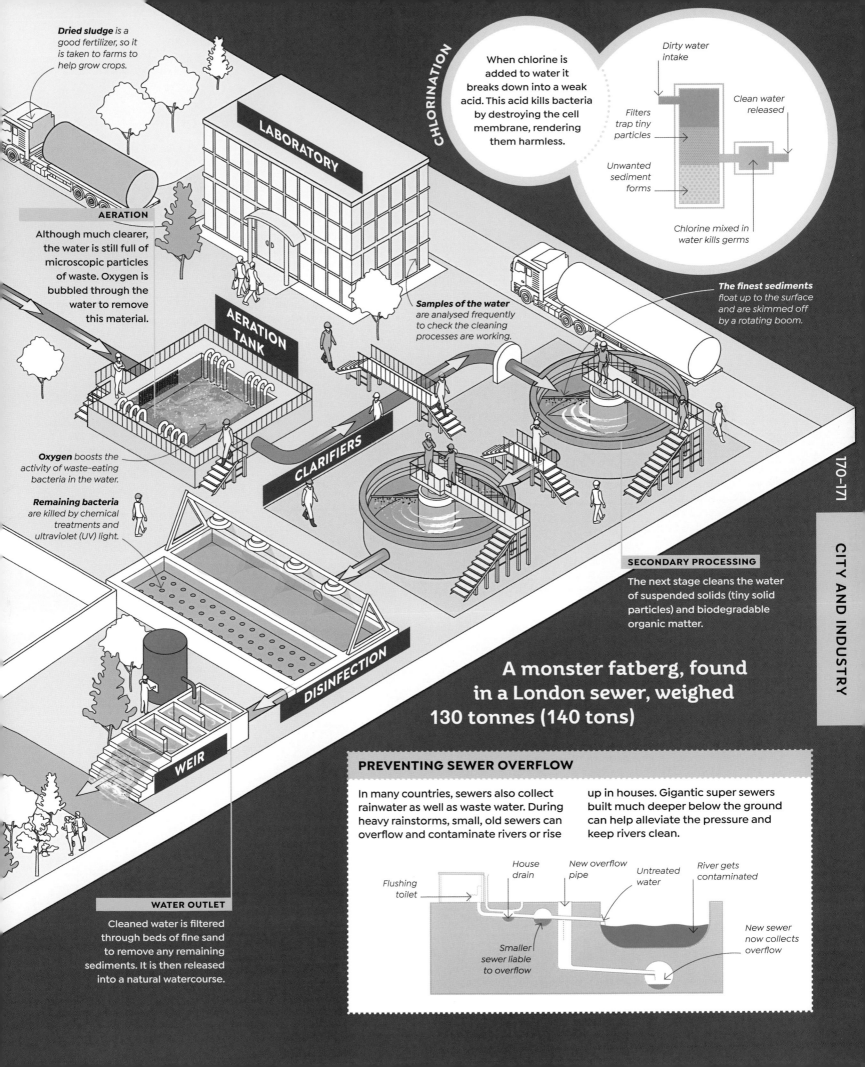

Dried sludge is a good fertilizer, so it is taken to farms to help grow crops.

When chlorine is added to water it breaks down into a weak acid. This acid kills bacteria by destroying the cell membrane, rendering them harmless.

Dirty water intake

Filters trap tiny particles

Clean water released

Unwanted sediment forms

Chlorine mixed in water kills germs

LABORATORY

AERATION

Although much clearer, the water is still full of microscopic particles of waste. Oxygen is bubbled through the water to remove this material.

AERATION TANK

Samples of the water are analysed frequently to check the cleaning processes are working.

The finest sediments float up to the surface and are skimmed off by a rotating boom.

Oxygen boosts the activity of waste-eating bacteria in the water.

CLARIFIERS

Remaining bacteria are killed by chemical treatments and ultraviolet (UV) light.

DISINFECTION

SECONDARY PROCESSING

The next stage cleans the water of suspended solids (tiny solid particles) and biodegradable organic matter.

A monster fatberg, found in a London sewer, weighed 130 tonnes (140 tons)

WEIR

PREVENTING SEWER OVERFLOW

In many countries, sewers also collect rainwater as well as waste water. During heavy rainstorms, small, old sewers can overflow and contaminate rivers or rise up in houses. Gigantic super sewers built much deeper below the ground can help alleviate the pressure and keep rivers clean.

Flushing toilet

House drain

New overflow pipe

Untreated water

River gets contaminated

Smaller sewer liable to overflow

New sewer now collects overflow

WATER OUTLET

Cleaned water is filtered through beds of fine sand to remove any remaining sediments. It is then released into a natural watercourse.

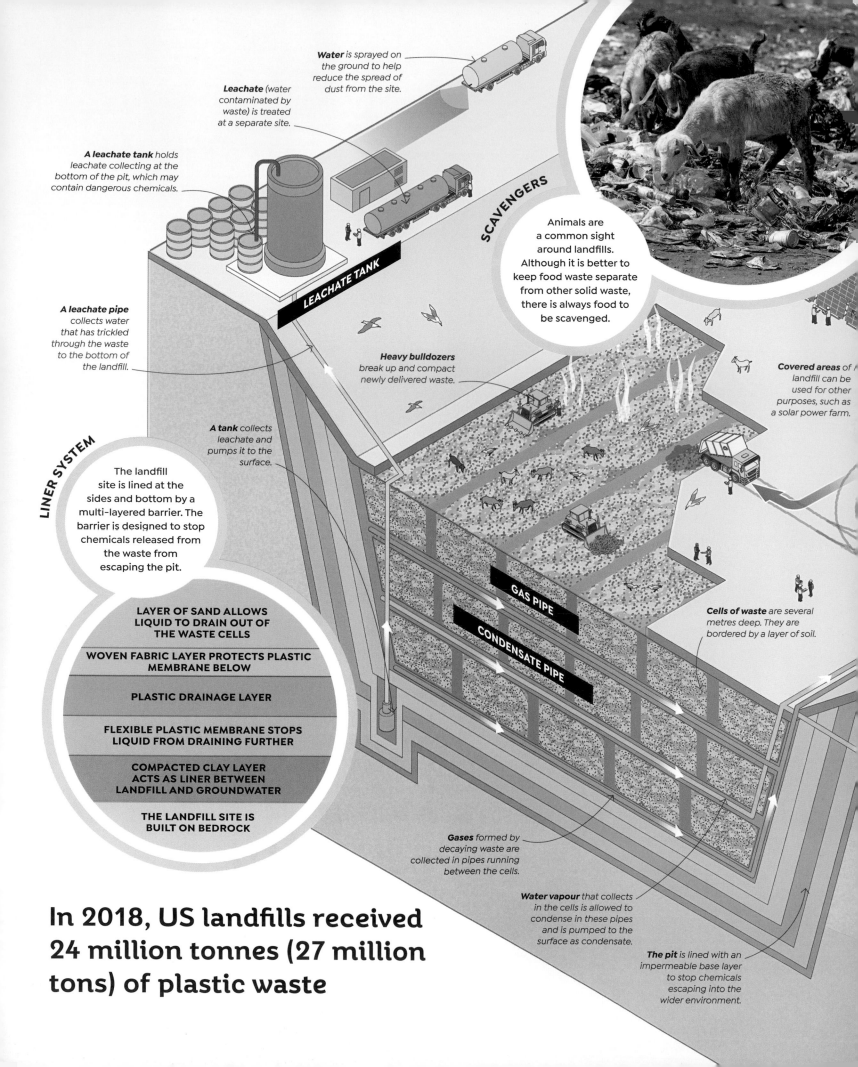

Water is sprayed on the ground to help reduce the spread of dust from the site.

Leachate (water contaminated by waste) is treated at a separate site.

A leachate tank holds leachate collecting at the bottom of the pit, which may contain dangerous chemicals.

A leachate pipe collects water that has trickled through the waste to the bottom of the landfill.

SCAVENGERS

LEACHATE TANK

Animals are a common sight around landfills. Although it is better to keep food waste separate from other solid waste, there is always food to be scavenged.

Heavy bulldozers break up and compact newly delivered waste.

A tank collects leachate and pumps it to the surface.

LINER SYSTEM

The landfill site is lined at the sides and bottom by a multi-layered barrier. The barrier is designed to stop chemicals released from the waste from escaping the pit.

Covered areas of landfill can be used for other purposes, such as a solar power farm.

GAS PIPE

CONDENSATE PIPE

Cells of waste are several metres deep. They are bordered by a layer of soil.

LAYER OF SAND ALLOWS LIQUID TO DRAIN OUT OF THE WASTE CELLS

WOVEN FABRIC LAYER PROTECTS PLASTIC MEMBRANE BELOW

PLASTIC DRAINAGE LAYER

FLEXIBLE PLASTIC MEMBRANE STOPS LIQUID FROM DRAINING FURTHER

COMPACTED CLAY LAYER ACTS AS LINER BETWEEN LANDFILL AND GROUNDWATER

THE LANDFILL SITE IS BUILT ON BEDROCK

Gases formed by decaying waste are collected in pipes running between the cells.

Water vapour that collects in the cells is allowed to condense in these pipes and is pumped to the surface as condensate.

The pit is lined with an impermeable base layer to stop chemicals escaping into the wider environment.

In 2018, US landfills received 24 million tonnes (27 million tons) of plastic waste

Landfill

Solid waste materials that cannot be reused or recycled are usually disposed of by burying them in the ground at a landfill site. Good sites are constructed to prevent pollution escaping from the waste and into the wider environment. Once filled, the site is covered over with soil and left for many years before being built on.

Electricity is transferred to the grid.

Incoming waste is delivered to the site by trucks.

Gas flares burn away excess flammable gases produced by the decomposing waste.

SITE ENTRANCE

MOBILE SCREENS

FLARE STATION AND CONDENSATE STORAGE

A deep groundwater monitoring well allows workers to check that unwanted chemicals are not leaking from the waste.

Gases released from the landfill site are stored in tanks and can be used as a fuel for generating electricity.

Mobile screens capture small items of waste that are blown away by wind.

GAS MONITOR

SUMP

GAS MONITOR

A sump collects condensate, which may be recirculated or collected and sprayed on the ground to control dust.

A gas monitor sunk deep in the ground beside the landfill looks for any gases escaping into the surrounding soil.

LANDFILL GAS-TO-ENERGY

The gas collected from landfill contains flammable substances, such as methane. Methane is a very powerful greenhouse gas, and it can be burned to convert it into carbon dioxide and water, which are less harmful. The heat released from the burning gas can be harnessed as a power source that generates electricity.

Gas produced by waste is collected in pipes

Clean gas burned to drive generators

Gas is cleaned, removing water vapour and impurities

A transformer creates a high-voltage current

Electricity made from waste is added to the power grid

Recycling

The role of a recycling centre is to separate out all the different recyclable materials that get mixed together during the collection process. These materials include metals, paper, cardboard, glass, and different kinds of plastic. Once separated, the materials are reprocessed elsewhere in order to be turned into raw materials that can be used to manufacture new items.

Computer analyses data

Laser

Mixed waste

Air jet sorts identified items

Collection bins for different types of waste

The way a laser beam reflects off an object tells the sorter what material it is. Jets of air are used to direct each piece to the correct collectors.

MIXED PAPER

NEWSPAPER

OPTICAL SORTER

SCREEN

OPTICAL SORTER

An optical sorter, using lasers, identifies which items are glass.

CARDBOARD

OPTICAL SORTER

SCREEN

OPTICAL SORTER

GLASS BREAKER

Human sorters look for contaminated items in mixed materials, such as food waste.

Glass items are crushed so that they take up less space.

A rotating screen sorts items by shape and size, such as flat cardboard.

Mixed waste arrives in refuse trucks. It is tipped onto the floor then fed into a conveyor.

Even cars can be recycled! Around 80 per cent of a vehicle can be re-used or re-purposed

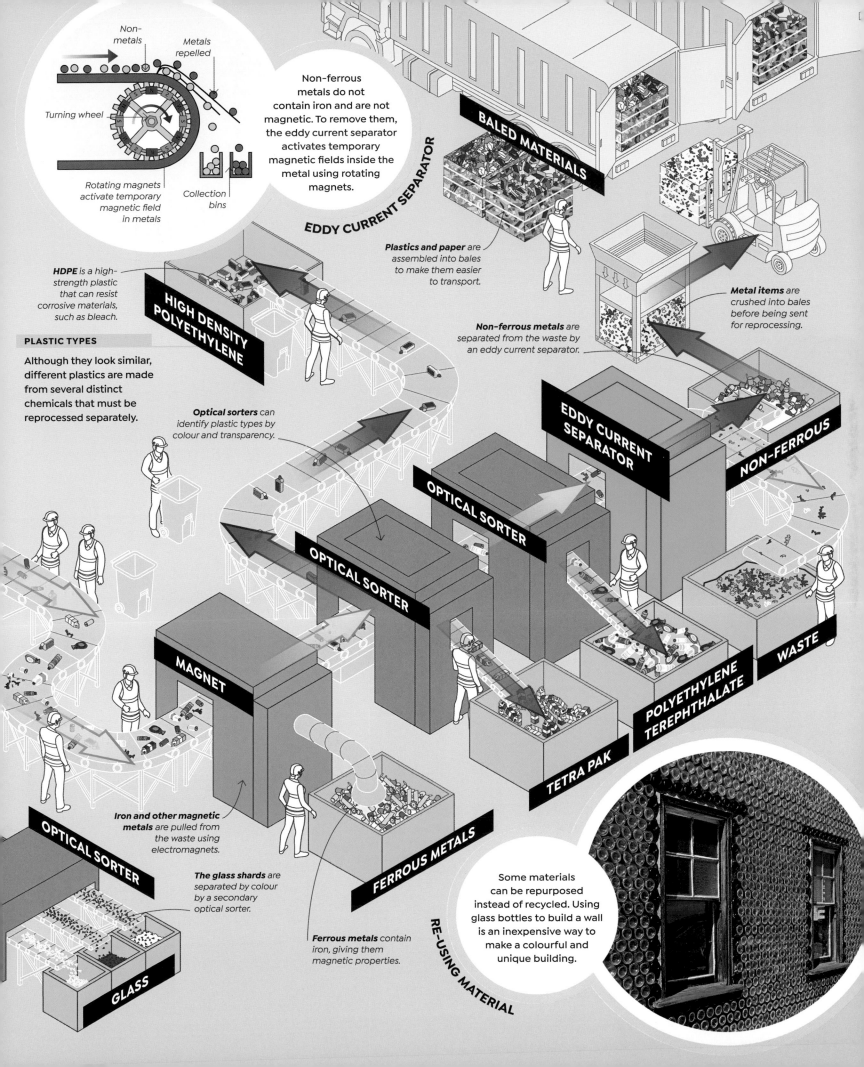

Non-ferrous metals do not contain iron and are not magnetic. To remove them, the eddy current separator activates temporary magnetic fields inside the metal using rotating magnets.

Non-metals

Metals repelled

Turning wheel

Rotating magnets activate temporary magnetic field in metals

Collection bins

EDDY CURRENT SEPARATOR

BALED MATERIALS

Plastics and paper are assembled into bales to make them easier to transport.

Metal items are crushed into bales before being sent for reprocessing.

Non-ferrous metals are separated from the waste by an eddy current separator.

HDPE is a high-strength plastic that can resist corrosive materials, such as bleach.

HIGH DENSITY POLYETHYLENE

PLASTIC TYPES

Although they look similar, different plastics are made from several distinct chemicals that must be reprocessed separately.

Optical sorters can identify plastic types by colour and transparency.

EDDY CURRENT SEPARATOR

NON-FERROUS

OPTICAL SORTER

OPTICAL SORTER

MAGNET

POLYETHYLENE TEREPHTHALATE

WASTE

TETRA PAK

Iron and other magnetic metals are pulled from the waste using electromagnets.

OPTICAL SORTER

The glass shards are separated by colour by a secondary optical sorter.

FERROUS METALS

Ferrous metals contain iron, giving them magnetic properties.

RE-USING MATERIAL

Some materials can be repurposed instead of recycled. Using glass bottles to build a wall is an inexpensive way to make a colourful and unique building.

GLASS

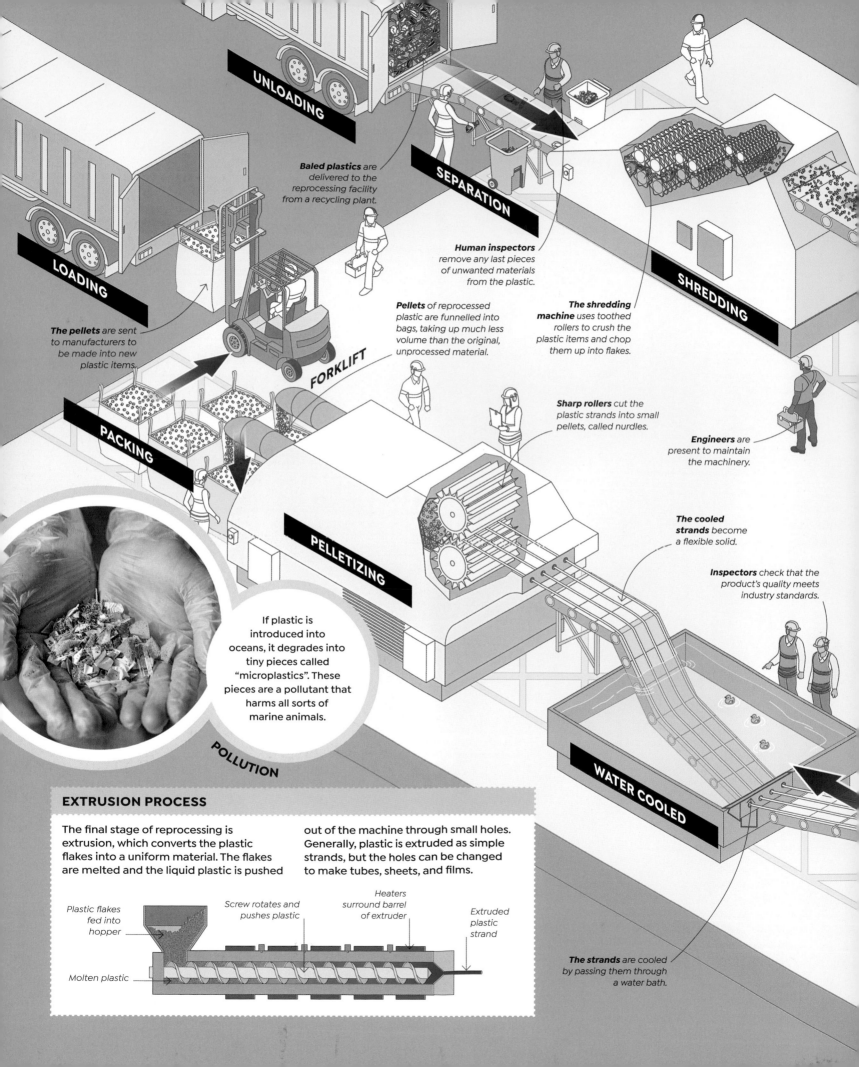

UNLOADING

Baled plastics are delivered to the reprocessing facility from a recycling plant.

SEPARATION

Human inspectors remove any last pieces of unwanted materials from the plastic.

SHREDDING

The **shredding machine** uses toothed rollers to crush the plastic items and chop them up into flakes.

LOADING

The **pellets** are sent to manufacturers to be made into new plastic items.

FORKLIFT

Pellets of reprocessed plastic are funnelled into bags, taking up much less volume than the original, unprocessed material.

Sharp rollers cut the plastic strands into small pellets, called nurdles.

Engineers are present to maintain the machinery.

PACKING

PELLETIZING

The cooled strands become a flexible solid.

Inspectors check that the product's quality meets industry standards.

If plastic is introduced into oceans, it degrades into tiny pieces called "microplastics". These pieces are a pollutant that harms all sorts of marine animals.

POLLUTION

WATER COOLED

The strands are cooled by passing them through a water bath.

EXTRUSION PROCESS

The final stage of reprocessing is extrusion, which converts the plastic flakes into a uniform material. The flakes are melted and the liquid plastic is pushed out of the machine through small holes. Generally, plastic is extruded as simple strands, but the holes can be changed to make tubes, sheets, and films.

Plastic flakes fed into hopper

Screw rotates and pushes plastic

Heaters surround barrel of extruder

Extruded plastic strand

Molten plastic

Materials reprocessing

Reprocessing is like manufacturing in reverse. The materials collected for recycling cannot be reused as they are. Instead, they must be cleaned and reformed into a material that can be used to create new products. Metals, glass, and plastics are all ideal for reprocessing and can go through this process many times.

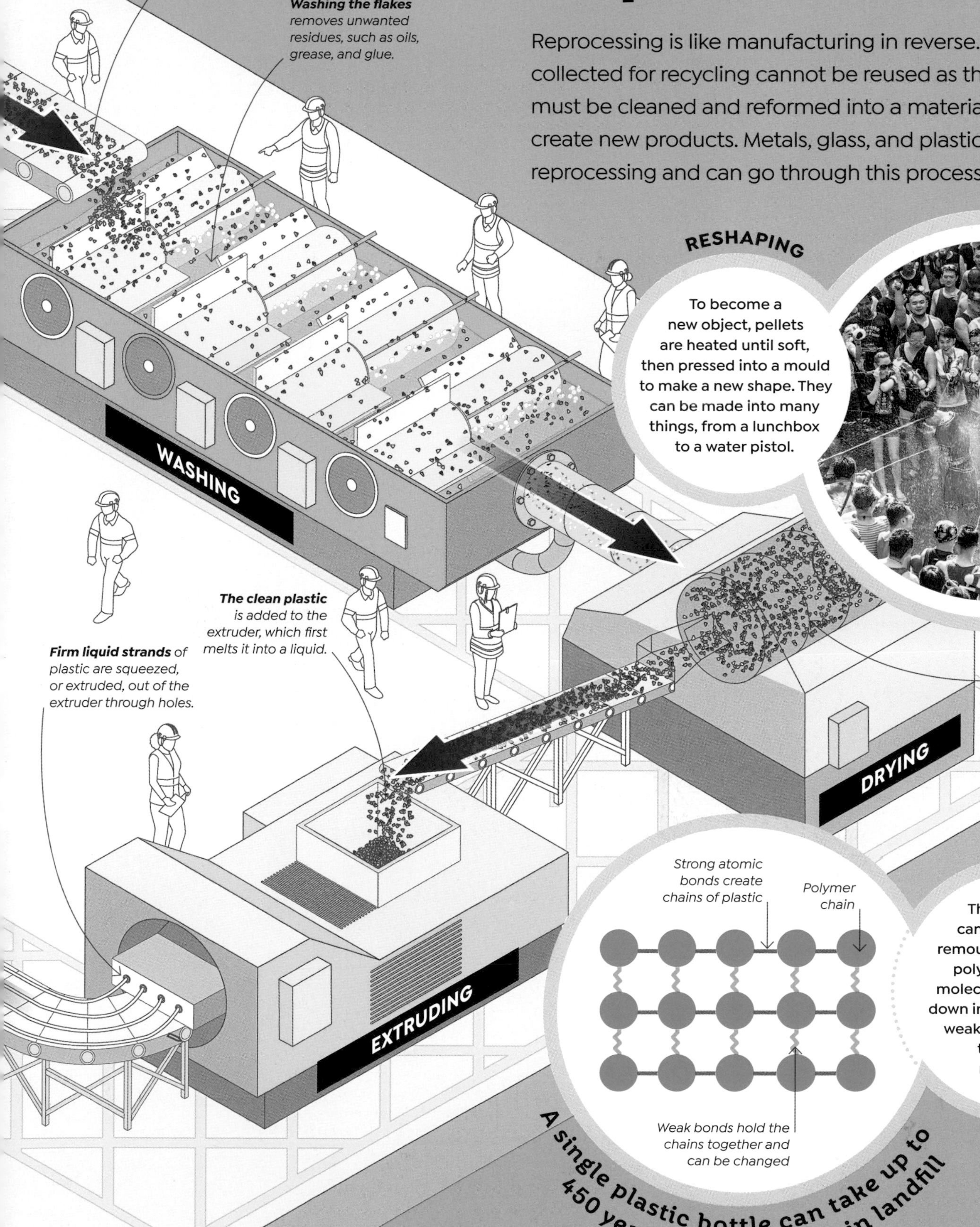

All plastic items are converted into consistently sized plastic flakes.

Washing the flakes removes unwanted residues, such as oils, grease, and glue.

WASHING

The clean plastic is added to the extruder, which first melts it into a liquid.

Firm liquid strands of plastic are squeezed, or extruded, out of the extruder through holes.

EXTRUDING

RESHAPING

To become a new object, pellets are heated until soft, then pressed into a mould to make a new shape. They can be made into many things, from a lunchbox to a water pistol.

The lightweight flakes are dried by being blown with warm air.

DRYING

THERMOPLASTICS

Thermoplastics can be heated and remoulded because the polymers (chains of molecules) do not break down in the heat, but have weak bonds that allow them to take new shapes.

Strong atomic bonds create chains of plastic

Polymer chain

Weak bonds hold the chains together and can be changed

A single plastic bottle can take up to 450 years to decompose in landfill

Living World

Beyond the human habitats of cities and farms is the natural environment of vast forests, deserts, and oceans. Each habitat works as a community of living organisms, from bacteria to bears, with competition and conflict, but also cooperation.

Bacteria

Bacteria are among the oldest and simplest forms of life on Earth. These single-celled microorganisms are found in all habitats – from hydrothermal vents to glaciers – and on and inside plants and animals. Like all life forms, bacteria are controlled by their genes – short lengths of DNA code. Unlike more complex organisms, bacteria have the special ability to pass genes to each other.

A membrane made from fat separates the inside of the cell from the outside. Only certain chemicals can pass through it.

A plasmid is a short strand of DNA in a closed loop. It contains extra genes that give the bacterium an advantage, such as resistance to antibiotics.

1 **A plasmid unravels** and one strand of its DNA passes through a sexual pilus to the recipient bacterium.

A stiff wall made of a network of sugars and proteins surrounds the cell.

Granules of food, such as starch and oils, are stored in the cytoplasm.

Ribosomes are the sites where the genetic code is read and the proteins the bacterium needs to grow and survive are built.

All of the bacterium's DNA is called the genome. Most of the genome is stored in a large, tangled loop.

The flagellar motor rotates the flagellum.

The stiff, tail-like flagellum can be used as a feeler or to move the bacterium by rotating like a propeller.

CELL WALL

CELL MEMBRANE

MAIN GENOME

DONOR BACTERIUM

CAPSULE

FLAGELLUM

A sexual pilus links the two cells until the DNA transfer is completed.

An outer capsule protects the cell. It can be a coating of slime or a stiff envelope.

Small hairlike pili (singular pilus) are used to cling to surfaces or other cells.

The cytoplasm is the fluid that fills the cell, and is mostly water.

BACILLI

Rod-shaped bacteria are known as bacilli (singular bacillus).

GENE DONATION

DONOR BACTERIUM

The process of transferring useful genes from cell to cell is called conjugation. One bacterium donates a strand of plasmid DNA to a nearby cell via a sexual pilus. The donated DNA gives the recipient new tools to survive.

DNA comes as a double strand, whether it is in the bacterium's main genome or one of its shorter plasmids. To donate genes, a bacterium unzips one of its plasmids, leaving a single strand that can leave the cell and enter the recipient bacterium. The remaining single-stranded plasmid is rebuilt into a double strand.

Donor strand of plasmid DNA leaves cell

DNA strands separate as chemical bonds break

PLASMID DNA

Each base pairs with its partner to restore the sequence

Free DNA subunits called bases rebuild the double strand

Spherical bacteria that grow in chains are called streptococci.

STREPTOCOCCI

ARCHAEA

In the 1970s, scientists discovered that certain microbes that look just like bacteria were in fact chemically distinct and utterly unrelated. Called Archaea, these microbes often live in extreme environments such as deep-sea volcanic rocks and hot spring water, as shown here at Grand Prismatic Spring in Yellowstone National Park, US.

Spherical bacteria are known as cocci (singular coccus).

COCCI

RECIPIENT BACTERIUM

This bacterium does not contain the new useful gene. Once it receives the donated DNA, the cell will become a donor bacterium and pass on the plasmid to others.

Spiral bacteria that move with flagella are called spirilla (singular spirillum).

SPIRILLA

❷ **Donated DNA** enters the recipient cell.

SEXUAL PILUS

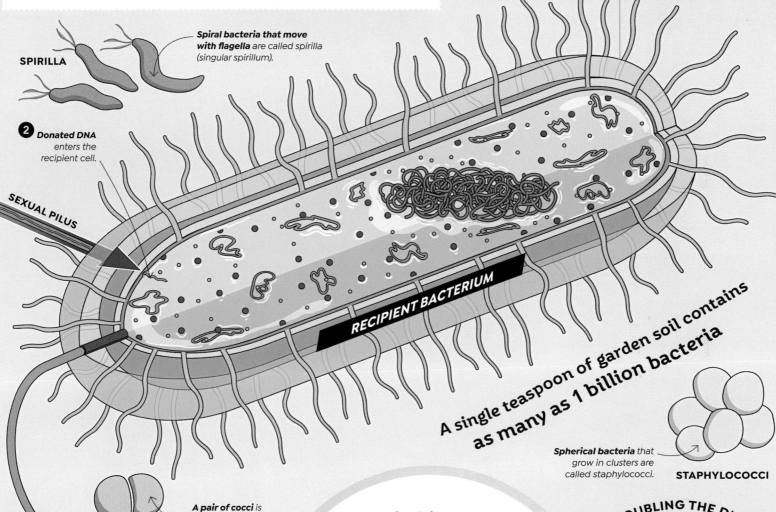

RECIPIENT BACTERIUM

A single teaspoon of garden soil contains as many as 1 billion bacteria

Spherical bacteria that grow in clusters are called staphylococci.

STAPHYLOCOCCI

A pair of cocci is called a diplococcus.

DIPLOCOCCUS

Spirochaetes are bacteria with twisted (spiral) cells.

SPIROCHAETES

Base A always pairs with T, and C with G

Copied strand of DNA

Donated strand of plasmid DNA entering cell

Duplicated plasmid identical to original

DOUBLING THE DNA

When the second bacterium receives the plasmid DNA, it needs to copy it to make a double strand. It uses the single strand as a template to build the second strand. The four chemical units, known as bases, which connect the strands always bond in specific pairs, so the sequence remains the same.

Plant and animal cells

The bodies of plants and animals are all made from microscopic building blocks called cells. A plant cell has several important differences from that of an animal, but they also share many things in common. Both types of cell contain even smaller units called organelles, where the processes necessary for life are performed.

PLANT CELL FEATURES

All plant cells have a thick wall made from cellulose. Many rigid cell walls together give a plant its solid shape. The leaves and stems of plants contain cells with chloroplasts, the organelles where photosynthesis takes place.

The cell wall provides support and structure.

2 *Specific proteins* are made on the rough ER. The genetic code is read at ribosomes, and the proteins are assembled.

1 *Most cell functions* require specific proteins to work. The nucleus sends out instructions to make these proteins.

Rough endoplasmic reticulum (ER) is a complex organelle made of a stack of interconnected membranes.

The nucleus stores DNA, which acts as a library of instructions for making specific proteins.

The nucleolus makes ribosomes.

Ribosomes make the ER appear "rough".

NUCLEUS

ROUGH ER

SMOOTH ER

Smooth endoplasmic reticulum (ER) makes and transports fats and some hormones.

CELL WALL

GOLGI BODY

3 *Protein* is taken to the Golgi body, which refines and parcels up proteins ready for action.

VESICLE

The Golgi body is an organelle made of a series of stacked membranes.

4 *The Golgi body* buds off a vesicle containing protein for transport around the cell or for sending outside, if the protein's job is done in a different part of the plant.

The cell membrane is a thin layer of fat. It forms a barrier that controls what goes into and out of the cell.

$$6CO_2 + 6H_2O \rightarrow C_6H_{12}O_6 + 6O_2$$

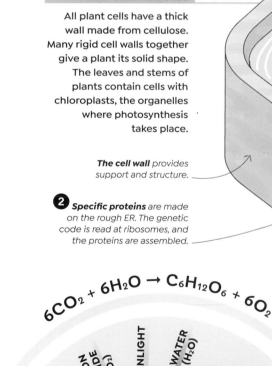

CHLOROPLAST

CARBON DIOXIDE (CO_2)

SUNLIGHT

WATER (H_2O)

GLUCOSE $(C_6H_{12}O_6)$

OXYGEN (O_2)

Pouches of chlorophyll

Plants use a process called photosynthesis to capture energy from sunlight and combine water and carbon dioxide into glucose fuel and oxygen.

PHOTOSYNTHESIS

Mitochondria are the organelles where respiration takes place, providing the cell with energy.

$$C_6H_{12}O_6 + 6O_2 \rightarrow 6CO_2 + 6H_2O$$

Folded inner membrane creates large surface area for chemical reactions

GLUCOSE ($C_6H_{12}O_6$)

OXYGEN (O_2)

WATER (H_2O)

CARBON DIOXIDE (CO_2)

MITOCHONDRION

CHEMICAL ENERGY

MITOCHONDRION

Cells release the energy they need from glucose fuel by the process of respiration. The reaction uses oxygen to split the glucose into water and carbon dioxide.

RESPIRATION

PROTOZOA

Plants and animals are eukaryotes, as are the single-celled organisms called protozoa, which share the same basic cell structure. Protozoa are highly varied, with tail-like flagella or hairlike cilia. Some, such as this amoeba, can change their shape by extending and retracting armlike projections called pseudopods.

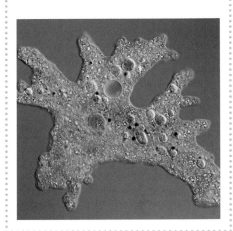

VACUOLE

The vacuole stores water and nutrients, and helps the plant to keep its shape by providing internal pressure.

CHLOROPLAST

Chloroplasts are the organelles where photosynthesis takes place. They contain a green pigment called chlorophyll, which gives plants their main colour.

A jelly-like fluid called cytoplasm fills the cell. It is mostly water.

A vesicle is a small sac of membrane filled with a particular protein.

LYSOSOME

Lysosomes contain enzymes that digest waste products.

Vesicles are made from the same material as the membrane and so can fuse to it.

Scientists estimate that the average human body contains about 37 trillion cells

Centrioles produce rope-like microtubules that pull cell into different shapes

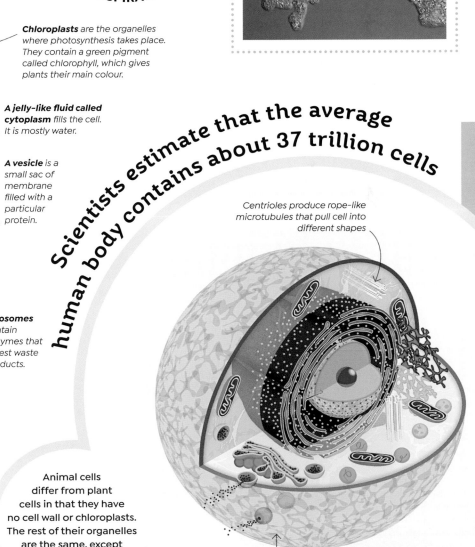

Flexible membrane allows cell to change shape

CELL MEMBRANE

5 **The vesicle fuses** with the cell membrane and releases the proteins to perform their task – which might be signalling to other cells to stimulate growth or develop flowers.

Animal cells differ from plant cells in that they have no cell wall or chloroplasts. The rest of their organelles are the same, except most plants do not have centrioles.

ANIMAL CELL

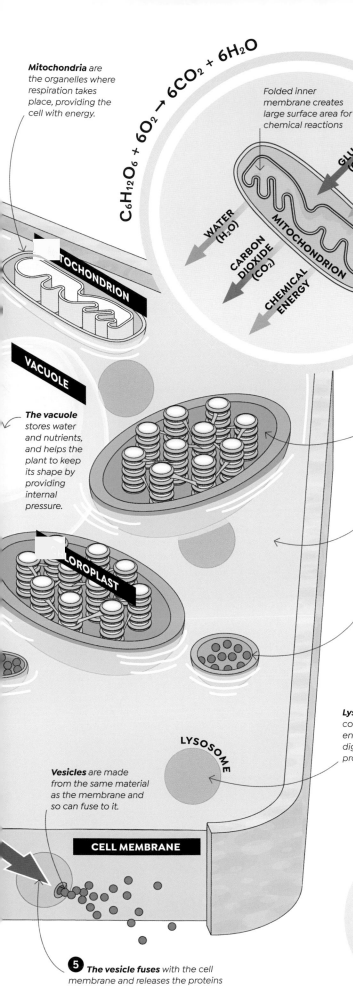

ANIMALIA

Animals are multicellular organisms, and most of them have nerves and move using muscles. They obtain their energy by eating food.

COMMON LOBSTER

Lobsters use their large pincers to catch smaller animals to eat.

PERCH

Perch have several fins, which they use to move through water.

LONG-TAILED MACAQUE

Sight is the most important sense used by macaques to find food.

GREY WOLF

Long legs enable wolves to run fast after prey.

AFRICAN WILDCAT

Cats use their nerve-rich whiskers to sense their surroundings.

LION

A muscular body helps lions to catch large animals.

TIGER

Tigers can move their ears to pinpoint a sound.

CHORDATA

Chordates all have a stiff rodlike notochord as they develop. In most chordates, the notochord becomes part of a flexible spine, also known as the vertebral column.

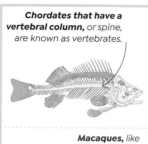

Chordates that have a vertebral column, or spine, are known as vertebrates.

Macaques, like all vertebrates, have an internal skeleton.

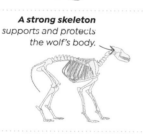

A strong skeleton supports and protects the wolf's body.

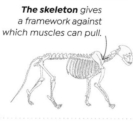

The skeleton gives a framework against which muscles can pull.

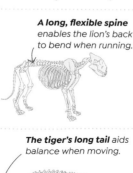

A long, flexible spine enables the lion's back to bend when running.

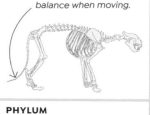

The tiger's long tail aids balance when moving.

MAMMALIA

Mammals are warm-blooded chordates that have hair on at least some of their body during their life. Adult females feed (suckle) their young with milk produced by mammary glands.

Female macaques feed milk to their young via soft teats, or nipples.

A wolf's body is covered in insulating fur.

African wildcats have up to five kittens in a litter.

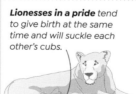

Lionesses in a pride tend to give birth at the same time and will suckle each other's cubs.

Tigers feed their cubs milk until they are six months old.

CARNIVORA

Carnivores are mammals that have specialized canine and molar teeth used for grasping, killing, and eating prey. Many primarily eat meat and have a body adapted for hunting.

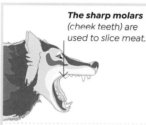

The sharp molars (cheek teeth) are used to slice meat.

Four long, sharp canines are used to stab prey.

Powerful jaws help with killing and eating.

The canines are revealed when snarling.

FELIDAE

Cats, or felids, are carnivores with short jaws, and well-developed claws used for holding prey, climbing trees, and fighting. In most cats, the claws are fully retractable.

Sharp, curved claws provide a good grip.

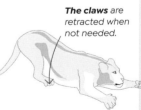

The claws are retracted when not needed.

Cats sharpen their claws by scratching.

| KINGDOM | PHYLUM | CLASS | ORDER | FAMILY |

WHAT IS A SPECIES?

A species is a group of organisms that share many similar physical characteristics and behaviours, although they are not identical. However, they are so similar that they are able to breed with one another and produce healthy young, such as the mute swans shown here. As a general rule, members of two different species cannot breed successfully.

TREE OF LIFE

The evolutionary links between life forms can be shown using a diagram called the tree of life. The diagram divides into branches to show that distinct groups evolved from a common ancestor. This tree shows the three largest classification groups, the domains Bacteria, Archaea, and Eukaryota. The last one has five branches known as kingdoms.

BACTERIA
Members of this domain are all simple, microscopic, single-celled organisms. They grow in number by dividing in two.

ARCHAEA
These single-celled organisms look similar to bacteria, but they use different chemicals to control their life processes.

EUKARYOTES
Eukaryotes have larger and more complex cells than bacteria and archaea. All multicellular organisms are members of this domain.

PROTOZOA
This is a hugely varied group of single-celled organisms, which includes amoebas and flagellates.

FUNGI
This kingdom comprises yeasts, moulds, and mushrooms, which are found on land and in water.

ANIMALS
All animals are multicellular organisms, which can move part or all of their body to get food to eat.

PLANTS
Plants are multicellular organisms that use photosynthesis to create food. Most are found on land.

CHROMISTS
Most chromists are seaweeds or single-celled algae that photosynthesize and live in water.

All members of the cat family are highly specialized hunters with curved claws

Classification

Life on Earth is organized using a system called classification, which groups organisms according to how they are related. All members of a group share a specific feature because they are descended from the first organism to evolve that innovation. That organism is known as their common ancestor. A species is the basic classification unit, and species are organized into groups of increasing size up to the highest level, which is called a domain.

PANTHERA

Members of the genus *Panthera* are large cats that have evolved flat and square vocal cords that respond more easily to passing air, allowing them to roar as well as purr.

When roaring, *the mouth is opened wide to project the sound.*

Tigers (and lions) *can roar as loud as 114 decibels – as loud as a rock concert.*

GENUS

PANTHERA TIGRIS

The tiger is the only member of the genus *Panthera* that has a striped coat when adult. The stripes camouflage tigers in sun-dappled vegetation, concealing them from prey.

SPECIES

BREEDS

A breed is an artificial grouping created by humans in a species of domestic animal or plant. Over many years, breeders are able to create organisms with specific features, such as a fluffy coat or sweet fruit, by choosing which pairs produce young. Despite their differences, the 100 or so breeds of domestic cat are all the same species, *Felis catus.*

Food web

A community of wildlife – made up of plants, animals, and microorganisms – can be represented as a food web. The web arranges organisms according to who is consuming what. By doing this, a food web shows how the energy that powers life and the nutrients needed to make living bodies flow through the community. Food webs divide wildlife into categories based on what they eat – and what eats them.

PRIMARY PRODUCERS

The food web begins here. Most producers are plants and algae that use photosynthesis to take the energy from sunlight to create food.

PRIMARY CONSUMERS

Animals must eat food to get the energy and nutrients they need to survive, and animals that eat producers are called primary consumers. They are also known as herbivores.

Arrows show the flow of energy and nutrients through the food web.

Zooplankton are tiny animals and protozoa that float in the ocean and eat phytoplankton. Some species eat other zooplankton and so are secondary consumers.

Phytoplankton are microalgae, tiny marine organisms that use photosynthesis to produce food. They drift in sunlit waters near the surface of the ocean.

Vast shoals of small crustaceans called krill swim up towards the surface at night to feed on the phytoplankton floating there.

Simple nutrients (minerals) are returned to the ocean (or the soil on land), where they are taken up by primary producers.

DECOMPOSERS

The nutrients in the remains of dead organisms are recycled back to the start of the food web by a category of organisms called decomposers. Fungi and bacteria are common decomposers.

Seaweeds are larger algae that grow on the seabed. They need sunlight to survive, just like plants on land, and so are found mostly in shallow waters close to the shore.

On shallow seabeds, some crabs and other primary consumers eat seaweed. Land-dwelling crabs have to wait until the tide is out to feed.

Decomposer bacteria ooze digestive enzymes and convert organic matter around their bodies to mineral waste.

MARINE SNOW

Marine snow is the name for the small fragments of waste and dead organisms that sink down from the upper zones of the ocean. It connects the food web to the deep ocean, transferring energy and nutrients, and is the main source of food for detritivores on the seabed. The Venus flytrap sea anemone's tentacles collect marine snow as it drifts past.

DETRITIVORES

When plants and animals die, their remains become food for a category of organisms called detritivores. Another term for them is scavenger. In the ocean, detritivores are most active on the seabed.

Sea pigs are relatives of sea urchins that live on the seabed scavenging for small fragments of food and waste that sink from above.

SECONDARY CONSUMERS

Secondary consumers are animals that eat primary consumers. In many food webs, secondary consumers eat plants as well as animals and so are described as omnivores.

TERTIARY CONSUMERS

Animals at this level of a food web are specialized hunters that target prey animals. They generally eat only meat and so are also known as carnivores.

The leopard seal is a voracious predator, eating a wide range of animals, including fish, penguins, and other seals.

APEX PREDATOR

An apex predator sits at the top of the food web and has no natural predators. Apex predators tend to be large animals that are few in number.

Baleen whales, the largest animals on Earth, are secondary consumers in ocean food webs. They scoop up vast mouthfuls of water and filter out any food, eating tonnes of krill every day.

Fish swimming in open water search for animals smaller than themselves to eat.

Penguins spend a long time out at sea to feed on animals such as fish, cuttlefish, and krill. They return to land or ice to rest and breed.

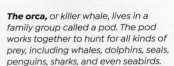

The orca, or killer whale, lives in a family group called a pod. The pod works together to hunt for all kinds of prey, including whales, dolphins, seals, penguins, sharks, and even seabirds.

Cuttlefish, which are relatives of squid and octopuses, eat animals that live in the water and on the seabed. When eating certain fish, they are also tertiary consumers.

Dolphins are all predators. These marine mammals vary their diet according to whether they live near the coast or in deep ocean water.

An average-sized orca eats about 225 kg (500 lb) of food every day

---

DEATH

WHALE FALL

The carcass of a dead whale provides an oasis of food on the seabed. It is too dark on most of the ocean floor for seaweeds to live, so many of the animals that live there are reliant on food falling from above.

The whale carcass becomes a haven for deep-sea life, such as worms, molluscs, and crabs, which live in the remains.

ZOMBIE WORMS

These deep-sea worms are specialist seabed detritivores. They use acid to bore into the bones of whale carcasses and then eat the fats inside.

Scavengers, including deep-sea octopuses, hagfish, and sharks, will travel a long distance for such a large supply of food as this.

A whale carcass will feed millions of animals over many months and years

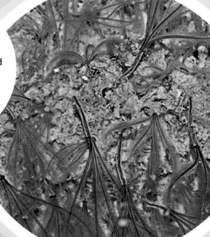

The carbon cycle

Life on Earth is based on the element carbon. All living organisms take in carbon in various forms – from the air, water, soil, and other organisms – and give it out again. Together with physical processes, such as weathering, this creates the carbon cycle. The cycle is naturally balanced, but human activity is upsetting it.

A single cow belches about 100 kg (220 lb) of methane every year

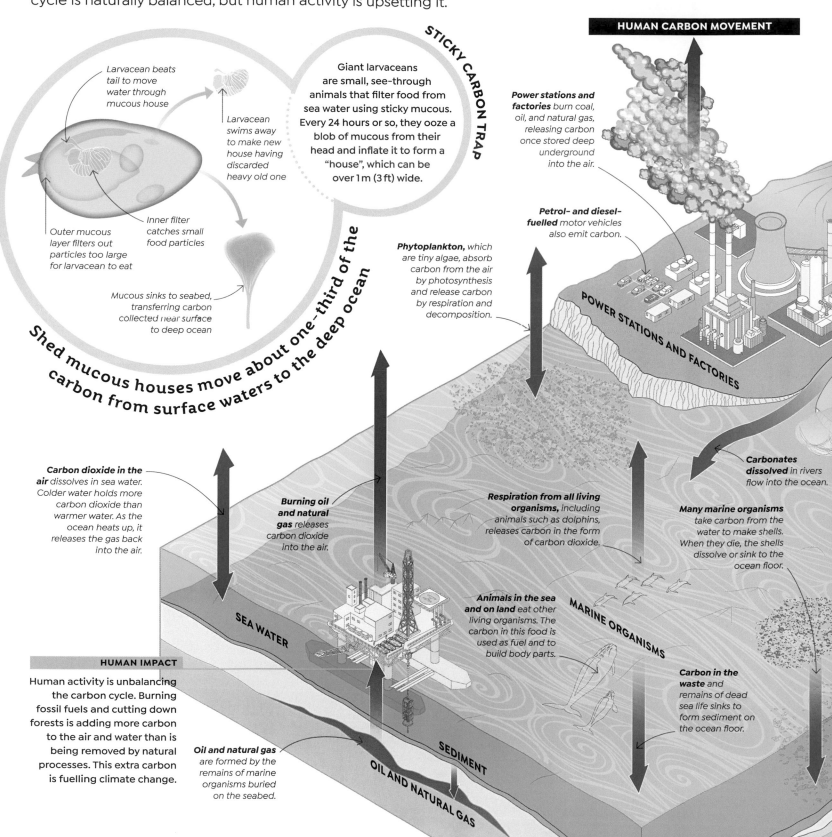

STICKY CARBON TRAP

Larvacean beats tail to move water through mucous house

Larvacean swims away to make new house having discarded heavy old one

Giant larvaceans are small, see-through animals that filter food from sea water using sticky mucous. Every 24 hours or so, they ooze a blob of mucous from their head and inflate it to form a "house", which can be over 1 m (3 ft) wide.

Inner filter catches small food particles

Outer mucous layer filters out particles too large for larvacean to eat

Mucous sinks to seabed, transferring carbon collected near surface to deep ocean

Shed mucous houses move about one-third of the carbon from surface waters to the deep ocean

HUMAN CARBON MOVEMENT

Power stations and factories *burn coal, oil, and natural gas, releasing carbon once stored deep underground into the air.*

Petrol– and diesel– fuelled *motor vehicles also emit carbon.*

POWER STATIONS AND FACTORIES

Phytoplankton, *which are tiny algae, absorb carbon from the air by photosynthesis and release carbon by respiration and decomposition.*

Carbon dioxide in the air *dissolves in sea water. Colder water holds more carbon dioxide than warmer water. As the ocean heats up, it releases the gas back into the air.*

Burning oil and natural gas *releases carbon dioxide into the air.*

Respiration from all living organisms, *including animals such as dolphins, releases carbon in the form of carbon dioxide.*

Carbonates dissolved *in rivers flow into the ocean.*

Many marine organisms *take carbon from the water to make shells. When they die, the shells dissolve or sink to the ocean floor.*

SEA WATER

Animals in the sea and on land *eat other living organisms. The carbon in this food is used as fuel and to build body parts.*

MARINE ORGANISMS

Carbon in the waste *and remains of dead sea life sinks to form sediment on the ocean floor.*

HUMAN IMPACT

Human activity is unbalancing the carbon cycle. Burning fossil fuels and cutting down forests is adding more carbon to the air and water than is being removed by natural processes. This extra carbon is fuelling climate change.

Oil and natural gas *are formed by the remains of marine organisms buried on the seabed.*

SEDIMENT

OIL AND NATURAL GAS

PHOTOSYNTHESIS

Plants and algae take carbon dioxide out of the air and water and use it to make sugars by photosynthesis. This process is the main way carbon enters the food chain.

Volcanic eruptions *release carbon dioxide into the atmosphere from carbon stored in rocks.*

Plants respire *all the time, releasing carbon dioxide into the air.*

VOLCANIC ERUPTION

Forests *cover about 30 per cent of Earth's land surface; the trees store carbon in their wood as they grow.*

Deforestation *releases carbon into the atmosphere if the trees are burned or decompose.*

FORESTS

RAIN

Carbon dioxide dissolves in rain, *creating acid that eats away at rocks, adding carbonates to river water.*

DIAMONDS

Diamonds are crystals of pure carbon that formed billions of years ago in Earth's mantle. Volcanic eruptions drag some diamonds nearer to the surface, where they can be mined.

Carbon dioxide *makes up about 0.04 per cent of the atmosphere. This gas is constantly being added and removed by other parts of the carbon cycle.*

Climate change *has led to an increase in the release of methane from tundra soils due to thawing of the permafrost and fires.*

Coal mining *moves carbon stored in sedimentary rock basins in Earth back to the surface.*

Peat soils *are formed by the decaying remains of plants in wetlands, such as swamps and bogs, and tundra.*

PEAT

Farm animals, *especially cattle, release carbon into the air as methane gas.*

FARMS

COAL

Coal *was formed from ancient plant remains buried before they rotted away.*

METHANE BUBBLES

Bubbles of methane gas are produced by bacteria on the bottom of Lake Abraham, Canada. They are trapped in ice as they approach the colder surface.

LIMESTONE

Carbonate minerals in sea shells *are compacted to form limestone.*

DECOMPOSITION

Dead organisms are eaten by scavengers, such as vultures and worms, and then decomposers, such as bacteria and fungi. Decomposers transfer the carbon stored in organisms back into the environment.

WEATHERING AND EROSION

Carbonates are minerals containing carbon found in limestone and dolomite rocks. Weathering and erosion, especially by water, eats away at these rocks, removing the carbonates. They are added to the soil or washed into the sea.

Decomposer bacteria *in many soils, such as those in rice paddies, produce methane gas as a waste product when breaking down organic matter.*

Grassland

A grassland forms wherever there is not enough rainfall to sustain a large number of trees, but where there is enough water to keep the land from becoming a desert. Fast-growing grasses are the dominant vegetation, and a huge number of animals rely on them for food.

SYNCHRONIZED BIRTHS

Wildebeest have a very short breeding season, which ensures the calves are born at around the same time. This increases their chances of avoiding being eaten.

SCAVENGERS

UMBRELLA ACACIA

Slow-growing acacia trees create islands of cool shade in a vast plain of grasses. The tree can grow at temperatures of 50 °C (122 °F) but also withstand low temperatures at night.

Cheetahs often use a termite mound as a lookout post, keeping a watchful eye for other predators as well as prey.

Warm air leaves mound

Vultures gather above the carcass, but they must wait for the lions to finish eating before they can scavenge the remains.

APEX PREDATORS

Lions hunt as a group. They hide in the longer grass of the African savanna, creeping up on their prey until they are close enough to attack.

GRAZERS

Grass-eating animals, such as wildebeest, have nowhere to hide, so they gather in huge herds for safety and are ready to run at the first sign of danger.

GRAZING HERD

SOLITARY HUNTER

COOPERATIVE HUNTERS

Cool air sucked into ventilation shaft.

Shallow tree roots spread out in all directions to take in rainwater as it trickles through the soil.

An aardvark, which eats ants and termites, sleeps hidden in a burrow during the day, emerging at night to feed.

TERMITE MOUND

Vast colonies of termites consume huge quantities of grass stalks. The insects live in underground nests below tall earth towers with a network of shafts that cause cool air to circulate inside.

The acacia's deeper taproots grow down to permanent sources of groundwater so the tree can survive the dry season.

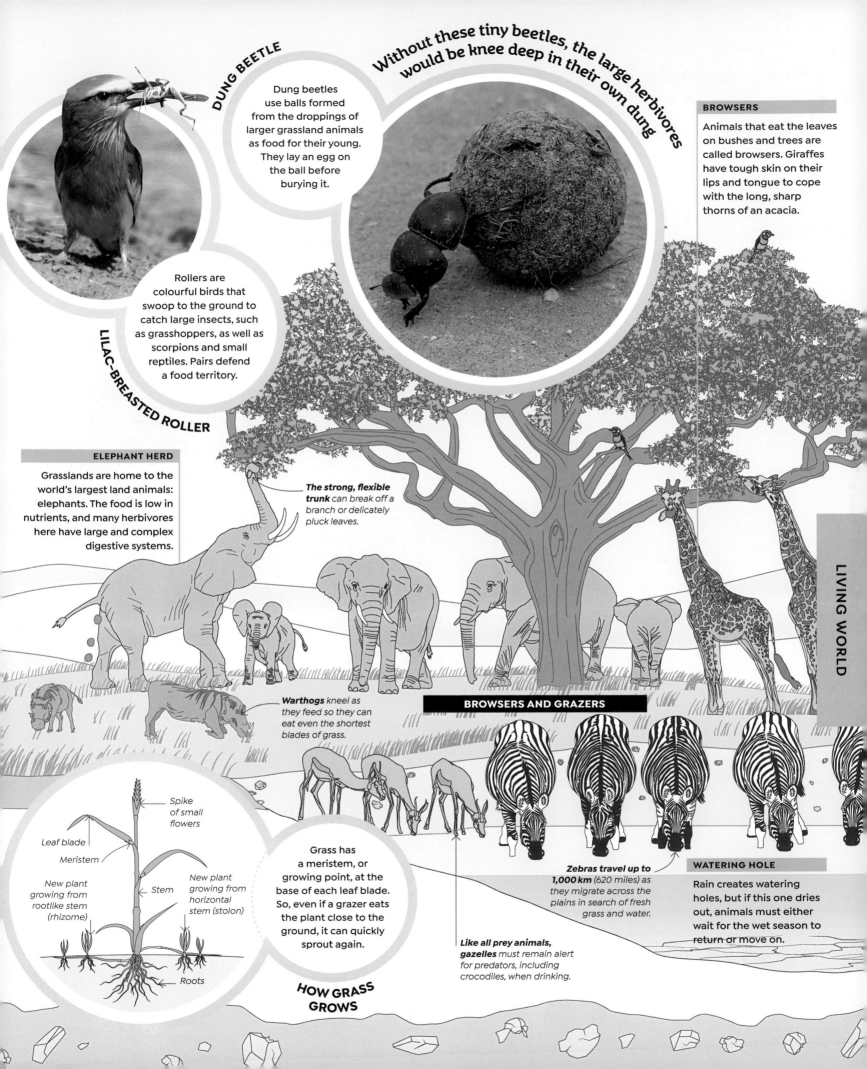

DUNG BEETLE

Dung beetles use balls formed from the droppings of larger grassland animals as food for their young. They lay an egg on the ball before burying it.

Without these tiny beetles, the large herbivores would be knee deep in their own dung

BROWSERS

Animals that eat the leaves on bushes and trees are called browsers. Giraffes have tough skin on their lips and tongue to cope with the long, sharp thorns of an acacia.

LILAC-BREASTED ROLLER

Rollers are colourful birds that swoop to the ground to catch large insects, such as grasshoppers, as well as scorpions and small reptiles. Pairs defend a food territory.

ELEPHANT HERD

Grasslands are home to the world's largest land animals: elephants. The food is low in nutrients, and many herbivores here have large and complex digestive systems.

The strong, flexible trunk can break off a branch or delicately pluck leaves.

Warthogs kneel as they feed so they can eat even the shortest blades of grass.

BROWSERS AND GRAZERS

Spike of small flowers

Leaf blade

Meristem

New plant growing from rootlike stem (rhizome)

Stem

New plant growing from horizontal stem (stolon)

Roots

Grass has a meristem, or growing point, at the base of each leaf blade. So, even if a grazer eats the plant close to the ground, it can quickly sprout again.

Zebras travel up to 1,000 km (620 miles) as they migrate across the plains in search of fresh grass and water.

WATERING HOLE

Rain creates watering holes, but if this one dries out, animals must either wait for the wet season to return or move on.

Like all prey animals, gazelles must remain alert for predators, including crocodiles, when drinking.

HOW GRASS GROWS

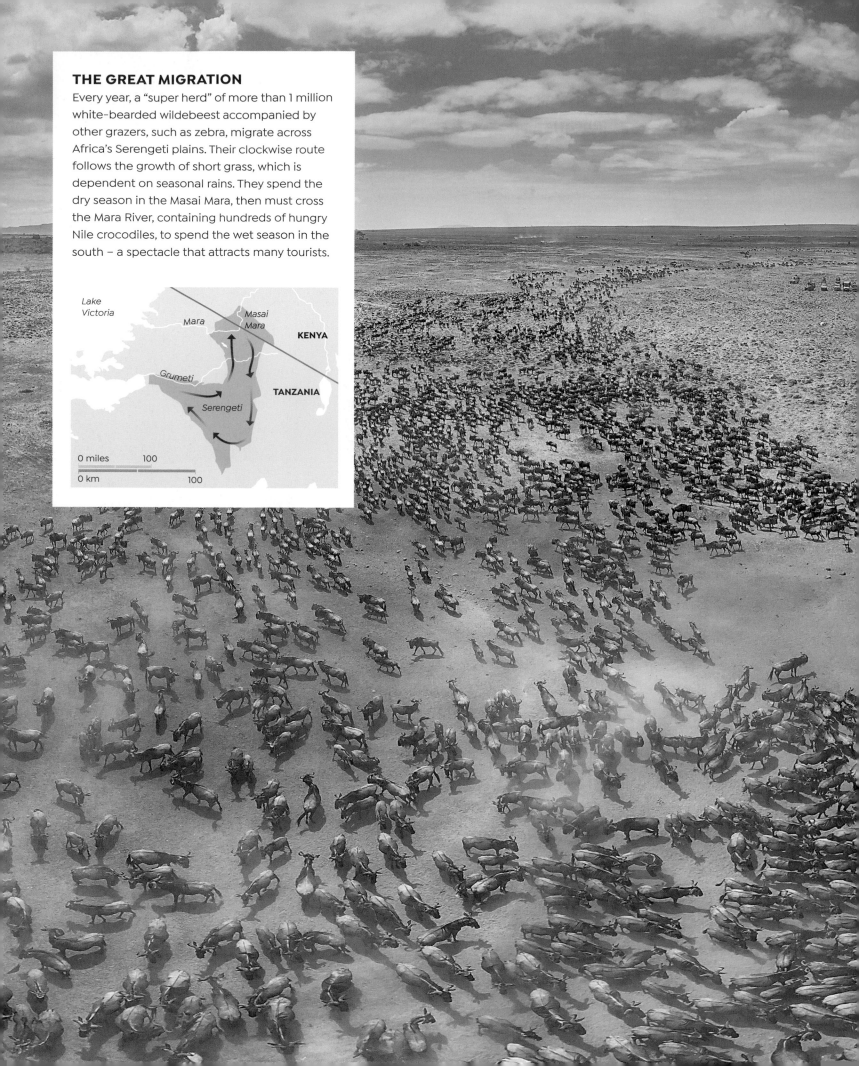

THE GREAT MIGRATION

Every year, a "super herd" of more than 1 million white-bearded wildebeest accompanied by other grazers, such as zebra, migrate across Africa's Serengeti plains. Their clockwise route follows the growth of short grass, which is dependent on seasonal rains. They spend the dry season in the Masai Mara, then must cross the Mara River, containing hundreds of hungry Nile crocodiles, to spend the wet season in the south – a spectacle that attracts many tourists.

Lake Victoria

Mara

Masai Mara

KENYA

Grumeti

TANZANIA

Serengeti

0 miles 100

0 km 100

RAIN SHADOW DESERTS

Some deserts form in the rain shadow of a tall mountain range. Moisture-laden air from the ocean must pass over the mountains to reach land on the other side. As the air rises, it cools, forms clouds, and rain falls. By the time the air reaches the land on the far side, it has dried out and seldom brings rain, and so a desert is created.

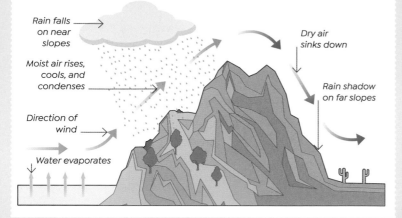

Rain falls on near slopes

Moist air rises, cools, and condenses

Direction of wind

Water evaporates

Dry air sinks down

Rain shadow on far slopes

SUCCULENTS

Succulents are plants that store water inside thick, fleshy body parts, such as the stem of a golden barrel cactus. The sharp spines of cacti are modified leaves.

Spines protect against grazers

Water stored in fleshy tissue

Waxy cuticle prevents water loss

Long roots collect water

Furry paws insulate the fennec fox against hot sand and give it traction when moving

To ambush small lizards, a desert horned viper conceals itself in the sand, leaving just its eyes and horns visible. It moves across dunes by sidewinding.

Each horn is a single modified scale, which may reduce glare from the sun.

A sandfish skink "swims" swiftly through sand by wriggling its body, but it can also use its short legs to move slowly on the surface.

Addax never need to drink water as they gain all the moisture they need from the plants they eat.

Their pale coat reflects heat and gives addax their alternative name of white antelope.

A fennec fox's large ears help it to radiate heat from its body and to listen for prey in and on the sand.

Also known as bitter apple, the desert gourd has round, spongy fruit, with bitter pulp and seeds rich in protein and fat.

Direction of travel

Head and front of body raised

Raised section of body

Sections of body push against ground

To move fast on a loose, sandy surface, some snakes use a method called sidewinding. Muscular waves lift sections of the snake's body and push it forward.

Saharan silver ants leave their nest to scavenge for just 10 minutes during the hottest part of the day, when predatory ant lizards are resting in the shade.

The desert gourd has a long tap root that reaches water deep underground, which means it can keep its leaves cool by evaporation.

During the day, a lesser Egyptian jerboa plugs the entrances to its burrow to keep out the heat and predators.

SAND

SIDEWINDING

A Saharan silver ant can travel 108 times its body length in one second

Desert

Any area of land that receives less than 25 cm (10 in) of rain in a year is a desert. Deserts are often very hot, during the day at least, but they can be very cold, and may be sandy, rocky, or even icy. The plants and animals that live in them have adapted to the hostile conditions in a variety of ways.

A unique wax on the leaves resists melting up to 70 °C (158 °F), which means they do not dry out in the extreme heat of the desert.

The fruit, or dates, hang in clusters, turning from yellow to reddish brown as they ripen.

DATE PALM

The sweet fruit of date palms helped humans to survive in the Sahara and Arabian deserts thousands of years ago. The wood can be used as timber and the leaves as thatching.

Sandgrouse usually nest far from oases and so must fly to a watering hole every day to drink and collect water to take back to their chicks.

As the trunk grows upwards, the tree sheds its lower leaves, leaving behind woody bases.

CAMEL TRAIN

Dromedaries were domesticated as pack animals around 4,000 years ago. They can survive without drinking water and food for weeks thanks to the fat stored in their hump.

A dromedary's nostrils can be closed to keep out sand.

DUNES

The broad, padded feet aid walking across hot sand.

HOW OASES ARE FORMED

Rain falling on distant hills flows through layers of porous rocks, known as aquifers. The water emerges at an oasis, either where the water table is near the surface or where pressure forces it up through a fault in the rock.

Rain falling on hills seeps into aquifers

Spring-fed oasis lies in depression close to water table

Oasis formed at fault

Groundwater flows slowly through aquifer

Impermeable rock prevents groundwater escaping

Water forced up at fault

OASIS

Male sandgrouse have absorbent breast feathers, which they use to gather water for their chicks.

SOURCE OF LIFE

An oasis is a source of water in a desert. The availability of water is the limiting factor for desert life, and so wildlife is scarce elsewhere.

IMPERMEABLE ROCK LAYERS

AQUIFER

IMPERMEABLE ROCK LAYER

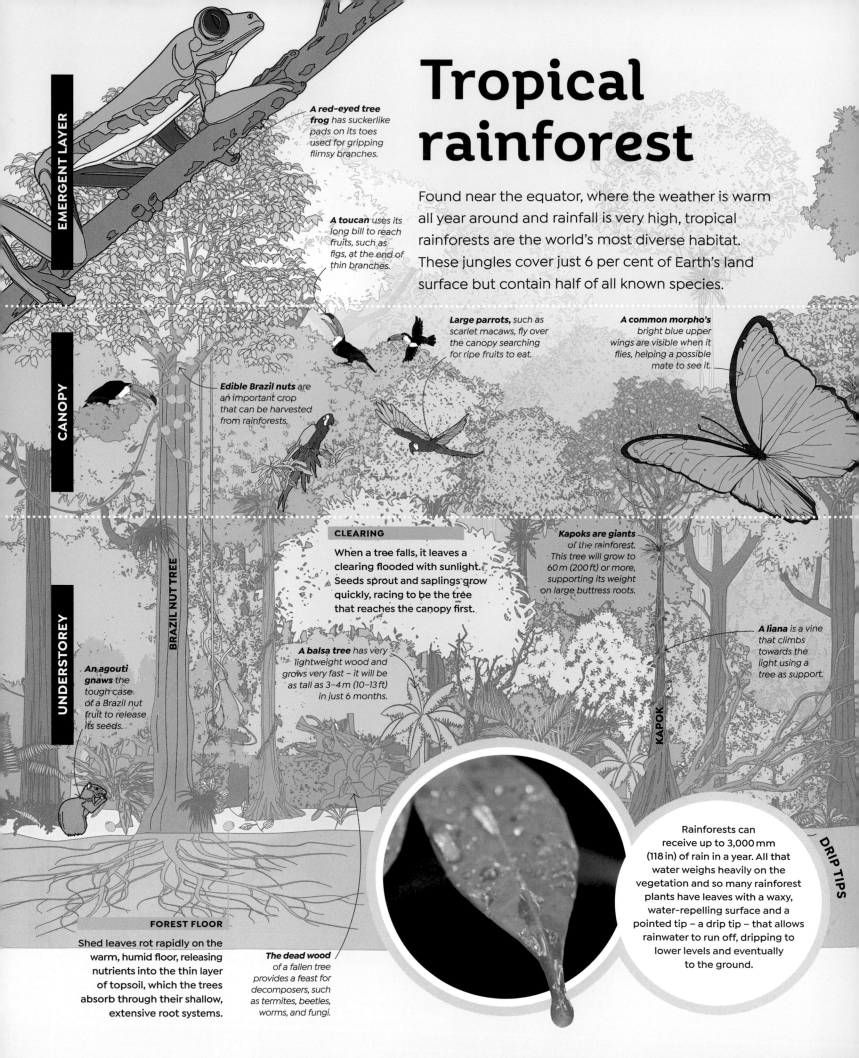

Tropical rainforest

Found near the equator, where the weather is warm all year around and rainfall is very high, tropical rainforests are the world's most diverse habitat. These jungles cover just 6 per cent of Earth's land surface but contain half of all known species.

EMERGENT LAYER

A red-eyed tree frog has suckerlike pads on its toes used for gripping flimsy branches.

A toucan uses its long bill to reach fruits, such as figs, at the end of thin branches.

CANOPY

Large parrots, such as scarlet macaws, fly over the canopy searching for ripe fruits to eat.

A common morpho's bright blue upper wings are visible when it flies, helping a possible mate to see it.

Edible Brazil nuts are an important crop that can be harvested from rainforests.

BRAZIL NUT TREE

CLEARING

When a tree falls, it leaves a clearing flooded with sunlight. Seeds sprout and saplings grow quickly, racing to be the tree that reaches the canopy first.

Kapoks are giants of the rainforest. This tree will grow to 60 m (200 ft) or more, supporting its weight on large buttress roots.

A liana is a vine that climbs towards the light using a tree as support.

UNDERSTOREY

An agouti gnaws the tough case of a Brazil nut fruit to release its seeds.

A balsa tree has very lightweight wood and grows very fast – it will be as tall as 3–4 m (10–13 ft) in just 6 months.

KAPOK

DRIP TIPS

Rainforests can receive up to 3,000 mm (118 in) of rain in a year. All that water weighs heavily on the vegetation and so many rainforest plants have leaves with a waxy, water-repelling surface and a pointed tip – a drip tip – that allows rainwater to run off, dripping to lower levels and eventually to the ground.

FOREST FLOOR

Shed leaves rot rapidly on the warm, humid floor, releasing nutrients into the thin layer of topsoil, which the trees absorb through their shallow, extensive root systems.

The dead wood of a fallen tree provides a feast for decomposers, such as termites, beetles, worms, and fungi.

One of the world's largest birds of prey, a harpy eagle is strong enough to snatch a monkey or sloth from the canopy in its talons.

NECTAR FEEDING

Many tropical plants rely on animals to transfer pollen between their flowers, and so they provide sweet nectar to attract them. As well as insects, forest pollinators include hummingbirds, bats, monkeys, and the kinkajou. Flowers that attract this nocturnal mammal tend to be large, white, and very fragrant, such as balsa flowers, which open for just one night.

Epiphytes, or air plants, such as orchids and bromeliads, live on trees but gain water from the moist air and nutrients from parrot and monkey droppings.

EMERGENT LAYER

The biggest trees rise above the canopy, some as tall as 75 m (250 ft), and capture the most sunlight.

CANOPY

The overlapping branches of tall evergreen trees create a "roof" that blocks most of the light. Eighty per cent of rainforest species live in the canopy.

A kinkajou uses its grasping feet and prehensile tail to move agilely around the trees.

Red howler monkeys call from the treetops at dawn or dusk to declare their troop's territory.

Slow-moving sloths forage for leaves at night, using their long, curved claws to hang from branches.

A rubber tree has a milky sap called latex, which can be converted into natural rubber.

A tapir hides in the dense understorey, her calf camouflaged by its striped and spotted coat.

Açai palms are cultivated for their berries and palm hearts.

UNDERSTOREY

A layer of smaller trees, shrubs, and ferns grows between the canopy and the mostly bare forest floor.

RUBBER TREE

FIG TREE

CACAO TREE

AÇAI PALM

The jaguar is the largest predator in the Amazon rainforest. It usually hunts at night for tapirs, deer, and other mammals.

Millions of leafcutter ants live in an underground nest, which contains several chambers where fungus is grown on leaf cuttings.

Leafcutter ants bite through leaves and carry fragments back to their nest. The ants use the leaves to cultivate fungus "gardens" as a source of food.

Leafcutter ants remove up to 15 per cent of leaves in the Amazon rainforest

LEAFCUTTER ANTS

Temperate forest

Temperate forests grow in regions that receive plenty of rain but do not get too hot or cold. These parts of the world experience four distinct seasons, and the life cycles of the forest's plants and animals are synchronized with the changes throughout the year.

SPRING BOUNTY

Insect eggs laid the previous year hatch in spring. The caterpillars and other young are an important food source for birds, such as this chickadee, and their chicks.

BUDS APPEAR

In early spring, the weather warms and the day length increases. The trees sprout new leaves and flower buds, and insects, such as aphids, hatch to eat them.

A pair of chickadees must find up to 570 caterpillars every day to rear their chicks

Deciduous trees, such as oaks, maples, and birches, grow a new set of leaves every year.

A barred owl usually roosts on a branch during the day, waking at night to hunt for rodents and other small prey.

A red-backed salamander lives in damp places, such as under a log, in leaf litter, or in a burrow.

LEAVES AND FLOWERS

By late spring, growth is at its fastest. Trees are in full leaf and their flowers start releasing pollen into the wind to pollinate, or fertilize, other trees.

White-tailed deer eat the saplings and other fresh shoots sprouting on the forest floor.

Spring flowers carpet the forest floor as sunshine streams down between the bare branches.

A male scarlet tanager is searching for food so it can fatten up in time for the breeding season in late spring and early summer.

A hole in a tree trunk provides a safe nesting place for birds such as woodpeckers and owls.

SHRUBS

OAK

BEECH

TRILLIUM

If it is caught by its tail by an owl, a salamander can shed part of the tail and escape

This spring flower races against time to bloom and reproduce before the leaves of the trees grow and prevent sunlight from reaching the forest floor.

A beech tree's roots spread out as much below ground as the branches above it, collecting water and providing support against storm winds.

SPRING

AUTUMN HARVEST

Many forest animals, such as this chipmunk, feast on the large supply of nuts and fruits produced in autumn, and some create food stores to see them through winter.

WHY LEAVES ARE USUALLY GREEN

Temperate forests are very green places in summer, due to a pigment called chlorophyll in the leaves. It absorbs sunlight as part of the process of photosynthesis. Chlorophyll absorbs red and blue light, but reflects green light, making the leaves look green.

Sunlight

Human eyes see reflected green light

Discs of chlorophyll held within chloroplast

Blue and red absorbed

Before leaves are shed, chlorophyll is removed by the tree and the leaves change to the colour of the red and brown pigments left behind.

A female scarlet tanager feeds her chicks huddled in a cup-shaped nest made of twigs and stems.

Woodpeckers use their pointed bill to dig out beetle grubs that are eating the soft wood under bark.

Wild turkeys scratch through the leaves and soil looking for seeds and insects to eat.

FRUIT AND NUTS

Pollinated flowers develop seeds enclosed inside a casing known as a nut or a fruit. The cases are packed with nutrients to fuel the growth of a new plant.

LEAF FALL

Winter days are too short and dull for photosynthesis, so deciduous trees drop their leaves in autumn to prevent them from being damaged by frosts.

In summer, fast-growing ferns spread over the forest floor.

BEECH

GROUND COVER

A chipmunk must remain alert for predators while gathering seeds from the ground. It stores what it cannot eat in its burrow.

OAK

MAPLE

A thick layer of leaf litter covers the forest floor and rots down, adding nutrients to the soil..

DECAYING LOG

The wood of a dead tree is a valuable source of food for wildlife. Beetle grubs burrow inside, and fungi grow over the wood, gradually rotting it away.

A chipmunk's burrow has a nest chamber, several food stores, and some drainage tunnels.

SUMMER

AUTUMN

Boreal forest

A wide, green belt of trees stretches across the northern continents below the Arctic tundra. Boreal forests, also known as taiga, are dominated by evergreen conifers, such as spruces, pines, and firs, which are adapted to survive the long, harsh winters and short, cool summers.

The Siberian taiga is so vast it contains as many trees as all of the world's rainforests combined

SPRUCE

PINE

SHAPED FOR SNOW

Conifer branches are bendy and grow sideways, creating a conical shape, so snow slides off when it gets too heavy instead of breaking a branch.

WINTER

Conifers reproduce using cones, and in early winter, the female cones dry out and open up, dropping seeds into the snow so they are ready to sprout after the spring thaw.

Reindeer spend the winter in forests eating twigs and strips of bark, as well as digging in the snow for mosses and lichens.

Pregnant reindeer keep their antlers until they give birth the following spring, whereas male reindeer shed their antlers in autumn.

Snow slides off branches when too much builds up.

A wood frog lies dormant under the snow.

Old cone shed the previous year.

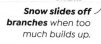

In winter, a stoat's white coat helps it blend in with the snow as it hunts for voles and other small prey.

A thick layer of fallen needles covers the soil, turning it acidic. Mosses are among the few plants that thrive on the ground here.

Roots spread out to anchor the tree in the thin layer of soil.

WINTER

Winters are long and cold, with temperatures well below freezing for up to eight months. The forest is blanketed in snow, and the days are short and often gloomy.

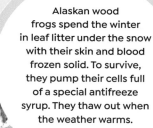

Alaskan wood frogs spend the winter in leaf litter under the snow with their skin and blood frozen solid. To survive, they pump their cells full of a special antifreeze syrup. They thaw out when the weather warms.

FROZEN ALIVE

Meadow voles dig networks of tunnels in the snow that include nesting areas lined with dry grasses, where females give birth to young.

LARCH

Evergreen conifers, such as white spruce, have waxy, needlelike leaves that retain water and resist frost. Older leaves are shed and replaced with new ones.

SPRUCE

INSECT INVASIONS

Spruce bark beetles emerge from infested trees in summer and fly to new hosts. These tiny insects burrow into the bark to mate and lay eggs, and release scent to attract more beetles to the tree. Their grubs will burrow through the tree's wood and could cause enough damage to kill it.

SAP RISES

In spring, the snow melts and the soil fills with liquid water. Roots take in water and flush the trees with fresh sap, priming them for rapid growth.

Small flocks of Siberian jays live in boreal forests all year around feeding on insects, berries, and seeds. In autumn, they store food for the winter behind loose bark.

Pollen released by male cones is carried by the wind to female cones, which are fertilized and develop seeds.

SUMMER

A larch, unlike evergreen trees, sheds its leaves before winter to save water, but this means it has grow new ones very quickly in spring.

A wolverine's powerful jaws enable it to kill and crush the bones of prey as large as reindeer, but in summer it targets smaller prey, such as birds and their eggs, and fruit.

In summer, the stoat's coat has turned brown, helping it to stay camouflaged.

MYCORRHIZAL NETWORK

A network of strands called hyphae is hidden in the soil. It belongs to a fungus and is only evident when the fungus produces its fruiting bodies, known as mushrooms or toadstools.

Hyphae pass water and nutrients from soil to a tree through the network and gain sugars from the tree in return.

Tree roots are connected to special fungi in a partnership called mycorrhizae. The fungal strands, or hyphae, in the soil create connections between forest trees. The trees share nutrients and chemical signals can be sent through this network, nicknamed the Wood Wide Web.

SUMMER

To make the most of the short growing season, evergreen trees keep their leaves all year, so they are ready to photosynthesize as soon as the days get longer and warmer.

WOOD WIDE WEB

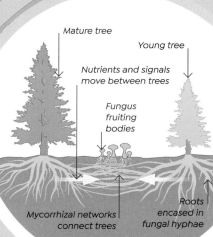

Mature tree

Young tree

Nutrients and signals move between trees

Fungus fruiting bodies

Mycorrhizal networks connect trees

Roots encased in fungal hyphae

Tundra

Land around the edge of the polar regions forms a habitat called tundra. It is so cold throughout the year that a constantly frozen subsoil layer, known as permafrost, prevents trees from growing. Only small, shallow-rooted plants are able to live here.

DWARF SHRUBS

Tundra plants tend to grow low to the ground to stay out of the cold, dry wind. This bearberry has small, thick leaves to help it hold onto precious water.

WINTER

HARSH HABITAT

The tundra's plant life grows out of a thin active layer of soil on top of the permafrost. For up to 10 months of the year, the plants are buried under a blanket of snow.

Herds of muskoxen, huge, shaggy relatives of sheep and goats, spend all year on the tundra.

SNOW

ACTIVE LAYER FROZEN IN WINTER

PERMAFROST

Plants lie dormant through the winter because it is too cold for their metabolism to work fast enough for them to grow.

Lemmings dig trackways through the snow as they continue to eat grass roots through the winter.

A long winter coat with dense insulating underwool shields the muskox against winds as strong as 120 kph (75 mph).

EXTENDED LIFE CYCLE

This hairy caterpillar cannot grow fast enough to transform into an adult tiger moth in one summer. Instead, that process takes several years, with the caterpillar spending each long winter frozen solid – but still alive.

Arctic terns migrate all the way from the Antarctic to feast on the profusion of insects that thrive in the tundra in summer.

SUMMER

WELCOME THAW

During the short summer, the snow melts away, and the upper layer of soil thaws. The tundra becomes a boggy wetland with surface water unable to soak below the permafrost.

Vast herds of reindeer have left the shelter of the boreal forest to graze on the tundra.

ACTIVE LAYER

Small, fast-growing plants, such as grasses, sedges, and mosses, sprout from the thawed soil and must reproduce before the freezing conditions return.

Reindeer are born in late spring, and the calf stays with its mother for about 6 months.

PERMAFROST

Winter temperatures in the Arctic tundra can fall as low as –50 °C (–60 °F)

A snowy owl finds lemmings and other small prey hidden under the snow by listening for the sounds they make.

Thick boots of fluffy feathers keep the owl's feet warm among the snow and ice.

An Arctic fox is an active hunter all year round, leaving its burrow during the day to prey on rodents, hares, and birds.

An Arctic hare digs in the snow for scraps of plant food. It has shorter ears than other hares to reduce the dangers of frostbite.

An Arctic ground squirrel spends winter hibernating inside a warm burrow dug into the top layer of soil.

PERMAFROST FEEDBACK LOOP

Climate change is causing permafrost to thaw. Methane stored in the peat soil of the permafrost is released into the air, causing it to warm. This melts more permafrost, which releases more methane, which leads to more melting, and so on, creating a feedback loop.

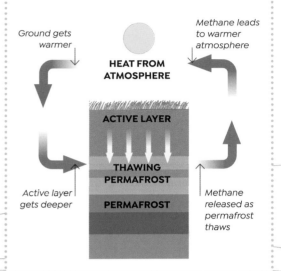

Ground gets warmer

Methane leads to warmer atmosphere

HEAT FROM ATMOSPHERE

ACTIVE LAYER

Active layer gets deeper

THAWING PERMAFROST

PERMAFROST

Methane released as permafrost thaws

FROZEN RIVER

SUMMER VISITORS

Migratory birds, such as this snow bunting, use the tundra as a summer breeding ground. They feed their chicks on the plentiful supply of insects in the marshy habitat.

The short growing season lasts just 50–60 days

Snow geese fly in after spending winter far to the south. The birds will lay eggs, raise their young, and then leave at the end of summer.

Mosquitoes swarm in their millions as these bloodsucking insects search for prey, such as reindeer, to feed on.

Arctic poppies and lupins are among the plants that bloom, producing nectar to attract pollinators, such as the Arctic bumble bee.

Brown bears fish for spawning salmon. This mother is teaching her cub how to catch them.

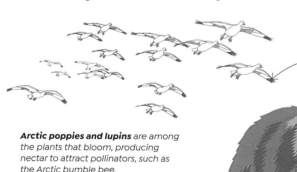

A ruddy turnstone forages for insect larvae in the mud.

Summer is spent eating seeds, fruits, and flowers as the Arctic ground squirrel fattens up for winter.

RIVER

Salmon swim up the shallow rivers to lay eggs, or spawn.

Freshwater habitat

Rainwater that finds its way into streams, rivers, lakes, and other places is described as fresh water. Freshwater habitats are a haven for many kinds of aquatic wildlife, including beavers. These skilled engineers dam rivers to reshape the landscape to suit their needs.

A heron waits patiently for a frog or fish to come close enough to grab with its long, slender bill.

FELLING TREES

A beaver uses its long, sharp incisors to gnaw through tree trunks. Once a tree falls, this large rodent chews off the branches and gnaws the trunk into smaller, more transportable, logs.

A channel leading from the pond to the wood has been dug by the beavers.

Mud plastered over the sticks freezes into a predator-proof surface in winter, but the beavers leave a ventilation hole so they do not suffocate.

Branches may be taken back to eat in the safety of the lodge or be stored for winter.

A male moose grazes on aquatic vegetation while wallowing in the cool water.

LODGE

A beaver repairs a breach in the dam with mud to keep the water in the pond at a constant level.

Common frogs are strong swimmers. They hunt on land but return to water to breed.

DOWNSTREAM

Heavy stones and logs stuck into the riverbed brace the dam on the downstream side.

A dam about 1.8 m (6 ft) high creates a pond about 0.9 m (3 ft) deep behind it, which means the water will not freeze to the bottom in winter.

An adult female nurses her young, known as kits, in the living chamber.

DAM

Dragonflies hunt other insects near ponds and streams. Females lay their eggs in the water in summer.

BEAVER DAM

Beavers build a dam across a shallow stream or river from logs, sticks, and stones stuck together with mud. The water flow slows, and a pond grows upstream of the dam.

Beavers can gnaw down a tree 1 m (3 ft) in diameter – only rarely has one been squashed by a falling trunk

BEAVER LODGE

A large dome of sticks and mud is built on top of a platform of stones, mud and sticks. Beavers are mostly nocturnal, and the family, or colony, sleeps in the lodge during the day.

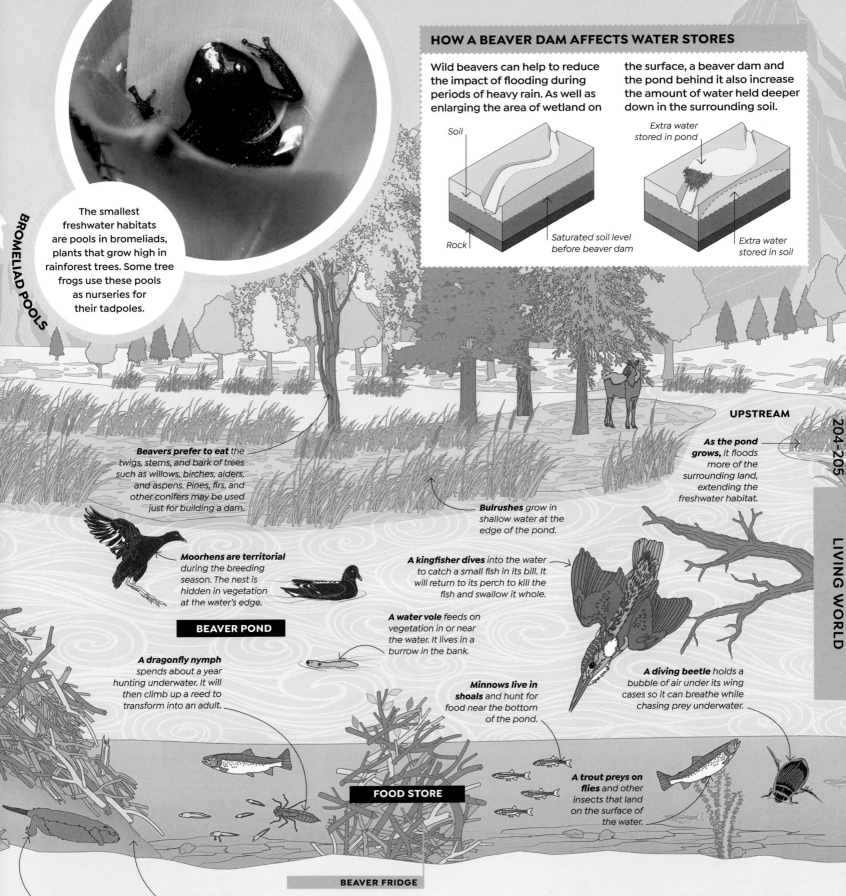

HOW A BEAVER DAM AFFECTS WATER STORES

Wild beavers can help to reduce the impact of flooding during periods of heavy rain. As well as enlarging the area of wetland on the surface, a beaver dam and the pond behind it also increase the amount of water held deeper down in the surrounding soil.

Soil

Rock

Saturated soil level before beaver dam

Extra water stored in pond

Extra water stored in soil

BROMELIAD POOLS

The smallest freshwater habitats are pools in bromeliads, plants that grow high in rainforest trees. Some tree frogs use these pools as nurseries for their tadpoles.

UPSTREAM

As the pond grows, it floods more of the surrounding land, extending the freshwater habitat.

Beavers prefer to eat the twigs, stems, and bark of trees such as willows, birches, alders, and aspens. Pines, firs, and other conifers may be used just for building a dam.

Bulrushes grow in shallow water at the edge of the pond.

A kingfisher dives into the water to catch a small fish in its bill. It will return to its perch to kill the fish and swallow it whole.

Moorhens are territorial during the breeding season. The nest is hidden in vegetation at the water's edge.

BEAVER POND

A water vole feeds on vegetation in or near the water. It lives in a burrow in the bank.

A diving beetle holds a bubble of air under its wing cases so it can breathe while chasing prey underwater.

A dragonfly nymph spends about a year hunting underwater. It will then climb up a reed to transform into an adult.

Minnows live in shoals and hunt for food near the bottom of the pond.

FOOD STORE

A trout preys on flies and other insects that land on the surface of the water.

BEAVER FRIDGE

A beaver propels itself through the water with its large, webbed rear feet, using its flattened, paddle-shaped tail like a rudder.

Two or more underwater tunnels allow the beavers to come and go from the lodge safe from predators, such as wolves, coyotes, and bears.

In preparation for winter, beavers store large clusters of branches close to the lodge. The food is kept fresh under the ice and can be retrieved as needed.

The world's biggest beaver dam, in Alberta, Canada, is 850 m (2,800ft) wide

POND LIFE

Freshwater animals often have very diverse life styles. River snails are passive feeders, filtering plankton through a siphon that also enables them to breathe in water. Unusually for a snail, females give birth to live young, which are miniature versions of the adult form. The young of damselflies (and dragonflies), known as nymphs, hatch from eggs and are ferocious predators, eating the larvae of other insects, and tadpoles. When the nymph is fully developed, it climbs out of the water, clings to a plant stem, and transforms into an adult through a process known as metamorphosis.

NYMPH

Adult emerges from split in skin of nymph

Eggs laid by female in water

Feathery gills enable nymph to breathe under water

EGGS

MOULT

Wings enable adult to fly over water in search of prey and a mate

ADULT

LIFE CYCLE OF A DAMSELFLY

Tidal zones

Where the ocean meets the land is a complex habitat. Twice a day, much of it is under salt water, but a few hours later it is exposed to the air again. The animals, plants, and seaweeds that live here must be able to cope with the endless cycle between these two extremes.

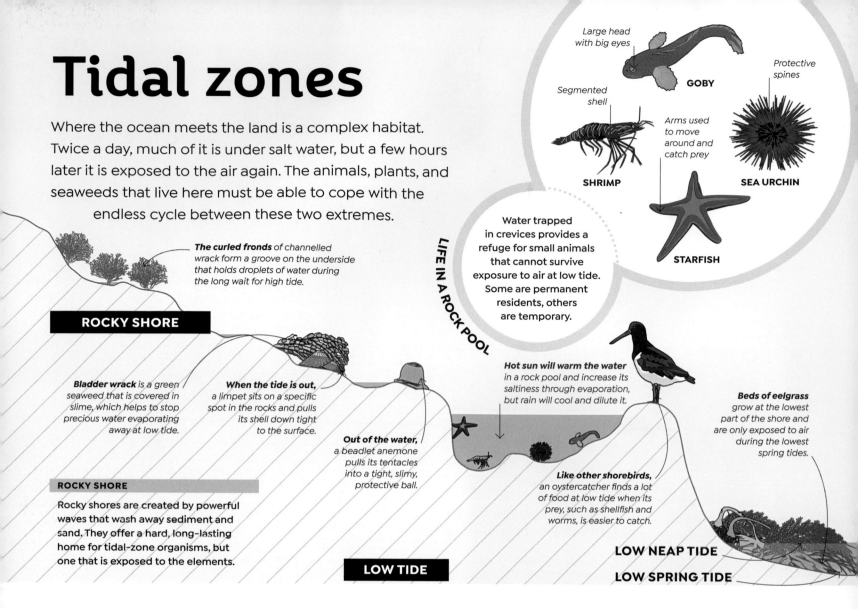

Large head with big eyes

GOBY

Segmented shell

SHRIMP

Arms used to move around and catch prey

Protective spines

SEA URCHIN

STARFISH

LIFE IN A ROCK POOL

Water trapped in crevices provides a refuge for small animals that cannot survive exposure to air at low tide. Some are permanent residents, others are temporary.

The curled fronds of channelled wrack form a groove on the underside that holds droplets of water during the long wait for high tide.

ROCKY SHORE

Bladder wrack is a green seaweed that is covered in slime, which helps to stop precious water evaporating away at low tide.

When the tide is out, a limpet sits on a specific spot in the rocks and pulls its shell down tight to the surface.

Out of the water, a beadlet anemone pulls its tentacles into a tight, slimy, protective ball.

Hot sun will warm the water in a rock pool and increase its saltiness through evaporation, but rain will cool and dilute it.

Like other shorebirds, an oystercatcher finds a lot of food at low tide when its prey, such as shellfish and worms, is easier to catch.

Beds of eelgrass grow at the lowest part of the shore and are only exposed to air during the lowest spring tides.

ROCKY SHORE

Rocky shores are created by powerful waves that wash away sediment and sand. They offer a hard, long-lasting home for tidal-zone organisms, but one that is exposed to the elements.

LOW TIDE

LOW NEAP TIDE

LOW SPRING TIDE

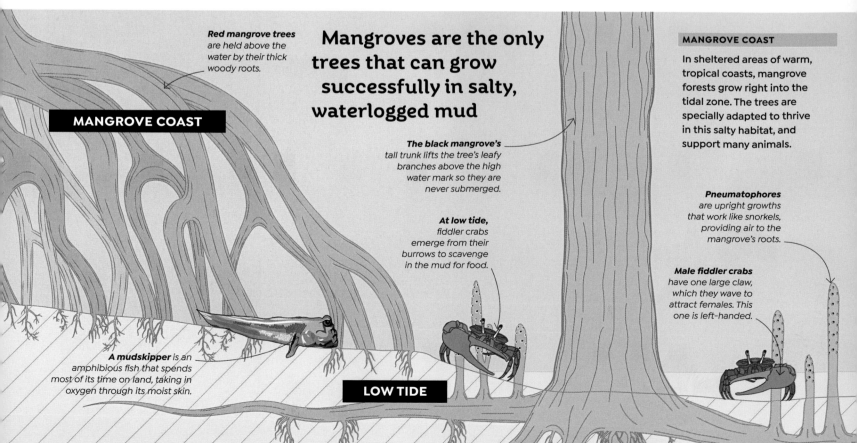

Mangroves are the only trees that can grow successfully in salty, waterlogged mud

Red mangrove trees are held above the water by their thick woody roots.

MANGROVE COAST

The black mangrove's tall trunk lifts the tree's leafy branches above the high water mark so they are never submerged.

At low tide, fiddler crabs emerge from their burrows to scavenge in the mud for food.

A mudskipper is an amphibious fish that spends most of its time on land, taking in oxygen through its moist skin.

MANGROVE COAST

In sheltered areas of warm, tropical coasts, mangrove forests grow right into the tidal zone. The trees are specially adapted to thrive in this salty habitat, and support many animals.

Pneumatophores are upright growths that work like snorkels, providing air to the mangrove's roots.

Male fiddler crabs have one large claw, which they wave to attract females. This one is left-handed.

LOW TIDE

TIDES

The tides are caused by the gravitational pull of the Moon, which pulls sea water into a bulge that sweeps across the oceans as the world turns. The Sun also has an effect. When both are aligned around the time of the full and new moons, they create extreme "spring" tides. More moderate "neap" tides form in between.

NEW MOON	FIRST QUARTER	FULL MOON	LAST QUARTER	NEW MOON
SPRING	NEAP	SPRING	NEAP	SPRING

TIDE HEIGHT

Giant kelp can grow 45 cm (18 in) in a day and be more than 50 m (160 ft) long

Seaweeds at the top of the shore are only fully submerged during the spring tides.

HIGH SPRING TIDE

HIGH NEAP TIDE

Kelp is a tall brown seaweed that floats upright, like a tree, when in the deep water at high tide.

Always growing low on the shore, red algae is a seaweed that is able to survive in the shadow of larger seaweeds.

Gas bladders help the bladder wrack's fronds float upright to catch the sunlight.

The unfurled tentacles of the anemone are covered in stingers that grab tiny fish and other small prey.

The limpet uses its muscular foot to move around and find algae to eat.

A small type of fish, a seahorse holds onto a blade of eelgrass with its prehensile tail.

LIMPET TEETH

To scrape up algae, the limpet extends its radula, an abrasive ribbon covered in tiny teeth. Scratches are left where it has grazed because the teeth are harder than rock.

HIGH TIDE

The saltwater crocodile – the largest reptile of all – is a fearsome hunter that searches for prey in the calm water of high tide.

A tangle of mangrove roots creates a shelter in which young fish can hide and grow.

HIGH TIDE

Coral reef

A tropical coral reef is a rich habitat found in warm, shallow, clear seas. The reef is a seafloor platform that is constructed from the stony remains of many generations of hard coral polyps – parts of Australia's famous Great Barrier Reef are estimated to be 500,000 years old. Corals are tiny relatives of jellyfish that live in colonies on the surface of the reef, which is also a haven for many other kinds of marine wildlife.

Meadows of seagrass grow in reef lagoons, and are an important source of food for turtles and manatees.

Young green sea turtles are partly carnivorous, eating jellyfish and sponges, for example, but adults graze inshore on seagrass.

LAGOON

REEF FLAT

A blue-ringed octopus has a highly venomous bite. If alarmed, its rings turn bright blue as a warning.

LAGOON

The lagoon is a shallow pool of seawater trapped between the coast and the reef. Its waters are sheltered and warm.

A fox coral is a soft coral, so its colony of polyps form ruffled shapes that sway gently in the currents.

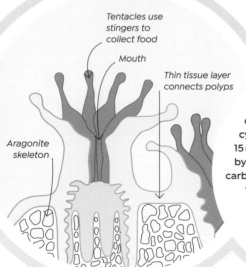

Tentacles use stingers to collect food

Mouth

Thin tissue layer connects polyps

Aragonite skeleton

Coral polyps are organized like upside-down jellyfish. They have a soft cylindrical body, mostly less than 15 mm (0.5 in) tall, that is supported by a skeleton of aragonite (calcium carbonate). The skeleton remains after the polyps die, creating a solid platform on which new corals will grow. Over many years, the skeletons build up into a stony reef.

SAND

A bird's nest coral forms a ball of hard, pricklelike branches.

A finger coral has many short, tube-shaped lobes.

The reef consists of coral remains compacted into limestone.

REEF BUILDERS

VOLCANIC ROCK

LIMESTONE REEF

COLD-WATER CORAL REEFS

Not all corals form reefs in warm tropical waters. Cold-water corals do not rely on zooxanthellae for nutrients. Instead, they gather zooplankton and krill from the water with their tentacles, and so can live in deep, dark waters. Most live around 300 m (1,000 ft) down, but can be found much deeper. They grow very slowly, but can create large reefs that support important wildlife communities, as at this reef in the Arctic Ocean.

Coral reefs support 25 per cent of all marine life

REEF CREST

This is the shallowest point on the reef, forming the barrier between the lagoon and the open sea. Waves break over this part of the reef so less wildlife lives here.

REEF FLAT

This section of the reef is closest to the coast and in the shallowest water. It is frequently exposed to the air as the tide goes out.

A tube sponge is a simple animal that draws water through its hollow body and filters out food.

Sea fans are soft corals that grow upright with flexible, spreading branches.

A blue tang uses its small, sharp teeth to scrape algae off the reef to eat.

Staghorn corals are common on the reef, but they are fragile and easily damaged by storms.

Brain corals can grow to 1.8 m (6 ft) tall and live for up to 900 years. They are important reef-building corals.

Moorish idols usually live alone or in pairs.

LIFE SUPPORT

Tiny algae called zooxanthellae live inside tropical corals, giving them their amazing colours. The algae provide their hosts with sugars made by photosynthesis.

RESCUING REEFS

Reefs are under threat from pollution and climate change. Conservationists are growing endangered corals, such as staghorn, in nurseries to ensure their survival.

REEF CREST

REEF FACE

A hammerhead shark's wide head allows the hunter to scan the seabed for electrical signals and scent produced by hidden prey.

Clownfish live among the stinging tentacles of sea anemones, which keep them safe from predators.

Table corals grow large, flat plates that expose as much of their surface as possible to sunlight, helping the zooxanthellae in the polyps to photosynthesize food for themselves and their host.

Brightly coloured parrotfish use their hard, beaklike jaws to crunch up live coral, but they also eat the algae that grow on the reef and compete with the coral polyps.

REEF FACE

This is the most crowded and productive part of the reef. The largest corals grow here, down to a depth of about 55 m (180 ft).

The Great Barrier Reef covers 345,000 sq km (133,000 sq miles) – it is the largest living structure on Earth

NIGHT

DAY

Cuvier's beaked whale can dive deeper – 2,992 m (9,816 ft) – and for longer – 3 hours and 42 minutes – than any other mammal.

Dolphins are predatory mammals that hunt mainly fish and squid near the surface of the ocean.

Phytoplankton are photosynthesizing bacteria and microscopic green algae that float in the sunlit zone.

Zooplankton are tiny animals and protozoans that feed on phytoplankton. Many of them are copepods, which are crustaceans. They swim deeper by day to avoid predatory fish.

VERTICAL MIGRATION

Many predatory Twilight Zone animals swim up towards the surface to hunt and feed every night. At dawn, they swim back down to hide in darker waters.

At up to 13 m (43 ft) long, giant and colossal squids are the largest invertebrates on Earth, but they are seldom seen.

Squid swim by squirting jets of water from their body.

Sharks hunt by sight, smell, and detecting movement and changes in electric fields.

Mackerel live in huge shoals that swim through the sunlit zone feeding on zooplankton.

Sponges are simple animals that are permanently attached to the seabed.

Sea urchins are spiny filter-feeders. They draw a current of seawater through their body and sieve out food particles.

A moon jellyfish swims by pulsations of its bell-shaped upper body and catches plankton in its tentacles.

Lanternfish are named for the glowing lights along their body, which they use to attract a mate and shoal together in the dark.

Glass sponges have a spiny skeleton made of silica, the same chemical found in sand and glass.

Plankton are photosynthesizing bacteria and green algae (phytoplankton) and tiny animals (zooplankton) that float in the water, drifting with ocean currents.

Antennae used like oars to move this zooplankton between twilight and sunlit zones

COPEPOD

Shell-like wall of silica surrounds single cell of this phytoplankton

DIATOM

This type of phytoplankton often glows in the dark

DINOFLAGELLATE

PLANKTON

Seaweeds are attached to the seabed, floating upright to catch as much light as possible.

SUNLIT ZONE

This surface layer of ocean is bright with sunlight during the day, providing energy for phytoplankton and seaweeds to survive by photosynthesis.

Starfish crawl slowly over the seabed preying on molluscs, sponges, and corals.

TWILIGHT ZONE

Even in the middle of the day, only a small amount of light reaches this deep. It is too gloomy for photosynthesis, but many animals live here.

At up to 27 cm (11 in) in diameter, colossal squid have the largest eyes of any animal

Ocean zones

The oceans are vast and are thousands of metres deep in most places. Oceanographers, the scientists who study oceans, divide the water into several zones based on depth. The water gets colder, darker, and pressure increases with depth and food becomes more scarce, and so life in each zone has adapted to survive in the different conditions.

DARK ZONE

Comb jellies live in deep water all over the world. They use light to attract a mate.

The piglet squid is named after its snout-like siphon, which squirts out a water jet when the squid swims.

Dumbo octopuses feed on snails and worms on the deep ocean floor.

Sea pigs walk on the seabed by pumping water from one leg to the next.

DARK ZONE

No light ever reaches below this depth and so the water is dark 24 hours a day. Animals that live here produce their own light to see and be seen.

Hagfish are deep-sea scavengers, eating the remains of larger animals that have sunk to the seabed from above.

4,000 M (13,100 FT)

ABYSSAL ZONE

Brittle stars are seabed scavengers. They crawl around searching for the remains of dead animals, and can swim when they need to.

Deep-sea corals get all the nutrients they need by sifting food from the water, so they do not need to live in the Sunlit Zone like other corals.

Deep-sea shrimp have special organs on their body that both emit and detect bioluminescence.

ABYSSAL ZONE

The ocean zone near the deep seabed is an abyss, a vast, mostly empty area. Life becomes less common with depth because there is less food around.

sea lilies are attached to the seabed by a long, slender stalk. They trap particles of food in their feathery arms.

6,000 M (19,700 FT)

HADAL ZONE

The Mariana snailfish lives at pressures 1,000 times greater than at sea level

The Mariana snailfish is the top predator in the Mariana Trench, and has been found as deep as 7,966 m (26,135 ft).

HADAL ZONE

The deepest ocean layer is in the trenches that plunge into the seabed. This zone is named after Hades, the ancient Greek god of the underworld.

LIGHT IN THE DARK

Many deep-sea organisms can produce coloured light, a process known as bioluminescence. This anglerfish uses a glowing lure to attract prey to its huge mouth.

The light in an anglerfish's lure is produced by bioluminescent bacteria living inside it

Urban habitat

About 3 per cent of Earth's land surface is covered by towns and cities. More than half of all humans on the planet live in or close to a city. Urban areas may be artificial habitats, but they share some features with wild places, and many plants and animals have adapted to live in them too.

Beehives can be kept on a roof. The insects forage widely, visiting city parks and gardens.

Gulls are often seen close to the coast, scavenging for food along the shore. That way of life means they are well-adapted to search for food waste left on the street.

The tops of tall buildings are ideal for gardens because they get a lot of sunlight.

A fox was found living on the 72nd floor of London's Shard, UK, while the skyscraper was being built

TOWN CENTRE

Peregrine falcons make nests on skyscrapers in cities. Away from cities, they nest on cliff ledges.

The vertical sides of buildings can be used to grow climbing plants. A green wall holds pockets of soil and grilles for stems to cling to.

The bark of a London plane peels off in large flakes, which may stop the breathing pores, or lenticels, becoming clogged by polluted air.

Peregrines soar above the streets and dive down at great speed to kill smaller birds flying below.

Hanging baskets create small flower gardens for insects high above the busy streets.

Urban pigeons are scavengers. The wild form of these birds is known as the rock dove and is found in dry, rocky habitats.

An urban red fox hunts for smaller animals, such as rodents, birds, and pet rabbits, as well as junk food.

CITY CENTRE

The tall buildings and narrow streets of a city are very like rocky cliffs and canyons. Birds such as gulls and pigeons thrive in this kind of urban habitat.

Grey squirrels have spread from their native eastern North American woodlands to cities across the US and in Europe.

Ponds and lakes provide breeding grounds for insects, and a home for ducks and other waterbirds.

A colony of African penguins at Boulders Beach in Simon's Town, South Africa, has become so crowded that some of them brave traffic to nest in the town.

The average American home has around 100 different species of insects, spiders, and other bugs living in it

Fruit trees, such as apples, cherries, and plums, provide nectar for bees and other insects in spring and fruit for many animals in autumn.

This wasp colony has hung its nest from a house beam instead of a tree branch.

Bats need dark places to rest, and at least 35 per cent of the world's more than 1,000 species of bat will use a building as a roost.

SUBURBAN HOME

A range of native plants in a garden can supply nectar for butterflies and food plants for their caterpillars.

A raccoon has dexterous forepaws that allow it to lift lids, release latches, and turn doorknobs in search of food.

Providing seeds, nuts, fat balls, and nectar will attract birds and other wildlife to a garden.

A nest box fitted to a tree or house provides a space for songbirds to raise chicks in locations where natural nesting sites are rare.

A house spider's natural habitat includes caves and tree hollows, but it has readily adapted to live in buildings.

A bird bath provides a little pool of fresh water for birds to drink and to wash in.

Hedges provide nesting and roosting sites for birds, berries in autumn, and food and shelter for other animals.

Lawns grow from healthy soil filled with worms, which are food for birds such as the American robin.

BUG HOTEL

Many bugs live in or around dead wood, but this is often cleared from gardens. A bug hotel provides wooden spaces in which insects can set up home.

Almost all wild brown rats live in close association with humans. They eat whatever they can find – even ice cream.

SUBURBAN HOME

Many people live in areas around cities called suburbs. The buildings are smaller, meaning more green spaces, and a garden can be a haven for wildlife.

URBAN FOX

A huge variety of animal species have made their home in towns and cities, attracted by the abundance of food, water, and shelter. Some, such as songbirds, are actively encouraged to visit gardens, while others, such as tiny ants on the ground, are rarely noticed. And others, such as the raccoons, foxes, and even bears that raid bins for food, are being seen more frequently. The red fox was introduced to Australia for sport in 1855 and is now widespread. Its population density depends on the resources available.

Pavement ants on New York's Broadway, US, eat 544 kg (2,100 lb) of discarded junk food in less than a year – the equivalent of 60,000 hot dogs

ARID RURAL AREA

URBAN AREA

RED FOX TERRITORY IN AUSTRALIA

In arid areas, food is scarce and each fox needs a hunting territory of 1.1 sq km (0.43 sq miles). However, a city, such as Melbourne, can support as many as 16 foxes per sq km (41 per sq mile).

Our
Planet

We inhabit only a tiny part of our home planet. Beneath our feet are vast, deep layers of hot, slow-moving rock and metal. Above us, a thin layer of gases provides oxygen to breathe and shields us from the cold, hostile environment of space.

There are two main types of crust: oceanic and continental. Oceanic crust, which forms most of the seabed, is relatively young, dense, and up to 10 km (6 miles) thick. Continental crust is lighter and up to 70 km (45 miles) deep. It is also more varied and older, including some rocks that are more than 4 billion years old.

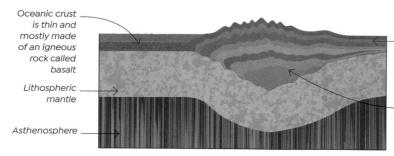

Oceanic crust is thin and mostly made of an igneous rock called basalt

Lithospheric mantle

Asthenosphere

Continental crust is made of many different rock types

Crust is thickest under mountain ranges

The mantle makes up about two-thirds of Earth's total mass and the core about one-third

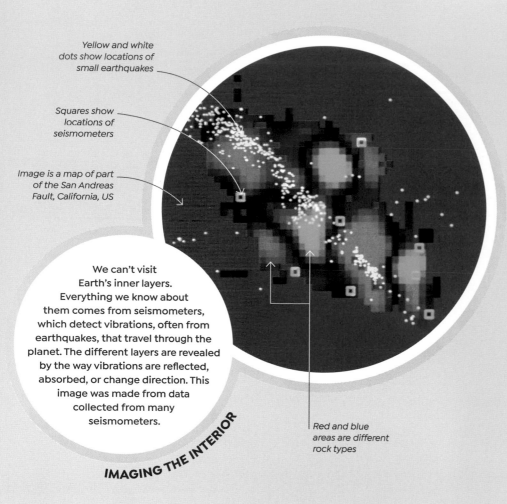

Yellow and white dots show locations of small earthquakes

Squares show locations of seismometers

Image is a map of part of the San Andreas Fault, California, US

We can't visit Earth's inner layers. Everything we know about them comes from seismometers, which detect vibrations, often from earthquakes, that travel through the planet. The different layers are revealed by the way vibrations are reflected, absorbed, or change direction. This image was made from data collected from many seismometers.

IMAGING THE INTERIOR

Red and blue areas are different rock types

At a spreading ridge, magma rises into gaps between plates and forms new crust.

At a hotspot, a supply of magma from the mantle creates a chain of volcanoes or volcanic islands on the crust above.

Convection currents in the mantle transfer heat towards the surface.

The temperature of Earth's inner core is about 5,500°C (10,000°F)

Earth's layers

Planet Earth formed about 4.5 billion years ago as a vast ball of red-hot materials. As the new planet cooled, the mixture of substances began to separate out, forming a series of layers. The heaviest materials, the metals, sank to the middle while lighter materials floated nearer to the surface. Earth still has this layered structure. The surface layer that we inhabit, called the crust, is like a thin skin above the thicker layers below.

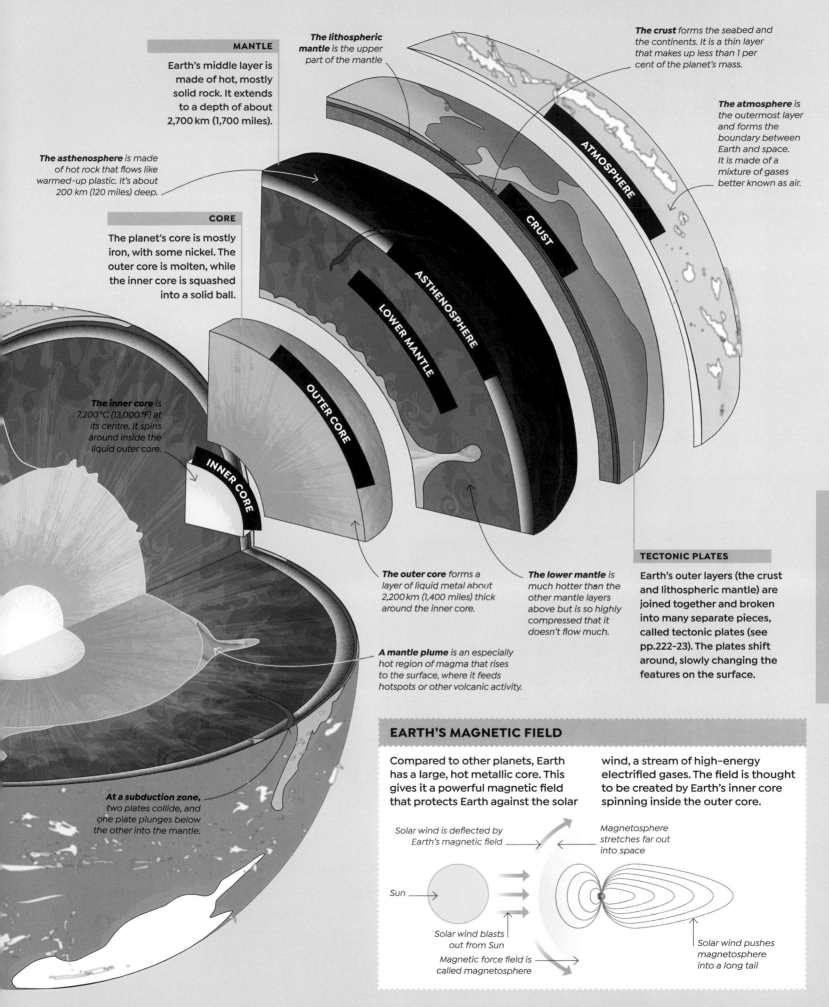

MANTLE

Earth's middle layer is made of hot, mostly solid rock. It extends to a depth of about 2,700 km (1,700 miles).

The lithospheric mantle is the upper part of the mantle

The crust forms the seabed and the continents. It is a thin layer that makes up less than 1 per cent of the planet's mass.

The asthenosphere is made of hot rock that flows like warmed-up plastic. It's about 200 km (120 miles) deep.

The atmosphere is the outermost layer and forms the boundary between Earth and space. It is made of a mixture of gases better known as air.

ATMOSPHERE

CRUST

CORE

The planet's core is mostly iron, with some nickel. The outer core is molten, while the inner core is squashed into a solid ball.

ASTHENOSPHERE

LOWER MANTLE

The inner core is 7,200°C (13,000°F) at its centre. It spins around inside the liquid outer core.

OUTER CORE

INNER CORE

The outer core forms a layer of liquid metal about 2,200 km (1,400 miles) thick around the inner core.

The lower mantle is much hotter than the other mantle layers above but is so highly compressed that it doesn't flow much.

TECTONIC PLATES

Earth's outer layers (the crust and lithospheric mantle) are joined together and broken into many separate pieces, called tectonic plates (see pp.222-23). The plates shift around, slowly changing the features on the surface.

A mantle plume is an especially hot region of magma that rises to the surface, where it feeds hotspots or other volcanic activity.

At a subduction zone, two plates collide, and one plate plunges below the other into the mantle.

EARTH'S MAGNETIC FIELD

Compared to other planets, Earth has a large, hot metallic core. This gives it a powerful magnetic field that protects Earth against the solar wind, a stream of high-energy electrified gases. The field is thought to be created by Earth's inner core spinning inside the outer core.

Solar wind is deflected by Earth's magnetic field

Magnetosphere stretches far out into space

Sun

Solar wind blasts out from Sun

Magnetic force field is called magnetosphere

Solar wind pushes magnetosphere into a long tail

Tectonic plates

Earth's rocky outer layers are broken up into many sections called plates. These move around, pushing on and grinding against their neighbours in a process called plate tectonics. Plate tectonics is very slow but it causes earthquakes and volcanic eruptions, and over millions of years it reshapes the surface of the planet, shifting landmasses and making oceans widen and shrink.

Earth has seven major plates, eight minor plates, and dozens of microplates

SOUTH AMERICAN PLATE

This tectonic plate covers most of the continent of South America and much of the seabed of the South Atlantic. It is moving westwards away from Africa at about 3 cm (1 in) a year.

As magma erupts along the plate boundary, it cools to create new rock on the seabed, forming an undersea mountain range called the Mid-Atlantic Ridge.

Volcanoes form above the plate boundary as magma rises up through the crust and breaks out onto the surface.

The Andes run along the entire western coast of South America. They are created as the South American Plate is squeezed and pushed up by the Nazca Plate sliding underneath.

A deep ocean trench is formed in the seabed where the denser oceanic crust plunges under the lighter continental crust.

Oceanic crust is about 5 km (3 miles) thick and so forms low-lying basins on Earth's surface that hold the oceans. The rock is also dense so it sinks below continental crust.

Continental crust is a lot thicker than oceanic crust – an average of 25 km (15 miles). The rock is also less dense so the plate floats higher on the mantle.

Lithospheric mantle is the outermost layer of the mantle. Made of solid rock, it is fused to the crust above.

The asthenosphere is mostly solid rock but it is so hot that the rocks start to flow.

ANDES MOUNTAIN CHAIN

OCEANIC TRENCH

CONTINENTAL CRUST

VOLCANO

LITHOSPHERIC MANTLE

ASTHENOSPHERE

Pockets of magma form as the subducting plate heats up and releases water into the mantle, causing it to melt.

The zone where the Nazca and South American plates collide is called a convergent boundary.

Subduction is a process where one plate moves beneath another and slides into the mantle.

The dense Nazca Plate slides under the lighter South American Plate and descends into the mantle.

This plateau in the central Andes is very dry and flat. The mountains on its western edge include some massive volcanoes formed by the subduction of the Nazca Plate.

ALTIPLANO

NAZCA PLATE

The Nazca Plate makes a section of the seabed of the western Pacific Ocean. As it plunges under South America, it is moving east at around 5 cm (2 in) a year.

The Mid-Atlantic Ridge follows a stepped path rather than a straight line. The ridge is divided into sections along lines called transform faults (see panel, below).

SPREADING RIFTS

When tectonic plates move apart, molten rock wells up between them, into a zone called a rift, and forms new crust. Most rifts are on the ocean floor but some, such as the Afar Depression in Ethiopia (shown here), are on land. The crust on the surface in this picture is made of salt crystals stained with sulfur.

MID-ATLANTIC RIDGE

The Mid-Atlantic Ridge is 16,000 km (10,000 miles) long.

OCEANIC CRUST

MANTLE UPWELLING

The African and South American plates are moving in opposite directions – this is called a divergent boundary.

An upwelling of magma from deep inside Earth pushes into the gap between two plates, driving them apart. The movement of plates is also caused as they descend under their own weight into the mantle.

AFRICAN PLATE

The African Plate covers the eastern Atlantic ocean and most of Africa. It is moving eastwards.

Magma is a mixture of molten and semi-molten rock.

The east coast of South America is a passive margin. This is where continental crust changes into oceanic crust but all held on the same plate.

TRANSFORM BOUNDARIES

A boundary where two plates move sideways past each other is called a transform boundary. A famous transform boundary is in California, US, between the North American and Pacific plates. The motion at these boundaries is seldom smooth. Often the plates become stuck until the forces driving them become too great. The rock breaks, and the plates suddenly jerk apart along a line called a transform fault, creating an earthquake. Transform faults are also found along the mid-Atlantic Ridge.

If Earth was the size of an apple, the tectonic plates would be the thickness of the apple's skin

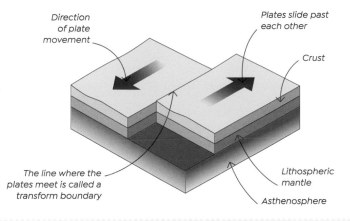

Direction of plate movement

Plates slide past each other

Crust

The line where the plates meet is called a transform boundary

Lithospheric mantle

Asthenosphere

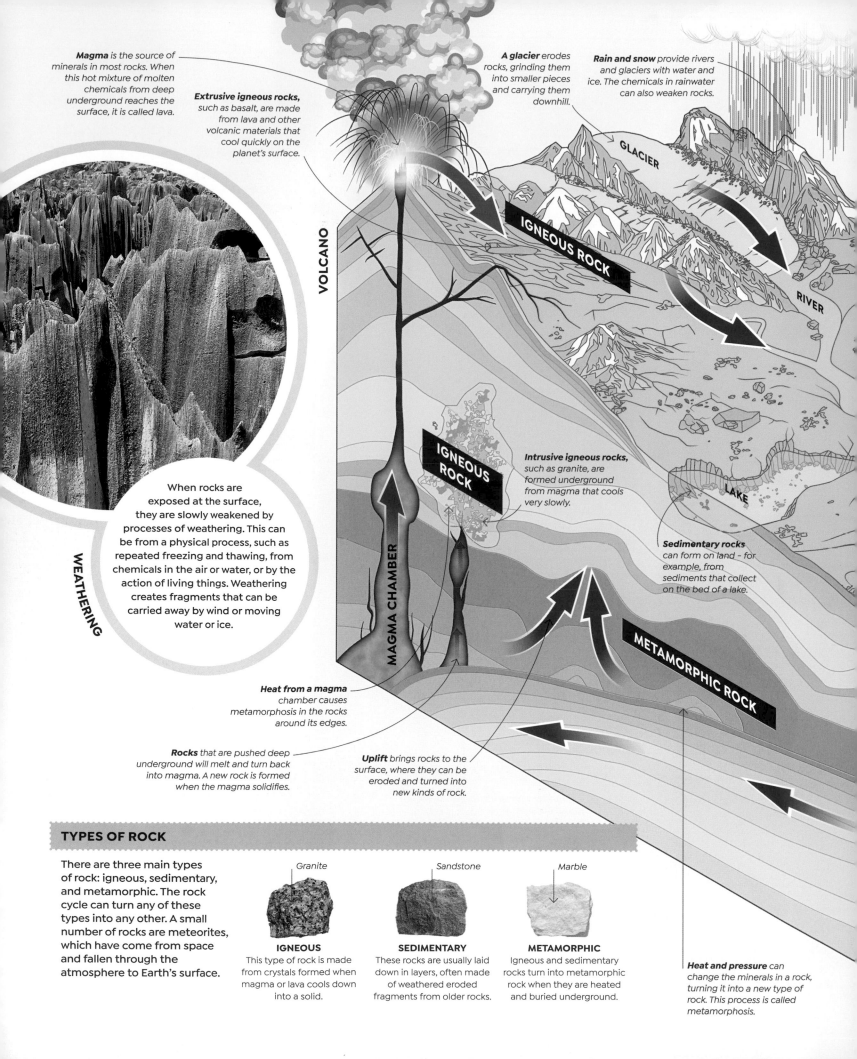

Magma is the source of minerals in most rocks. When this hot mixture of molten chemicals from deep underground reaches the surface, it is called lava.

Extrusive igneous rocks, such as basalt, are made from lava and other volcanic materials that cool quickly on the planet's surface.

A glacier erodes rocks, grinding them into smaller pieces and carrying them downhill.

Rain and snow provide rivers and glaciers with water and ice. The chemicals in rainwater can also weaken rocks.

GLACIER

IGNEOUS ROCK

RIVER

VOLCANO

When rocks are exposed at the surface, they are slowly weakened by processes of weathering. This can be from a physical process, such as repeated freezing and thawing, from chemicals in the air or water, or by the action of living things. Weathering creates fragments that can be carried away by wind or moving water or ice.

WEATHERING

IGNEOUS ROCK

Intrusive igneous rocks, such as granite, are formed underground from magma that cools very slowly.

LAKE

Sedimentary rocks can form on land – for example, from sediments that collect on the bed of a lake.

MAGMA CHAMBER

METAMORPHIC ROCK

Heat from a magma chamber causes metamorphosis in the rocks around its edges.

Rocks that are pushed deep underground will melt and turn back into magma. A new rock is formed when the magma solidifies.

Uplift brings rocks to the surface, where they can be eroded and turned into new kinds of rock.

TYPES OF ROCK

There are three main types of rock: igneous, sedimentary, and metamorphic. The rock cycle can turn any of these types into any other. A small number of rocks are meteorites, which have come from space and fallen through the atmosphere to Earth's surface.

Granite

IGNEOUS
This type of rock is made from crystals formed when magma or lava cools down into a solid.

Sandstone

SEDIMENTARY
These rocks are usually laid down in layers, often made of weathered eroded fragments from older rocks.

Marble

METAMORPHIC
Igneous and sedimentary rocks turn into metamorphic rock when they are heated and buried underground.

Heat and pressure can change the minerals in a rock, turning it into a new type of rock. This process is called metamorphosis.

The rock cycle

Earth's rocks are constantly being created, destroyed, and transformed from one type into another in a process called the rock cycle. All rocks are made from mixtures of different minerals. The way the minerals are assembled in a rock tells rock experts called geologists how that rock was made.

Eroded particles are transported to the sea

Particles are deposited on the sea floor

Compaction squeezes out most of the water and reduces the spaces between grains

Chemicals dissolved in the water become solid and fill the gaps to create a strong cement

Fragments of rock, called clasts, that are created by weathering and erosion are carried downhill by rivers.

FROM SEDIMENT TO ROCK

If they are not disturbed, layers of sediment will turn into solid sedimentary rock. The process begins with rock fragments settling to the ground or seabed. As more are added, the fragments are compressed and come closer together. Deeper still, the temperature goes up, causing chemical reactions that cement the fragments together.

Chemicals dissolved in water are deposited as layers of sediment as the water evaporates. The sediment may eventually become new rock.

Waves and currents in sea water erode rocks at the shoreline. They also move sediment along the shore or carry it out to sea.

Limestone is a sedimentary rock that forms from the bodies of dead animals or when minerals precipitate out of water in shallow seas or lakes.

LAKE BED

Larger fragments carried down from high ground, such as sand grains, are deposited as a river approaches the coast.

SEDIMENTARY ROCK

Smaller clasts, such as clays, are washed out to sea, where they eventually settle to the seabed as thick layers of sediment.

The oldest rocks on Earth are slabs of greenstone from Canada that are 4.28 billion years old

Sedimentary layers, or strata, are buried by newer layers above. Eventually the great weight compacts the sediment into blocks of rock.

The movement of tectonic plates pulls sedimentary rocks that formed near the surface downwards into Earth's interior.

The extreme forces involved in mountain building can make the crust buckle into structures called folds. The tops of these folds create ridges. The forces can also create fault lines, or deep cracks in the rock. Rocks pushing past each other at these faults can create tremors and even earthquakes.

Rocks are squeezed together

Isoclines are very tight, steep folds

In an overturned fold, rocks on lower part of fold are turned upside-down

Older rock is pushed over younger rock at a thrust fault

Rocks move sideways at a lateral fault

Anticline fold forms a crest

Syncline fold forms a trough

Fault line is a deep crack in the rock

A face is a steep side of a mountain.

The snowline is the lower limit of where it is so cold that snow is present all year round.

A valley is a lowland area between two peaks that has been cut out of the rock by a river.

Foothills are the lower peaks of a mountain range, nearer the lowland areas.

TREELINE

RIVER

A flat, lowland plain is often located next to a mountain range on the surface of the lower, subducting plate.

The headwaters of rivers are located in the highlands.

The treeline is the upper limit of where trees can grow. Above this boundary it is too cold, windy, and dry.

INDIAN PLATE

The continental crust and lithospheric mantle together form a tectonic plate. In Asia, as the Indian Plate has moved north, it has been pushed below the Eurasian Plate, forming the Himalayas over a period of more than 50 million years.

PLAIN

CONTINENTAL CRUST

LITHOSPHERIC MANTLE

The asthenosphere is a solid layer of the mantle where the heat and pressure is so great that it behaves like a liquid.

ASTHENOSPHERE

Mountain range

Most mountain ranges form where two tectonic plates push together. As they collide, the rocks of Earth's crust bulge upwards to heights of over 8,000 m (26,000 ft). The folded, twisted rocks crack and erode over time into long ridge lines of sharp mountain peaks that follow the course of the plate boundary.

BATHOLITHS

Half Dome in Yosemite Valley, US, is an example of a batholith – a mountain composed of a vast, single mass of granite or other rock that originally formed underground when a chamber of magma cooled. Softer rock surrounding the hard granite eroded away over many thousands of years to reveal this giant, dome-shaped mountain.

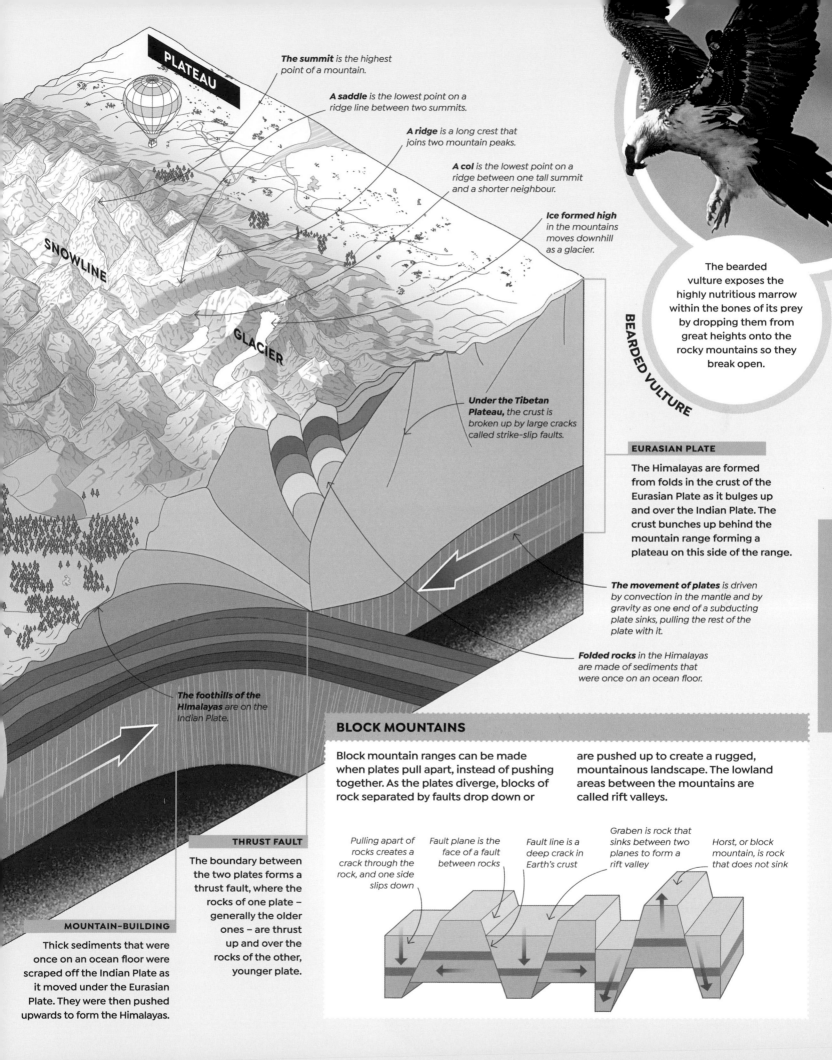

PLATEAU

The summit is the highest point of a mountain.

A saddle is the lowest point on a ridge line between two summits.

A ridge is a long crest that joins two mountain peaks.

A col is the lowest point on a ridge between one tall summit and a shorter neighbour.

Ice formed high in the mountains moves downhill as a glacier.

SNOWLINE

GLACIER

Under the Tibetan Plateau, the crust is broken up by large cracks called strike-slip faults.

BEARDED VULTURE

The bearded vulture exposes the highly nutritious marrow within the bones of its prey by dropping them from great heights onto the rocky mountains so they break open.

EURASIAN PLATE

The Himalayas are formed from folds in the crust of the Eurasian Plate as it bulges up and over the Indian Plate. The crust bunches up behind the mountain range forming a plateau on this side of the range.

The movement of plates is driven by convection in the mantle and by gravity as one end of a subducting plate sinks, pulling the rest of the plate with it.

Folded rocks in the Himalayas are made of sediments that were once on an ocean floor.

The foothills of the Himalayas are on the Indian Plate.

THRUST FAULT

The boundary between the two plates forms a thrust fault, where the rocks of one plate – generally the older ones – are thrust up and over the rocks of the other, younger plate.

MOUNTAIN-BUILDING

Thick sediments that were once on an ocean floor were scraped off the Indian Plate as it moved under the Eurasian Plate. They were then pushed upwards to form the Himalayas.

BLOCK MOUNTAINS

Block mountain ranges can be made when plates pull apart, instead of pushing together. As the plates diverge, blocks of rock separated by faults drop down or are pushed up to create a rugged, mountainous landscape. The lowland areas between the mountains are called rift valleys.

Pulling apart of rocks creates a crack through the rock, and one side slips down

Fault plane is the face of a fault between rocks

Fault line is a deep crack in Earth's crust

Graben is rock that sinks between two planes to form a rift valley

Horst, or block mountain, is rock that does not sink

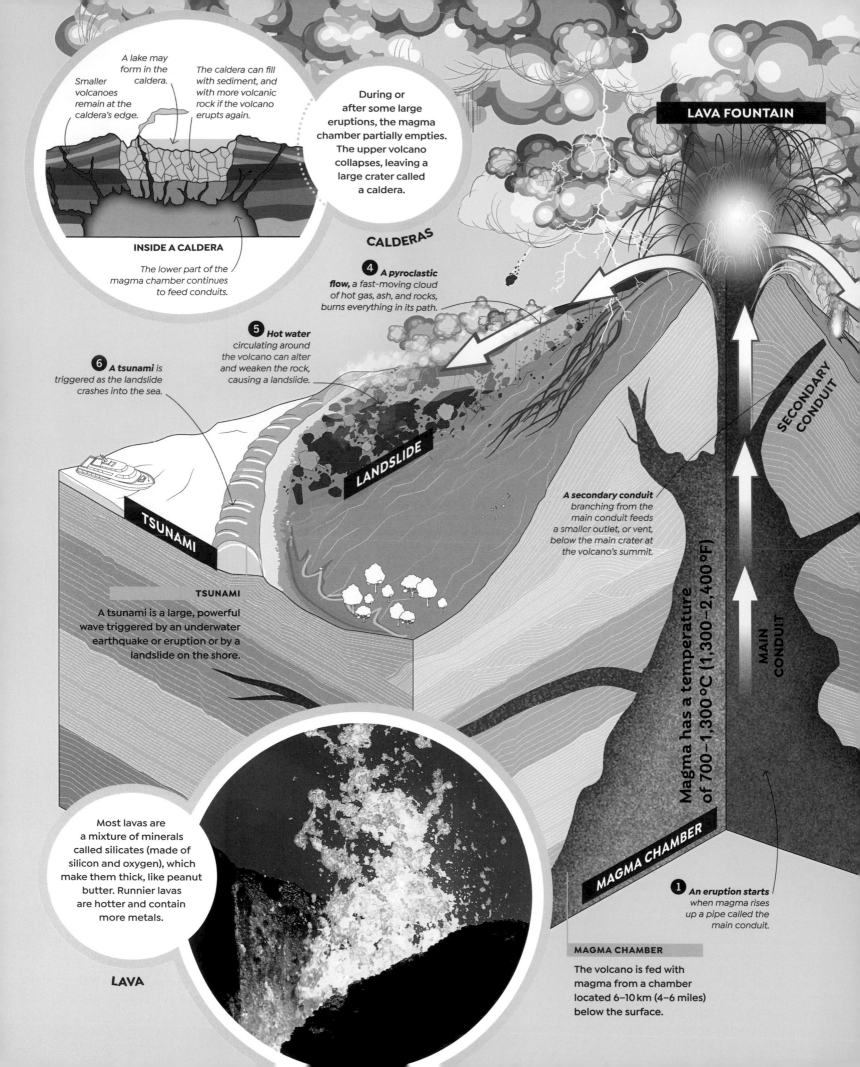

A lake may form in the caldera.

Smaller volcanoes remain at the caldera's edge.

The caldera can fill with sediment, and with more volcanic rock if the volcano erupts again.

During or after some large eruptions, the magma chamber partially empties. The upper volcano collapses, leaving a large crater called a caldera.

LAVA FOUNTAIN

INSIDE A CALDERA

The lower part of the magma chamber continues to feed conduits.

CALDERAS

4 *A pyroclastic flow*, a fast-moving cloud of hot gas, ash, and rocks, burns everything in its path.

5 *Hot water* circulating around the volcano can alter and weaken the rock, causing a landslide.

6 *A tsunami* is triggered as the landslide crashes into the sea.

LANDSLIDE

A secondary conduit branching from the main conduit feeds a smaller outlet, or vent, below the main crater at the volcano's summit.

SECONDARY CONDUIT

TSUNAMI

TSUNAMI

A tsunami is a large, powerful wave triggered by an underwater earthquake or eruption or by a landslide on the shore.

Magma has a temperature of 700–1,300°C (1,300–2,400°F)

MAIN CONDUIT

Most lavas are a mixture of minerals called silicates (made of silicon and oxygen), which make them thick, like peanut butter. Runnier lavas are hotter and contain more metals.

LAVA

MAGMA CHAMBER

1 *An eruption starts* when magma rises up a pipe called the main conduit.

MAGMA CHAMBER

The volcano is fed with magma from a chamber located 6–10 km (4–6 miles) below the surface.

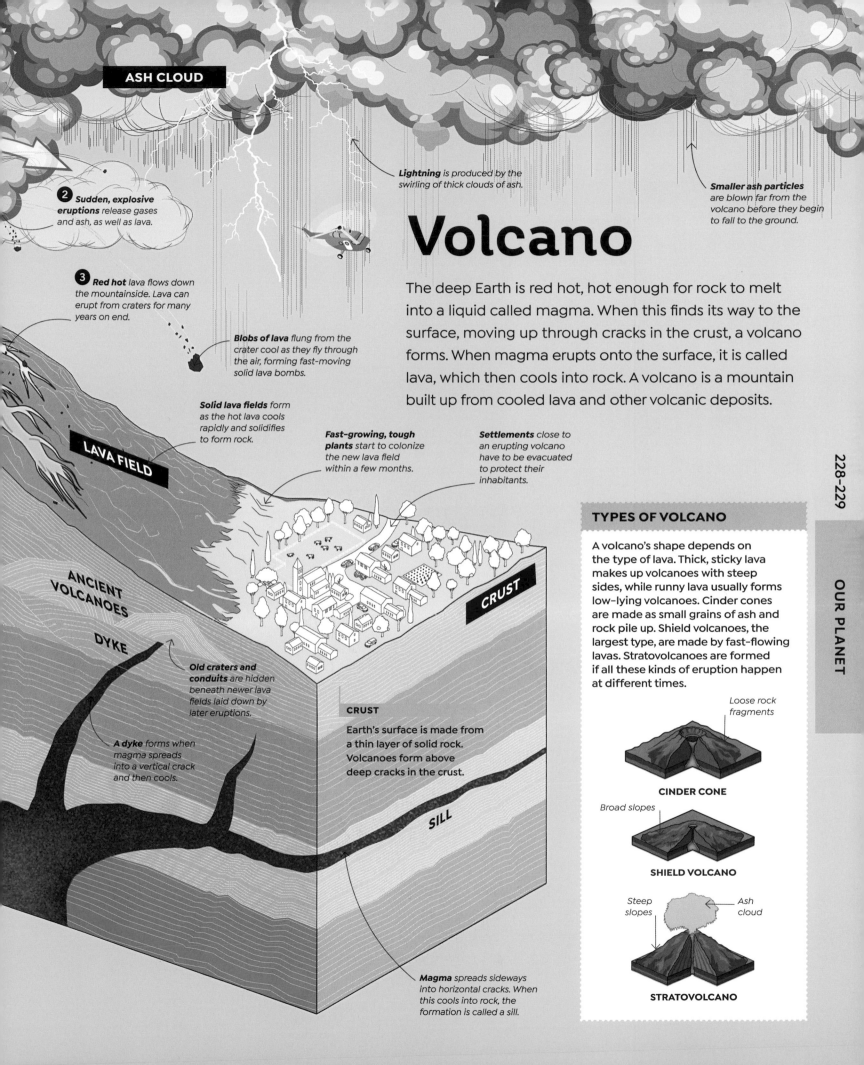

2 *Sudden, explosive eruptions* release gases and ash, as well as lava.

Lightning is produced by the swirling of thick clouds of ash.

Smaller ash particles are blown far from the volcano before they begin to fall to the ground.

3 *Red hot* lava flows down the mountainside. Lava can erupt from craters for many years on end.

Blobs of lava flung from the crater cool as they fly through the air, forming fast-moving solid lava bombs.

Volcano

The deep Earth is red hot, hot enough for rock to melt into a liquid called magma. When this finds its way to the surface, moving up through cracks in the crust, a volcano forms. When magma erupts onto the surface, it is called lava, which then cools into rock. A volcano is a mountain built up from cooled lava and other volcanic deposits.

Solid lava fields form as the hot lava cools rapidly and solidifies to form rock.

LAVA FIELD

Fast-growing, tough plants start to colonize the new lava field within a few months.

Settlements close to an erupting volcano have to be evacuated to protect their inhabitants.

CRUST

ANCIENT VOLCANOES

DYKE

Old craters and conduits are hidden beneath newer lava fields laid down by later eruptions.

A dyke forms when magma spreads into a vertical crack and then cools.

CRUST

Earth's surface is made from a thin layer of solid rock. Volcanoes form above deep cracks in the crust.

SILL

Magma spreads sideways into horizontal cracks. When this cools into rock, the formation is called a sill.

TYPES OF VOLCANO

A volcano's shape depends on the type of lava. Thick, sticky lava makes up volcanoes with steep sides, while runny lava usually forms low-lying volcanoes. Cinder cones are made as small grains of ash and rock pile up. Shield volcanoes, the largest type, are made by fast-flowing lavas. Stratovolcanoes are formed if all these kinds of eruption happen at different times.

Loose rock fragments

CINDER CONE

Broad slopes

SHIELD VOLCANO

Steep slopes

Ash cloud

STRATOVOLCANO

RIVERS OF FIRE

The erupting Tolbachik volcano in Russia makes for a spectacular sight. Some volcanoes erupt violently, blasting clouds of ash, rock, gas, and lava bombs into the air. Others erupt more quietly but continuously, pouring rivers of lava out from cracks and fissures. The strength of the eruption depends on gas dissolved in the lava, and whether the lava is runny or viscous.

Lava erupts
from fissures

HAWAIIAN

Small ash
cloud

Lava ejected
in clumps

STROMBOLIAN

Moderately
high cloud of
gas and ash

Lava
bombs

VULCANIAN

Violent blasts can
reach stratosphere

Rain
of ash

PLINIAN

BLOWING ITS TOP

Eruptions are measured by an explosivity index, with Hawaiian volcanoes least explosive and Plinian volcanoes the most.

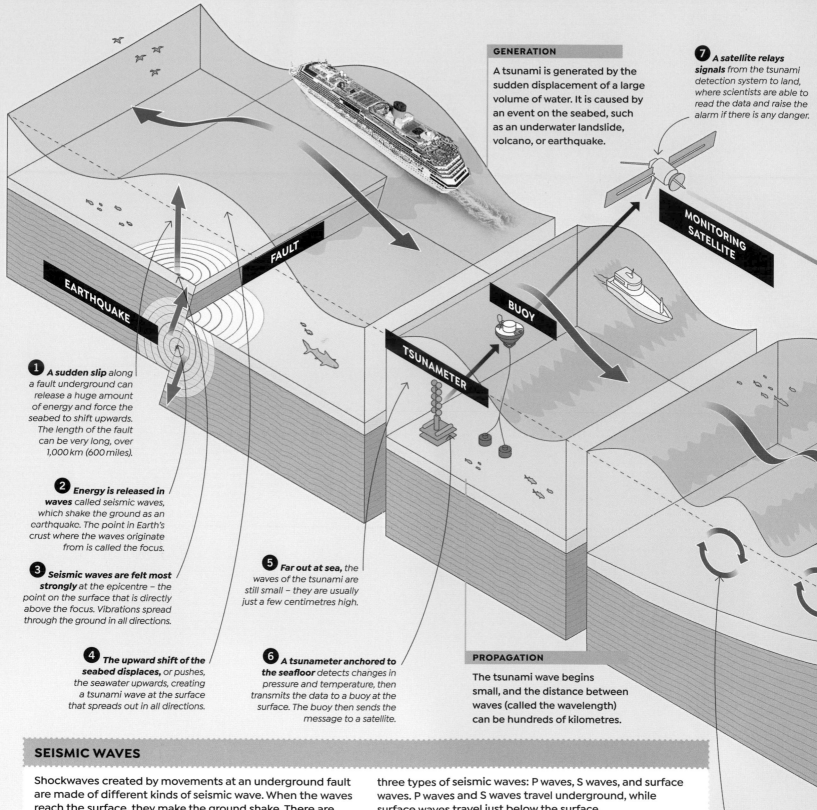

GENERATION

A tsunami is generated by the sudden displacement of a large volume of water. It is caused by an event on the seabed, such as an underwater landslide, volcano, or earthquake.

7 *A satellite relays signals* from the tsunami detection system to land, where scientists are able to read the data and raise the alarm if there is any danger.

MONITORING SATELLITE

FAULT

EARTHQUAKE

BUOY

TSUNAMETER

1 *A sudden slip* along a fault underground can release a huge amount of energy and force the seabed to shift upwards. The length of the fault can be very long, over 1,000 km (600 miles).

2 *Energy is released in waves* called seismic waves, which shake the ground as an earthquake. The point in Earth's crust where the waves originate from is called the focus.

3 *Seismic waves are felt most strongly* at the epicentre – the point on the surface that is directly above the focus. Vibrations spread through the ground in all directions.

4 *The upward shift of the seabed displaces,* or pushes, the seawater upwards, creating a tsunami wave at the surface that spreads out in all directions.

5 *Far out at sea,* the waves of the tsunami are still small – they are usually just a few centimetres high.

6 *A tsunameter anchored to the seafloor* detects changes in pressure and temperature, then transmits the data to a buoy at the surface. The buoy then sends the message to a satellite.

PROPAGATION

The tsunami wave begins small, and the distance between waves (called the wavelength) can be hundreds of kilometres.

8 *The water in ocean waves* moves in a circular motion as the tsunami's energy travels through the water. The sea water itself does not head towards the land.

SEISMIC WAVES

Shockwaves created by movements at an underground fault are made of different kinds of seismic wave. When the waves reach the surface, they make the ground shake. There are three types of seismic waves: P waves, S waves, and surface waves. P waves and S waves travel underground, while surface waves travel just below the surface.

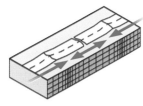

P WAVES

P (primary) waves are the fastest waves. They move underground by squeezing and stretching the rock.

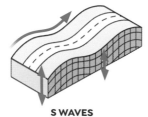

S WAVES

S (secondary) waves move slowly underground. They cause the ground to rise and fall like ripples.

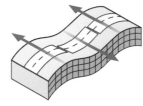

LOVE WAVES

These waves are a type of surface wave that make land shake from side to side.

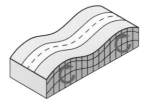

RAYLEIGH WAVES

Rayleigh waves are surface waves that make the ground roll in circular movements, like ocean waves.

Earthquake and tsunami

Earth's tectonic plates are constantly moving past each other, which can cause stress to build up at their boundaries. If the stress becomes too great, the rocks can break along fault lines, releasing a burst of energy that violently shakes the ground. When this happens near or under the ocean, it can trigger a tsunami – a huge ocean wave that can flood far inland.

Tsunami is a Japanese word meaning "harbour wave"

INUNDATION

Near the shore, the waves get closer together and can reach over 10 m (30 ft) tall. The tsunami hits the shore with huge force and can flood inland by several kilometres.

Tsunamis can travel across entire oceans at over 800 kph (500 mph). Modern tsunami warning systems are positioned throughout the Pacific and Indian Oceans to give people on land precious warning of potential danger.

TSUNAMI WARNING

MONITORING STATION

An early warning allows people in coastal communities to evacuate to high ground, such as an evacuation tower.

Some modern tsunami-resistant buildings are constructed with collapsible walls that allow water through without destroying the main structure of the house.

9 *As the waves approach the shore,* they begin to make contact with the rising seabed, which forces them to slow down and grow taller.

COLOSSAL FORCE

Tsunamis don't typically break like coastal waves, but instead they surge far inland with a huge amount of energy. They are capable of tearing down trees and homes, and even carrying boats and cars with them as they go.

Houses may be built on stilts so the water from a tsunami can flow underneath without causing significant damage.

River basin

As its name suggests, a river basin is like a large bowl within which water from many sources collects to flow downhill through rivers. Small streams, each starting from a source on high ground, join together to form larger rivers. Eventually, all the water that falls as rain or snow within the basin will flow out to sea through the same river.

Soft rocks erode faster than hard rocks. Water acts like an excavator in the soft rock of a waterfall's plunge pool, and the waterfall retreats upstream as the hard rock above collapses. Rapids occur where eroded soft and uneroded hard rock form an uneven surface.

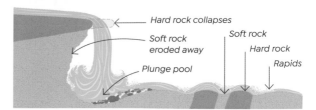

Hard rock collapses

Soft rock eroded away

Soft rock

Hard rock

Plunge pool

Rapids

DELTA WETLANDS

River deltas are filled with moist, nutrient-rich sediment and are havens for all sorts of flora and fauna. Botswana's Okavango Delta is so important to local wildlife that their reproductive cycles have adapted to coincide with the arrival of floods in winter to ensure they have a better chance of survival.

Meander bends form by a process of erosion and sediment deposition as the river's volume and energy make it move sideways.

The place where two or more rivers join is called a confluence.

Floodplains are areas of low-lying flat land that are submerged when a river overflows.

A meander's flat, low inside bank is created by sediment deposits.

A meander's outside bank is high and steep, because it is eroded by faster-moving water than the inside bank.

MEANDER

OXBOW LAKE

An oxbow lake is a meander that has been cut off from a river's main channel.

The Amazon's river basin covers 7 million square km (2.7 million square miles)

DRAINAGE DIVIDE

DELTA

LOWER COURSE

A drainage divide is a feature such as a ridge that marks the edge of the area drained by a river, called the watershed or catchment. Rainwater landing on one side of the divide will flow into a different river from water landing on its other side.

Many towns and cities began near rivers, which provided a source of water, a means of transport, and fertile soil for farming.

Rivers reaching the sea can break up into channels divided by muddy islands of silt formed from sediment deposits. This is a river delta.

A river's mouth is where it finally meets the sea, or flows into another, larger body of water, such as a lake.

LOWER COURSE

As it nears the sea, a river gets wider and straighter. Its volume and the amount of sediment it carries increase.

Mountain ranges are the source of many rivers. At least 10 major rivers start in the Himalayas, for example.

Most rivers begin as small springs high up in hills and mountains. This is known as a river's source.

Glaciers are slowly moving masses of ice. In warm months they partially melt, and the water flows into rivers.

Tributaries are smaller streams that feed into the main river channel.

GLACIER

Few things can resist water's powers of erosion. For example, the Colorado River has cut down through 300 m (1,000 ft) of rock to carve out this bend.

Snow melt in spring flows downhill into the river, greatly increasing its volume.

Lakes may develop where meltwater collects in a valley hollow. As they fill, they overflow and feed into rivers.

Streams are mini rivers. They are smaller, narrower, and often temporary.

STREAM

GORGE

UPPER COURSE

When a river flows over land layered with hard and soft rock, it undercuts and erodes the soft rock to make a waterfall.

RAPIDS

Gorges (steep-sided valleys) form where waterfalls wear away the surrounding earth and rock.

Rapids emerge when the erosion of soft rock on the river bed leaves hard rock to protrude up, disrupting the water's flow.

MIDDLE COURSE

VALLEY SHAPES

In a river basin's upper reaches, its waters only have enough energy to erode downwards, carving out a steep V-shape. As the river gathers size in its middle course, its growing energy is expended sideways, making its valley shallower. By a river's lower course the valley has almost been worn down to a flat plain.

UPPER COURSE

This is where a river forms and is usually the steepest part of a river basin. Small streams meet here to create a larger river.

Vertical (downwards) erosion cuts a narrow valley

Water volume is low, but flow is turbulent

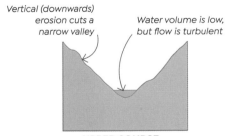

UPPER COURSE

MIDDLE COURSE

Running through gently sloping land often prone to flooding, rivers meander in sweeping curves across the landscape.

Lateral (sideways) erosion widens valley

Water volume increases and slows

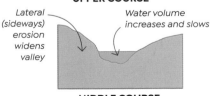

MIDDLE COURSE

BRAIDED RIVERS

Braided rivers occur where a river's load of silt and sand is too heavy for it to carry. Dumped sediment forms into small islands, breaking up the river into small streams, or braids.

River's volume at its greatest

Less erosion and more deposition occur

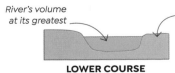

LOWER COURSE

IN FULL FLOOD

Rivers flood when a sudden peak in rainfall or snowmelt descends from the channels that supply them. This raises the height of the water in the riverbed, causing it to overflow. If confined in a narrow channel, as in this gorge on the Jinsha River in China, the speed of flow increases rapidly, turning a calm flow into a raging torrent. In flatter areas a river will burst its banks, covering the surrounding land with a depth of water and depositing mud and debris from upstream. Floods can have devastating impacts on people and property in surrounding areas.

72 MILLION 2010
147 MILLION 2030
221 MILLION 2050

PEOPLE AFFECTED BY FLOODS

Studies by the World Resources Institute predict that the damage caused to people and property by floods could rise significantly by 2050.

A cenote is a natural pool formed when a sinkhole collapses and exposes the groundwater beneath. Cenotes are particularly common in Mexico, where people flock to swim in their picturesque turquoise waters. The word "cenote" is from ancient Mayan.

CENOTES

Exposed limestone where large blocks are separated by deep fissures is called limestone pavement.

LIMESTONE PAVEMENT

A sinking stream is one that flows over the surface then suddenly disappears as its water drops into a cave system.

Water from rivers, streams, and rain seeps underground to create the caves beneath the surface.

LIMESTONE

Stalactites form on the roof of a cave when drips of water leave behind tiny crystals, which build up into a downward-pointing spike.

Columns form where stalactites growing downwards meet stalagmites growing upwards.

Water seeps underground through tiny fissures, or cracks, in the rock.

Stalagmites form when drips of water from the cave roof deposit minerals on the ground, gradually growing into columns over time.

WATER TABLE

A gour is a shallow pool that fills a step in a cascade, often trickling water down to the step below.

Water saturates the ground below a line called the water table. When a cave is below the water table, it is full of water.

FISSURES

SPELEOTHEMS

Speleothems, such as stalactites, are intricately shaped cave features. They form when minerals dissolved in water moving through a cave are deposited as solid crystals.

Narrow areas form passages that connect chambers. Underground streams can travel through these passages.

Cave drapery is a type of speleothem that looks like a hanging curtain or cloth.

GOUR

Caves

Elaborate underground labyrinths are hidden beneath some of Earth's landscapes. Caves can form in a few ways but most of the planet's biggest cave systems form when water seeps into limestone rock to create a kind of landscape known as karst. Carbon dioxide dissolved in the water makes it slightly acidic, and it gradually erodes minerals in the rock to create hollow spaces.

CHAMBER

Large spaces in a cave system are called chambers or caverns. Often these are formed where the original rocks are already weakened by cracks, making them collapse, or where several streams meet to wash away more rock.

Cascades are a series of step-like deposits of minerals that form where cave streams flow down a steep, rugged slope.

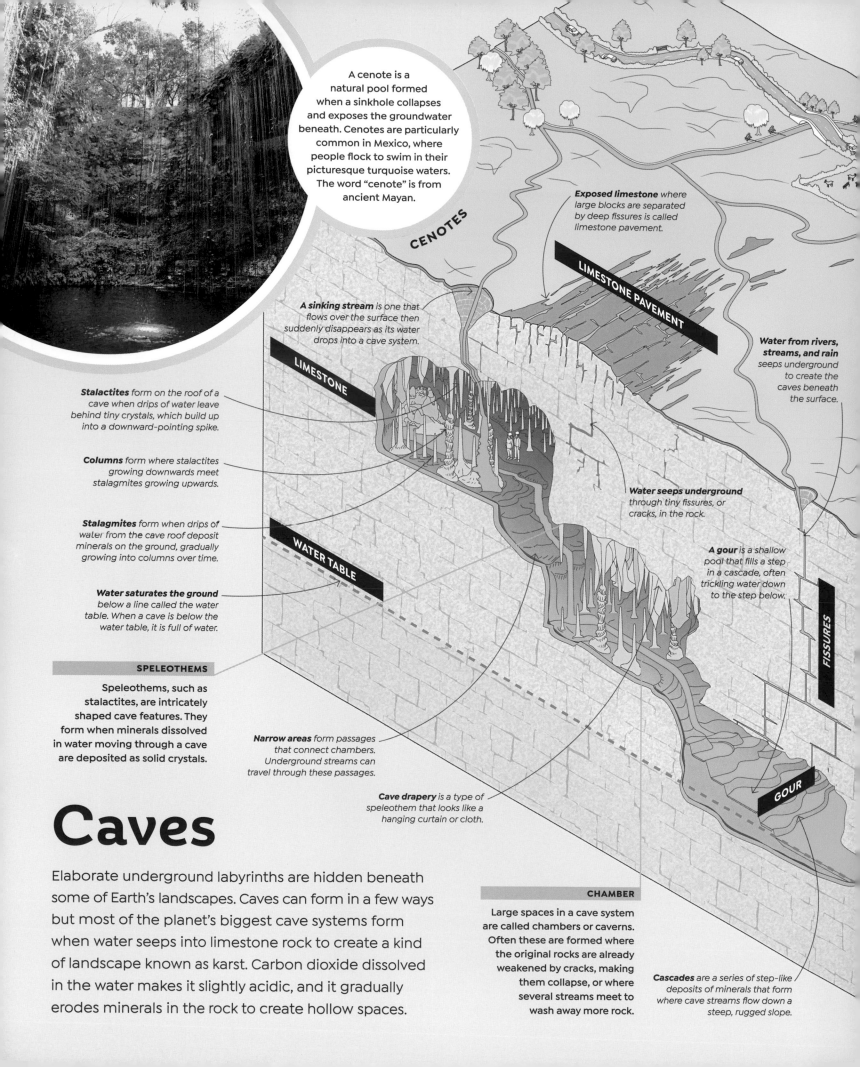

CAVE LIFE

Caves make the perfect shelter for many animals, from bats and bears to spiders and glowworms, due to their darkness, constant temperature, and protection from the elements. The lesser horseshoe bat (right) comes to caves to roost and hibernate.

Mammoth Cave in Kentucky, US, is the **longest cave in the world**

TROPICAL KARST

The heavy rainfall of tropical regions means karst landscapes are eroded more rapidly than in temperate areas. As sinkholes form across a tropical karst plain, they merge to form sunken areas around hills, called fengcong karst, and eventually isolated towers, called fenglin karst.

Sinkhole

Small caves

KARST PLAIN

Fengcong karst hill

Sinkholes merge

FENGCONG KARST

Fenglin karst tower

FENGLIN KARST

SINKHOLE

Erosion of limestone at the surface creates hollows called sinkholes. Sinkholes are often the way water enters a cave system.

Vertical shafts *are formed by water eroding straight through the soft limestone.*

An underground river, *fed by water seeping through sinkholes and fissures, erodes a passage through the limestone.*

Impermeable rock *forces the flow of water to the surface, forming a spring.*

A sinkhole may collapse *if the rock between a sinkhole and a cave below becomes too thin to support itself.*

SINKHOLE

SINKHOLE

VERTICAL SHAFT

DRY CAVE

UNDERGROUND LAKE

IMPERMEABLE ROCK

Water cannot flow *into impermeable rock, such as granite.*

This dry cave *is above the water table and has become cut off from a supply of surface water.*

An underground lake *fills chambers that meet the water table.*

GLACIER CAVES

Temporary caves can also form inside glaciers when ice melts at the surface and drains through to the base. Slightly warmer than the glacial ice, the water melts a channel through the middle of the glacier.

SUBMERGED CAVE

Submerged chambers *below the water table can be visited by cave diving.*

LIMESTONE

Limestone is a sedimentary rock made of calcium carbonate that dissolves in naturally acidic water, making it easy for water to move downwards, eroding the rock as it goes.

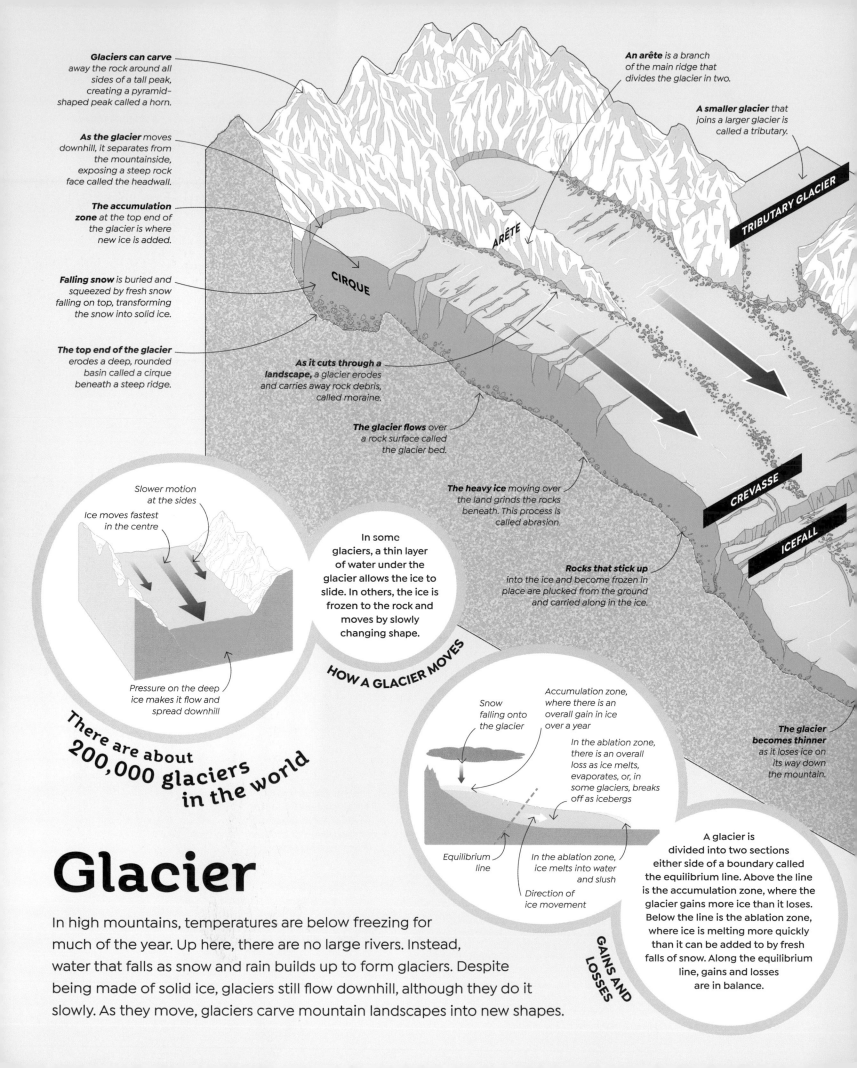

Glaciers can carve away the rock around all sides of a tall peak, creating a pyramid-shaped peak called a horn.

As the glacier moves downhill, it separates from the mountainside, exposing a steep rock face called the headwall.

The accumulation zone at the top end of the glacier is where new ice is added.

Falling snow is buried and squeezed by fresh snow falling on top, transforming the snow into solid ice.

The top end of the glacier erodes a deep, rounded basin called a cirque beneath a steep ridge.

An arête is a branch of the main ridge that divides the glacier in two.

A smaller glacier that joins a larger glacier is called a tributary.

TRIBUTARY GLACIER

ARÊTE

CIRQUE

As it cuts through a landscape, a glacier erodes and carries away rock debris, called moraine.

The glacier flows over a rock surface called the glacier bed.

The heavy ice moving over the land grinds the rocks beneath. This process is called abrasion

Rocks that stick up into the ice and become frozen in place are plucked from the ground and carried along in the ice.

CREVASSE

ICEFALL

Slower motion at the sides

Ice moves fastest in the centre

Pressure on the deep ice makes it flow and spread downhill

In some glaciers, a thin layer of water under the glacier allows the ice to slide. In others, the ice is frozen to the rock and moves by slowly changing shape.

HOW A GLACIER MOVES

The glacier becomes thinner as it loses ice on its way down the mountain.

There are about **200,000 glaciers** in the world

Snow falling onto the glacier

Accumulation zone, where there is an overall gain in ice over a year

In the ablation zone, there is an overall loss as ice melts, evaporates, or, in some glaciers, breaks off as icebergs

Equilibrium line

In the ablation zone, ice melts into water and slush

Direction of ice movement

A glacier is divided into two sections either side of a boundary called the equilibrium line. Above the line is the accumulation zone, where the glacier gains more ice than it loses. Below the line is the ablation zone, where ice is melting more quickly than it can be added to by fresh falls of snow. Along the equilibrium line, gains and losses are in balance.

GAINS AND LOSSES

Glacier

In high mountains, temperatures are below freezing for much of the year. Up here, there are no large rivers. Instead, water that falls as snow and rain builds up to form glaciers. Despite being made of solid ice, glaciers still flow downhill, although they do it slowly. As they move, glaciers carve mountain landscapes into new shapes.

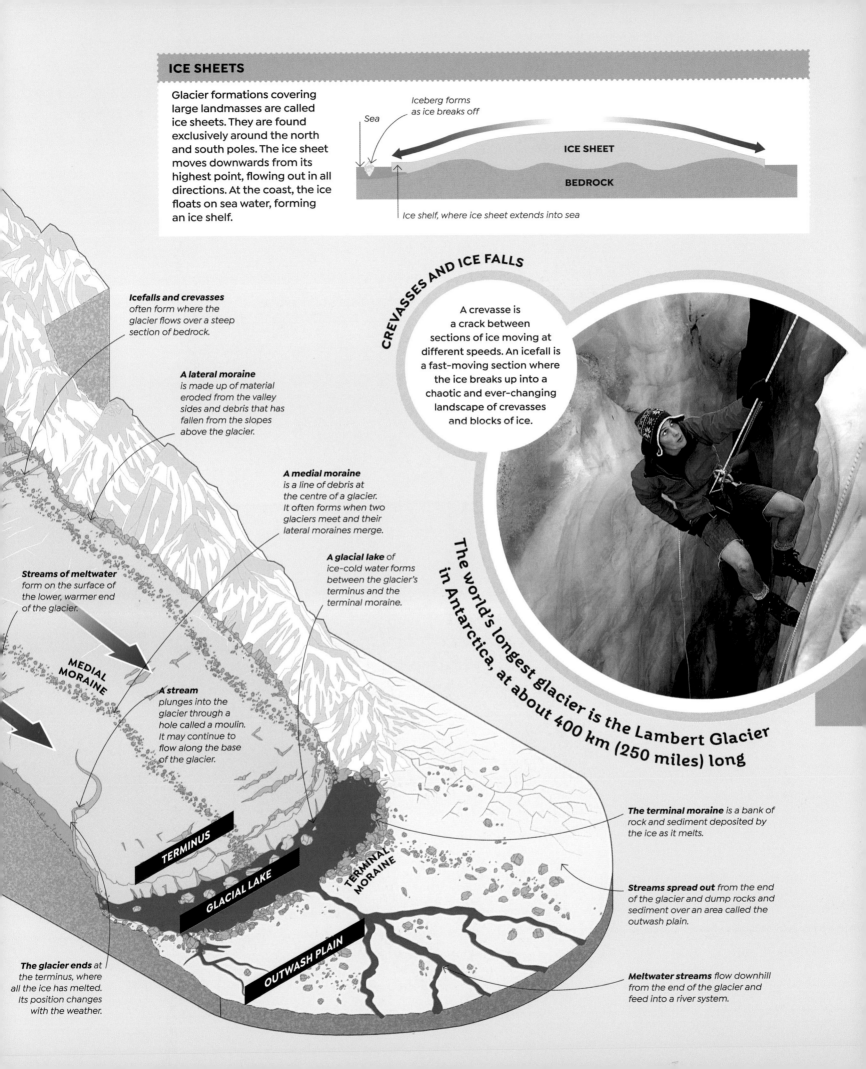

ICE SHEETS

Glacier formations covering large landmasses are called ice sheets. They are found exclusively around the north and south poles. The ice sheet moves downwards from its highest point, flowing out in all directions. At the coast, the ice floats on sea water, forming an ice shelf.

Sea

Iceberg forms as ice breaks off

ICE SHEET

BEDROCK

Ice shelf, where ice sheet extends into sea

CREVASSES AND ICE FALLS

A crevasse is a crack between sections of ice moving at different speeds. An icefall is a fast-moving section where the ice breaks up into a chaotic and ever-changing landscape of crevasses and blocks of ice.

The world's longest glacier is the Lambert Glacier in Antarctica, at about 400 km (250 miles) long

Icefalls and crevasses often form where the glacier flows over a steep section of bedrock.

A lateral moraine is made up of material eroded from the valley sides and debris that has fallen from the slopes above the glacier.

A medial moraine is a line of debris at the centre of a glacier. It often forms when two glaciers meet and their lateral moraines merge.

A glacial lake of ice-cold water forms between the glacier's terminus and the terminal moraine.

Streams of meltwater form on the surface of the lower, warmer end of the glacier.

A stream plunges into the glacier through a hole called a moulin. It may continue to flow along the base of the glacier.

MEDIAL MORAINE

TERMINUS

GLACIAL LAKE

TERMINAL MORAINE

OUTWASH PLAIN

The glacier ends at the terminus, where all the ice has melted. Its position changes with the weather.

The terminal moraine is a bank of rock and sediment deposited by the ice as it melts.

Streams spread out from the end of the glacier and dump rocks and sediment over an area called the outwash plain.

Meltwater streams flow downhill from the end of the glacier and feed into a river system.

FLOATING HAZARD

Icebergs are chunks of ice that have broken off an ice sheet or glacier. They can range in size from 5 m (16 ft) across to that of a small country, with smaller pieces called "bergy bits" (about the size of a house) or "growlers" (the size of a car). It may look like the iceberg in the picture is towering over the ship, but the ship is distant, and the iceberg, just a growler, is right in front of the camera. Around 90 per cent of an iceberg is hidden below the water, so it is still dangerous. As icebergs drift from the poles towards the equator, they crack, roll over, shrink, and melt.

TABULAR   **WEDGE**   **DOME**

DRYDOCK   **PINNACLE**   **BLOCKY**

ICEBERG TYPES

Most icebergs break off as tabular or blocky pieces and gradually change shape as they are affected by melting and weathering.

OCEAN CONVEYOR BELT

The ocean conveyor belt is a current system that slowly mixes surface waters into the deep oceans. Warm water expands and spreads out from the equator towards the poles. There it cools and sinks, before flowing along the seabed back to the equator, where it warms up and rises to the surface to begin the cycle again.

Water's heat lost to air

Warm surface current

Cold, deep current

It takes 1,000 years for water to complete one loop of the ocean conveyor belt

Direction of Earth's rotation

Current in northern hemisphere is deflected to right

Current in southern hemisphere is deflected to left

Equator

Ocean and air currents (the wind) don't flow in straight lines but are deflected by the Coriolis effect, a phenomenon caused by the rotation of Earth from west to east. As the surface of the planet moves, the flow of both water and air are dragged to the right in the northern hemisphere and to the left in the southern hemisphere.

CORIOLIS EFFECT

WARM CURRENTS

The currents that flow from the equator towards the poles generally carry warm water. The water is warm thanks to the intense sunshine at the equator.

The Great Pacific Garbage Patch is a mass of more than a trillion pieces of floating plastic junk washed together by a gyre. It covers an area larger than the size of Texas.

PACIFIC OCEAN

EQUATORIAL COUNTERCURRENT

The equatorial countercurrent is driven by wind. It flows eastward near the equator in the Pacific, Atlantic, and Indian oceans.

A gyre is a vast loop created by several linked currents that circulate water around an ocean.

The Humboldt Current creates a fertile area of ocean. Its cold water is full of nutrients.

Cold currents bring cold, dry weather. Coasts nearby are often deserts, as here in western South America.

SOUTH AMERICA

CIRCUMPOLAR CURRENT

SOUTHERN OCEAN

ATLANTIC OCEAN

ANTARCTICA

THERMOHALINE CIRCULATION

Ocean currents can be created by differences in water density. This is called a thermohaline circulation, because the differences in density are caused by temperature (thermo-) and saltiness (-haline). Cold, salty water is heavier than warmer water and always sinks. Sinking water makes room at the surface for lighter, warmer water to rise. This happens in a constant cycle of colder, denser water sinking and warmer, lighter water rising.

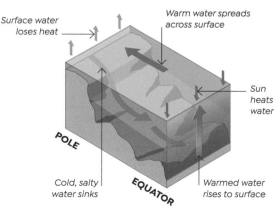

Surface water loses heat

Warm water spreads across surface

Sun heats water

POLE

EQUATOR

Cold, salty water sinks

Warmed water rises to surface

Where currents meet, their surface waters crash into each other. The impact and the pressure forces the water downwards, a process called downwelling that helps deliver oxygen to the sea's lower depths.

The Gulf Stream is the fastest ocean current, with a top speed of 9 kph (5.6 mph)

Ocean currents

The water in the world's oceans is mixed by currents. They are usually horizontal, moving on or near the surface, but can be vertical, too, where water sinks to the seafloor in one place and rises to the surface elsewhere. Currents are more obvious at the surface, partly created by strong winds that blow over the water. Surface currents form a network of river-like streams that flow between the continents.

COLD CURRENTS

Ocean currents that flow towards the equator tend to be cold. Their water comes from the polar seas, which are cold year round.

ARCTIC OCEAN

NORTH AMERICA

GULF STREAM

COASTAL UPWELLING

Coastal upwelling water is filled with the nutrient-rich remains of dead animals and plants from the ocean floor. Where it rises to the surface, great numbers of fish, birds, and higher predators, such as whales, come to feast.

EUROPE

The Gulf Stream carries warm water from the Gulf of Mexico to the seas of western Europe, making the climate warm.

The equator divides the northern and southern hemispheres. Temperatures, weather, and currents are moderate here.

AFRICA

The ocean's surface is not completely flat. Warm, salty parts can bulge up to 2 m (6 ft) above colder waters at the poles.

The Monsoon Current in the Indian Ocean changes direction with the seasons, as winds blow away from land in winter and towards it in summer.

ASIA

This dark patch is an area of high salinity. Paler areas show lower salinity.

EQUATORIAL COUNTERCURRENT

INDIAN OCEAN

The Circumpolar Current creates a continuous loop around Antarctica. It moves more water than any other current.

AUSTRALIA AND OCEANIA

PACIFIC OCEAN

EQUATOR

OUR PLANET

SALINITY

Chemicals washed out of rocks by rivers make oceans salty, or saline. An ocean's salinity also depends on how much non-salty rainwater falls into it, and how much water is lost by evaporation (which leaves salt behind).

Upwelling happens when the wind blows away warm surface water, and deeper, cooler water rises to the surface.

Volcanic islands

In some places under the oceans, molten rock called magma pushes its way up through Earth's crust at places called hotspots or along the boundaries between tectonic plates to form new rock on the seabed. If enough lava escapes it can form an underwater mountain or even a mountain range – and when these mountains break the sea's surface their tips appear as islands.

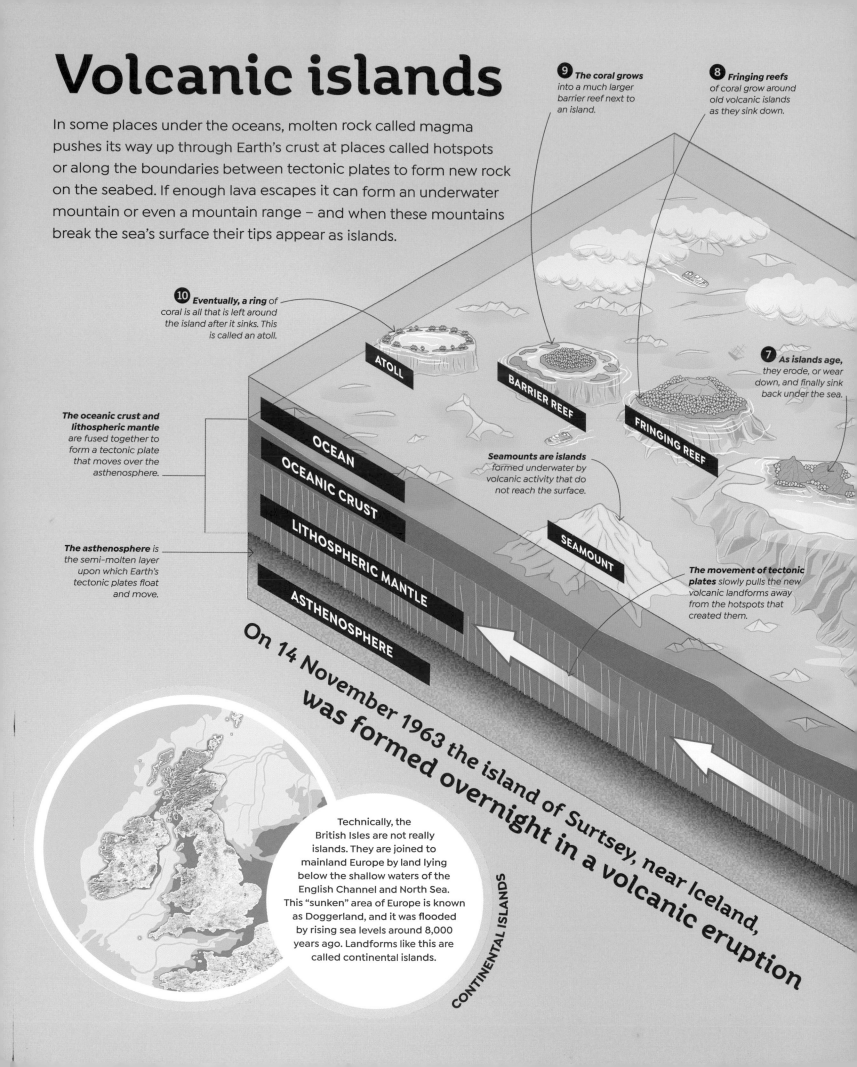

9 *The coral grows* into a much larger barrier reef next to an island.

8 *Fringing reefs* of coral grow around old volcanic islands as they sink down.

7 *As islands age,* they erode, or wear down, and finally sink back under the sea.

10 *Eventually, a ring* of coral is all that is left around the island after it sinks. This is called an atoll.

ATOLL

BARRIER REEF

FRINGING REEF

The oceanic crust and lithospheric mantle are fused together to form a tectonic plate that moves over the asthenosphere.

Seamounts are islands formed underwater by volcanic activity that do not reach the surface.

OCEAN

OCEANIC CRUST

LITHOSPHERIC MANTLE

SEAMOUNT

The asthenosphere is the semi-molten layer upon which Earth's tectonic plates float and move.

ASTHENOSPHERE

The movement of tectonic plates slowly pulls the new volcanic landforms away from the hotspots that created them.

On 14 November 1963 the island of Surtsey, near Iceland, was formed overnight in a volcanic eruption

Technically, the British Isles are not really islands. They are joined to mainland Europe by land lying below the shallow waters of the English Channel and North Sea. This "sunken" area of Europe is known as Doggerland, and it was flooded by rising sea levels around 8,000 years ago. Landforms like this are called continental islands.

CONTINENTAL ISLANDS

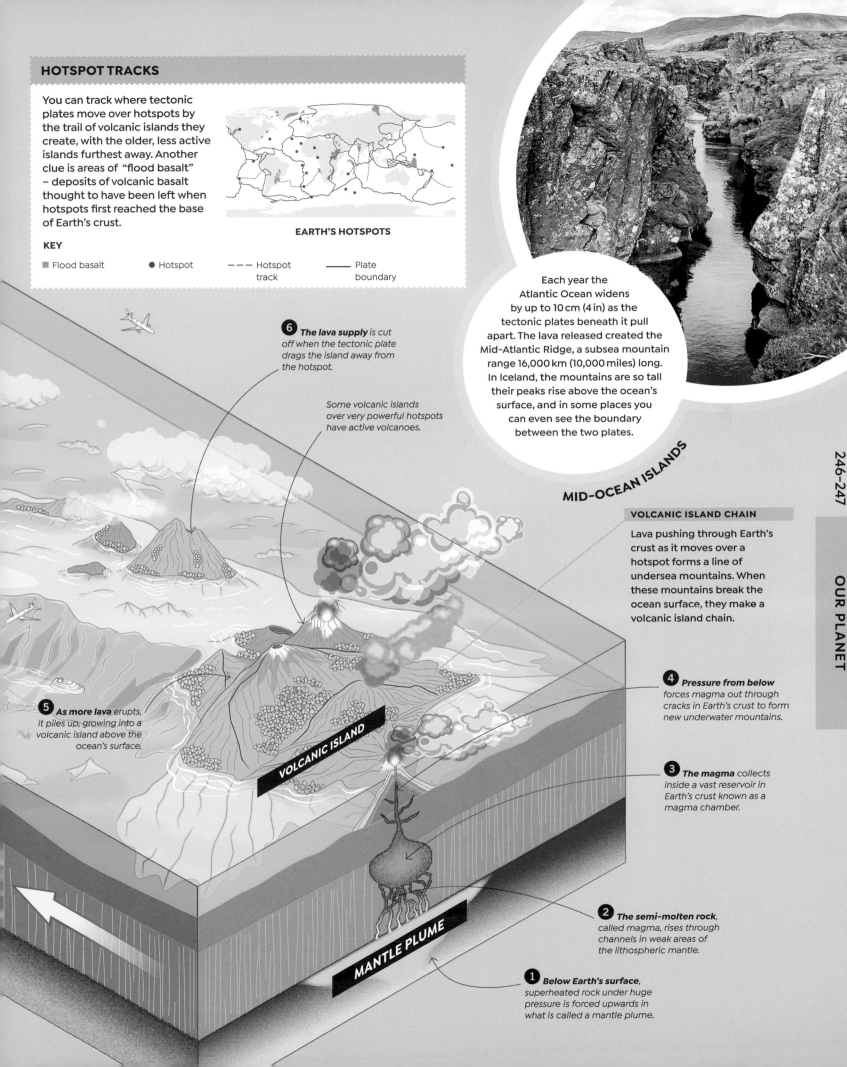

HOTSPOT TRACKS

You can track where tectonic plates move over hotspots by the trail of volcanic islands they create, with the older, less active islands furthest away. Another clue is areas of "flood basalt" – deposits of volcanic basalt thought to have been left when hotspots first reached the base of Earth's crust.

EARTH'S HOTSPOTS

KEY

■ Flood basalt ● Hotspot - - - Hotspot track —— Plate boundary

6 *The lava supply* is cut off when the tectonic plate drags the island away from the hotspot.

Some volcanic islands over very powerful hotspots have active volcanoes.

Each year the Atlantic Ocean widens by up to 10 cm (4 in) as the tectonic plates beneath it pull apart. The lava released created the Mid-Atlantic Ridge, a subsea mountain range 16,000 km (10,000 miles) long. In Iceland, the mountains are so tall their peaks rise above the ocean's surface, and in some places you can even see the boundary between the two plates.

MID-OCEAN ISLANDS

VOLCANIC ISLAND CHAIN

Lava pushing through Earth's crust as it moves over a hotspot forms a line of undersea mountains. When these mountains break the ocean surface, they make a volcanic island chain.

5 *As more lava* erupts, it piles up, growing into a volcanic island above the ocean's surface.

VOLCANIC ISLAND

4 *Pressure from below* forces magma out through cracks in Earth's crust to form new underwater mountains.

3 *The magma* collects inside a vast reservoir in Earth's crust known as a magma chamber.

MANTLE PLUME

2 *The semi-molten rock,* called magma, rises through channels in weak areas of the lithospheric mantle.

1 *Below Earth's surface,* superheated rock under huge pressure is forced upwards in what is called a mantle plume.

The seabed

Deep below the surface of the ocean, the seabed is rich with fascinating features, from canyons cutting into the continental shelf to entire mountain ranges that stretch for thousands of kilometres across the seafloor. The oceans cover more than 70 per cent of Earth's surface, but more than 80 per cent of this watery world is yet to be explored.

Survey ships use echo sounders to measure the depth of the ocean. They send sound waves to the seabed, which then bounce back to the ship. The time it takes for the waves to return reveals how deep the ocean is. This information is then used to construct a map of the seafloor.

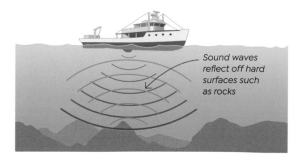

Sound waves reflect off hard surfaces such as rocks

SEABED EXPLORATION

More people have visited the Moon than the deepest parts of the ocean floor. Ocean explorers use small craft called submersibles to travel to the seabed – a round trip that takes several hours. Submersibles are built to withstand the extreme pressure of the deep ocean that would otherwise crush both the craft and the explorers.

TRENCH

At convergent plate boundaries, where one plate moves under its neighbour, the seabed plunges down to form a deep trench. Trenches like this are the deepest parts of the seabed.

A fault line is a crack in the crust that forms where different sections of seabed move at different speeds or in different directions.

A volcanic island forms when a volcano grows tall enough to rise above the surface of the water.

Abyssal hills are small hills that rise only a few hundred metres above the abyssal plain.

TRENCH

A seamount is an undersea volcano that does not break the surface. Many seamounts are now extinct.

VOLCANIC ARC

VOLCANIC ARC

Volcanic eruptions near a subduction zone can create a string of volcanoes along the plate boundary. The volcanoes grow larger as extra rock is added by new eruptions, forming seamounts and islands.

A volcano can form on the seabed above a subduction zone, as hot magma erupts from the seafloor and solidifies.

A subduction zone is where one tectonic plate is forced beneath another at a convergent boundary. As the plate enters Earth's hot interior, it causes melting of the mantle to make magma.

CONTINENTAL RISE

Sediment and debris that fall down the continental slope create a gently rising region of seabed called the continental rise, located between the continental slope and abyssal plain.

CONTINENTAL SHELF

The shallow region of seabed close to the coast is called the continental shelf. It is part of a continent.

The coast is where the water meets land. Coastal water shapes the land, eroding rock and providing rich habitats.

Continental crust can be very old, and is thicker and more buoyant than oceanic crust.

ABYSSAL PLAIN

Much of the deep ocean beyond the continental shelf is covered by the abyssal plain. This mostly flat area is covered in sediment.

COAST

SUBMARINE CANYON

A submarine canyon is a deep notch in the continental shelf. Some are deeper than the Grand Canyon in the US.

CONTINENTAL CRUST

LITHOSPHERIC MANTLE

ASTHENOSPHERE

OCEAN

A guyot is a seamount (an extinct undersea volcano) with a summit that has been eroded by waves into a flat surface.

ABYSSAL PLAIN

GUYOT

MID-OCEAN RIDGE

CONTINENTAL SLOPE

The continental slope marks the border of the continental shelf, dropping away in a steep slope that plunges down to the deep ocean floor. It also forms the edge of a continent.

Sediment, made of rock and soil particles washed off the land and remains of marine organisms, sits on the seabed.

A deep-sea fan branches out from the mouth of a submarine canyon. It is made from sediment that has washed off the land.

Oceanic crust is thinner than continental crust, at just 5 km (3 miles) thick, and is made mostly from a dense rock called basalt.

OCEANIC CRUST

The asthenosphere is the part of the mantle that is so hot it can flow, even though it is solid. At mid-ocean ridges, as the tectonic plates spread apart, it melts as it rises, erupting lava on the seafloor.

The lithospheric mantle is a solid upper layer of the mantle that sits atop the asthenosphere.

MID-OCEAN RIDGE

Mid-ocean ridges occur at divergent plate boundaries, where molten rock from the asthenosphere rises up to fill the gap between the plates. As the lava builds up, a mountainous ridge forms along the seabed.

On average, the seabed is 3,688 m (12,100 ft) deep. The deepest point is Challenger Deep, near Guam, which is 10,935 m (35,876 ft) deep.

SUBMARINE CANYON LIFE

Submarine canyons have walls that stretch up to 2,600 m (8,500 ft) tall. They are havens for wildlife, as they allow organic material, such as dead plants and marine creatures, to travel down to the deep sea. These rich nutrients support an extensive food web that ranges from corals, like this mushroom soft coral, to whales and otters.

Hydrothermal vent

The ocean depths are, for the most part, cold and empty. In a few places, however, jets of super-hot water gush out of the seabed through holes called hydrothermal vents. These mysterious places are havens for microbes and other creatures that thrive in hot, mineral-rich water, far from the light of the sun.

THE ORIGIN OF LIFE?

Many scientists think life began inside hydrothermal vents. Although they seem like extreme places to us, they were one of the most stable habitats on the young Earth. Inside the vent chimneys, simple chemicals might have reacted together in the hot, wet environment to form the chemicals used by life, such as DNA and proteins.

As they rise, the molecules become more complex

Simple cell containing building blocks for life

Chemicals react with minerals in vent walls

Simple chemicals   Warm water

INSIDE A VENT CHIMNEY

BLACK SMOKER

The hottest vents release what looks like clouds of black smoke. In fact, they are made of chemicals that turn into dark particles in the cold seawater.

The vent octopus is the top predator. It eats crabs and other shellfish.

Vent clams grow bacteria in their gills that supply them with food.

① *The vent is fed* by cold seawater trickling down into deep cracks, or fissures, in the seabed.

FISSURES

Rocks beneath the seabed are heated by a magma chamber deeper down.

② *Water is heated* by hot rocks. This heat is the source of energy for vent wildlife.

White "smoke" is made of chemicals rich in silicon and calcium.

The water inside a hydrothermal vent is hot enough to melt lead

If the water in the vent is cooler than 300°C (570°F), it creates a "white smoker". These are usually slower-flowing than black smokers and grow smaller chimneys.

WHITE SMOKERS

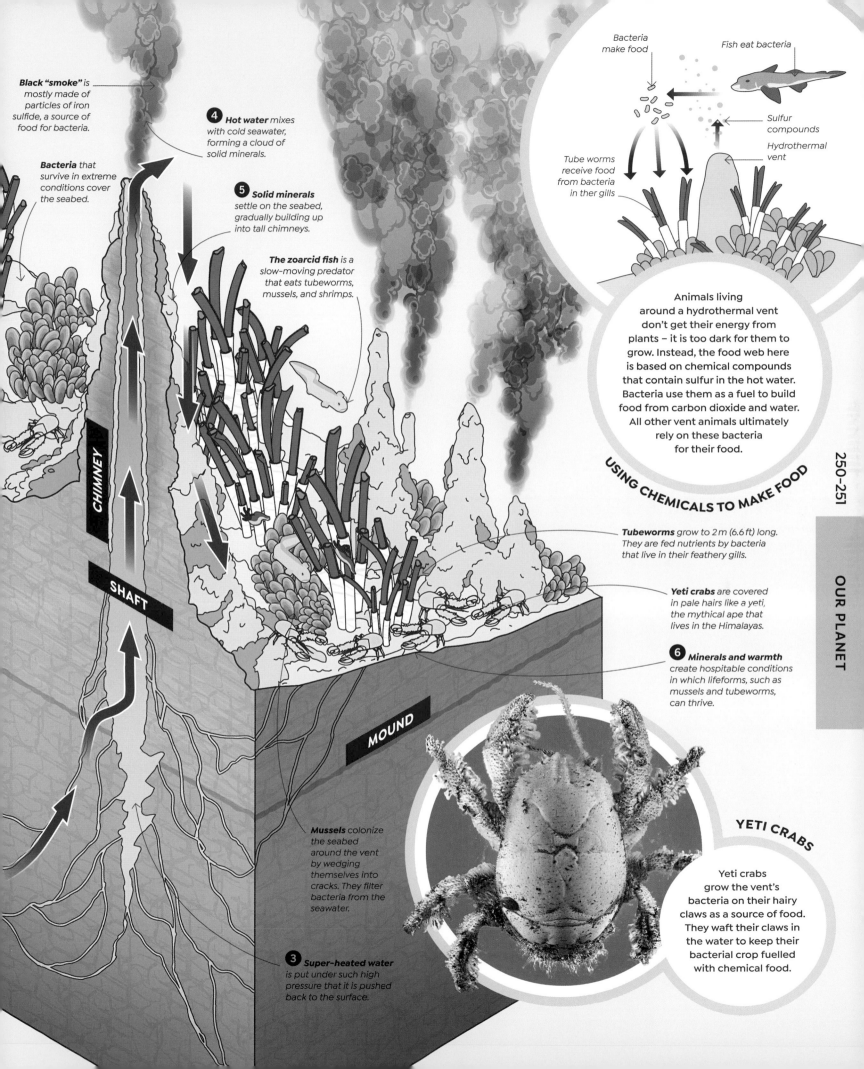

Black "smoke" is mostly made of particles of iron sulfide, a source of food for bacteria.

Bacteria that survive in extreme conditions cover the seabed.

4 **Hot water** mixes with cold seawater, forming a cloud of solid minerals.

5 **Solid minerals** settle on the seabed, gradually building up into tall chimneys.

The zoarcid fish is a slow-moving predator that eats tubeworms, mussels, and shrimps.

CHIMNEY

SHAFT

MOUND

Mussels colonize the seabed around the vent by wedging themselves into cracks. They filter bacteria from the seawater.

3 **Super-heated water** is put under such high pressure that it is pushed back to the surface.

Bacteria make food

Fish eat bacteria

Sulfur compounds

Hydrothermal vent

Tube worms receive food from bacteria in ther gills

Animals living around a hydrothermal vent don't get their energy from plants – it is too dark for them to grow. Instead, the food web here is based on chemical compounds that contain sulfur in the hot water. Bacteria use them as a fuel to build food from carbon dioxide and water. All other vent animals ultimately rely on these bacteria for their food.

USING CHEMICALS TO MAKE FOOD

Tubeworms grow to 2 m (6.6 ft) long. They are fed nutrients by bacteria that live in their feathery gills.

Yeti crabs are covered in pale hairs like a yeti, the mythical ape that lives in the Himalayas.

6 **Minerals and warmth** create hospitable conditions in which lifeforms, such as mussels and tubeworms, can thrive.

YETI CRABS

Yeti crabs grow the vent's bacteria on their hairy claws as a source of food. They waft their claws in the water to keep their bacterial crop fuelled with chemical food.

Wetlands are coastal areas that are partly or completely underwater, so are less affected by the erosion of tides and waves. Coastal wetlands include mangrove swamps and salt- and freshwater marshes, like Mexico's wetlands. These areas have a rich variety of wildlife, from wading birds to dangerous predators such as crocodiles.

WETLAND COASTS

Dunes are made by wind piling up heaps of sand. The sheltered gap between dunes is called a slack.

Wind strength and direction has a major role in shaping a coastal landscape.

DUNES

Estuaries are where rivers meet the sea. They are rich in flora and fauna, which thrive on the mix of fresh river water and salty seawater.

Spits are long deposits of sand that are joined to the land at one end.

DEPOSITION

Rivers, waves, and tides deposit large amounts of material along the shoreline, making it an ever-changing landscape.

LONGSHORE DRIFT

BAY

Longshore drift is the process by which waves flowing back and forth at an angle to the beach move material up and along the shore.

BARRIER ISLAND

TRANSPORTATION

Waves carry sand, silt, and pebbles. Most of this sediment falls to the seabed offshore, but some stays in the water, ready to be deposited onshore.

Barrier islands are deposits of sand and silt that lie parallel to the coastline.

A coastal landslide in Alaska, US, in 1958 produced the biggest wave ever recorded, at 30.4 m (100 ft) high

TYPES OF WAVES

Waves are made by tides (caused by the gravitational pull of the Moon and Sun) and wind. Strong tidal surges, tsunamis, or high winds lead to destructive waves that damage coastlines by flooding or swamping them with debris; normal tides and lighter winds lead to constructive waves that help build, shape, and maintain coastlines.

On shallow shores, fast-moving water at the top of the wave topples over slow water at the bottom

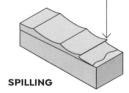

SPILLING

On steeper shores, the top of a wave rises high and then breaks in a circular motion

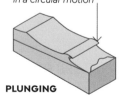

PLUNGING

On very steep shores, incoming waves are forced up very high, making them collapse in on themselves

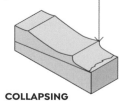

COLLAPSING

When a large body of water hits a shallow shore, it swells into a wall of surging waves, like a tsunami or a tidal bore

SURGING

Unlike coasts created by wave action, glacial coasts form when massive glaciers carve through a landscape and make their way to the sea. When the glacier melts, it leaves behind a steep-sided coastal valley, known as a fjord. Its beaches are made of the rough, rocky deposits of sediment left by the glacier as it bulldozed everything before it.

GLACIAL COASTS

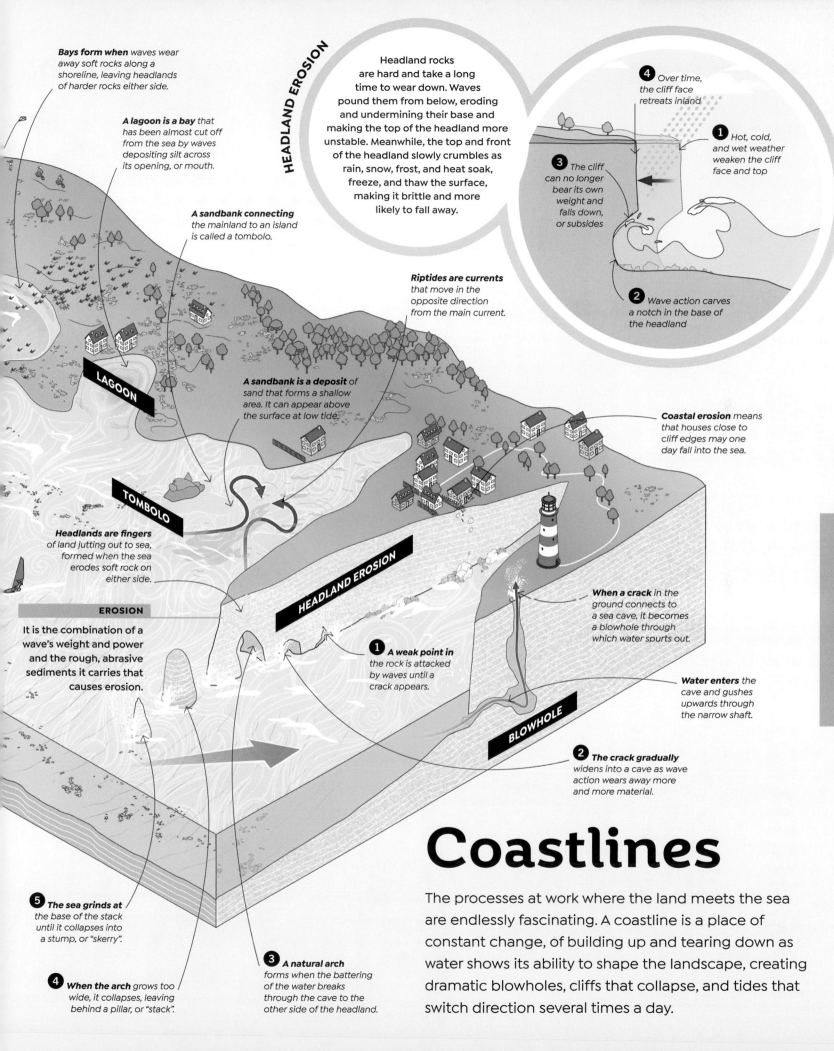

Bays form when waves wear away soft rocks along a shoreline, leaving headlands of harder rocks either side.

A lagoon is a bay that has been almost cut off from the sea by waves depositing silt across its opening, or mouth.

A sandbank connecting the mainland to an island is called a tombolo.

Headland rocks are hard and take a long time to wear down. Waves pound them from below, eroding and undermining their base and making the top of the headland more unstable. Meanwhile, the top and front of the headland slowly crumbles as rain, snow, frost, and heat soak, freeze, and thaw the surface, making it brittle and more likely to fall away.

4 Over time, the cliff face retreats inland

1 Hot, cold, and wet weather weaken the cliff face and top

3 The cliff can no longer bear its own weight and falls down, or subsides

2 Wave action carves a notch in the base of the headland

Riptides are currents that move in the opposite direction from the main current.

A sandbank is a deposit of sand that forms a shallow area. It can appear above the surface at low tide.

Coastal erosion means that houses close to cliff edges may one day fall into the sea.

LAGOON

TOMBOLO

Headlands are fingers of land jutting out to sea, formed when the sea erodes soft rock on either side.

HEADLAND EROSION

When a crack in the ground connects to a sea cave, it becomes a blowhole through which water spurts out.

EROSION

It is the combination of a wave's weight and power and the rough, abrasive sediments it carries that causes erosion.

1 **A weak point in** the rock is attacked by waves until a crack appears.

Water enters the cave and gushes upwards through the narrow shaft.

BLOWHOLE

2 **The crack gradually** widens into a cave as wave action wears away more and more material.

5 **The sea grinds at** the base of the stack until it collapses into a stump, or "skerry".

4 **When the arch** grows too wide, it collapses, leaving behind a pillar, or "stack".

3 **A natural arch** forms when the battering of the water breaks through the cave to the other side of the headland.

Coastlines

The processes at work where the land meets the sea are endlessly fascinating. A coastline is a place of constant change, of building up and tearing down as water shows its ability to shape the landscape, creating dramatic blowholes, cliffs that collapse, and tides that switch direction several times a day.

The atmosphere

The atmosphere is one of the things that makes life on our planet possible. A mix of gases held in place by Earth's gravity, it acts as a shield that stops heat from the Sun cooking the planetary surface. It is also a protective bubble that conserves the gases in the air, especially oxygen, that we need to survive.

1,500 °C (2,700 °F)

2,000 °C (3,600 °F)

700 KM

Earth

Star

Light from star

Light rays are distorted as they pass through layers with differerent temperature and density

EXOSPHERE

THERMOSPHERE

TWINKLING STARS

When light from a star enters the atmosphere, its rays are bent, or refracted, by the layers of hot and cold air they pass through. The star's brightness and even colour appear to change. This twinkling effect is also called scintillation.

The International Space Station has been carrying out vital research since its launch in 1998.

INTERNATIONAL SPACE STATION

WEATHER SATELLITE

Weather satellites observe and record data on Earth's climate.

Satellites in geostationary orbits remain in one fixed point when viewed from Earth and send and receive TV and telecoms signals.

The Hubble Telescope was launched in 1990 and has photographed the Universe's most distant stars and galaxies.

SATELLITE

HUBBLE SPACE TELESCOPE

IONOSPHERE

EXOSPHERE

Most satellites orbit in this layer. It holds tiny traces of gas and atomic particles. Beyond is the vacuum of outer space. Temperatures reach 1,500 °C (2,700 °F).

AURORAS

These shimmering curtains of green, red, yellow, or white light appear above the polar regions when electrically charged particles from the Sun interact with particles of gases, such as nitrogen and oxygen, in Earth's atmosphere.

Auroras can last for just a few minutes or for many hours.

IONOSPHERE

This layer consists of the thermosphere and parts of the mesosphere and exosphere. Solar radiation electrically charges, or ionizes, the gas atoms in this layer.

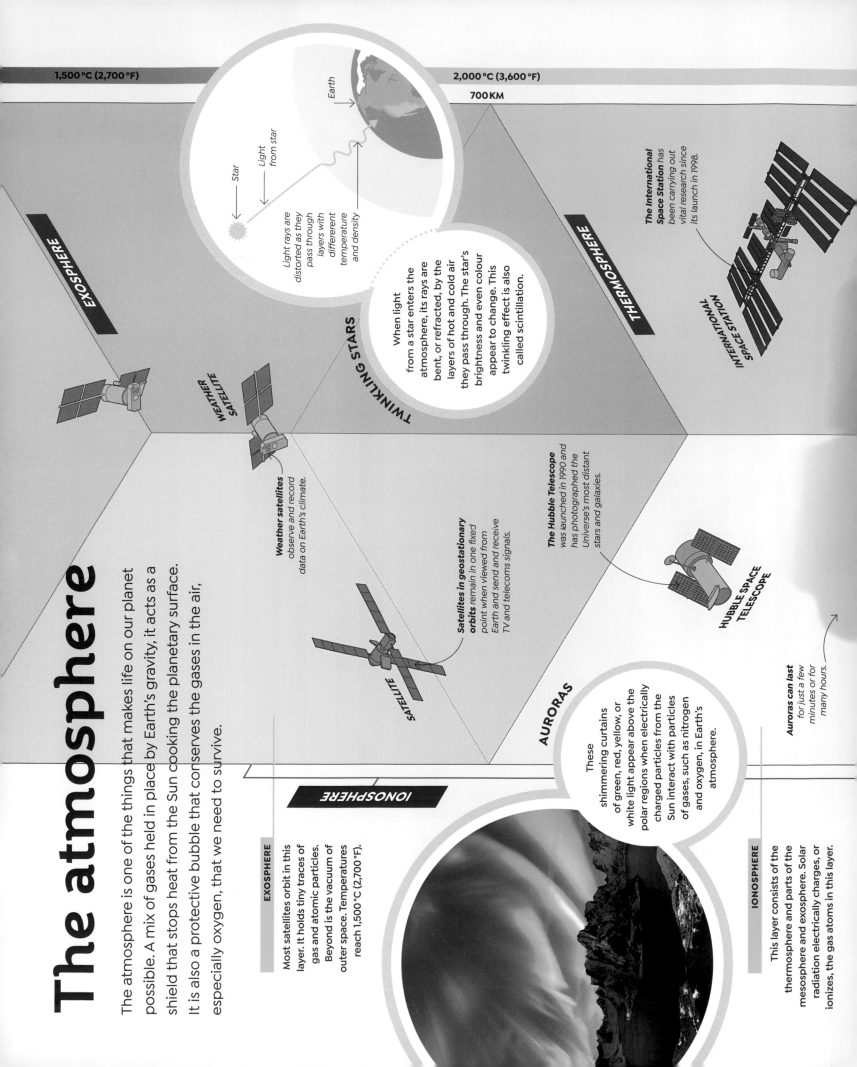

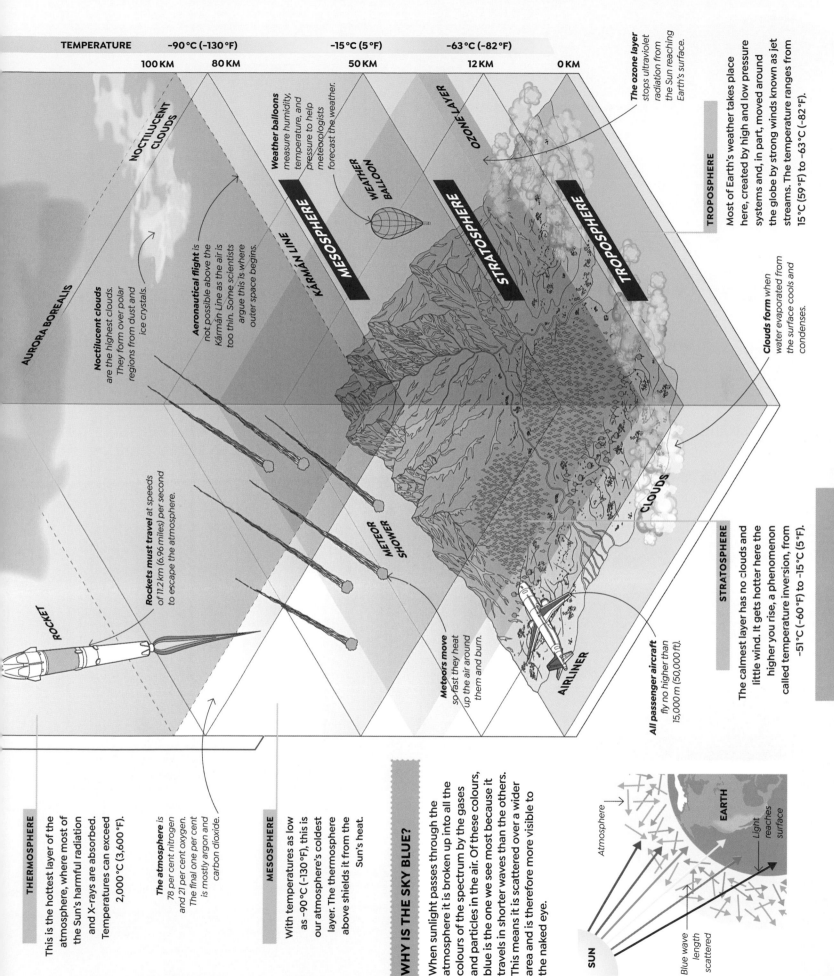

OUR PLANET

TEMPERATURE   -90°C (-130°F)   -15°C (5°F)   -63°C (-82°F)

100 KM   80 KM   50 KM   12 KM   0 KM

AURORA BOREALIS

NOCTILUCENT CLOUDS

Noctilucent clouds are the highest clouds. They form over polar regions from dust and ice crystals.

Weather balloons measure humidity, temperature, and pressure to help meteorologists forecast the weather.

Aeronautical flight is not possible above the Kármán Line as the air is too thin. Some scientists argue this is where outer space begins.

KÁRMÁN LINE

MESOSPHERE

WEATHER BALLOON

OZONE LAYER

STRATOSPHERE

TROPOSPHERE

The ozone layer stops ultraviolet radiation from the Sun reaching Earth's surface.

TROPOSPHERE

Most of Earth's weather takes place here, created by high and low pressure systems and, in part, moved around the globe by strong winds known as jet streams. The temperature ranges from 15°C (59°F) to -63°C (-82°F).

Clouds form when water evaporated from the surface cools and condenses.

ROCKET

Rockets must travel at speeds of 11.2 km (6.96 miles) per second to escape the atmosphere.

METEOR SHOWER

Meteors move so fast they heat up the air around them and burn.

AIRLINER

All passenger aircraft fly no higher than 15,000m (50,000ft).

CLOUDS

STRATOSPHERE

The calmest layer has no clouds and little wind. It gets hotter here the higher you rise, a phenomenon called temperature inversion, from -51°C (-60°F) to -15°C (5°F).

THERMOSPHERE

This is the hottest layer of the atmosphere, where most of the Sun's harmful radiation and X-rays are absorbed. Temperatures can exceed 2,000°C (3,600°F).

The atmosphere is 78 per cent nitrogen and 21 per cent oxygen. The final one per cent is mostly argon and carbon dioxide.

MESOSPHERE

With temperatures as low as -90°C (-130°F), this is our atmosphere's coldest layer. The thermosphere above shields it from the Sun's heat.

WHY IS THE SKY BLUE?

When sunlight passes through the atmosphere it is broken up into all the colours of the spectrum by the gases and particles in the air. Of these colours, blue is the one we see most because it travels in shorter waves than the others. This means it is scattered over a wider area and is therefore more visible to the naked eye.

SUN

EARTH

Atmosphere

Light reaches surface

Blue wave length scattered

VOLCANIC STEAM

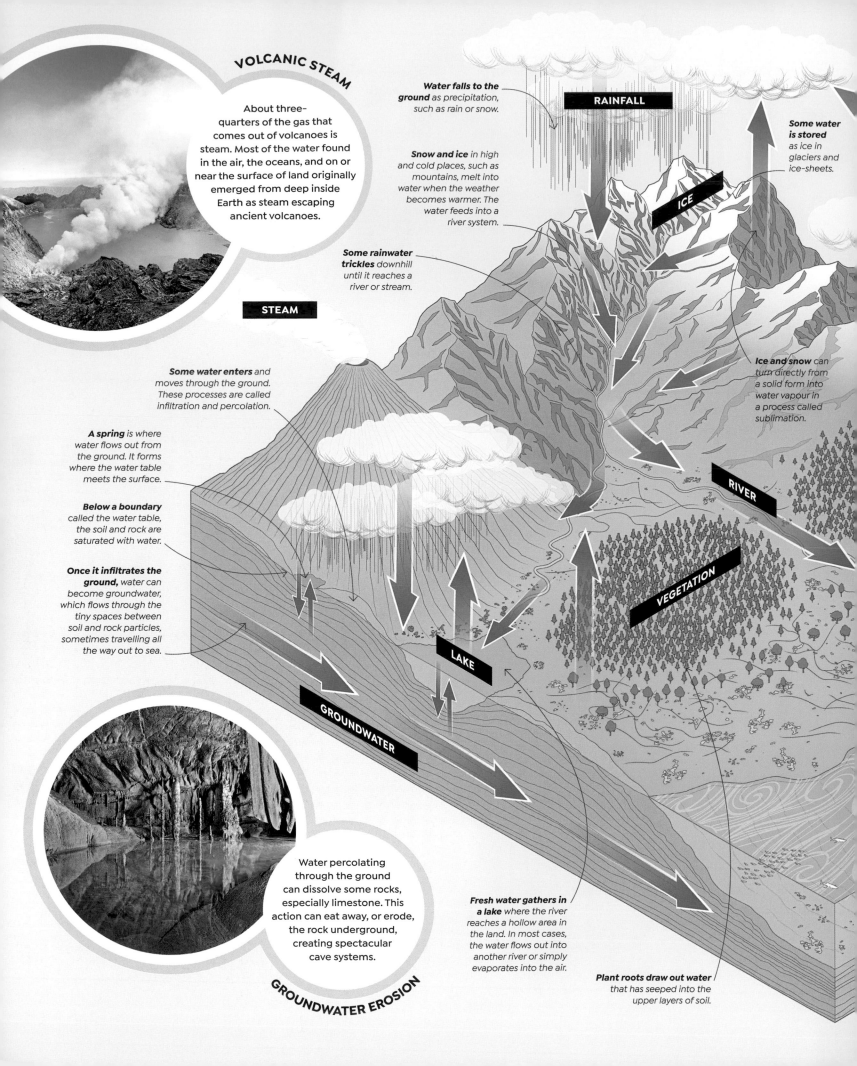

About three-quarters of the gas that comes out of volcanoes is steam. Most of the water found in the air, the oceans, and on or near the surface of land originally emerged from deep inside Earth as steam escaping ancient volcanoes.

STEAM

Water falls to the ground as precipitation, such as rain or snow.

RAINFALL

Snow and ice in high and cold places, such as mountains, melt into water when the weather becomes warmer. The water feeds into a river system.

ICE

Some water is stored as ice in glaciers and ice-sheets.

Some rainwater trickles downhill until it reaches a river or stream.

Ice and snow can turn directly from a solid form into water vapour in a process called sublimation.

Some water enters and moves through the ground. These processes are called infiltration and percolation.

A spring is where water flows out from the ground. It forms where the water table meets the surface.

RIVER

Below a boundary called the water table, the soil and rock are saturated with water.

VEGETATION

Once it infiltrates the ground, water can become groundwater, which flows through the tiny spaces between soil and rock particles, sometimes travelling all the way out to sea.

LAKE

GROUNDWATER

Water percolating through the ground can dissolve some rocks, especially limestone. This action can eat away, or erode, the rock underground, creating spectacular cave systems.

GROUNDWATER EROSION

Fresh water gathers in a lake where the river reaches a hollow area in the land. In most cases, the water flows out into another river or simply evaporates into the air.

Plant roots draw out water that has seeped into the upper layers of soil.

The water cycle

The amount of water on Earth is fixed – it is not being created or destroyed. Instead it is in constant circulation between the atmosphere, the land, and the oceans, changing from liquid to gas and solid and back again in a process called the water cycle. The whole cycle is driven by energy from sunlight.

Trees and other plants *release water vapour into the air through their leaves in a process called transpiration.*

Water vapour condenses into clouds of water droplets when the air temperature drops. The droplets form around tiny specks of dust or fungal spores floating in the air.

The Sun's heat converts liquid water on the surface of the ocean into water vapour in a process called evaporation.

Rivers carry water from highland areas to the ocean, where the cycle begins again.

OCEAN WATER

FLOODING

When rainwater or snowmelt is too great to be contained by rivers or infiltrate the ground, flooding occurs, where water breaks through riverbanks and spreads temporarily over the land.

97 per cent of Earth's water is contained in the oceans

Most of the world's water is liquid that fills deep ocean basins between the continents.

68 per cent of fresh water on Earth is stored in ice caps and glaciers

ARTESIAN WELLS

Groundwater can be tapped by an artesian well using natural high pressure. The pressure is created when groundwater from highlands flows down into lowlands through porous rock layers, and becomes trapped between layers of impermeable rock (rock that doesn't allow water to pass through). Drilling an artesian well into this high-pressure water forces it to the surface.

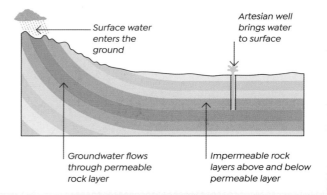

Surface water enters the ground

Artesian well brings water to surface

Groundwater flows through permeable rock layer

Impermeable rock layers above and below permeable layer

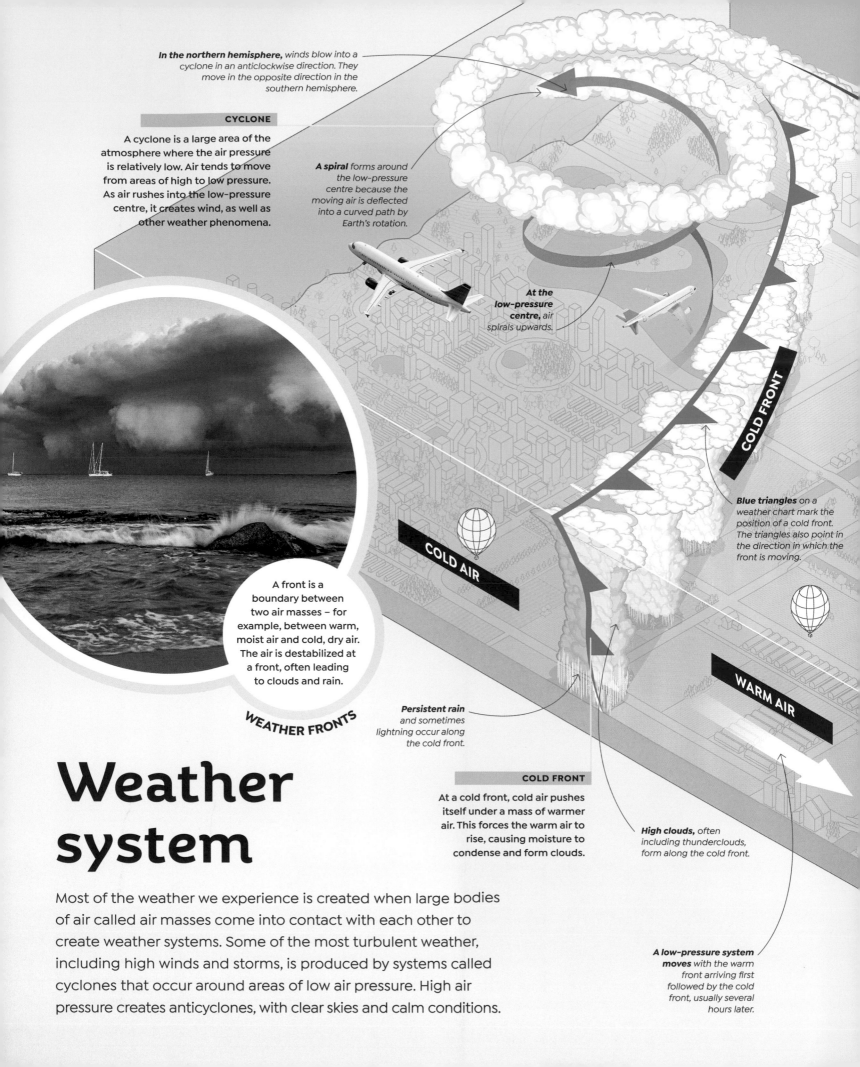

In the northern hemisphere, *winds blow into a cyclone in an anticlockwise direction. They move in the opposite direction in the southern hemisphere.*

CYCLONE

A cyclone is a large area of the atmosphere where the air pressure is relatively low. Air tends to move from areas of high to low pressure. As air rushes into the low-pressure centre, it creates wind, as well as other weather phenomena.

A spiral *forms around the low-pressure centre because the moving air is deflected into a curved path by Earth's rotation.*

At the low-pressure centre, *air spirals upwards.*

COLD FRONT

Blue triangles *on a weather chart mark the position of a cold front. The triangles also point in the direction in which the front is moving.*

A front is a boundary between two air masses – for example, between warm, moist air and cold, dry air. The air is destabilized at a front, often leading to clouds and rain.

COLD AIR

WEATHER FRONTS

WARM AIR

Persistent rain *and sometimes lightning occur along the cold front.*

COLD FRONT

At a cold front, cold air pushes itself under a mass of warmer air. This forces the warm air to rise, causing moisture to condense and form clouds.

High clouds, *often including thunderclouds, form along the cold front.*

Weather system

Most of the weather we experience is created when large bodies of air called air masses come into contact with each other to create weather systems. Some of the most turbulent weather, including high winds and storms, is produced by systems called cyclones that occur around areas of low air pressure. High air pressure creates anticyclones, with clear skies and calm conditions.

A low-pressure system moves *with the warm front arriving first followed by the cold front, usually several hours later.*

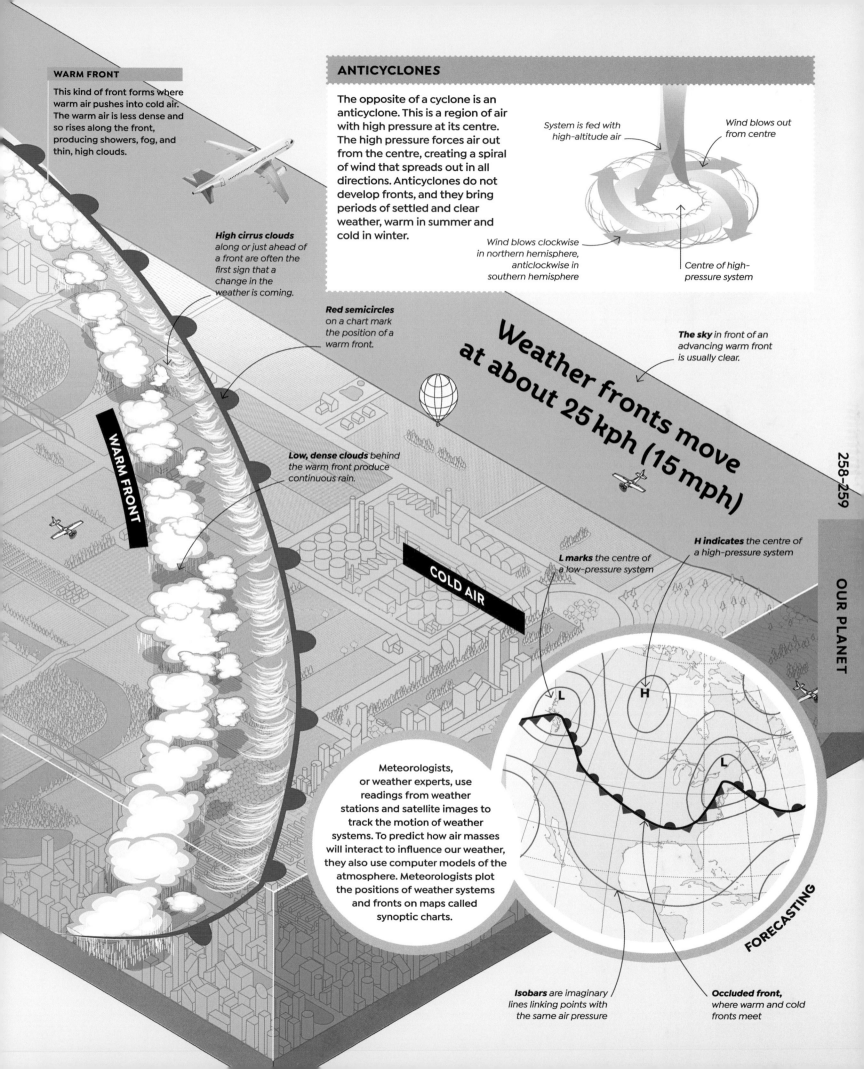

WARM FRONT

This kind of front forms where warm air pushes into cold air. The warm air is less dense and so rises along the front, producing showers, fog, and thin, high clouds.

ANTICYCLONES

The opposite of a cyclone is an anticyclone. This is a region of air with high pressure at its centre. The high pressure forces air out from the centre, creating a spiral of wind that spreads out in all directions. Anticyclones do not develop fronts, and they bring periods of settled and clear weather, warm in summer and cold in winter.

System is fed with high-altitude air

Wind blows out from centre

Wind blows clockwise in northern hemisphere, anticlockwise in southern hemisphere

Centre of high-pressure system

High cirrus clouds along or just ahead of a front are often the first sign that a change in the weather is coming.

Red semicircles on a chart mark the position of a warm front.

WARM FRONT

Low, dense clouds behind the warm front produce continuous rain.

COLD AIR

Weather fronts move at about 25 kph (15 mph)

The sky in front of an advancing warm front is usually clear.

L marks the centre of a low-pressure system

H indicates the centre of a high-pressure system

Meteorologists, or weather experts, use readings from weather stations and satellite images to track the motion of weather systems. To predict how air masses will interact to influence our weather, they also use computer models of the atmosphere. Meteorologists plot the positions of weather systems and fronts on maps called synoptic charts.

FORECASTING

Isobars are imaginary lines linking points with the same air pressure

Occluded front, where warm and cold fronts meet

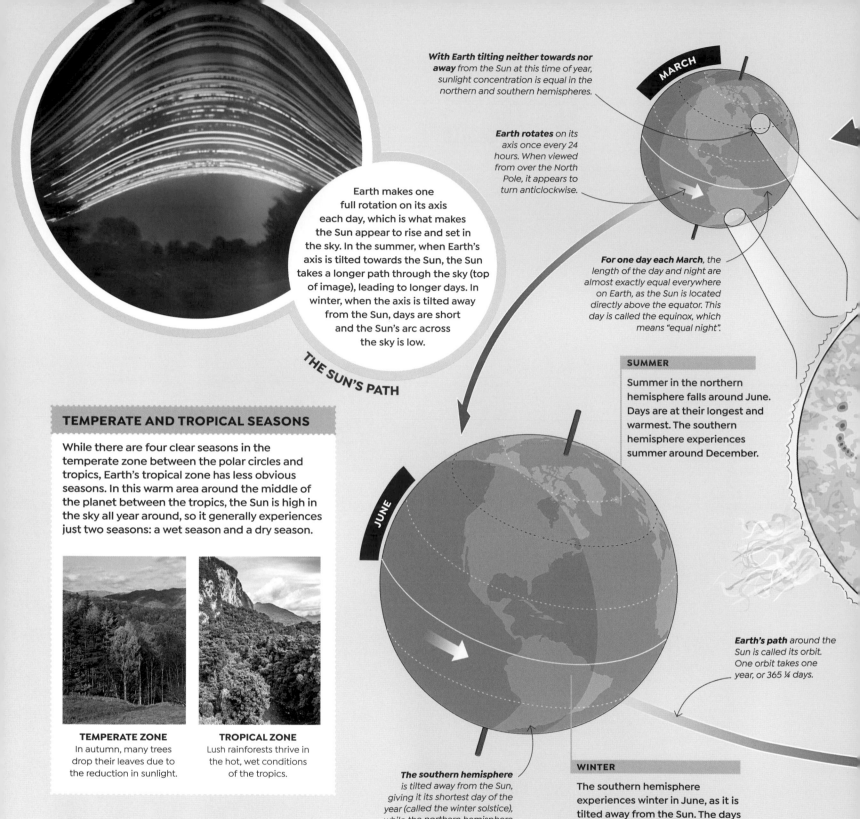

With **Earth tilting neither towards nor away** from the Sun at this time of year, sunlight concentration is equal in the northern and southern hemispheres.

MARCH

Earth rotates on its axis once every 24 hours. When viewed from over the North Pole, it appears to turn anticlockwise.

Earth makes one full rotation on its axis each day, which is what makes the Sun appear to rise and set in the sky. In the summer, when Earth's axis is tilted towards the Sun, the Sun takes a longer path through the sky (top of image), leading to longer days. In winter, when the axis is tilted away from the Sun, days are short and the Sun's arc across the sky is low.

For one day each March, the length of the day and night are almost exactly equal everywhere on Earth, as the Sun is located directly above the equator. This day is called the equinox, which means "equal night".

THE SUN'S PATH

SUMMER

Summer in the northern hemisphere falls around June. Days are at their longest and warmest. The southern hemisphere experiences summer around December.

TEMPERATE AND TROPICAL SEASONS

While there are four clear seasons in the temperate zone between the polar circles and tropics, Earth's tropical zone has less obvious seasons. In this warm area around the middle of the planet between the tropics, the Sun is high in the sky all year around, so it generally experiences just two seasons: a wet season and a dry season.

JUNE

TEMPERATE ZONE
In autumn, many trees drop their leaves due to the reduction in sunlight.

TROPICAL ZONE
Lush rainforests thrive in the hot, wet conditions of the tropics.

Earth's path around the Sun is called its orbit. One orbit takes one year, or 365 ¼ days.

The southern hemisphere is tilted away from the Sun, giving it its shortest day of the year (called the winter solstice), while the northern hemisphere experiences its longest day (the summer solstice).

WINTER

The southern hemisphere experiences winter in June, as it is tilted away from the Sun. The days are at their shortest and coolest. Winter for the northern hemisphere occurs around December.

Seasons

Over a year, the weather conditions on Earth's surface go through a cycle of changes called the seasons. These are caused by a tilt on Earth's spin axis. As Earth orbits the Sun over a year, different parts of its surface lean towards and away from the Sun. This means that a particular place on Earth is heated more intensely at some times of year than others.

If Earth's axis was not tilted, the planet would experience no seasonal changes

The tilt of Earth's axis varies between 22.1° and 24.5° every 41,000 years

When a hemisphere is tilted away from the Sun sunlight is less direct, so it is spread over a wider area when it meets Earth. This means the sunlight is less bright and strong.

At this time of year, the North Pole is in total darkness for 24 hours a day, as it tilts away from the Sun.

In December, the Sun is located as far south of the equator as possible, directly over the Tropic of Capricorn. The North Pole tilts away from the Sun, leading to the shortest day in the north and the longest day in the south.

DECEMBER

SUNLIGHT

For at least one day each year, the Sun does not set or rise north of this line, called the Arctic Circle. The equivalent line in the southern hemisphere is the Antarctic Circle.

Sunlight is always intense at the equator, where the Sun's rays are direct and concentrated over a small area.

South of the equator, the seasons are opposite to the seasons in the north.

SUN

The Tropic of Cancer marks the northernmost point at which the Sun can be directly overhead. The equivalent line in the southern hemisphere is called the Tropic of Capricorn.

ARCTIC CIRCLE

TROPIC OF CANCER

EQUATOR

TROPIC OF CAPRICORN

SEPTEMBER

AUTUMN

The northern hemisphere experiences autumn around September, meaning days are growing cooler and shorter. Autumn for the southern hemisphere is around March.

MIDNIGHT SUN

The impact of Earth's tilt is greatest near the poles, where summer days are so long that for at least one day during the season the Sun does not set. On the longest day of the year, you can watch as the Sun approaches the horizon towards midnight, before rising again without ever setting.

The equator is a line around Earth midway between the North and South poles. Seasonal changes are less obvious here.

SPRING

In September, the southern hemisphere is in spring, meaning days are becoming warmer and longer. Spring for the northern hemisphere is around March.

Earth rotates around an imaginary line called an axis. Earth's axis is tilted from the vertical by 23.5°.

For one day of September each year, day and night are of almost equal length everywhere, as the Sun is positioned directly over the equator and Earth's axis is tilted neither towards nor away from the Sun.

The greenhouse effect is impacted by how much light natural surfaces reflect, or their albedo. Ice reflects a lot of energy, helping to cool the planet.

ALBEDO

NATURAL GREENHOUSE EFFECT

The greenhouse effect is crucial to life on Earth. Its warming effect ensures that liquid water covers much of the surface. Without it, Earth would be an ice planet.

SUN

Some of the heat given out from Earth's surface is radiated back into space. This balances with the light energy coming in to keep the planet at a constant temperature.

Without the natural greenhouse effect, Earth's average temperature would be −20 °C (−4 °F)

Clouds block light from reaching the surface and so have a cooling effect.

GREENHOUSE GASES

Some of the sunlight scatters straight off Earth's atmosphere and back out to space.

Some of the heat that radiates from the surface is absorbed by the greenhouse gases, such as carbon dioxide, water vapour, and methane. This makes the atmosphere warmer.

Clouds reflect heat rising up from the ground, trapping warm air low down.

NATURAL

Land absorbs most of the energy carried in the sunlight that hits it. This energy makes the land warm up.

OCEAN

ICE

LAND

Water absorbs less of the energy in sunlight than land, and reflects more of it straight back again.

FOREST

Heat radiates from Earth's surface as invisible infrared radiation. It is then absorbed by greenhouse gases and re-radiated towards Earth.

Ice reflects nearly all of the sunlight that shines on it. This is why it looks white, and why ice only melts slowly, even in full sunlight.

When volcanic ash spreads through the air, it can reduce the brightness of sunlight reaching Earth. This process is called global dimming.

GLOBAL DIMMING

Forests and other plants naturally absorb carbon dioxide out of the air. This is crucial in controlling the amount of greenhouse gas in the air.

Greenhouse effect

A greenhouse is a structure that allows sunlight to shine in but stops the heat inside from escaping. Some gases in Earth's atmosphere have the same effect, trapping heat and making the planet warmer than it would be otherwise. These gases are known as greenhouse gases. Human activity is disrupting the natural greenhouse effect and causing the planet to warm up dangerously.

All of the energy that warms Earth comes from the sunlight and heat radiating from the Sun.

As well as light and heat, solar radiation contains ultraviolet light. Most of this is blocked from reaching the surface by the atmosphere.

SOLAR RADIATION

Extra greenhouse gases absorb more heat and reduce the amount that escapes into space.

GREENHOUSE GASES

HUMAN IMPACT

Humans are adding greenhouse gases to the air in unnatural amounts. This increases the warming of the greenhouse effect and is changing the climate of the entire planet.

With more greenhouse gases in the air, the whole planet is gradually warming.

HUMAN IMPACT

The two main greenhouse gases in the atmosphere are carbon dioxide and methane.

Burning fuel for heating, transport, and generating electricity releases extra carbon dioxide into the air.

CITY

FARMING

WETLANDS

Deforestation reduces the amount of carbon dioxide that plants can take out of the air. This increases the amount of greenhouse gases in the air even more.

A city forms a heat island because heat escapes from buildings. Materials such as concrete also absorb and then release more heat than natural surfaces.

Livestock from farming release large amounts of greenhouse gases.

Wetlands are stores of carbon dioxide and methane. Destroying them adds to climate change.

Ice melts as the planet warms up. With less ice cover, more of the energy in sunlight is absorbed by Earth's surface.

Crude oil is a fossil fuel, along with coal and natural gas. It contains carbon that became trapped underground millions of years ago. Burning these fuels releases that trapped carbon as a greenhouse gas.

ICE

In the last 250 years, the amount of carbon dioxide in the atmosphere has risen by 50 per cent

Our home planet is dwarfed by the rest of the Universe. Spacecraft and satellites allow us to look back at Earth and explore the rest of the Solar System, as well as to see far out into space beyond the limits of our own galaxy.

Space

Astronomers have found evidence of a cloud of icy, rocky objects left over from the formation of the Solar System 4.6 billion years ago. The Oort Cloud, as it is named, is at the very edge of the Solar System – between 2,000 and 200,000 times further from the Sun than Earth. When Oort Cloud objects are disturbed by collisions, they fall in towards the Sun, becoming comets.

The outer edge of the Oort Cloud is halfway to the nearest star

Objects in the Oort Cloud orbit the Sun at all angles

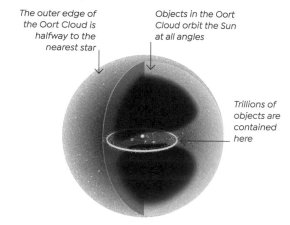

Trillions of objects are contained here

Pluto, a dwarf planet, is nestled inside the Kuiper Belt – a disc of accumulated matter such as dust and gas.

The Solar System formed 4.6 billion years ago – 8 billion years after the Milky Way

Comets are small objects made of rock and ice.

COMET

GIANT PLANETS

Neptune is the planet most distant from the Sun and has a blue atmosphere due to the presence of methane gas.

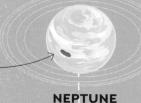

NEPTUNE

Solar System

The Solar System is dominated by our nearest star, the Sun, which is so massive that its gravity keeps millions of objects in orbit around it. These objects include four small, rocky planets, with thin, gaseous atmospheres, and four giant gas planets, with liquid or solid cores. Also in orbit around the Sun are millions of smaller objects, such as asteroids, comets, and dwarf planets. All these objects, with the Sun at the centre, make up the Solar System.

SATURN

Like all giant planets, Saturn has a system of rings made of rock and ice.

Uranus has a unique tilt – its axis of rotation tilts at nearly 90 degrees to its orbit (Earth's tilt is 23.5 degrees).

URANUS

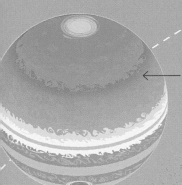

A gas giant, Jupiter is the largest planet of all: more than three hundred times the mass of Earth.

JUPITER

Our home planet, Earth, is the only place in the Universe known to harbour life and is mostly covered with liquid water.

The Sun is a hot, glowing ball of gas with a surface temperature of around 5,500°C (9,900°F).

THE SUN

EARTH

The Asteroid Belt contains more than 1 million small, mostly irregularly shaped rocky objects called asteroids.

Orbits are created by the Sun's gravity pulling planets towards itself in a curved path.

Mercury is the smallest planet in the Solar System and takes just 88 days to revolve once around the Sun.

MERCURY

ROCKY PLANETS

MARS

Mars is the outermost rocky planet in our Solar System.

VENUS

Venus is about the same size as Earth and has an atmosphere filled with droplets of sulphuric acid.

The Sun is so massive that it contains 99.8 per cent of the Solar System's mass

THE ICE LINE

Within a certain distance from the Sun, called the ice line (or frost line), an orbiting planet receives enough heat to maintain liquid water on its surface. Generally, rocky planets are within the ice line, but gas and ice giants are not.

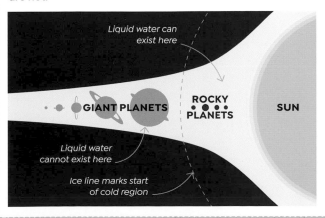

Liquid water can exist here

GIANT PLANETS

ROCKY PLANETS

SUN

Liquid water cannot exist here

Ice line marks start of cold region

PLANETARY MOONS

Just as planets orbit the Sun, so most planets in our Solar System have moons in orbit around them. Earth has one, called the Moon, but Jupiter and Saturn have more than 60 moons each.

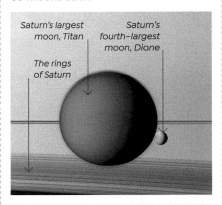

Saturn's largest moon, Titan

Saturn's fourth-largest moon, Dione

The rings of Saturn

The orbits of planets in the Solar System are spaced further apart as the distance from the Sun increases.

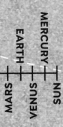

NEPTUNE

URANUS

SATURN

JUPITER

MARS

VENUS

MERCURY

EARTH

SUN

The Sun

The Sun sits at the centre of the Solar System, with all the planets, moons, comets, and other objects in orbit around it. It is a star: a huge ball of gas that glows brightly because it is very hot. The temperature at the visible surface, or photosphere, is 5,500°C (9,900°F). Nuclear reactions at the centre, or core, release huge amounts of energy, keeping the core at 15 million°C (27 million°F).

The corona varies in size and shape and is not usually visible to the naked eye.

In the convective zone, hotter gas rises through cooler gas, then cools and falls back again.

In the radiative zone, energy travels as electromagnetic radiation.

CONVECTIVE ZONE

Circular currents of gases radiate energy to the top of the convective zone, then cool and sink towards the radiative zone.

The core is dense enough and hot enough for nuclear fusion to take place.

CORE

CONVECTIVE ZONE

RADIATIVE ZONE

THE CORE

The process of fusion inside the core converts hydrogen to helium, releasing heat and light.

NUCLEAR FUSION IN THE SUN

At the extreme temperatures and pressures in the Sun's core, the nuclei (central parts) of hydrogen atoms join together, or fuse, forming nuclei of helium atoms. This nuclear fusion reaction releases energy, and it is this energy that keeps the Sun hot. There is enough hydrogen left to power the Sun for another five billion years.

Hydrogen atom with one neutron

Helium atom produced

Hydrogen atom with two neutrons

Hydrogen atoms fuse

An extra neutron is emitted

Massive amount of energy emitted

RADIATIVE ZONE

Energy generated in the core travels slowly through the extremely dense radiative zone, diffusing outwards as it goes.

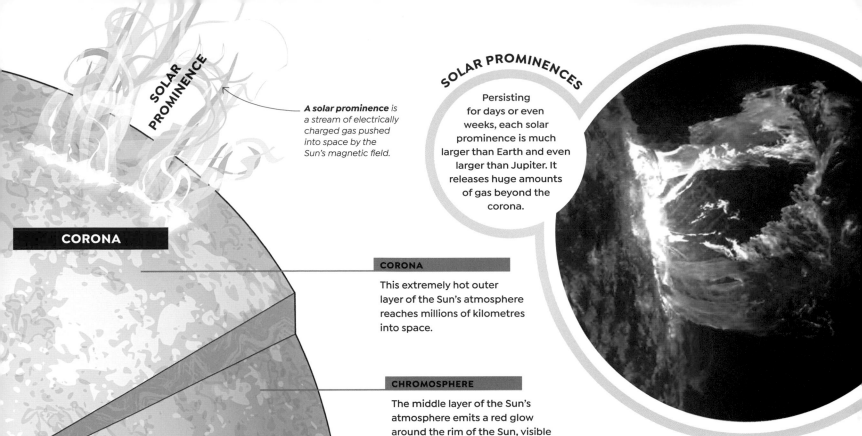

SOLAR PROMINENCE

A solar prominence is a stream of electrically charged gas pushed into space by the Sun's magnetic field.

SOLAR PROMINENCES

Persisting for days or even weeks, each solar prominence is much larger than Earth and even larger than Jupiter. It releases huge amounts of gas beyond the corona.

CORONA

CORONA

This extremely hot outer layer of the Sun's atmosphere reaches millions of kilometres into space.

CHROMOSPHERE

CHROMOSPHERE

The middle layer of the Sun's atmosphere emits a red glow around the rim of the Sun, visible only during a Solar eclipse.

About 1 million Earths could fit inside the Sun

Other elements include small amounts of oxygen, carbon, iron, and neon.

HELIUM

HYDROGEN

COMPOSITION OF THE SUN

The Sun is made almost entirely of the chemical elements hydrogen and helium. All the other elements together make up less than 2 per cent of its mass.

PHOTOSPHERE

Sunspots are slightly cooler areas on the photosphere, which typically persist for a few weeks.

PHOTOSPHERE

The lowest layer of the Sun's atmosphere is the innermost layer we can see. It emits most of the light that reaches Earth.

SOLAR ECLIPSES

Normally, the full Moon is slightly above or below the Sun as seen from Earth, but sometimes it lines up exactly so that it blocks the Sun's light. This is a solar eclipse.

During a solar eclipse, the Moon casts a shadow on Earth. In parts of the world where the Moon fully blocks the Sun, the eclipse is "total", and it goes dark in the day.

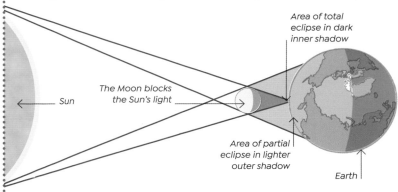

Area of total eclipse in dark inner shadow

Sun

The Moon blocks the Sun's light

Area of partial eclipse in lighter outer shadow

Earth

The planets

There are eight planets in the Solar System, including our own planet, Earth. The four nearest the Sun are small, rocky planets. The other four are giant planets, with solid or liquid cores surrounded by deep, dense atmospheres. Rocky planets have few moons, or none at all, while each giant planet has many moons.

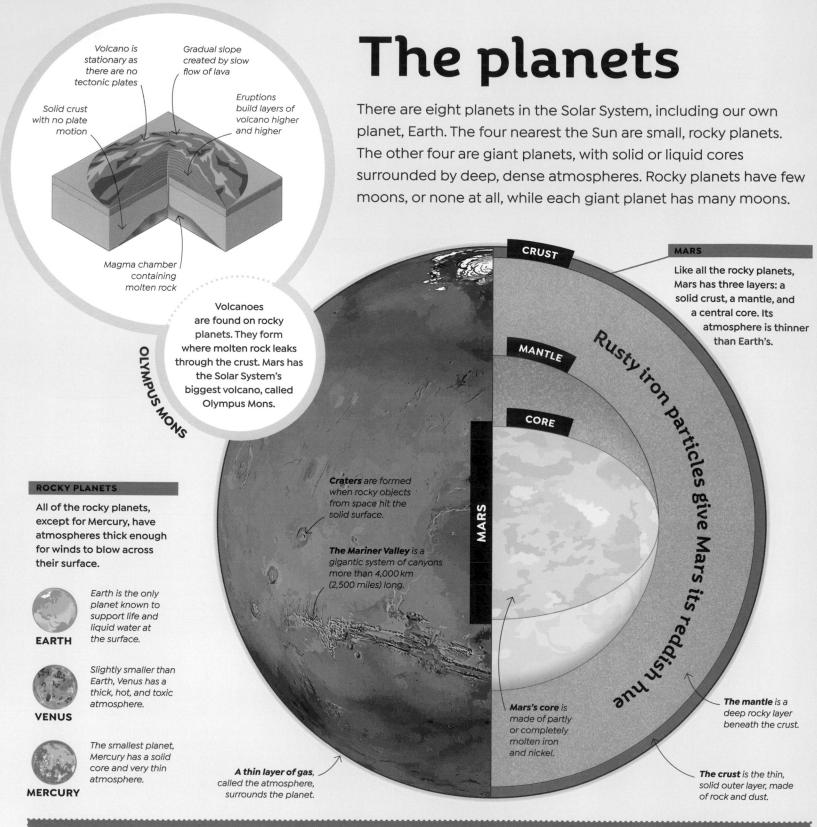

Volcano is stationary as there are no tectonic plates

Gradual slope created by slow flow of lava

Solid crust with no plate motion

Eruptions build layers of volcano higher and higher

Magma chamber containing molten rock

OLYMPUS MONS

Volcanoes are found on rocky planets. They form where molten rock leaks through the crust. Mars has the Solar System's biggest volcano, called Olympus Mons.

ROCKY PLANETS

All of the rocky planets, except for Mercury, have atmospheres thick enough for winds to blow across their surface.

EARTH
Earth is the only planet known to support life and liquid water at the surface.

VENUS
Slightly smaller than Earth, Venus has a thick, hot, and toxic atmosphere.

MERCURY
The smallest planet, Mercury has a solid core and very thin atmosphere.

CRUST

MANTLE

CORE

MARS

Craters are formed when rocky objects from space hit the solid surface.

The Mariner Valley is a gigantic system of canyons more than 4,000 km (2,500 miles) long.

A thin layer of gas, called the atmosphere, surrounds the planet.

MARS

Like all the rocky planets, Mars has three layers: a solid crust, a mantle, and a central core. Its atmosphere is thinner than Earth's.

Rusty iron particles give Mars its reddish hue

Mars's core is made of partly or completely molten iron and nickel.

The mantle is a deep rocky layer beneath the crust.

The crust is the thin, solid outer layer, made of rock and dust.

THEIA IMPACT

The Moon is Earth's only moon; Mars has two moons, while Mercury and Venus have none. The Moon probably formed from debris thrown up after a large rocky object, which scientists have named Theia, crashed into our planet soon after the Solar System formed, about 4.5 billion years ago.

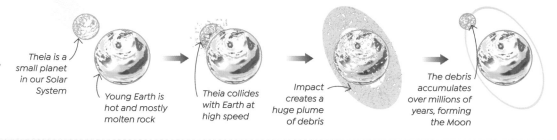

Theia is a small planet in our Solar System

Young Earth is hot and mostly molten rock

Theia collides with Earth at high speed

Impact creates a huge plume of debris

The debris accumulates over millions of years, forming the Moon

GIANT PLANETS

All giant planets have rings made of chunks of ice and rock. Saturn and Jupiter are gas giants. Uranus and Neptune are ice giants.

The atmosphere of Uranus is mostly water ice, ammonia, and methane.

URANUS

Neptune has a methane-rich atmosphere, giving it a blue colour.

NEPTUNE

The second largest planet after Jupiter, Saturn has the most spectacular set of rings.

SATURN

CYCLONES ON JUPITER

NASA's Juno probe, currently orbiting Jupiter's poles, has captured incredible pictures of gigantic cyclones spinning at the planet's south pole. The cyclones are a massive 1,000 km (600 miles) in diameter and cluster together. They are produced by hot gases expanding and rising through Jupiter's atmosphere.

Auroras form at the poles, caused by the planet's strong magnetic field.

ATMOSPHERE

OUTER MANTLE

INNER MANTLE

CORE

JUPITER

The upper atmosphere is 5,000 km (3,000 miles) thick.

Hydrogen gas makes up 90 per cent of the upper atmosphere by volume.

Inner core of dense, solid rock.

JUPITER

Jupiter is mostly gas and liquid. Like the other giant planets, its atmosphere becomes more dense towards the centre.

Great Red Spot is an enormous storm system.

Winds blow in different directions above and below the bands

Bands of white and brown clouds form in the upper atmosphere

Warmed white clouds rise through the cooler brown clouds

JUPITER'S CLOUDS

Just like clouds on Earth, Jupiter's clouds are made of countless tiny droplets and ice crystals. But they are not made of water. The brown clouds are mists of droplets that are made of compounds of sulphur; the white clouds are made of crystals of frozen ammonia. Warmed from below, the white clouds rise up, forming bands above the brown clouds below.

Hydrogen is in liquid form at the high pressures beneath the upper atmosphere.

Metallic hydrogen, a form of hydrogen that conducts electricity, forms at very high pressure.

Jupiter has the shortest day in the Solar System at only nine hours and 56 minutes long

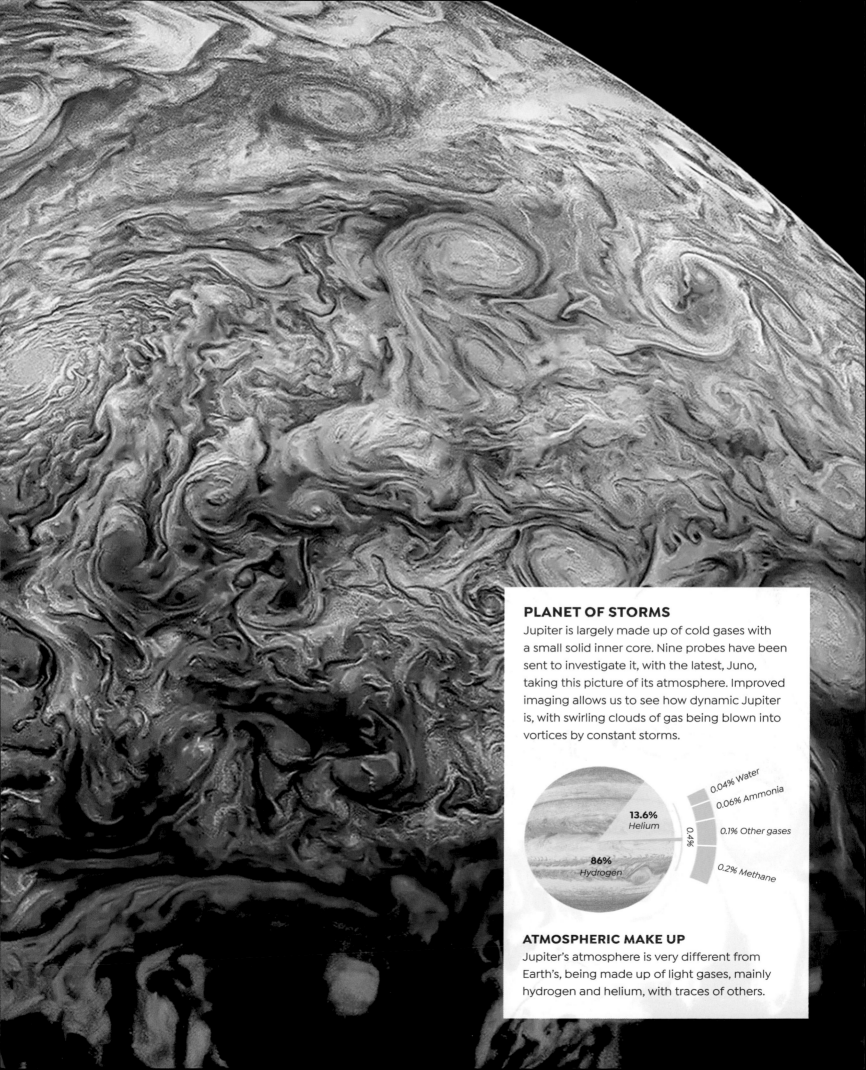

PLANET OF STORMS

Jupiter is largely made up of cold gases with a small solid inner core. Nine probes have been sent to investigate it, with the latest, Juno, taking this picture of its atmosphere. Improved imaging allows us to see how dynamic Jupiter is, with swirling clouds of gas being blown into vortices by constant storms.

13.6% *Helium*

0.4%

86% *Hydrogen*

0.04% Water

0.06% Ammonia

0.1% Other gases

0.2% Methane

ATMOSPHERIC MAKE UP

Jupiter's atmosphere is very different from Earth's, being made up of light gases, mainly hydrogen and helium, with traces of others.

A meteoroid is any object in space from the size of a speck of dust all the way up to a small asteroid.

METEOR

If a meteoroid burns up as it enters Earth's atmosphere it is called a meteor. Meteors emit a streak of bright light.

The bright atmosphere around the nucleus is called the coma.

Rock and ice form the centre of a comet. As it approaches the Sun, the ice melts and evaporates, releasing vapour and dust.

A meteorite is a meteoroid that has survived the journey through the atmosphere and impacts the ground.

Any extremely bright meteor is called a bolide. A bolide is formed by a large meteoroid that would form a crater if it reached the surface.

66 million years ago, a massive asteroid struck Earth, leading to a mass extinction

Occasionally, large meteorites hit Earth, leaving craters in the ground, just like the craters on the Moon. This was more common in the early history of the Solar System.

METEORITE CRATER

DUST TAIL

Asteroids, comets, and meteors

It is not only planets and their moons that orbit the Sun – there are also chunks of material left over from the formation of the Solar System. Large and small rocks are called asteroids and meteoroids; icy, dusty rocks that grow tails when they near the Sun are called comets. Some meteoroids hit Earth, burning up in the atmosphere as streaks of light called meteors, or shooting stars.

COMET TAILS

A comet produces two tails when it is near the Sun. One is made of dust and one from ionized (electrically charged) water vapour and other gases.

SHOOTING STARS

When meteoroids enter the atmosphere, they heat up and give off a bright glow for a few seconds – a meteor, or shooting star. Most meteors are caused by debris left behind by comets' dust tails. Earth passes through some comets' debris trails each year at the same time, leading to visible and predictable "meteor showers".

ASTEROID

Asteroids are minor planets (large space rocks) in the inner Solar System. Most are found in a belt between the orbits of Mars and Jupiter.

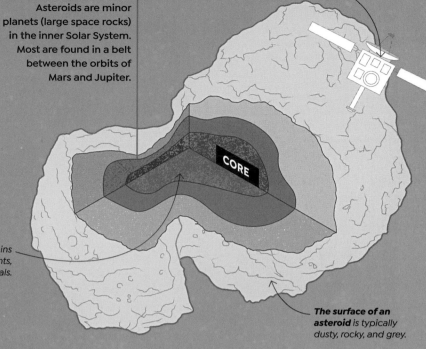

In 2005, the Hayabusa probe landed on an asteroid, called Itokawa and collected samples from its surface.

CORE

The core contains heavier elements, such as metals.

The surface of an asteroid is typically dusty, rocky, and grey.

Halley's comet can be seen every 75 years

A shockwave, called bow shock, is created by a stream of charged particles – the solar wind – pushing away the ionized vapour and gases.

The plasma tail forms when fast-moving particles emitted from the Sun interact with ionized particles from the comet's coma.

PLASMA TAIL

The plasma tail is straight and points directly away from the Sun.

A curved dust tail forms from solid particles released as the comet warms.

COMET ORBITS

Comets orbit the Sun in very elliptical orbits. Most spend hundreds of years in the outer Solar System before coming close enough to the Sun for tails to form.

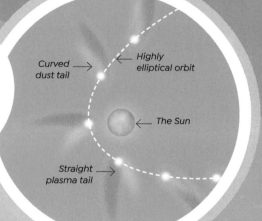

Curved dust tail

Highly elliptical orbit

The Sun

Straight plasma tail

NASA'S DART

In the extremely unlikely event that an asteroid crashed into Earth, it could wipe out our civilization, so astronomers track large objects that come anywhere near Earth. If they spot one that might hit, space engineers could send a spacecraft to nudge the asteroid into a different orbit so that it would miss our planet. In 2022, as part of the Double Asteroid Redirection Test mission (DART), NASA successfully crashed a spacecraft into an asteroid, Dimorphos, as a test of this new technology.

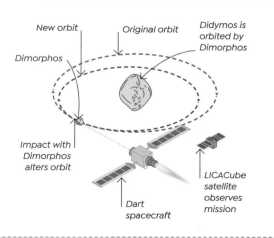

New orbit

Original orbit

Didymos is orbited by Dimorphos

Dimorphos

Impact with Dimorphos alters orbit

Dart spacecraft

LICACube satellite observes mission

Stars

A star is a huge ball of plasma (electrically charged gas) that is so hot it glows brightly. It is kept hot by nuclear reactions at its core. Our Sun is a star, and a few thousand other stars are visible at night, but there are billions more stars in our galaxy. A star's size determines how much light it emits, how long it glows, and what happens to it when it stops shining.

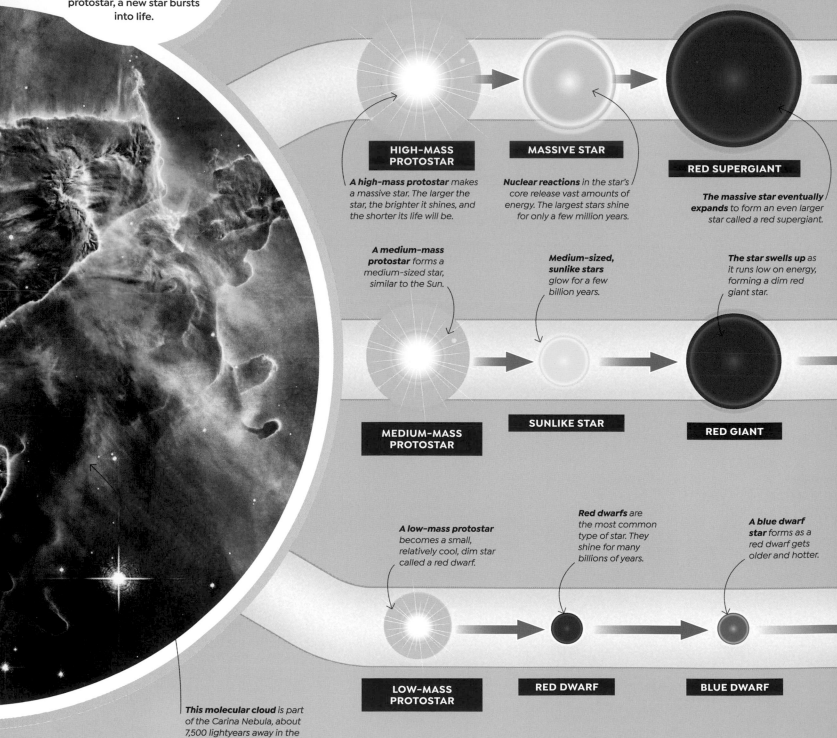

HIGH-MASS PROTOSTAR

A high-mass protostar makes a massive star. The larger the star, the brighter it shines, and the shorter its life will be.

MASSIVE STAR

Nuclear reactions in the star's core release vast amounts of energy. The largest stars shine for only a few million years.

RED SUPERGIANT

The massive star eventually expands to form an even larger star called a red supergiant.

A medium-mass protostar forms a medium-sized star, similar to the Sun.

Medium-sized, sunlike stars glow for a few billion years.

The star swells up as it runs low on energy, forming a dim red giant star.

MEDIUM-MASS PROTOSTAR

SUNLIKE STAR

RED GIANT

A low-mass protostar becomes a small, relatively cool, dim star called a red dwarf.

Red dwarfs are the most common type of star. They shine for many billions of years.

A blue dwarf star forms as a red dwarf gets older and hotter.

LOW-MASS PROTOSTAR

RED DWARF

BLUE DWARF

This molecular cloud is part of the Carina Nebula, about 7,500 lightyears away in the southern constellation Carina. Hot young stars sculpt the cloud into amazing shapes.

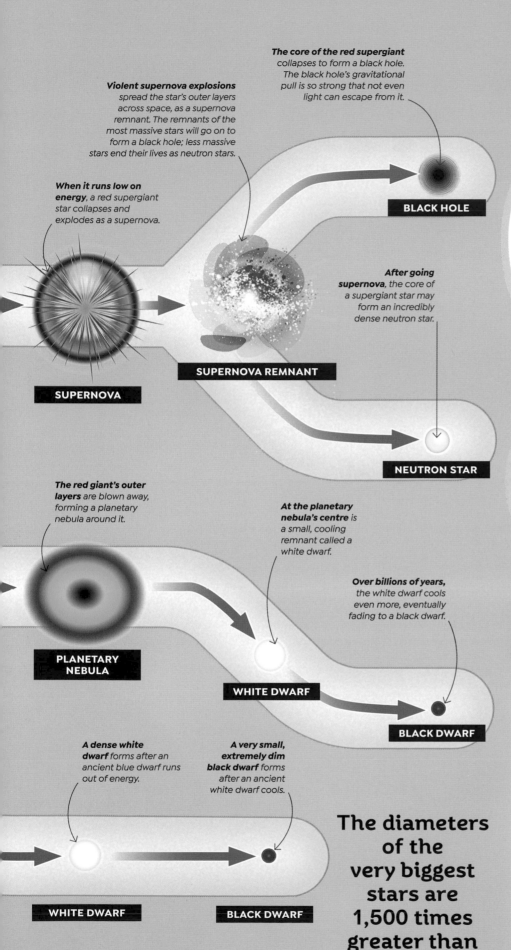

The core of the red supergiant collapses to form a black hole. The black hole's gravitational pull is so strong that not even light can escape from it.

Violent supernova explosions spread the star's outer layers across space, as a supernova remnant. The remnants of the most massive stars will go on to form a black hole; less massive stars end their lives as neutron stars.

When it runs low on energy, a red supergiant star collapses and explodes as a supernova.

After going supernova, the core of a supergiant star may form an incredibly dense neutron star.

BLACK HOLE

SUPERNOVA REMNANT

SUPERNOVA

NEUTRON STAR

The red giant's outer layers are blown away, forming a planetary nebula around it.

At the planetary nebula's centre is a small, cooling remnant called a white dwarf.

Over billions of years, the white dwarf cools even more, eventually fading to a black dwarf.

PLANETARY NEBULA

WHITE DWARF

BLACK DWARF

A dense white dwarf forms after an ancient blue dwarf runs out of energy.

A very small, extremely dim black dwarf forms after an ancient white dwarf cools.

WHITE DWARF

BLACK DWARF

The diameters of the very biggest stars are 1,500 times greater than the diameter of the Sun

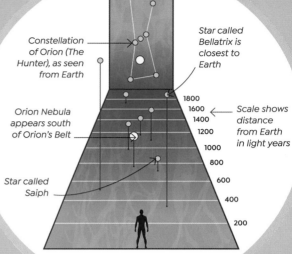

Constellation of Orion (The Hunter), as seen from Earth

Star called Bellatrix is closest to Earth

Orion Nebula appears south of Orion's Belt

Scale shows distance from Earth in light years

Star called Saiph

1800
1600
1400
1200
1000
800
600
400
200

Astronomers divide the night sky into regions called constellations that contain imaginary patterns of stars, some depicting mythical characters or animals dating from ancient times. Stars that look near each other from Earth are not close together in space – constellations would look very different if seen from a planet around a different star.

CONSTELLATIONS

EXOPLANETS

An exoplanet is any planet orbiting a star other than the Sun. The first confirmed exoplanet discoveries – of two planets orbiting the star PSR B1 257+12 in the constellation Virgo, 2,300 light years away – were made in 1992. Since then, astronomers have discovered around 5,000 more exoplanets. These exoplanets fall into categories that are similar to the planets in our own Solar System: there are small and large rocky planets ("Earths"), large ice giants ("Neptunes"), and huge gas giants ("Jupiters").

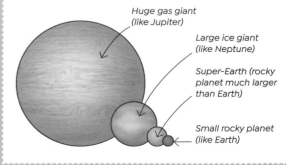

Huge gas giant (like Jupiter)

Large ice giant (like Neptune)

Super-Earth (rocky planet much larger than Earth)

Small rocky planet (like Earth)

Supernova

Sometimes a very large star reaches the end of its life in an extremely violent and bright explosion called a supernova. New chemical elements made during a supernova event are scattered into space in the dying star's outer layers. At the centre, the rest of the star's mass is compressed into a neutron star or a black hole.

TYPICAL SUPERNOVA

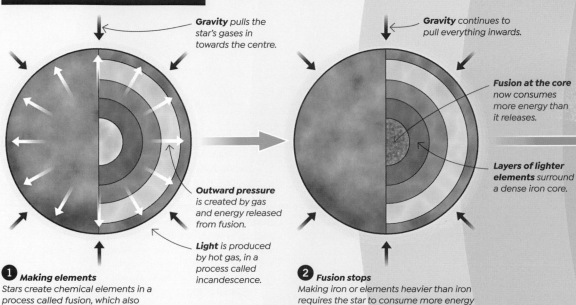
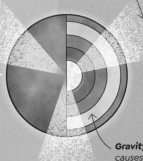

Gravity pulls the star's gases in towards the centre.

Outward pressure is created by gas and energy released from fusion.

Light is produced by hot gas, in a process called incandescence.

1 *Making elements*
Stars create chemical elements in a process called fusion, which also releases energy that keeps the star from collapsing.

Gravity continues to pull everything inwards.

Fusion at the core now consumes more energy than it releases.

Layers of lighter elements surround a dense iron core.

2 *Fusion stops*
Making iron or elements heavier than iron requires the star to consume more energy than it produces. As iron is created in the core, the star approaches the end of its life.

Particles called neutrinos carry energy away from the core of the star.

Gravity causes the cooling core to shrink very quickly.

3 *Core collapses*
The core cools, and now nothing is able to prevent gravity from pulling the core in on itself. It collapses, until it is extremely dense and can compact no more.

BLACK HOLES

The cores of most supernovas collapse only so far, forming a neutron star. But the very biggest stars have so much mass that they continue to collapse until all their matter is squashed into an infinitesimal space called a singularity. This extremely dense object is called a black hole, because its gravity is so strong that not even light can escape from it. Visualizing gravity as the warping of spacetime, the fabric of the Universe, a black hole creates an infinitely deep well.

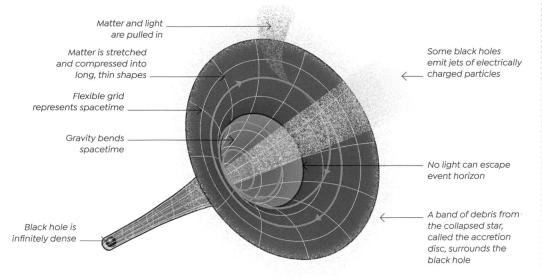

Matter and light are pulled in

Matter is stretched and compressed into long, thin shapes

Flexible grid represents spacetime

Gravity bends spacetime

Black hole is infinitely dense

Some black holes emit jets of electrically charged particles

No light can escape event horizon

A band of debris from the collapsed star, called the accretion disc, surrounds the black hole

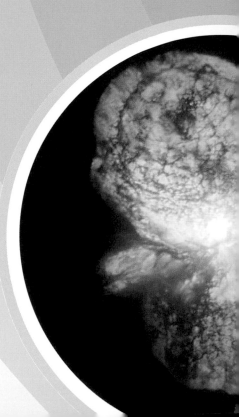

Nearby planets *are destroyed by the energetic stream of intensely hot gases.*

The star's outer layers *are blown away.*

New heavy elements *made during the explosion are scattered across space.*

At the centre *is a neutron star or black hole.*

The release of energy *makes the supernova shine as brightly as a whole galaxy of stars.*

4 **Star explodes**
The collapsed core rebounds, sending out shockwaves. This causes new fusion, forming heavier elements, which are scattered across space in a huge explosion.

SUPERNOVA REMNANTS

During a supernova, the outer layers of a dying star are expelled into space, forming a vast and beautiful cloud. The Crab Nebula is the remnant of a supernova that occurred in 1054 CE, which was so bright that it could be seen by the naked eye during daytime.

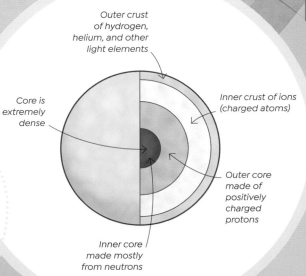

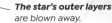

Many of the chemical elements in our bodies were produced in supernovas

READY TO EXPLODE

Over the past two centuries, the brightness of this star, Eta Carinae, has varied wildly. Astronomers predict that it will go supernova in the next few millennia.

NEUTRON STAR

The core of a star that has gone supernova is pulled ever tighter. Matter inside the core is initially made of protons, neutrons, and electrons. The pressure forces the protons and electrons together, so they form more neutrons. In the end, the core is mostly made of neutrons, preventing the further collapse of all but the most massive stars.

Outer crust of hydrogen, helium, and other light elements

Core is extremely dense

Inner crust of ions (charged atoms)

Outer core made of positively charged protons

Inner core made mostly from neutrons

Galaxies

Our planet is part of a vast system of stars, planets, dust, and gas, called the Milky Way Galaxy. There are billions of other galaxies in the Universe. The Milky Way is a spiral galaxy, with a central bulge surrounded by a flat disc divided into several spiral arms. Everything in it orbits the centre, where a huge black hole is located. The galaxy may be partly made of an as-yet unexplained kind of matter called dark matter.

THE MILKY WAY'S HALO

Clusters of very old stars exist in a spherical region, called the stellar halo. Extending beyond the stellar halo, is a galactic corona, made of thin, hot gas.

Location of Solar System

Spherical halo

Clusters of old stars

Central bulge

Galactic disc has warped edges

HALO STAR ORBIT

Bulge stars are in random orbits, so the bulge itself is more or less spherical.

BULGE STAR ORBIT

CENTRAL BULGE

At the very centre of the galaxy is a supermassive black hole. It has a mass 4 million times larger than the Sun's.

THE GALACTIC CENTRE

Disc-shaped galaxies have a central bulge more densely packed with stars than the rest of the disc. At the centre is a supermassive black hole.

Spiral arms contain lots of gas and dust, and are areas of active starbirth.

PERSEUS ARM

ORION ARM

Regions between the arms contain much less matter than the arms and the central bulge.

OUTER ARM

DISC STAR ORBIT

SPIRAL ARMS

The Milky Way has spiral arms where most of the matter is concentrated. The arms are stable features and do not gradually twist around each other.

Our Solar System is located in the galaxy's Orion Arm.

Gravity brings stars towards the disc, their momentum carries them through it – then gravity brings them back again.

Our star, the Sun, is one of more than 100 billion stars in the Milky Way Galaxy

Halo stars' orbits are randomly oriented.

TYPES OF GALAXY

Astronomers group galaxies into three main types. Elliptical galaxies are spherical or elliptical (egg-shaped). They contain old stars, and no new stars are being born in them. Disc-shaped spirals contain a lot of young, hot stars, giving them a blue-white appearance. Galaxies that are neither spiral nor elliptical are called irregular.

 **ELLIPTICAL**

 **SPIRAL**

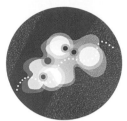 **IRREGULAR**

MILKY WAY

SCUTUM CENTAURUS ARM

Disc stars bob up and down as they orbit.

The closest galaxy
outside the Milky Way is 25,000 light years from the Sun

Dark matter is a hypothetical substance that cannot be seen, but has a gravitational influence on other objects that can be observed. Theory suggests that early in the Universe's history, dark matter collapsed under its own gravity to form huge halos (yellow in this computer simulation) that attracted normal matter to form galaxies.

DARK MATTER

SPACE

QUASARS

A quasar is a galactic centre that emits huge amounts of light and radiation. A quasar emits thousands of times as much radiation as all the stars in our galaxy. The radiation from a quasar is produced by stars, gas, and dust reaching extremely high temperatures as they fall towards a supermassive black hole. Jets of high-speed particles spiral out above and below the quasar.

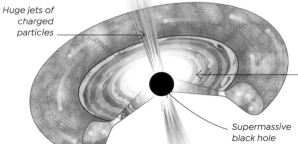

Huge jets of charged particles

Matter falls towards central black hole

Supermassive black hole located in centre of galaxy

THE BIG BANG

The theory proposes that the Universe began with a high-energy explosive event, the Big Bang, but it does not say *why* it could have arisen out of nothing.

INFLATION

A tiny fraction of a second after the Big Bang, the Universe expanded incredibly rapidly, from smaller than an atom to the size of a grapefruit.

At the end of inflation, the electromagnetic force and the weak force separate, and electrons, positrons, and photons come into existence.

CMB RADIATION

The Big Bang theory predicts that radiation emitted when atoms first formed should still be detectable, its waves stretched by the expansion of space to become microwaves. This cosmic microwave background (CMB) was discovered in 1964.

The strong force breaks away, and the Universe is filled with a "soup" of quarks and gluons.

During inflation, the Universe increases in size by one hundred trillion trillion times.

Protons and neutrons appear, each consisting of three quarks bound tightly together.

Atomic nuclei, of hydrogen and helium, form, made of protons and neutrons bound together.

FORCES

Today, there are four fundamental forces. The strong nuclear force, gravity, and electromagnetism all affect how particles interact, while the weak nuclear force governs radioactive decay. In the early Universe, these forces all separated from a single combined superforce.

Gravity is the first force to separate from the superforce.

The Big Bang

The Big Bang theory is the prevailing scientific theory for the origin of the Universe. The theory suggests that the Universe started expanding 13.8 billion years ago from an extremely hot, dense point. It describes how all space, time, and matter came to be. There is a great deal of scientific evidence to support the Big Bang theory, from the interactions of tiny particles to observations of the Universe at the grandest of scales.

ONE TRILLIONTH OF A SECOND AFTER THE BIG BANG

ONE MILLIONTH OF A SECOND AFTER THE BIG BANG

1–3 MINUTES AFTER THE BIG BANG

380,000 YEARS AFTER THE BIG BANG

The Universe is still too hot for protons and neutrons to form.

No atoms can form until the Universe cools to a temperature at which electrons can attach to nuclei.

In the beginning, all the Universe's energy was contained in a space smaller than a proton

Radiation is released when electrons and nuclei combine to make atoms.

PARTICLE PHYSICS

Physicists try to recreate the conditions in the first second of the Universe by smashing subatomic particles together. We can see their tracks in particle detectors.

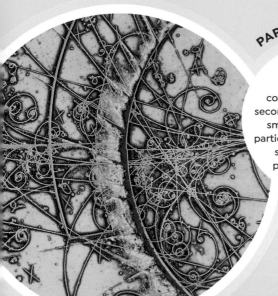

THE JAMES WEBB SPACE TELESCOPE

When astronomers look into space, they also look back in time, because light and other radiation from distant parts of the Universe takes billions of years to reach us. The orbiting James Webb Space Telescope, whose mirror is shown right, will image the early stars and galaxies that emitted the first light in the Universe and may reveal when they formed.

SUBATOMIC PARTICLES

Although atoms did not form until at least 380,000 years after the Big Bang, many smaller (subatomic) particles appeared during the first second of the Universe's existence. Some particles have an identical "twin" particle with an opposite electric charge. These opposite twins are called antiparticles.

POSITRON
Positively charged antiparticle of the electron.

ELECTRON
Negatively charged subatomic particle.

PHOTON
A tiny packet of electromagnetic radiation, such as light.

GLUON
Carrier of the strong force. It "sticks" quarks together.

QUARK
Particle that makes up protons and neutrons.

ANTIQUARK
Antiparticle of the quark, found in antiprotons and antineutrons.

ANTIPROTON
Negatively charged antiparticle of the proton.

PROTON
Positively charged particle made up of quarks.

NEUTRON
Particle with no net electric charge, made up of quarks.

ANTINEUTRON
Antiparticle of the neutron, made up of antiquarks.

Atoms of hydrogen and helium form, now that the Universe is sufficiently cool.

DARK UNIVERSE

Until the first stars burst into life, the Universe was utterly dark, because there were no sources of light.

Stars start to burn, after gravity causes vast clouds of hydrogen and helium to collapse and nuclear reactions to begin inside.

The first galaxies come together as gravity pulls huge numbers of stars into vast groups.

Our own galaxy, the Milky Way, contains hundreds of billions of stars, including the Sun.

380,000–2 MILLION YEARS AFTER THE BIG BANG

500–600 MILLION YEARS AFTER THE BIG BANG

2–3 BILLION YEARS AFTER THE BIG BANG

THE PRESENT

The Universe is nearly three times as old as the Sun

EXPANDING SPACE

As space expands, each galaxy moves away from all the others

The two-dimensional surface of the balloon represents three-dimensional space

Scientists came up with the Big Bang theory after noticing that galaxies all around us are moving away from Earth. This suggests that space itself is expanding and cooling, and that it was once much smaller and hotter. To imagine the expansion of space, picture a balloon with galaxies drawn on it. As it inflates, the galaxies on the balloon spread apart.

Space is still expanding, so we observe galaxies in every direction moving away from us.

PRESENT DAY

Today, the Universe is still expanding. Galaxies are colliding, stars are dying, and new ones are forming.

Optical telescope

Astronomers' telescopes have curved mirrors or lenses to gather and focus light from planets, stars, galaxies, and other objects in space. These are called primary mirrors and lenses, and the larger their diameter, the more light they gather. Secondary mirrors or lenses produce magnified images of the objects, which can be seen by the eye or captured by sensors like those in a digital camera. Astronomers use other different of telescopes to collect radio waves, X-rays, and other kinds of radiation (see pp.286–87).

Some large telescopes have mirrors made of more than 90 segments that move separately from each other

CHOOSING A SITE

Observatories are often sited at high altitude, to cut the amount of atmosphere the light they receive has to pass through. These telescopes are on an extinct volcano in Hawaii.

OBSERVATORY BUILDING

Astronomers work inside a large building that also houses the powerful computers that control the telescope and process the images it captures.

6 *Powerful computers* process and store the digital images.

COMPUTER ROOM

7 *Astronomers study images* from the telescope on their computers.

REFLECTORS AND REFRACTORS

Most large telescopes are reflectors: they use curved mirrors as the primary, or objective, to collect the light. Many smaller telescopes are refractors, with a lens as the primary. The objective focuses the light, producing an image, and a powerful lens magnifies that image for the eye to see (or a sensor to detect and record).

Light from an astronomical object, such as a star

Image forms inside telescope tube, at focal point of objective

Eyepiece lens magnifies image for the eye to see

A refractor has a lens as its objective to gather light and focus it to produce an image

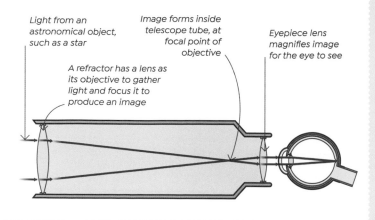

The world's largest single telescope mirror is 10.4 m (35 ft) in diameter

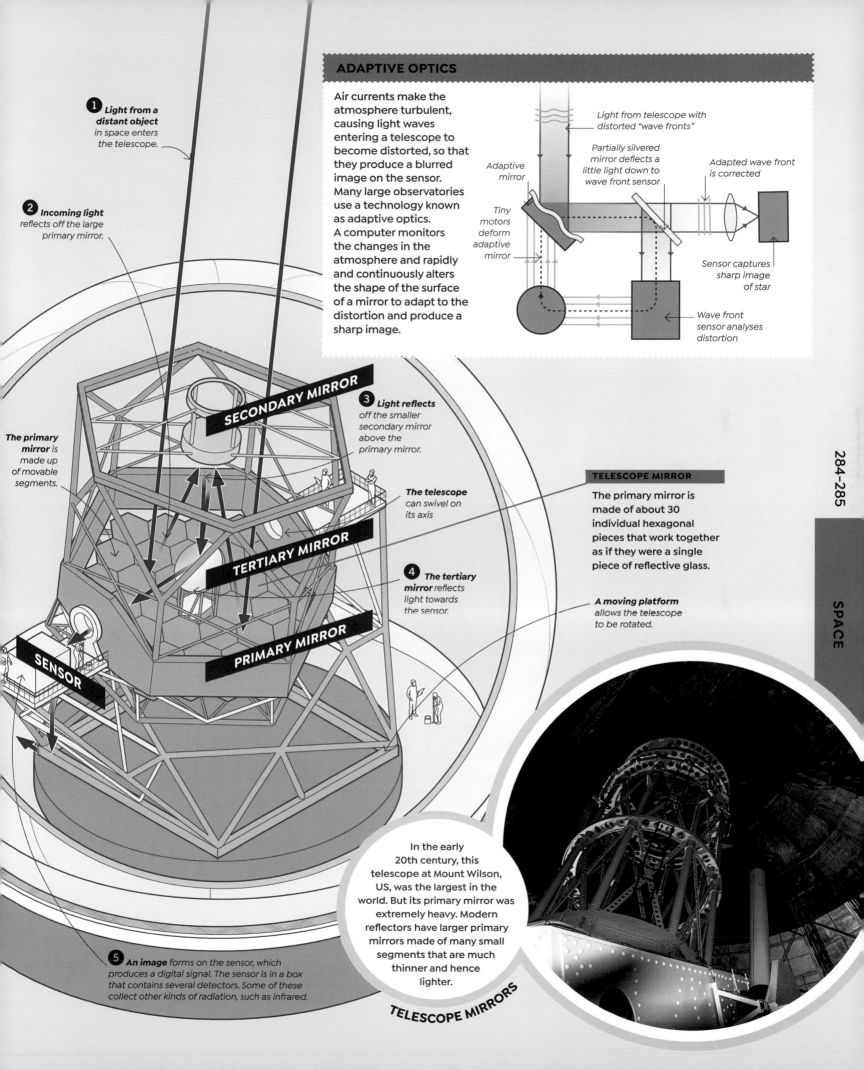

① **Light from a distant object** in space enters the telescope.

② **Incoming light** reflects off the large primary mirror.

284–285

SPACE

ADAPTIVE OPTICS

Air currents make the atmosphere turbulent, causing light waves entering a telescope to become distorted, so that they produce a blurred image on the sensor. Many large observatories use a technology known as adaptive optics. A computer monitors the changes in the atmosphere and rapidly and continuously alters the shape of the surface of a mirror to adapt to the distortion and produce a sharp image.

Light from telescope with distorted "wave fronts"

Partially silvered mirror deflects a little light down to wave front sensor

Adaptive mirror

Adapted wave front is corrected

Tiny motors deform adaptive mirror

Sensor captures sharp image of star

Wave front sensor analyses distortion

SECONDARY MIRROR

The primary mirror is made up of movable segments.

③ **Light reflects** off the smaller secondary mirror above the primary mirror.

The telescope can swivel on its axis

TERTIARY MIRROR

④ **The tertiary mirror** reflects light towards the sensor.

PRIMARY MIRROR

TELESCOPE MIRROR

The primary mirror is made of about 30 individual hexagonal pieces that work together as if they were a single piece of reflective glass.

A moving platform allows the telescope to be rotated.

SENSOR

⑤ **An image** forms on the sensor, which produces a digital signal. The sensor is in a box that contains several detectors. Some of these collect other kinds of radiation, such as infrared.

In the early 20th century, this telescope at Mount Wilson, US, was the largest in the world. But its primary mirror was extremely heavy. Modern reflectors have larger primary mirrors made of many small segments that are much thinner and hence lighter.

TELESCOPE MIRRORS

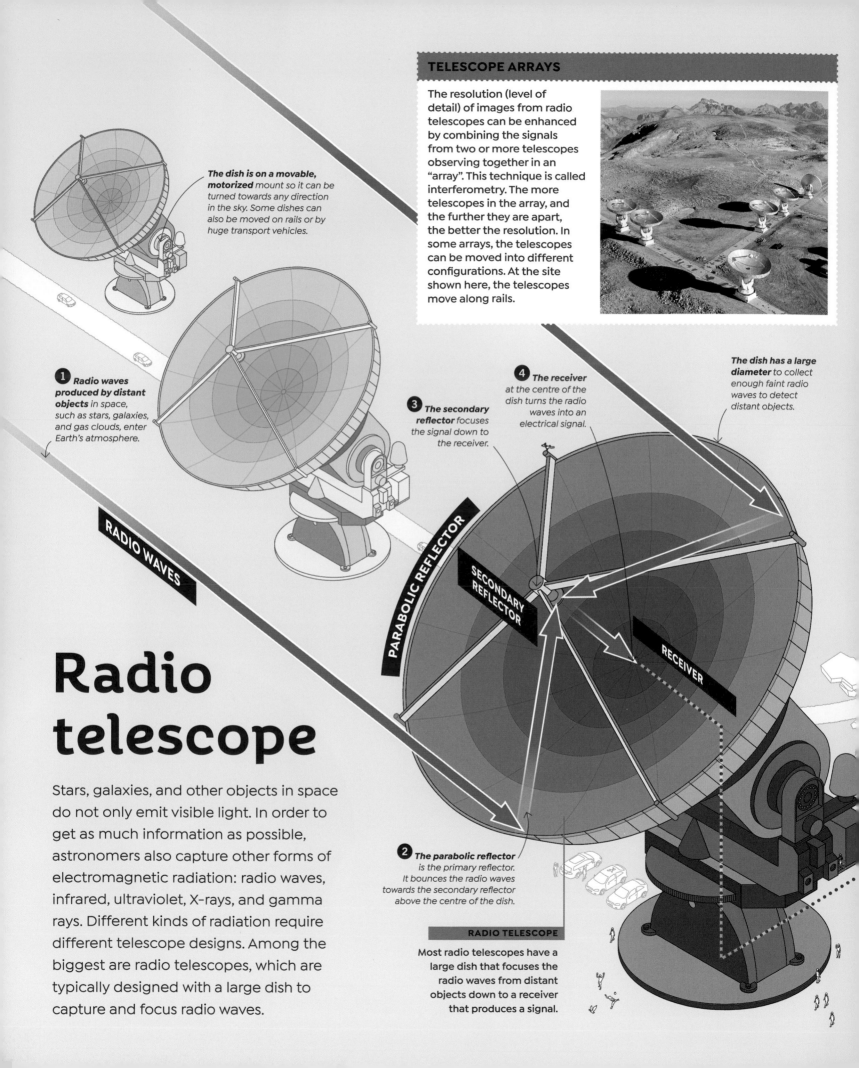

The dish is on a movable, motorized mount so it can be turned towards any direction in the sky. Some dishes can also be moved on rails or by huge transport vehicles.

1 **Radio waves produced by distant objects** in space, such as stars, galaxies, and gas clouds, enter Earth's atmosphere.

RADIO WAVES

4 **The receiver** at the centre of the dish turns the radio waves into an electrical signal.

3 **The secondary reflector** focuses the signal down to the receiver.

The dish has a large diameter to collect enough faint radio waves to detect distant objects.

PARABOLIC REFLECTOR

SECONDARY REFLECTOR

RECEIVER

Radio telescope

Stars, galaxies, and other objects in space do not only emit visible light. In order to get as much information as possible, astronomers also capture other forms of electromagnetic radiation: radio waves, infrared, ultraviolet, X-rays, and gamma rays. Different kinds of radiation require different telescope designs. Among the biggest are radio telescopes, which are typically designed with a large dish to capture and focus radio waves.

2 **The parabolic reflector** is the primary reflector. It bounces the radio waves towards the secondary reflector above the centre of the dish.

RADIO TELESCOPE

Most radio telescopes have a large dish that focuses the radio waves from distant objects down to a receiver that produces a signal.

SPACE TELESCOPES

Radio waves pass through Earth's atmosphere almost unaffected, but light, infrared, ultraviolet, and X-rays are partly blocked. This is why astronomers launch telescopes into space, above the atmosphere, like the Hubble Space Telescope, shown here.

6 *The signal reaches the observing centre,* where it is stored and processed by powerful supercomputers.

At the observing centre, astronomers control the telescopes and study the signals they receive. They may also receive signals from radio telescopes elsewhere.

OBSERVATION CENTRE

Other telescopes, arranged in an array, gather radio waves from the same object at the same time.

Fibre-optic cables carry the digital signals from all the telescopes in the array.

DIGITAL SIGNAL

The dish of the world's biggest single radio telescope is 500 m (1,650 ft) across

5 *The signal* from the receiver is sent to the observing centre. It is now a digital signal that can be processed by the astronomers' computers.

RADIO IMAGES

New stars are made from vast clouds of mostly hydrogen gas. Hydrogen emits a particular frequency of radio waves, which can be detected by radio telescopes. In this remarkable picture of the Whirlpool Galaxy, the white parts are from an optical telescope; the red areas, from an array of radio telescopes, highlight clouds of hydrogen gas.

MANY KINDS OF LIGHT

Some features of astronomical objects are visible only in images captured by infrared telescopes, while others may be highlighted in images captured by radio, ultraviolet, or X-ray telescopes. Astronomers often combine images from different telescopes. This image, like the image on the far right, shows the Whirlpool Galaxy, but it includes information from more types of radiation to reveal extra detail.

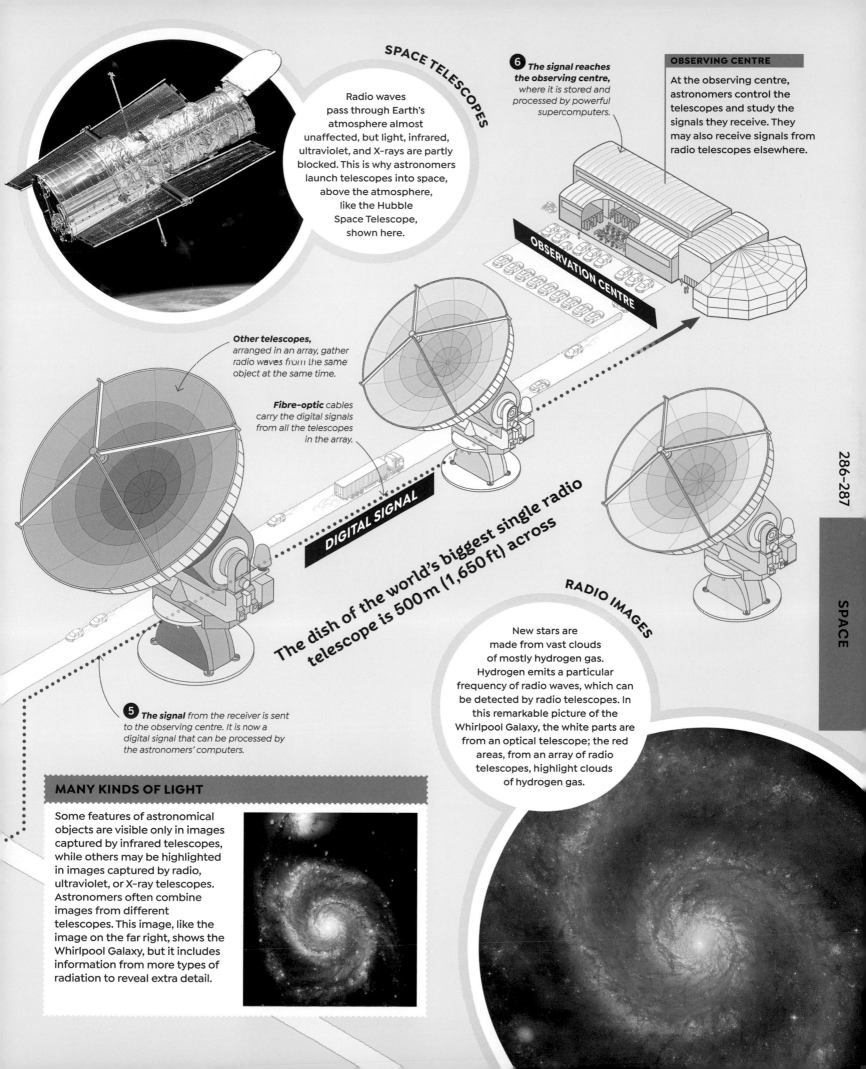

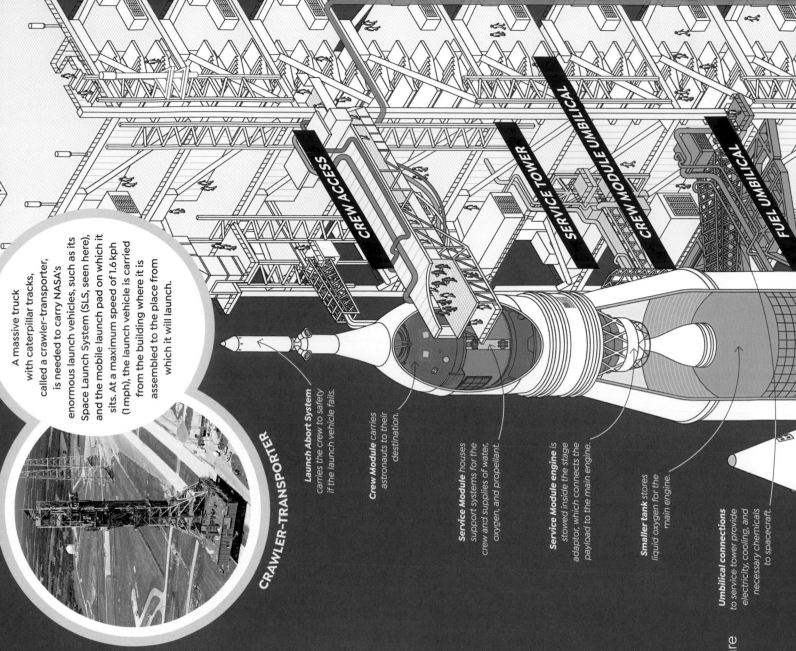

SERVICE TOWER

CREW MODULE UMBILICAL

FUEL UMBILICAL

A massive truck with caterpillar tracks, called a crawler-transporter, is needed to carry NASA's enormous launch vehicles, such as its Space Launch System (SLS, seen here), and the mobile launch pad on which it sits. At a maximum speed of 1.6kph (1mph), the launch vehicle is carried from the building where it is assembled to the place from which it will launch.

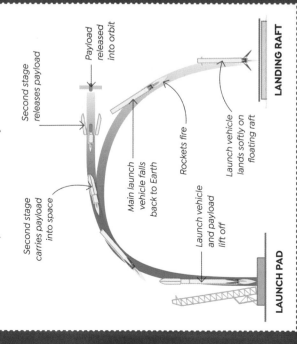

CRAWLER-TRANSPORTER

Launch Abort System carries the crew to safety if the launch vehicle fails.

Crew Module carries astronauts to their destination.

Service Module houses support systems for the crew and supplies of water, oxygen, and propellant.

Service Module engine is stowed inside the stage adaptor, which connects the payload to the main engine.

Smaller tank stores liquid oxygen for the main engine.

Umbilical connections to service tower provide electricity, cooling, and necessary chemicals to spacecraft.

REUSABLE ROCKETS

To make spaceflight more affordable and less wasteful, some modern launch vehicles are reusable. After lifting the payload above the atmosphere, a reusable launch vehicle then falls back down to Earth. Small rocket engines slow its descent, so that it lands softly.

Second stage carries payload into space

Second stage releases payload

Payload released into orbit

Main launch vehicle falls back to Earth

Rockets fire

Launch vehicle and payload lift off

Launch vehicle lands softly on floating raft

LAUNCH PAD

LANDING RAFT

A launch rocket can produce the same amount of power as 18 Boeing 747 airliners

Rocket

In order to lift heavy payloads above Earth's atmosphere and into space, rockets need to be huge and carry lots of fuel. Most launch vehicles are divided into several sections, called stages, each propelled by powerful rocket engines. The stages fall away one by one after exhausting their fuel.

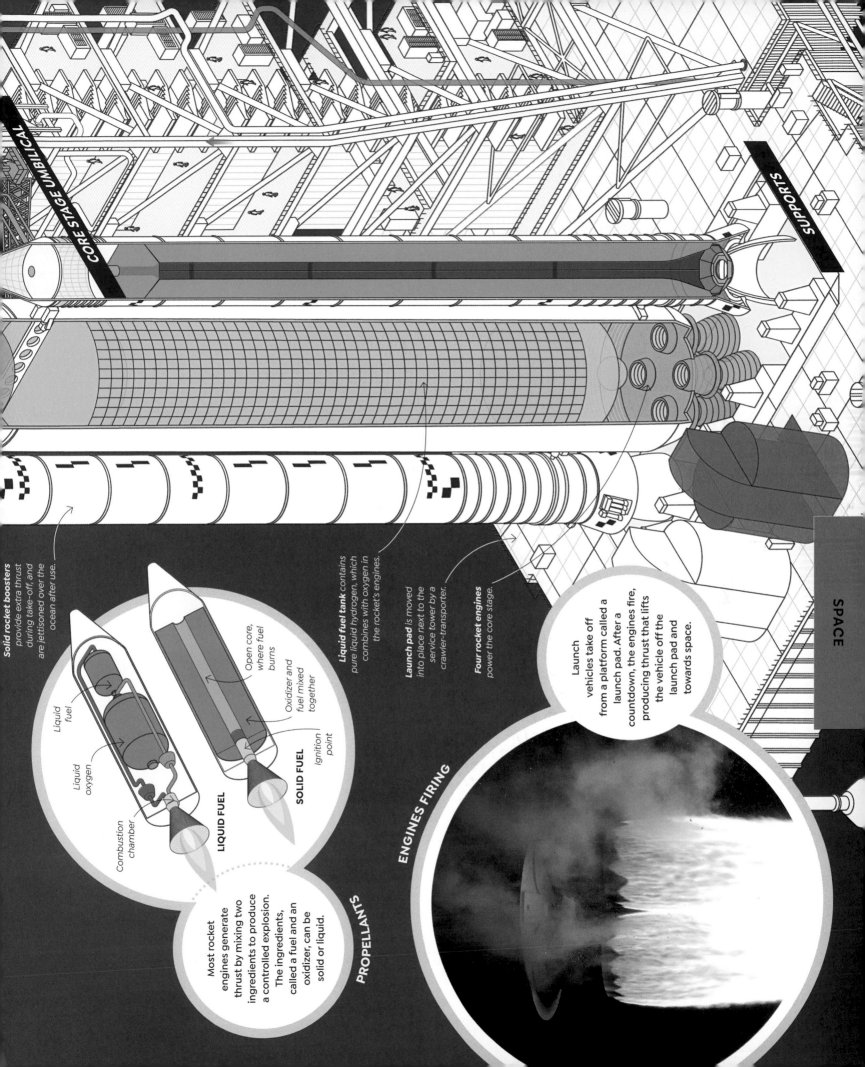

Solid rocket boosters provide extra thrust during take-off, and are jettisoned over the ocean after use.

Liquid fuel tank contains pure liquid hydrogen, which combines with oxygen in the rocket's engines.

Launch pad is moved into place next to the service tower by a crawler-transporter.

Four rocket engines power the core stage.

Open core, where fuel burns

Oxidizer and fuel mixed together

Liquid fuel

Liquid oxygen

Combustion chamber

Ignition point

LIQUID FUEL

SOLID FUEL

PROPELLANTS

Most rocket engines generate thrust by mixing two ingredients to produce a controlled explosion. The ingredients, called a fuel and an oxidizer, can be solid or liquid.

ENGINES FIRING

Launch vehicles take off from a platform called a launch pad. After a countdown, the engines fire, producing thrust that lifts the vehicle off the launch pad and towards space.

SPACE

ESCAPING EARTH

A Falcon 9 rocket blasts off on a mission to resupply the ISS. The Dragon capsule that sits at the top can carry seven astronauts and up to 6 tonnes of food and equipment to low Earth orbit. If humans are to go back to the Moon, or even Mars, bigger rockets with larger payloads will be needed.

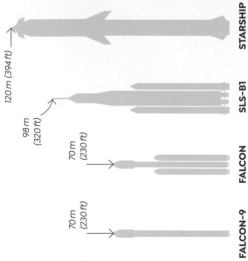

70m (230ft)

FALCON-9

70m (230ft)

FALCON HEAVY

98m (320ft)

120m (394ft)

SLS-B1

STARSHIP

HEAVY LIFTERS

New rockets, such as the Falcon Heavy and SLS, are now undergoing test launches. Starship is being designed to be fully reusable.

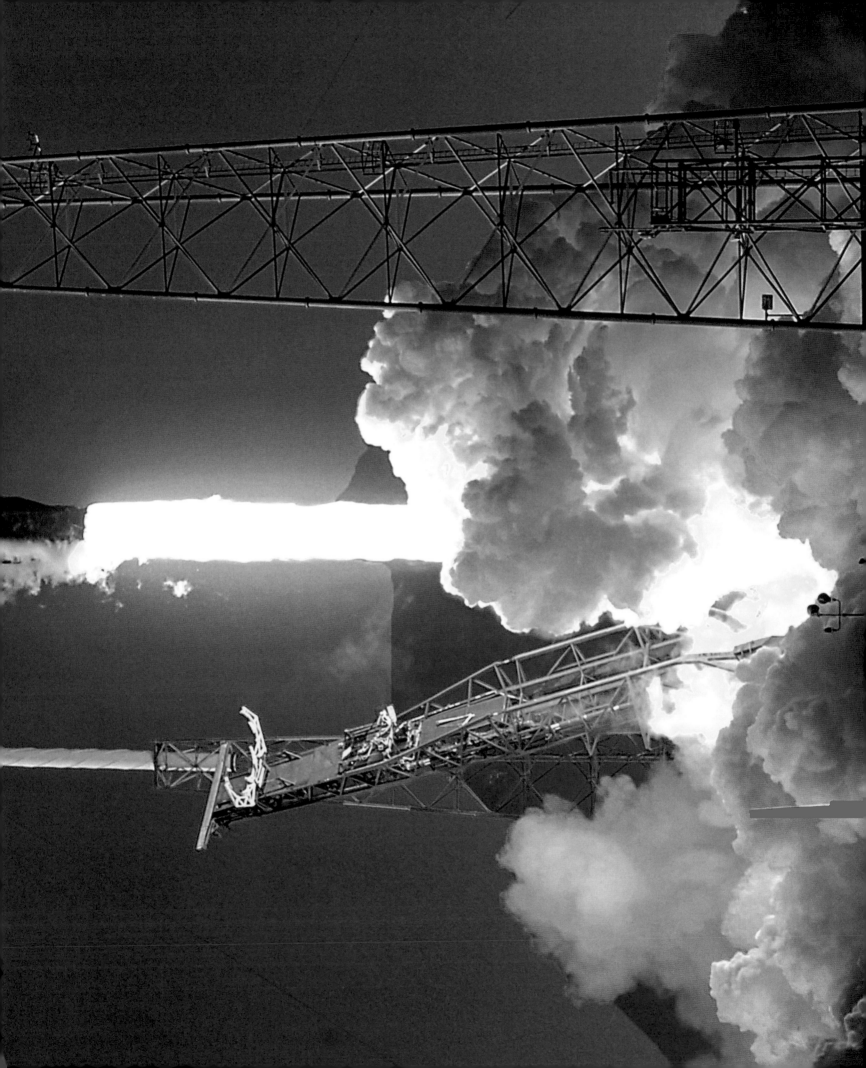

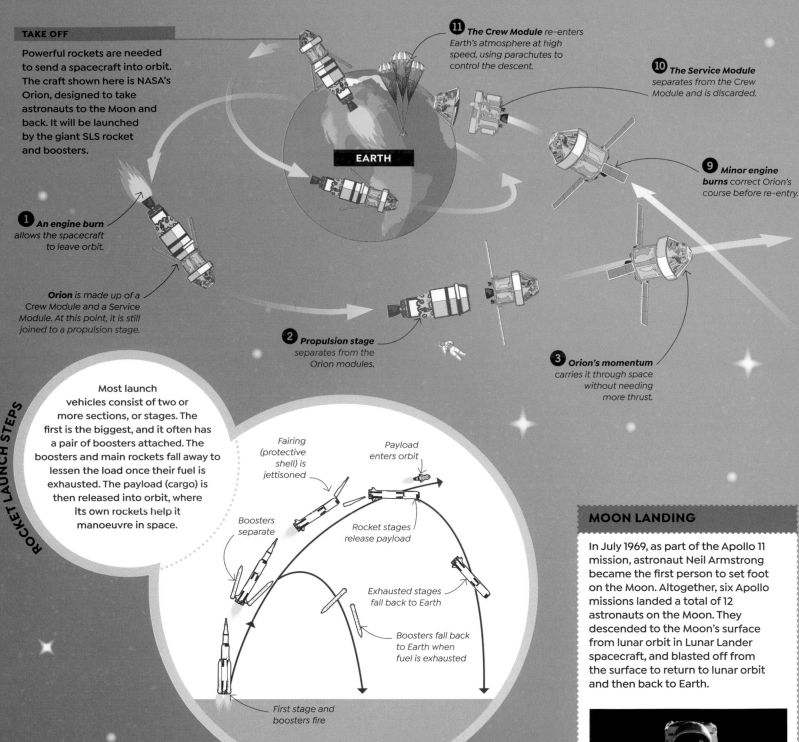

TAKE OFF

Powerful rockets are needed to send a spacecraft into orbit. The craft shown here is NASA's Orion, designed to take astronauts to the Moon and back. It will be launched by the giant SLS rocket and boosters.

11 *The Crew Module re-enters Earth's atmosphere at high speed, using parachutes to control the descent.*

10 *The Service Module separates from the Crew Module and is discarded.*

EARTH

9 *Minor engine burns correct Orion's course before re-entry.*

1 *An engine burn allows the spacecraft to leave orbit.*

Orion is made up of a Crew Module and a Service Module. At this point, it is still joined to a propulsion stage.

2 *Propulsion stage separates from the Orion modules.*

3 *Orion's momentum carries it through space without needing more thrust.*

ROCKET LAUNCH STEPS

Most launch vehicles consist of two or more sections, or stages. The first is the biggest, and it often has a pair of boosters attached. The boosters and main rockets fall away to lessen the load once their fuel is exhausted. The payload (cargo) is then released into orbit, where its own rockets help it manoeuvre in space.

Fairing (protective shell) is jettisoned

Payload enters orbit

Boosters separate

Rocket stages release payload

Exhausted stages fall back to Earth

Boosters fall back to Earth when fuel is exhausted

First stage and boosters fire

MOON LANDING

In July 1969, as part of the Apollo 11 mission, astronaut Neil Armstrong became the first person to set foot on the Moon. Altogether, six Apollo missions landed a total of 12 astronauts on the Moon. They descended to the Moon's surface from lunar orbit in Lunar Lander spacecraft, and blasted off from the surface to return to lunar orbit and then back to Earth.

Space flight

Once lifted above the atmosphere by rockets, a spacecraft goes into orbit. Satellites and space stations remain in orbit; they can change their orbit's altitude by changing their speed. Other spacecraft – such as space probes or crewed vehicles headed for the Moon – speed up enough to escape Earth's gravity altogether. These missions require the spacecraft to perform many complex manoeuvres in space.

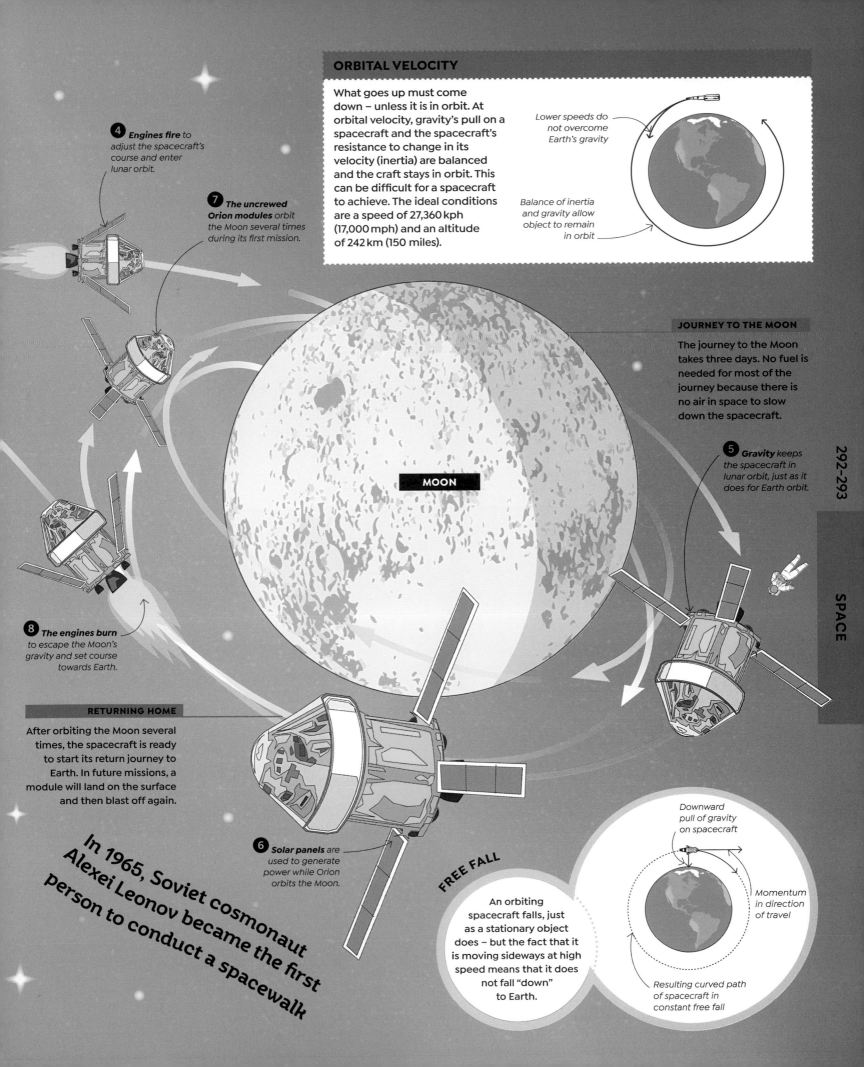

ORBITAL VELOCITY

What goes up must come down – unless it is in orbit. At orbital velocity, gravity's pull on a spacecraft and the spacecraft's resistance to change in its velocity (inertia) are balanced and the craft stays in orbit. This can be difficult for a spacecraft to achieve. The ideal conditions are a speed of 27,360 kph (17,000 mph) and an altitude of 242 km (150 miles).

Lower speeds do not overcome Earth's gravity

Balance of inertia and gravity allow object to remain in orbit

4 *Engines fire* to adjust the spacecraft's course and enter lunar orbit.

7 *The uncrewed Orion modules* orbit the Moon several times during its first mission.

MOON

JOURNEY TO THE MOON

The journey to the Moon takes three days. No fuel is needed for most of the journey because there is no air in space to slow down the spacecraft.

5 *Gravity* keeps the spacecraft in lunar orbit, just as it does for Earth orbit.

8 *The engines burn* to escape the Moon's gravity and set course towards Earth.

RETURNING HOME

After orbiting the Moon several times, the spacecraft is ready to start its return journey to Earth. In future missions, a module will land on the surface and then blast off again.

6 *Solar panels* are used to generate power while Orion orbits the Moon.

In 1965, Soviet cosmonaut Alexei Leonov became the first person to conduct a spacewalk

FREE FALL

An orbiting spacecraft falls, just as a stationary object does – but the fact that it is moving sideways at high speed means that it does not fall "down" to Earth.

Downward pull of gravity on spacecraft

Momentum in direction of travel

Resulting curved path of spacecraft in constant free fall

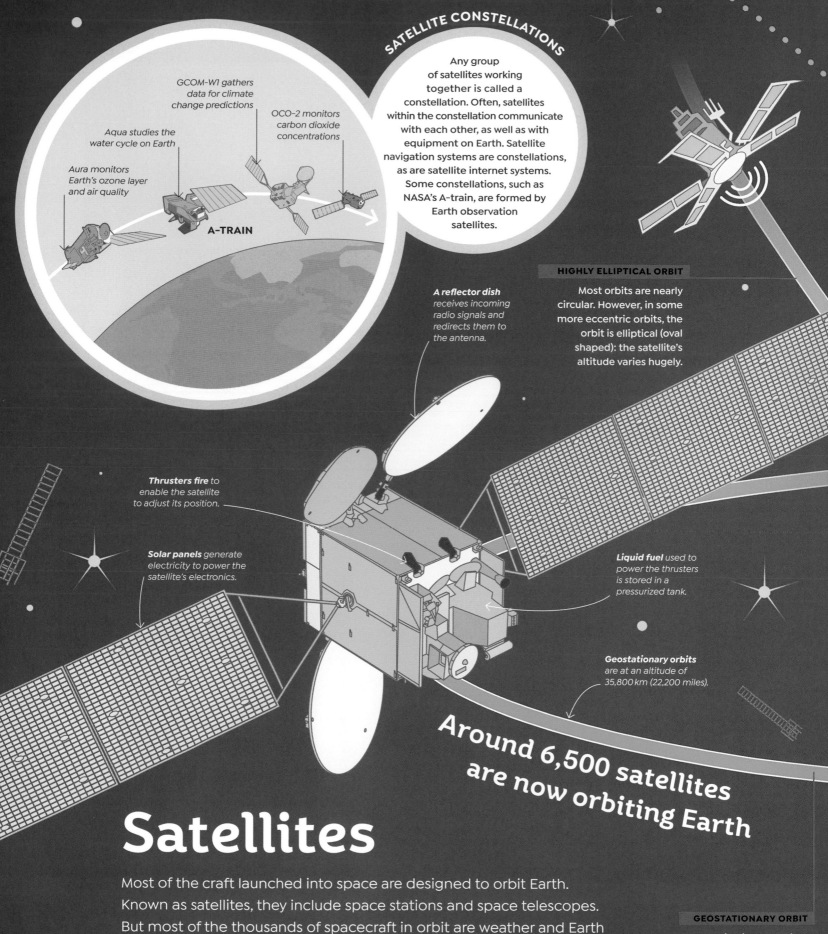

SATELLITE CONSTELLATIONS

Aura monitors Earth's ozone layer and air quality

Aqua studies the water cycle on Earth

GCOM-W1 gathers data for climate change predictions

OCO-2 monitors carbon dioxide concentrations

A-TRAIN

Any group of satellites working together is called a constellation. Often, satellites within the constellation communicate with each other, as well as with equipment on Earth. Satellite navigation systems are constellations, as are satellite internet systems. Some constellations, such as NASA's A-train, are formed by Earth observation satellites.

A reflector dish receives incoming radio signals and redirects them to the antenna.

HIGHLY ELLIPTICAL ORBIT

Most orbits are nearly circular. However, in some more eccentric orbits, the orbit is elliptical (oval shaped): the satellite's altitude varies hugely.

Thrusters fire to enable the satellite to adjust its position.

Solar panels generate electricity to power the satellite's electronics.

Liquid fuel used to power the thrusters is stored in a pressurized tank.

Geostationary orbits are at an altitude of 35,800 km (22,200 miles).

Around 6,500 satellites are now orbiting Earth

Satellites

Most of the craft launched into space are designed to orbit Earth. Known as satellites, they include space stations and space telescopes. But most of the thousands of spacecraft in orbit are weather and Earth observation satellites, which monitor conditions on the planet from above the atmosphere, and communications satellites, which relay television and internet communications signals.

GEOSTATIONARY ORBIT

Communications satellites in geostationary orbits remain at the same point in the sky when viewed from Earth.

Single-use fuel tank is jettisoned and falls back to Earth

Aluminium alloy shell

An estimated 523,000 pieces of **debris currently orbit Earth**

When a satellite is no longer working, it may be de-orbited, in which case it burns up in the atmosphere. But many satellites remain in orbit and become space junk. Also considered space junk are pieces of spacecraft that have broken off or been discarded after launch. Some are as small as flecks of paint, or as large as entire rocket stages.

TRANSFER ORBITS

Satellites sometimes need to move from one orbit to another. Firing onboard rocket engines speeds up the craft, sending it into a highly elliptical transfer orbit that merges with the new orbit. The craft is moving slowly at the high point of its orbit, and so to prevent it falling back down, the engines burn again, so that the satellite matches the speed of the second orbit.

New orbital path achieved

Transfer orbit merges with new geostationary orbit

Satellite is in a low Earth orbit after launch

Engine burn takes satellite into an elliptical transfer orbit

Polar orbits *take a satellite over both poles, and are used for weather and Earth observation satellites.*

Broken satellites *burn up when entering Earth's atmosphere due to heating from the friction of the air.*

Low Earth orbit *only gives satellites a small field of view.*

Solar cells

Modular design allows CubeSats to be stacked

LOW EARTH ORBIT

With an altitude of less than 2,000 km (1,200 miles), low Earth orbit is populated by space stations and some space telescopes.

Sun-synchronous orbits *are low-Earth, polar orbits in which the satellite always passes over the same spot at the same time of day.*

Small satellites for scientific research, called CubeSats, are just 10 cm (4 in) wide, making them cheap to launch, typically as part of a bigger mission.

CUBESATS

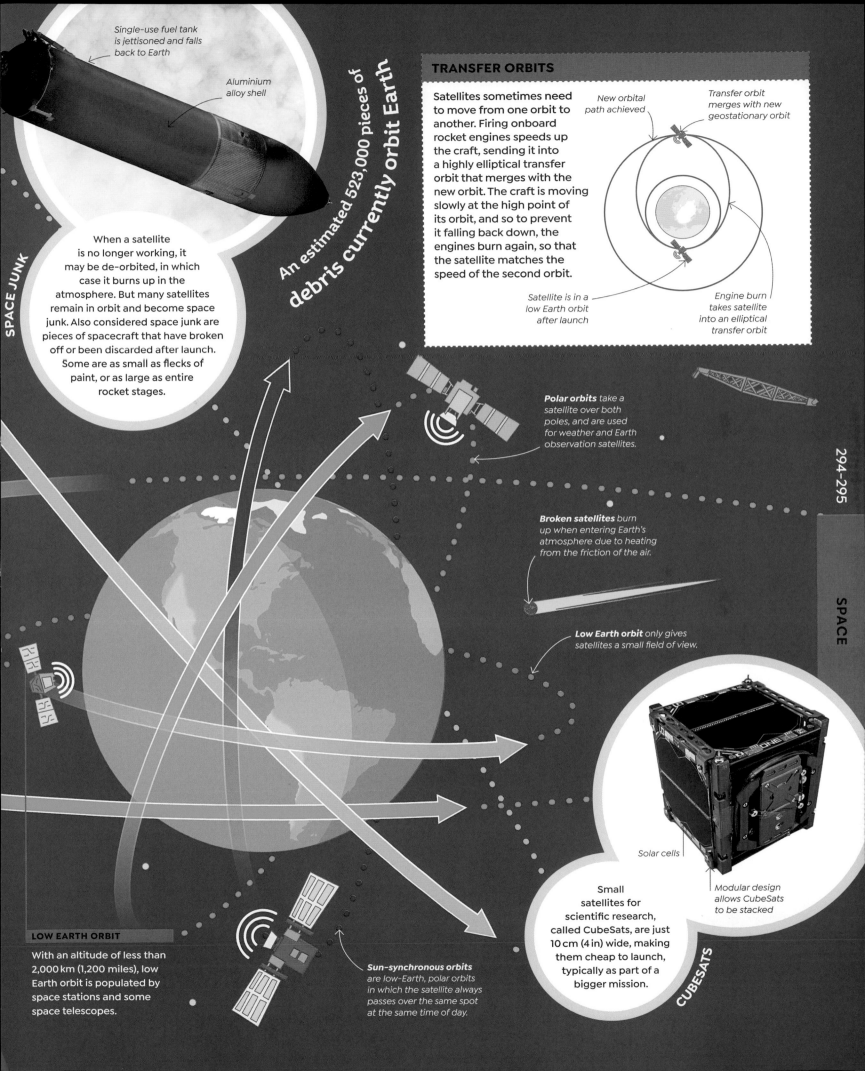

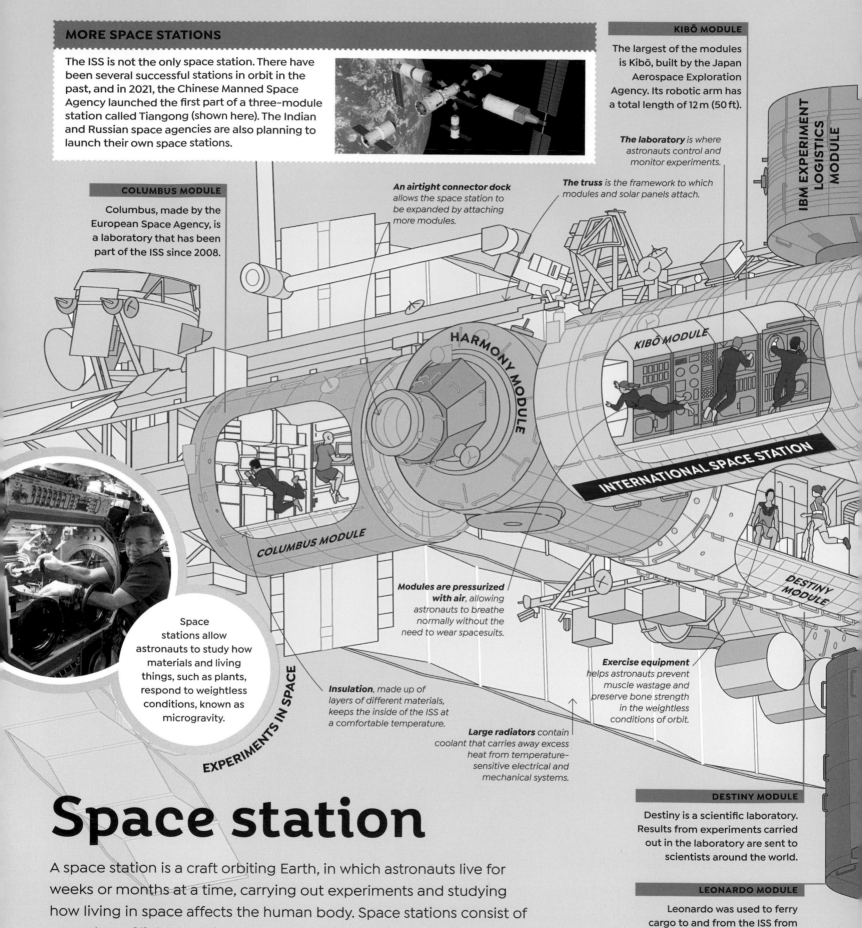

KIBŌ MODULE

The largest of the modules is Kibō, built by the Japan Aerospace Exploration Agency. Its robotic arm has a total length of 12 m (50 ft).

The laboratory is where astronauts control and monitor experiments.

COLUMBUS MODULE

Columbus, made by the European Space Agency, is a laboratory that has been part of the ISS since 2008.

An airtight connector dock allows the space station to be expanded by attaching more modules.

The truss is the framework to which modules and solar panels attach.

IBM EXPERIMENT LOGISTICS MODULE

HARMONY MODULE

KIBŌ MODULE

COLUMBUS MODULE

INTERNATIONAL SPACE STATION

DESTINY MODULE

Space stations allow astronauts to study how materials and living things, such as plants, respond to weightless conditions, known as microgravity.

EXPERIMENTS IN SPACE

Insulation, made up of layers of different materials, keeps the inside of the ISS at a comfortable temperature.

Modules are pressurized with air, allowing astronauts to breathe normally without the need to wear spacesuits.

Large radiators contain coolant that carries away excess heat from temperature-sensitive electrical and mechanical systems.

Exercise equipment helps astronauts prevent muscle wastage and preserve bone strength in the weightless conditions of orbit.

DESTINY MODULE

Destiny is a scientific laboratory. Results from experiments carried out in the laboratory are sent to scientists around the world.

LEONARDO MODULE

Leonardo was used to ferry cargo to and from the ISS from 2001 until 2011, when it became a permanent part of the station. It is now used to store spare parts and supplies.

Space station

A space station is a craft orbiting Earth, in which astronauts live for weeks or months at a time, carrying out experiments and studying how living in space affects the human body. Space stations consist of a number of linked sections called modules. The largest space station is the International Space Station (ISS) – a collaboration between 15 countries. It has been continuously lived in since 2000.

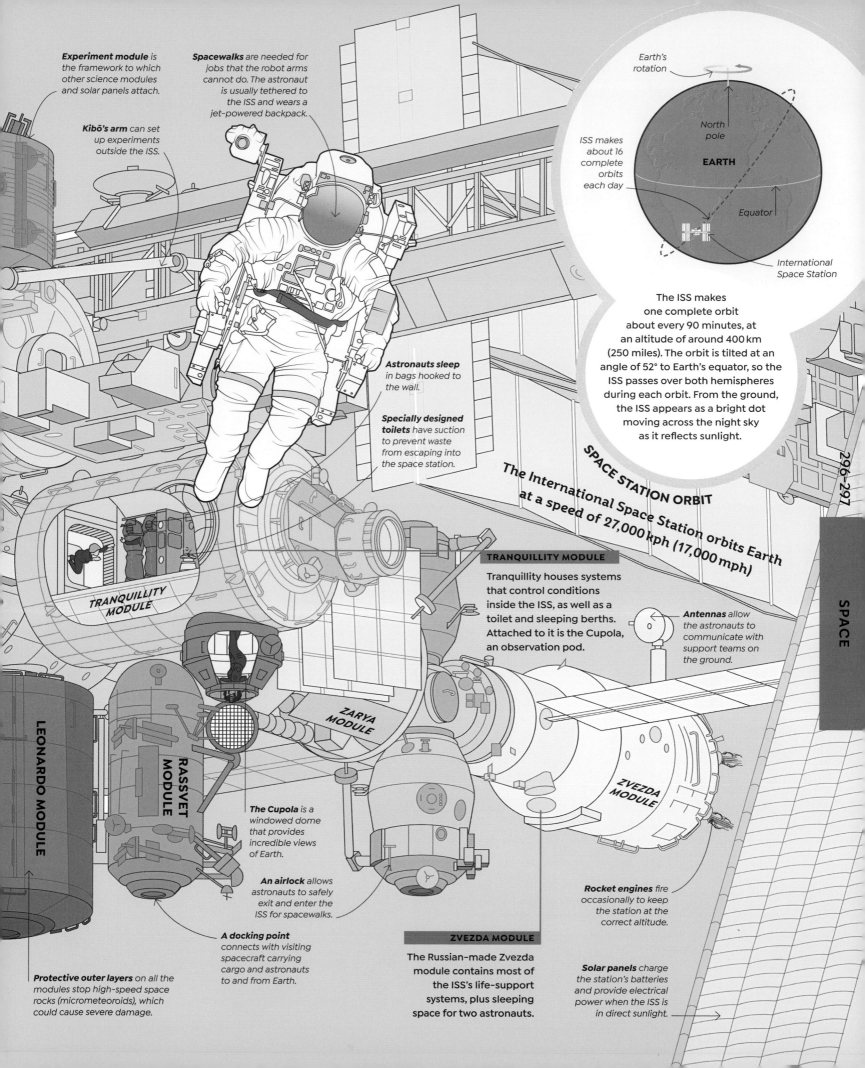

Experiment module is the framework to which other science modules and solar panels attach.

Kibō's arm can set up experiments outside the ISS.

Spacewalks are needed for jobs that the robot arms cannot do. The astronaut is usually tethered to the ISS and wears a jet-powered backpack.

Astronauts sleep in bags hooked to the wall.

Specially designed toilets have suction to prevent waste from escaping into the space station.

Earth's rotation

North pole

EARTH

ISS makes about 16 complete orbits each day

Equator

International Space Station

The ISS makes one complete orbit about every 90 minutes, at an altitude of around 400 km (250 miles). The orbit is tilted at an angle of 52° to Earth's equator, so the ISS passes over both hemispheres during each orbit. From the ground, the ISS appears as a bright dot moving across the night sky as it reflects sunlight.

SPACE STATION ORBIT
The International Space Station orbits Earth at a speed of 27,000 kph (17,000 mph)

SPACE

TRANQUILLITY MODULE

TRANQUILLITY MODULE
Tranquillity houses systems that control conditions inside the ISS, as well as a toilet and sleeping berths. Attached to it is the Cupola, an observation pod.

Antennas allow the astronauts to communicate with support teams on the ground.

LEONARDO MODULE

RASSVET MODULE

ZARYA MODULE

ZVEZDA MODULE

The Cupola is a windowed dome that provides incredible views of Earth.

An airlock allows astronauts to safely exit and enter the ISS for spacewalks.

A docking point connects with visiting spacecraft carrying cargo and astronauts to and from Earth.

Protective outer layers on all the modules stop high-speed space rocks (micrometeoroids), which could cause severe damage.

ZVEZDA MODULE
The Russian-made Zvezda module contains most of the ISS's life-support systems, plus sleeping space for two astronauts.

Rocket engines fire occasionally to keep the station at the correct altitude.

Solar panels charge the station's batteries and provide electrical power when the ISS is in direct sunlight.

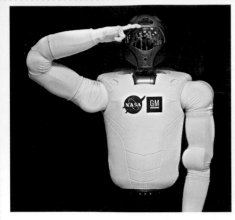

NASA's Robonaut is a humanoid robot designed to work alongside humans in space, carrying out many of the duties of an astronaut. It spent seven years aboard the International Space Station and performed routine and repetitive tasks using simple tools.

Spacesuit

When astronauts spend time outside a space station in orbit, or when walking on the Moon, they need to be protected against the harsh environment of space. They wear sophisticated spacesuits that create an environment in which they can stay alive and move about freely to carry out their duties. A spacesuit provides astronauts with pressurized oxygen to breathe and water to drink and to cool their bodies. It also shields them from harmful radiation.

HELMET

The rigid backpack contains the life-support system.

A reserve oxygen bottle can be used if a spacewalk takes longer than anticipated.

A water bag contains clean water for drinking and for cooling the suit.

The scrubbing cartridge contains lithium hydroxide, which absorbs exhaled carbon dioxide.

A system of pipes circulates oxygen, exhaled gases, and water.

A water filter purifies water circulating in the suit.

A moisture collector tank stores used water from sweat.

BACKPACK

A radio transmitter and receiver allows astronauts to communicate with ground controllers and other astronauts.

The primary oxygen tank supplies the astronaut with breathable oxygen.

A battery provides power for water pumps and radio.

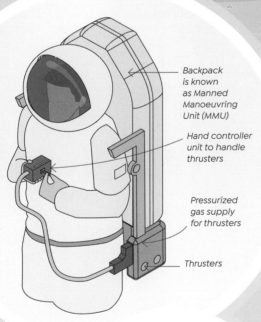

Backpack is known as Manned Manoeuvring Unit (MMU)

Hand controller unit to handle thrusters

Pressurized gas supply for thrusters

Thrusters

Astronauts can carry out untethered spacewalks, floating free in space, using jet packs. Most astronauts are tethered to their spacecraft during spacewalks but wear a jetpack as a safety feature. The jetpacks have small, gas-powered thrusters that allow the astronauts to get back to the spacecraft if the tether breaks.

UNTETHERED JETPACK

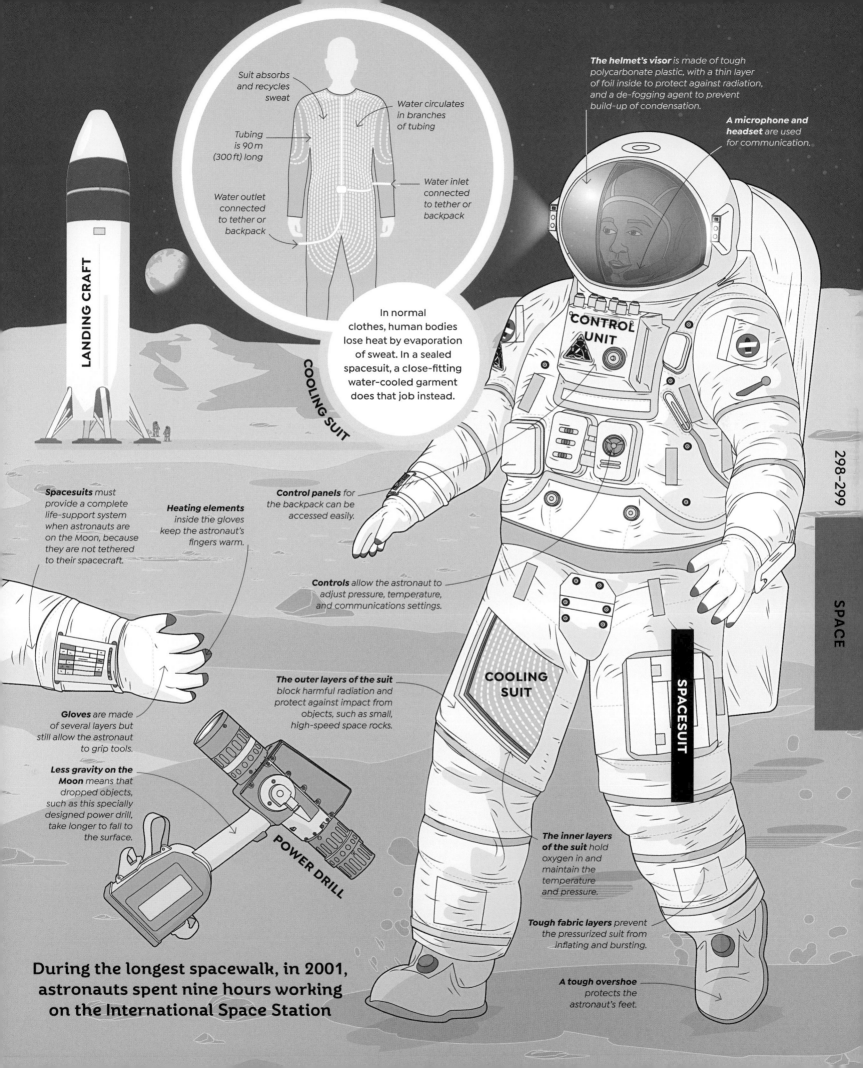

LANDING CRAFT

Suit absorbs and recycles sweat

Water circulates in branches of tubing

Tubing is 90 m (300 ft) long

Water inlet connected to tether or backpack

Water outlet connected to tether or backpack

In normal clothes, human bodies lose heat by evaporation of sweat. In a sealed spacesuit, a close-fitting water-cooled garment does that job instead.

COOLING SUIT

The helmet's visor is made of tough polycarbonate plastic, with a thin layer of foil inside to protect against radiation, and a de-fogging agent to prevent build-up of condensation.

A microphone and headset are used for communication.

CONTROL UNIT

Spacesuits must provide a complete life-support system when astronauts are on the Moon, because they are not tethered to their spacecraft.

Heating elements inside the gloves keep the astronaut's fingers warm.

Control panels for the backpack can be accessed easily.

Controls allow the astronaut to adjust pressure, temperature, and communications settings.

Gloves are made of several layers but still allow the astronaut to grip tools.

Less gravity on the Moon means that dropped objects, such as this specially designed power drill, take longer to fall to the surface.

The outer layers of the suit block harmful radiation and protect against impact from objects, such as small, high-speed space rocks.

COOLING SUIT

SPACESUIT

POWER DRILL

The inner layers of the suit hold oxygen in and maintain the temperature and pressure.

Tough fabric layers prevent the pressurized suit from inflating and bursting.

A tough overshoe protects the astronaut's feet.

During the longest spacewalk, in 2001, astronauts spent nine hours working on the International Space Station

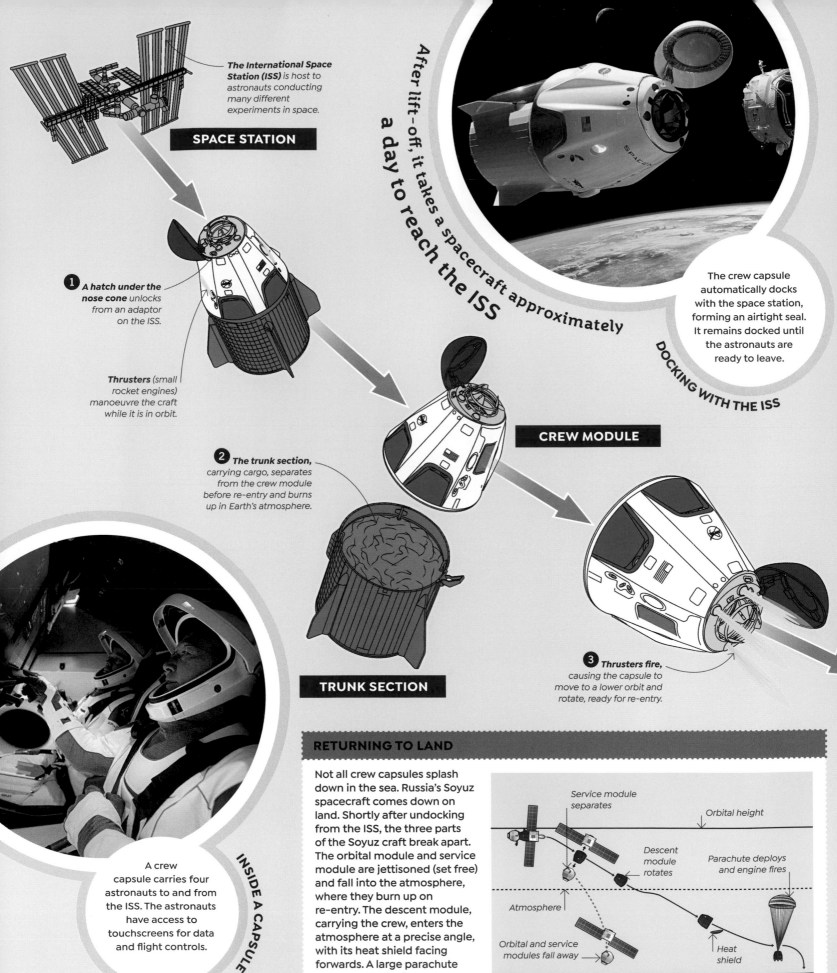

The International Space Station (ISS) is host to astronauts conducting many different experiments in space.

SPACE STATION

After lift-off, it takes a spacecraft approximately a day to reach the ISS

① *A hatch under the nose cone* unlocks from an adaptor on the ISS.

Thrusters (small rocket engines) manoeuvre the craft while it is in orbit.

The crew capsule automatically docks with the space station, forming an airtight seal. It remains docked until the astronauts are ready to leave.

DOCKING WITH THE ISS

CREW MODULE

② *The trunk section,* carrying cargo, separates from the crew module before re-entry and burns up in Earth's atmosphere.

TRUNK SECTION

③ *Thrusters fire,* causing the capsule to move to a lower orbit and rotate, ready for re-entry.

A crew capsule carries four astronauts to and from the ISS. The astronauts have access to touchscreens for data and flight controls.

INSIDE A CAPSULE

RETURNING TO LAND

Not all crew capsules splash down in the sea. Russia's Soyuz spacecraft comes down on land. Shortly after undocking from the ISS, the three parts of the Soyuz craft break apart. The orbital module and service module are jettisoned (set free) and fall into the atmosphere, where they burn up on re-entry. The descent module, carrying the crew, enters the atmosphere at a precise angle, with its heat shield facing forwards. A large parachute and a rocket engine help to slow its descent.

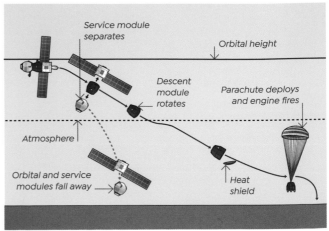

Service module separates

Orbital height

Descent module rotates

Parachute deploys and engine fires

Atmosphere

Orbital and service modules fall away

Heat shield

Re-entry vehicle

When re-entering Earth's atmosphere after time in space, the spacecraft that carry astronauts back to Earth must face unique challenges. They have to withstand dangerous amounts of heat caused by friction with air particles, and they need to slow down to a safe speed before landing on the ground or splashing into the sea.

CAPSULE RECOVERY

After splashing down into the sea, the capsule is recovered and most of it reused in future missions. The heat shield is too damaged to be reused.

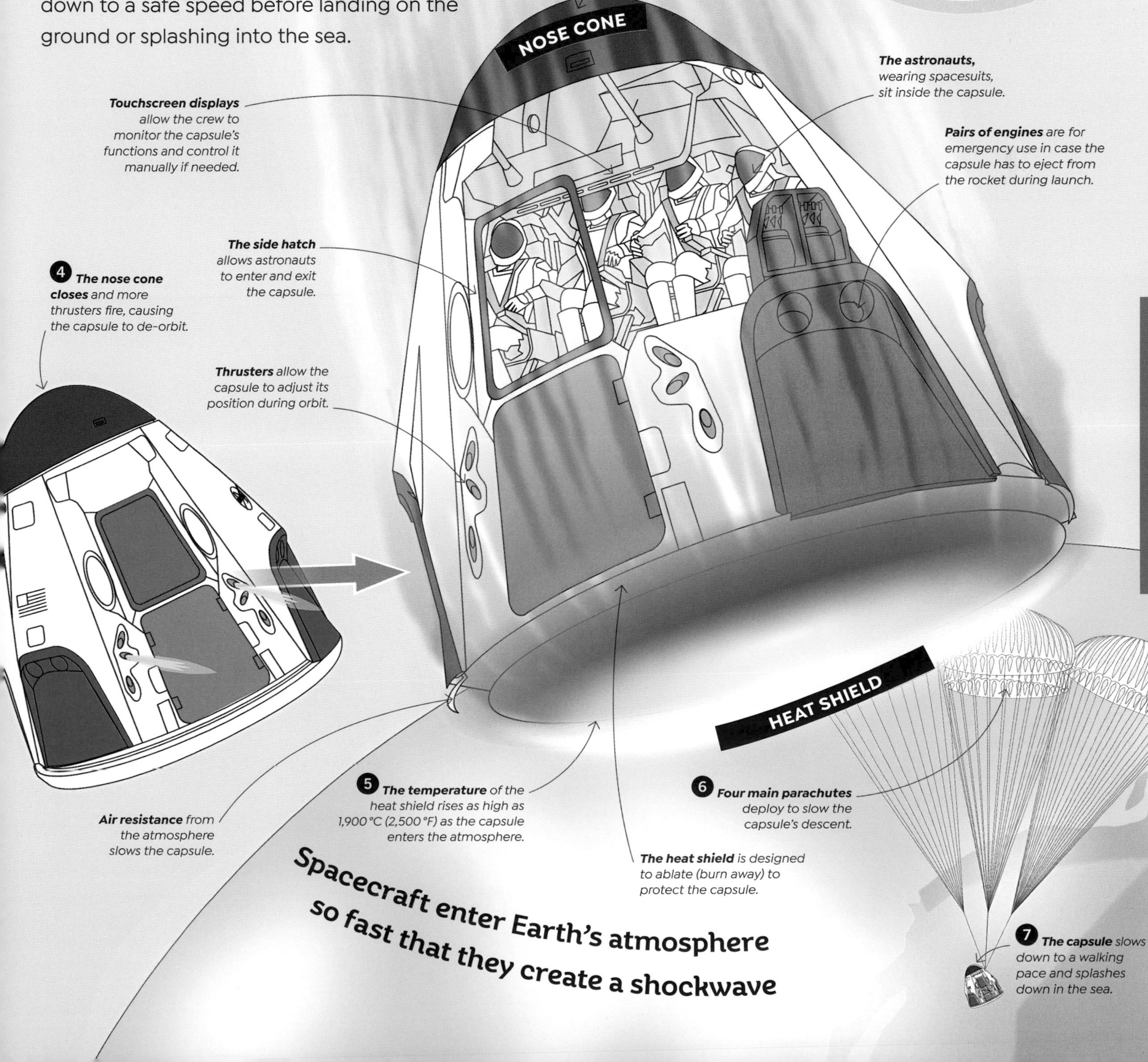

The closed nose cone protects the docking mechanism and back-up parachutes.

NOSE CONE

Touchscreen displays allow the crew to monitor the capsule's functions and control it manually if needed.

The astronauts, wearing spacesuits, sit inside the capsule.

Pairs of engines are for emergency use in case the capsule has to eject from the rocket during launch.

The side hatch allows astronauts to enter and exit the capsule.

4 **The nose cone closes** and more thrusters fire, causing the capsule to de-orbit.

Thrusters allow the capsule to adjust its position during orbit.

Air resistance from the atmosphere slows the capsule.

5 **The temperature** of the heat shield rises as high as 1,900 °C (2,500 °F) as the capsule enters the atmosphere.

The heat shield is designed to ablate (burn away) to protect the capsule.

HEAT SHIELD

6 **Four main parachutes** deploy to slow the capsule's descent.

7 **The capsule** slows down to a walking pace and splashes down in the sea.

Spacecraft enter Earth's atmosphere so fast that they create a shockwave

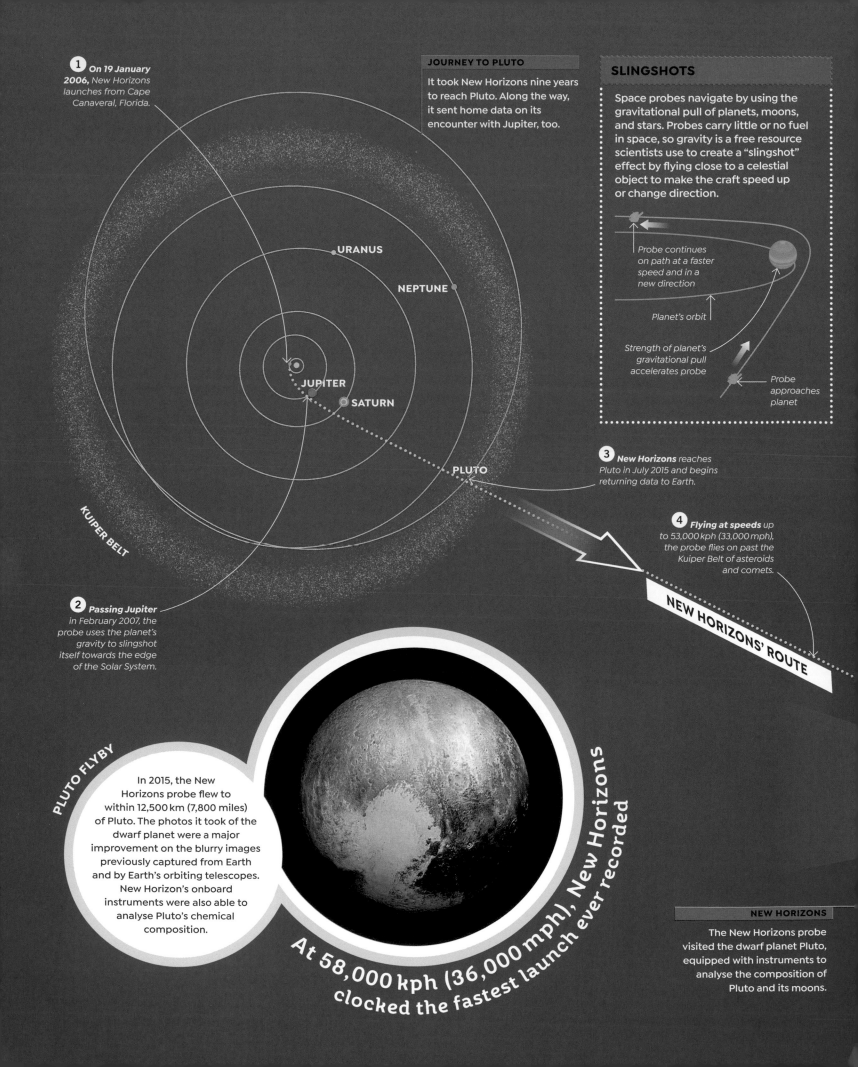

1 *On 19 January 2006, New Horizons launches from Cape Canaveral, Florida.*

JOURNEY TO PLUTO

It took New Horizons nine years to reach Pluto. Along the way, it sent home data on its encounter with Jupiter, too.

SLINGSHOTS

Space probes navigate by using the gravitational pull of planets, moons, and stars. Probes carry little or no fuel in space, so gravity is a free resource scientists use to create a "slingshot" effect by flying close to a celestial object to make the craft speed up or change direction.

Probe continues on path at a faster speed and in a new direction

Planet's orbit

Strength of planet's gravitational pull accelerates probe

Probe approaches planet

URANUS

NEPTUNE

JUPITER

SATURN

KUIPER BELT

PLUTO

3 *New Horizons reaches Pluto in July 2015 and begins returning data to Earth.*

4 *Flying at speeds up to 53,000 kph (33,000 mph), the probe flies on past the Kuiper Belt of asteroids and comets.*

2 *Passing Jupiter in February 2007, the probe uses the planet's gravity to slingshot itself towards the edge of the Solar System.*

NEW HORIZONS' ROUTE

PLUTO FLYBY

In 2015, the New Horizons probe flew to within 12,500 km (7,800 miles) of Pluto. The photos it took of the dwarf planet were a major improvement on the blurry images previously captured from Earth and by Earth's orbiting telescopes. New Horizon's onboard instruments were also able to analyse Pluto's chemical composition.

At 58,000 kph (36,000 mph), New Horizons clocked the fastest launch ever recorded

NEW HORIZONS

The New Horizons probe visited the dwarf planet Pluto, equipped with instruments to analyse the composition of Pluto and its moons.

Space probe

A space probe is an uncrewed craft that travels the Solar System and beyond, recording images and gathering data about the Universe to send back to Earth, usually through radio signals. Some space probes return to Earth, while others, like NASA's New Horizons, take a one-way journey.

CRASH LANDING

NASA's Deep Impact space probe was sent to intercept the comet Tempel 1 in 2005. On reaching the comet, Deep Impact fired an "Impactor" device onto Tempel 1 that collected vital information about the comet's core. Deep Impact itself took 500,000 images during its mission before contact with the probe was lost in 2013.

The low gain antenna *is a two-way communications device used to keep in contact with Earth early in the mission.*

The medium gain antenna *is an emergency backup communications system.*

The SWAP (solar wind around Pluto) *device measures how many of the Sun's low-energy particles reach Pluto.*

PEPPSI *(the Pluto energetic particle spectrometer science investigation) records how many of the Sun's high-level energy particles reach Pluto.*

The radio science equipment *(or REX) records Pluto's atmospheric pressure and temperature, and also measures its diameter.*

New Horizon's power source *is a radioisotope thermoelectric generator. It runs on a tiny amount of nuclear fuel, producing 250 watts of electricity at launch.*

A feedhorn *concentrates signals captured from Pluto, or other objects, by the antenna and beams them back to Earth.*

REX

GENERATOR

ANTENNA

PEPPSI

SWAP

NEW HORIZONS SPACE PROBE

LORRI

LORRI (long range reconnaissance imager) *is a digital camera and telescope with a 20.8 cm (8.2 in) lens designed to survive the hostile environment of space.*

ALICE

RALPH

ALICE *is an ultraviolet imaging spectrometer that allows New Horizons to analyse the make-up of Pluto's atmosphere.*

Thrusters *let the probe change position to align its cameras and to point its antenna back to Earth.*

Known as RALPH, *this device is a visible and infrared imager and spectrometer that captures images and assesses them.*

A star tracker *traces the positions of stars, to help the probe to orient and adjust its location.*

TALKING TO EARTH

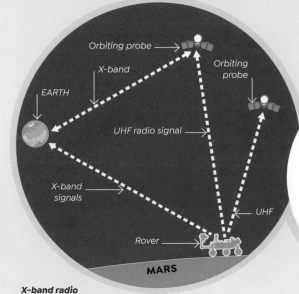

Orbiting probe

X-band

Orbiting probe

EARTH

UHF radio signal

X-band signals

UHF

Rover

MARS

Rovers receive orders from engineers on Earth, and send back images and information using radio signals. Some signals travel directly between Earth and the rover, but most are relayed by probes orbiting Mars. Three ground stations in different places on Earth ensure that at least one station is always in direct line-of-sight with Mars as Earth rotates.

X-band radio antennas can communicate directly with radio dishes on Earth.

The high-resolution camera has a laser beam to clear dust from rocks in order to get a better view, and a spectrometer to work out what the rocks are made of.

CAMERA

RADIO ANTENNA

A UHF radio antenna communicates with probes orbiting Mars.

The power source generates electricity using heat emitted by radioactive plutonium.

The ground-penetrating radar can detect water 10 m (33 ft) below the surface.

POWER SOURCE

A panoramic camera captures wide-angle 3D views of the Martian landscape.

A weather station measures the wind speed and direction, the temperature and humidity, and the size of dust particles in the atmosphere.

LASER BEAM

An upward-pointing camera took photos during the rover's descent to the surface.

BODY

MARS ROVER

The flexible suspension allows the rover to stay level while it moves over uneven surfaces.

A storage space holds samples collected from the rock, soil, and atmosphere.

Wide wheel rims have raised strips to give extra grip.

PERSEVERANCE

The rover Perseverance touched down on Mars in 2021. It is about the size of a family car, but it can only move at speeds of up to 0.15 kph (0.1 mph).

Six wheels allow the rover to turn 360 degrees on the spot.

Curved titanium spokes allow the wheel to flex (bend) when travelling over small rocks.

The rover Opportunity travelled more than 45 km (28 miles) on Mars between 2004 and 2018

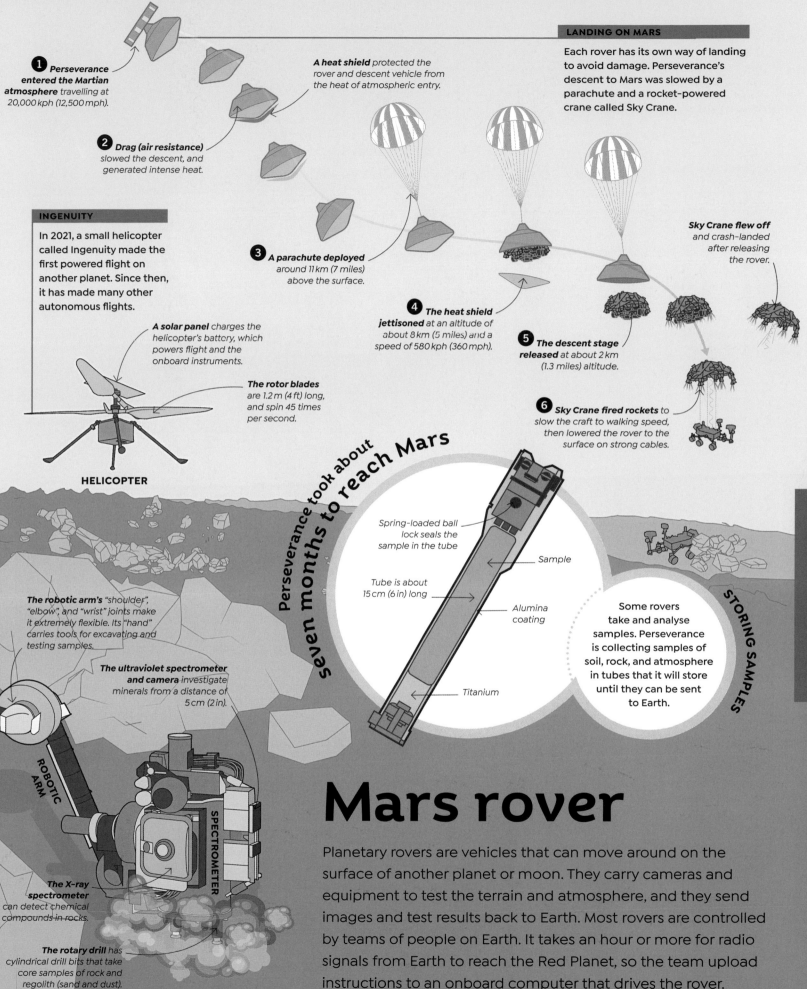

Each rover has its own way of landing to avoid damage. Perseverance's descent to Mars was slowed by a parachute and a rocket-powered crane called Sky Crane.

1 *Perseverance entered the Martian atmosphere* travelling at 20,000 kph (12,500 mph).

A heat shield protected the rover and descent vehicle from the heat of atmospheric entry.

2 *Drag (air resistance)* slowed the descent, and generated intense heat.

3 *A parachute deployed* around 11 km (7 miles) above the surface.

4 *The heat shield jettisoned* at an altitude of about 8 km (5 miles) and a speed of 580 kph (360 mph).

5 *The descent stage released* at about 2 km (1.3 miles) altitude.

6 *Sky Crane fired rockets* to slow the craft to walking speed, then lowered the rover to the surface on strong cables.

Sky Crane flew off and crash-landed after releasing the rover.

INGENUITY

In 2021, a small helicopter called Ingenuity made the first powered flight on another planet. Since then, it has made many other autonomous flights.

A solar panel charges the helicopter's battery, which powers flight and the onboard instruments.

The rotor blades are 1.2 m (4 ft) long, and spin 45 times per second.

HELICOPTER

Perseverance took about seven months to reach Mars

The robotic arm's "shoulder", "elbow", and "wrist" joints make it extremely flexible. Its "hand" carries tools for excavating and testing samples.

The ultraviolet spectrometer and camera investigate minerals from a distance of 5 cm (2 in).

ROBOTIC ARM

SPECTROMETER

The X-ray spectrometer can detect chemical compounds in rocks.

The rotary drill has cylindrical drill bits that take core samples of rock and regolith (sand and dust).

Spring-loaded ball lock seals the sample in the tube

Sample

Tube is about 15 cm (6 in) long

Alumina coating

Titanium

STORING SAMPLES

Some rovers take and analyse samples. Perseverance is collecting samples of soil, rock, and atmosphere in tubes that it will store until they can be sent to Earth.

Mars rover

Planetary rovers are vehicles that can move around on the surface of another planet or moon. They carry cameras and equipment to test the terrain and atmosphere, and they send images and test results back to Earth. Most rovers are controlled by teams of people on Earth. It takes an hour or more for radio signals from Earth to reach the Red Planet, so the team upload instructions to an onboard computer that drives the rover.

SNAPSHOT FROM MARS

Mars may be the first planet to be visited by humans, but before that can happen, more needs to be known about its environment. Nasa's rover Curiosity, pictured here, has ten instruments on board that detect radiation, monitor wind and atmospheric movement, chemically analyse soil and rock samples, take temperature readings, and look for water. It also has 17 cameras that send pictures back to Earth, including the occasional selfie.

Index

Page numbers in **bold** indicate main topics.

Acknowledgments

DK would like to thank the following people for their contributions to this book: Tom Jackson for his work on the contents; Bharti Bedi, Tom Booth, and Ian Fitzgerald for additional text; Steve Setford for additional editing; Sharon Spencer and Duncan Turner for design work; Satish Gaur, Tarun Sharma, and Rajdeep Singh for DTP design; Ann Baggaley for proof-reading; and Elizabeth Wise for compiling the index.

The publisher would like to thank the following for their kind permission to reproduce their photographs:

(Key: a-above; b-below/bottom; c-centre; f-far; l-left; r-right; t-top)

10 Dreamstime.com: Ferli Achirulli Kamaruddin (tl). **13 Science Photo Library:** Edward Kinsman (br). **14 Getty Images:** Addictive Stock / Jose Luis Carrascosa (cra). **15 Getty Images / iStock:** Viorika (cl). **16-17 Shutterstock.com:** Paul Aiken. **19 123RF.com:** Csak Istvan (tl). **23 Getty Images / iStock:** ti-ja / E+ (tr). **24-25 Getty Images:** Jakob Sanne / 500px Prime. **27 Alamy Stock Photo:** Science Photo Library (br). **29 Alamy Stock Photo:** Science Photo Library / Steve Gschmeissner. **30 Dreamstime.com:** Mike_kiev (bc). **32-33 Science Photo Library:** Steve Gschmeissner. **34 Getty Images:** Karen Bleier / AFP (bl). **35 Science Photo Library:** Steve Gschmeissner (br). **37 Alamy Stock Photo:** Massimo Parisi (br). **39 Science Photo Library:** NIBSC (br). **40 Alamy Stock Photo:** Victor Okhumale (bl). **Science Photo Library:** David Scharf (tr). **43 Science Photo Library:** Edelmann (tc). **46 Dreamstime.com:** Larry Jordan (cl). **47 Dreamstime.com:** Andrii Afanasiev (bl). **49 Alamy Stock Photo:** dpa picture alliance / Julian Stratenschulte (tr). **50-51 Alamy Stock Photo:** Apurva Madia. **51 Shutterstock.com:** katesid (cra). **52 Dreamstime.com:** Majkl85 (bl). **53 Alamy Stock Photo:** Hans Georg Eiben / Flonline digitale Bildagentur GmbH (br). **54 Dreamstime.com:** Tenrook (tl). **Getty Images:** golf was here / Moment (bc). **56 Getty Images:** Catherine Ledner / DigitalVision (br). **57 Getty Images / iStock:** hayatikayhan (cb). **58 Alamy Stock Photo:** le Moal Olivier (tl). **59 Getty Images / iStock:** sturti (tr). **62 Dreamstime.com:** Valmedia Creatives (tl). **Getty Images:** Education Images / Universal Images Group Editorial (bc). **63 Dorling Kindersley:** Based on Metabowerke GmbH (Metabo) drill (br). **Getty Images / iStock:** ferrantraite / E+ (cra). **64-65 Dreamstime.com:** Cristianzamfir. **67 Shutterstock.com:** David Pereiras (br). **69 Dreamstime.com:** Destina156 (bc). **Getty Images / iStock:** Salomonus_ (cr). **75 Getty Images / iStock:** leungchopan (tr). **76 Online Crane University** (bc). **79 Alamy Stock Photo:** John Henshall (tr). **80-81 Getty Images:** Ratnakorn Piyasirisorost / Moment. **82 Dreamstime.com:** Nadtochiy (crb). **Getty Images:** suraark / Moment Open (bl). **83 TK Elevator:** (bl). **84 Getty Images / iStock:** andresr / E+ (bl). **86 123RF.com:** Macrovector (Reference for surgical robot, control console). **Dreamstime.com:** Chanawit (bl). **87 Getty Images / iStock:** gorodenkoff (tr). **88 Dreamstime.com:** Angel Claudio (cl). **89 Dreamstime.com:** Alexandre Zveiger (br). **90 Alamy Stock Photo:** Edmund Sumner-VIEW (cla). **Getty Images:** Javier Soriano / AFP (clb). **91 Alamy Stock Photo:** Konrad Zelazowski (tr). **92 Getty Images / iStock:** imaginima / E+ (tl). **94 Getty Images:** Luis Alvarez / DigitalVision (bc). **95 Getty Images / iStock:** FatCamera / E+ (br); SamuelBrownNG (tr). **96 123RF.com:** Marian Vejcik (cl). **98-99 Getty Images:** Jackal Pan / Moment. **100 Alamy Stock Photo:** Matthew Richardson (crb). **106 Getty Images / iStock:** Avalon_Studio / E+ (tl). **109 Alamy Stock Photo:** Maximilian Weinzierl (tr). **110 123RF.com:** Dean Drobot (tl). **112 Getty Images / iStock:** yuelan (bc). **115 Shutterstock.com:** Sk Hasan Ali (cr). **116 Alamy Stock Photo:** Cultura Creative RF / Steve Woods Photography (cla). **117 Alamy Stock Photo:** Matthias Scholz (cra). **Getty Images / iStock:** sambrogio / E+ (tc). **119 Getty Images / iStock:** mbbirdy / E+ (tl). **120 Dreamstime.com:** Fiona Ayerst / Fionaayerst (br). **Pixabay:** Scholty1970 (tr). **121 Alamy Stock Photo:** US Navy Photo (c). **122 Alamy Stock Photo:** Cynthia Lee (tl). **Getty Images:** Songphol Thesakit / Moment (bc). **123 Truth Box Architects:** Nat Rea (cr). **Wikimedia Commons:** AlMare (bl). **125 Alamy Stock Photo:** Viacheslav Iakobchuk (br). **127 Alamy Stock Photo:** Eraza Collection (cr). **129 Getty Images:** The Sydney Morning Herald / Fairfax Media (bl). **131 Getty Images:** China News Service (bl). **132 Getty Images:** Visual China Group (cl). **133 Dreamstime.com:** Irina Borsuchenko. **134-135 Getty Images:** Bloomberg. **136 Dreamstime.com:** Perseo8888 (tr). **137 Alamy Stock Photo:** William Arthur (ca, ca/Sheep, ca/Sheep 2). **Getty Images / iStock:** RosaFrei (crb). **138 Dreamstime.com:** Anny Ben (fcla); Katerina Kovaleva (cla); Nevinates (ca). **Getty Images / iStock:** Chaiyaporn1144 (tr). **140-141 Getty Images / iStock:** JohnnyGreig / E+. **142 Epiroc:** (clb). **143 Shutterstock.com:** Sunshine Seeds (ca); waniuszka (br). **144-145 Getty Images:** Georgy Rozov / EyeEm. **146 Dreamstime.com:** Roman Zaiets (cl). **149 Shutterstock.com:** DedMityay (tc). **150-151 Getty Images:** Monty Rakusen / Image Source. **152 Alamy Stock Photo:** Everett Collection Historical (bc). **Getty Images / iStock:** sambrogio / E+ (tl). **153 Dorling Kindersley:** Roller cone bit based on Schlumberger (tc). **154 Getty Images:** Westend61 (br). **157 Alamy Stock Photo:** dpa picture alliance archive (bl). **Dreamstime.com:** Pavel Dolgikh (tl). **158 Getty Images / iStock:** CharlieChesvick / E+ (tl). **161 Alamy Stock Photo:** aerial-photos.com (tr). **163 Dreamstime.com:** Chris Labasco (cb). **164-165 Getty Images:** Nigel Killeen / Moment. **166 Getty Images:** Visual China Group (cl). **168 Getty Images / iStock:** ronemmons (br). **169 Alamy Stock Photo:** Tim Hill (tr). **170 Getty Images:** Adrian Dennis / AFP (bc). **172 Alamy Stock Photo:** Ros Drinkwater (tr). **175 Alamy Stock Photo:** Steve Hamblin (br). **176 123RF.com:** David Pereiras Villagr (clb). **177 Dreamstime.com:** James Kelley (cr). **181 Dreamstime.com:** Photo263 (tc). **183 Getty Images / iStock:** micro_photo (cra). **184 Dreamstime.com:** Indukall (tr). **185 Dreamstime.com:** Nils Jacobi (br). **186 Alamy Stock Photo:** PF-(usna1) (bl). **187 Shutterstock.com:** Dr Gregory Rouse (br). **189 Alamy Stock Photo:** Kevin Schafer (br); Bjrn Wylezich (tr). **190 Dreamstime.com:** Slowmotiongli (tr). **191 Dreamstime.com:** Dazztan1 (tl); Michael Sheehan / Bondsza (tc). **192-193 AirPano images:** LLC. **194-195 Dreamstime.com:** Agami Photo Agency (cla). **195 Dreamstime.com:** Agami Photo Agency (ca). **196 naturepl.com:** Gerry Ellis (bc). **naturepl.com:** Christian Ziegler (tc). **197 123RF.com:** wollertz (bc). **198 Dreamstime.com:** Pkzphotos (tr). **199 Alamy Stock Photo:** Susan Feldberg (cla). **200 Janet M. Storey, Carleton University:** (bc). **201 Dreamstime.com:** Danler